OXFORD THEOLOGICAL MONOGRAPHS

OXFORD THEOLOGICAL MONOGRAPHS

FAITH, REASON, AND REVELATION IN THE THOUGHT OF THEODORE BEZA

Jeffrey Mallinson (2003)

RICHARD HOOKER AND REFORMED THEOLOGY
A Study of Reason, Will, and Grace

Nigel Voak (2003)

THE COUNTESS OF HUNTINGDON'S CONNEXION

Alan Harding (2003)

THE APPROPRIATION OF DIVINE LIFE IN CYRIL OF ALEXANDRIA

Daniel A. Keating (2004)

THE MACARIAN LEGACY
The Place of Macarius-Symeon in the Eastern Christian Tradition

Marcus Plested (2004)

PSALMODY AND PRAYER IN THE WRITINGS OF EVAGRIUS PONTICUS

Luke Dysinger, OSB (2005)

ORIGEN ON THE SONG OF SONGS AS THE SPIRIT OF SCRIPTURE
The Bridegroom's Perfect Marriage-Song

J. Christopher King (2005)

AN INTERPRETATION OF HANS URS VON BALTHASAR
Eschatology as Communion

Nicholas J. Healy (2005)

DURANDUS OF ST POURÇAIN
A Dominican Theologian in the Shadow of Aquinas

Isabel Iribarren (2005)

THE TROUBLES OF TEMPLELESS JUDAH

Jill Middlemas (2005)

TIME AND ETERNITY IN MID-THIRTEENTH-CENTURY THOUGHT

Rory Fox (2006)

THE SPECIFICATION OF HUMAN ACTIONS IN ST THOMAS AQUINAS

Joseph Pilsner (2006)

THE WORLDVIEW OF PERSONALISM
Origins and Early Development

Jan Olof Bengtsson (2006)

The Eusebians

The Polemic of Athanasius of Alexandria and the Construction of the 'Arian Controversy'

DAVID M. GWYNN

OXFORD
UNIVERSITY PRESS

OXFORD
UNIVERSITY PRESS

Great Clarendon Street, Oxford OX2 6DP

Oxford University Press is a department of the University of Oxford.
It furthers the University's objective of excellence in research, scholarship,
and education by publishing worldwide in

Oxford New York

Auckland Cape Town Dar es Salaam Hong Kong Karachi
Kuala Lumpur Madrid Melbourne Mexico City Nairobi
New Delhi Shanghai Taipei Toronto

With offices in

Argentina Austria Brazil Chile Czech Republic France Greece
Guatemala Hungary Italy Japan Poland Portugal Singapore
South Korea Switzerland Thailand Turkey Ukraine Vietnam

Published in the United States
by Oxford University Press Inc., New York

First published 2007

British Library Cataloguing in Publication Data
Data available

Library of Congress Cataloging-in-Publication Data
Gwynn, David M. (David Morton), 1975–
The Eusebians : the polemic of Athanasius of Alexandria and the
construction of the Arian controversy / David M. Gwynn.
p. cm. — (Oxford theological monographs)
ISBN–13: 978–0–19–920555–4 (alk. paper)
ISBN–10: 0–19–920555–8 (alk. paper)
1. Athanasius, Saint, Patriarch of Alexandria, d. 373. 2. Arianism. 3. Theology,
Doctrinal—History—Early church, ca. 30–600. 4. Eusebius, of Caesarea, Bishop of
Caesarea, ca. 260–ca. 340. I. Title.
BR65.A446G89 2006
273′.4—dc22
2006027695

Typeset by
SPI Publisher Services, Pondicherry, India
Printed in Great Britain
on acid-free paper by
Biddles Ltd., King's Lynn, Norfolk

ISBN 978–0–19–920555–4

In memory of Norman James Edmonstone Austin

Teacher, Inspiration, and Friend

Preface

This monograph derives directly from my Oxford doctoral thesis, submitted in 2003 and entitled '*Hoi peri Eusebion*: The Polemic of Athanasius of Alexandria and the early "Arian Controversy"'. I have updated the bibliography and certain sections of my argument, particularly to allow for the recent important works of Lewis Ayres and John Behr, and I have incorporated various modifications recommended by examiners and reviewers.

The present work is not intended to be a general study of the career of Athanasius or of the controversies that divided the fourth-century Church. My aim is more specific, to present a systematic literary, historical, and theological re-evaluation of the polemical writings of Athanasius and their influence upon modern interpretations of the so-called 'Arian Controversy'. The particular focus of this study is the origins and evolution of Athanasius' presentation of those whom he regarded as 'heretics' as a single 'Arian party', *hoi peri Eusebion* ('the ones around Eusebius' or the 'Eusebians'). These are the men, named after their alleged leader Eusebius, bishop of Nicomedia, whom Athanasius held responsible for his own condemnation at the Council of Tyre in 335, and whom from that date onwards he accused of manipulating episcopal and imperial politics in order to persecute the 'orthodox' and to impose their 'heresy' upon the Church. My examination of Athanasius' polemic and of what little external evidence survives against which that polemic can be compared reveals that the 'Eusebians' who play so prominent a role in modern scholarly accounts of the 'Arian Controversy' were in fact neither a 'party' nor 'Arian'. Athanasius' image of a fourth-century Church polarized between his own 'orthodoxy' and the 'Arianism' of the 'Eusebians' is a polemical construct, and the distortions inherent within that construct must be recognized if we are to fully understand the fourth-century Church.

My hope is that my conclusions will contribute to the ongoing reinterpretation of the events and participants of the fourth-century controversies. In that process of reinterpretation, we must do justice to the contribution of those whom Athanasius and later generations would come to condemn as 'Arian' and also do justice to Athanasius himself. It is inevitable that a study focused almost exclusively upon Athanasius' polemical writings will offer only a partial reflection of the true theological and ecclesiastical importance of the bishop of Alexandria within Christian tradition. But I continue to believe that it is only if we see past the polemical and distorted construction of the 'Arian Controversy', created primarily by Athanasius himself, that we can fully appreciate Athanasius' own achievement in the emergence of Christian 'orthodoxy' in the crucial formative period in which he lived.

I am deeply grateful to all those without whose assistance I could never have completed my original thesis nor brought this monograph to the point of publication. My supervisor Dr Mark Edwards (Christ Church) has continued to offer his support and advice, and his comments have consistently forced me to extend my research and to correct and strengthen my conclusions. Professor Averil Cameron (Keble College) assisted my first arrival to Oxford, and has ever since been outstandingly generous with her encouragement and critical suggestions. At an early stage in my research, I was extremely fortunate that the Reverend Professor Christopher Stead agreed to read a preliminary version of my argument, and I would once again like to express my thanks for his time and his valuable suggestions. Professor Maurice Wiles and Archbishop Rowan Williams were extremely acute and helpful doctoral examiners, and Reverend Professor Stuart Hall read through my original manuscript and made a number of important comments and corrections. The responsibility for any remaining errors is, needless to say, entirely my own.

For his supervision of my first struggles with the fourth-century Church and for his continuing encouragement since, I would further like to thank Dr Paul McKechnie of Auckland University, and likewise all the other scholars who supported my initial studies in New Zealand, particularly Dr Tom Stevenson (also in Auckland) and Dr Stuart Lawrence (of Massey University, Palmerston North). In my years in Oxford I have received guidance and assistance from many individuals, among whom I must thank Professor Elizabeth Jeffreys, Dr James Howard-Johnston, Dr Bryan Ward-Perkins, Dr Peter Heather, and Dr Roger Tomlin. The colleagues and friends who have heard and commented on the arguments that I present here are too numerous to record in full, but my thanks again to you all, particularly Alan Dearn, James George, Scott Johnson, Susanne Bangert, Judith Gilliland, Eleni Lianta, Anthi Papagiannaki, and Teresa Shawcross. I must also express my gratitude both to Keble College, where I wrote my original thesis, and to Christ Church, whose generosity in granting me a Junior Research Fellowship allowed me the opportunity to adapt that thesis into monograph form. And of course I am grateful to Oxford University Press for accepting this monograph for publication, and above all to my editor Lucy Qureshi, whose enthusiasm and patience throughout this long process have been equally appreciated.

I trust that my family already know how deeply I appreciate all their love and support. In particular, to my parents Margaret and Robin, and to Jenny and Steve, thank you.

I have deliberately omitted one name from these acknowledgements thus far. The late Professor Norman Austin was my first supervisor at Massey University, and it was he who drew me into the classical and late antique worlds and who opened up to me the delights for both learning and teaching that those centuries offered. I can never repay everything that I owe to Norman and the example that he set me, but it is to him that this monograph is dedicated.

David M. Gwynn

Christ Church, Oxford
Summer 2006

Contents

List of Abbreviations

AJAH	*American Journal of Ancient History*
Byz	*Byzantion*
CH	*Church History*
GRBS	*Greek, Roman, and Byzantine Studies*
HThR	*Harvard Theological Review*
IThQ	*Irish Theological Quarterly*
JAC	*Jahrbuch für Antike und Christentum*
JAC.E	*Jahrbuch für Antike und Christentum, Ergänzungsband*
JEA	*Journal of Egyptian Archaeology*
JECS	*Journal of Early Christian Studies*
JEH	*Journal of Ecclesiastical History*
JRS	*Journal of Roman Studies*
JThS, OS	*Journal of Theological Studies,* Old Series
JThS, NS	*Journal of Theological Studies,* New Series
RSR	*Recherches de science religieuse*
SJTh	*Scottish Journal of Theology*
StP	*Studia Patristica*
ThS	*Theological Studies*
VC	*Vigiliae Christianae*
ZKG	*Zeitschrift für Kirchengeschichte*
ZNW	*Zeitschrift für die neutestamentaliche Wissenschaft und die Künde der älteren Kirche*
ZPE	*Zeitschrift für Papyrologie und Epigraphik*

Introduction

Few figures in the history of Christianity have aroused such controversy within their own lifetimes or wielded such influence upon the judgements of later generations as Athanasius of Alexandria (bishop 328–73). In the traditional interpretation of the so-called 'Arian Controversy' that divided the fourth-century Church, Athanasius is the champion of 'orthodoxy'. He it was who all but single-handedly resisted the spread of the 'Arian heresy' that threatened to deny the divinity of the Son of God, and so ensured the ultimate triumph of the Nicene Creed, composed by the first ecumenical Council of Nicaea in 325 under the auspices of Constantine, the first Christian Roman emperor.

This interpretation of Athanasius' career, which originated in the writings of the bishop himself, became over the century that followed his death the largely unchallenged foundation for later assessments both of Athanasius as an individual and of the period in which he lived. Already less than ten years after he died, Athanasius' steadfast defence of the Nicene faith was commemorated in a *Funeral Oration* by Gregory of Nazianzus.[1] The fifth-century ecclesiastical historians Socrates, Sozomen, and Theodoret, whose works provide the only detailed narrative accounts of the fourth-century controversies, likewise derived their interpretations of those years to a large extent from Athanasius' own writings.[2] It is therefore hardly surprising that for centuries few writers saw any need to challenge what had become the accepted representation of the heroic bishop of Alexandria and of the 'Arian Controversy'.[3]

[1] Gregory of Nazianzus, *Oration* XXI, *c.*380.

[2] The extent of Athanasius' influence upon the ecclesiastical historians is readily apparent from their accounts of his career and their quotations from his writings. It thus needs to be emphasized that these fifth-century sources cannot provide external confirmation for Athanasius' own presentation of the fourth-century controversies.

[3] For a study of medieval and early modern attitudes towards Athanasius and the 'Arian Controversy', see Slusser (1993). Those attitudes are well encapsulated in the panegyrical presentations of Athanasius given by William Bright (1877) in the

The critical reaction to this prevailing hagiography of Athanasius emerged at the beginning of the twentieth century through the work of the great German historians Eduard Schwartz and Otto Seeck,[4] and modern attitudes towards Athanasius have varied widely. A number of scholars, of whom the most influential is Charles Kannengiesser,[5] have reacted in turn against the critical challenge to Athanasius, whom they continue to uphold as a moral exemplar and saint.[6] At the other extreme, T. D. Barnes has likened the bishop of Alexandria to a 'modern gangster'.[7] R. P. C. Hanson presents Athanasius as an ambivalent character of theological genius and divisive violence,[8] while John Behr has now returned to the older verdict of Harnack, that if Athanasius is judged 'by the standards of his time, we can discover nothing ignoble or mean about him'.[9] The present monograph offers a further contribution to this debate, and to the ongoing reinterpretation of the fourth-century controversies and their participants. For it is the measure of Athanasius' importance that any reassessment of the man, his theology, and his writings inevitably leads to a reassessment of the times in which he lived.

Athanasius was born in the closing years of the third century,[10] and died in 373. His life thus spanned a period of momentous change for

Dictionary of Christian Biography, and by Archibald Robertson (1892) in the introduction to the *Nicene and Post-Nicene Fathers* translation of Athanasius' works (lxvi–viii).

[4] Schwartz (1959) (first pub. 1904–11) and Seeck (1911). There are convenient surveys of early twentieth-century scholarship on Athanasius in Cross (1945) 3–11, Schneemelcher (1950), and Tetz (1979*b*) 23–9.

[5] Sadly, Professor Kannengiesser's long-awaited biography of Athanasius will not appear in time to be considered here. In his *Prolegomena* to that biography (2002), he challenges the recent critical approach to Athanasius, and declares that 'a biography of Athanasius would have to meet the standards of a spiritual synthesis bringing the bishop back from a last, and posthumous, century-long exile, which alienated him in our lifetime from his true self under the pressure of a rejection of traditional dogmatism, carrying on its own secularist and post-Christian dogma' (30).

[6] See among others Twomey (1982), Arnold (1991), and Ng (2001).

[7] Barnes (1981) 230. Barnes developed this interpretation of Athanasius in far greater detail first in his Patristics Conference paper of 1987 (1989), and then above all in his *Athanasius and Constantius* (1993).

[8] Hanson (1988*b*), especially 239–73.

[9] Behr (2004) 167, quoting Harnack (1898) 45.

[10] Athanasius' exact date of birth is uncertain. His age was a subject of debate at the time of his accession to the episcopate in 328, when his opponents are reported to have alleged that he had not yet reached the canonical age of 30 (*Festal Index* III). It is thus probable that he was born near the very end of the third century (Barnes (1993) 10).

the Roman Empire and the Christian Church. The conversion of Constantine (emperor 306–37) in 312 transformed the status of Christianity,[11] and in size, wealth, and power the Church steadily expanded throughout the reigns of Constantine and of his sons Constantine II (337–40), Constans (337–50), and Constantius II (337–61). The brief reign of Julian 'the Apostate' (361–3), the last pagan Roman emperor, could not halt this expansion, and the Church continued to grow in the east after Julian, under Jovian (363–4), Valens (364–78), and Theodosius I (378–95).

The new prominence of Christianity, however, also gave a new importance to the doctrinal and ecclesiastical conflicts that had always threatened to divide the Church. The greatest of these conflicts in the fourth century began in Alexandria *c.*321,[12] with a dispute between Alexander, bishop of Alexandria, and his presbyter Arius concerning the nature of the divinity of the Son and the relationship of the Son to the Father. This dispute then spread throughout the eastern Church in the years before Constantine conquered the east by defeating his rival Licinius in 324. Arius himself was condemned at Nicaea in 325, and the doctrines attributed to him were anathematized, while the Son was declared to be *homoousios* ('of one essence') with the Father. Yet despite this verdict, the doctrinal expression of the relationship of the Son to the Father remained a subject of ongoing debate, and over the decades that followed various positions emerged among those who taught that the Son was *homoios kat' ousian* ('like according to essence'), *homoios* ('like') or *anomoios* ('unlike') to the Father. Ecclesiastical rivalries added further fuel to these conflicts, and helped to cause the failure of repeated conciliar efforts to end the debates, notably the planned joint councils of the eastern and western Church at Serdica in 343 and at Ariminum and Seleucia in 359. The disputes had still not ceased by the time of Athanasius' death in 373, and indeed continued to exert influence even after the formal settlement of the doctrinal

[11] The reign of Constantine and his impact on the Church have always been a subject for great scholarly controversy. Among the most important recent contributions to these debates are Barnes (1981), Elliott (1996), Drake (2000), and Odahl (2004).

[12] For the chronology of the early 'Arian Controversy' adopted here, see Ch. 3.

debates with the reaffirmation of a slightly modified Nicene Creed at the second ecumenical Council of Constantinople in 381.[13]

For almost the entire period of these long and complex debates, Athanasius was a figure of huge controversy. He attended the Council of Nicaea in 325 as a young deacon and aide to bishop Alexander of Alexandria,[14] but his election to succeed Alexander on the latter's death in 328 faced immediate opposition within Egypt,[15] notably from the Melitians, a schismatic sect that had emerged in 305–6 during the Great Persecution.[16] Already in 332, Athanasius was summoned to the court of Constantine to defend himself over charges of extortion and violence against these Melitians, and similar charges recurred in 334, and culminated in his condemnation at the Council of Tyre in 335, and his exile by the emperor to 'the ends of the world' (Trier). Athanasius returned to Egypt on Constantine's death in late 337, but fled again in 339, going to Rome. He was defended by a Council called by Bishop Julius of Rome in 340, condemned by the 'Dedication' Council of Antioch in 341, defended by the western 'half' of the Council of Serdica in 343, condemned by the eastern 'half' of that same council, and finally returned to Alexandria in 346. After a decade of relative peace, Athanasius was then exiled once more by Constantine's son Constantius II in 356, and although he returned under the amnesty to Christian exiles ordered by Julian in 362, he subsequently experienced further short periods of exile under that emperor in 362–3, and again under Valens

13 The standard modern accounts of the fourth-century controversies are Simonetti (1975) and Hanson (1988*b*), to which have now been added Ayres (2004*b*) and Behr (2004) 61–122.

14 The role played by Athanasius at the Council of Nicaea, much exaggerated in later hagiography from the *Funeral Oration* of Gregory of Nazianzus onwards, would appear to have been minor. The earliest allusion to his activity at the Council occurs in the *Encyclical Letter* of the Council of Alexandria in 338 (quoted in Athanasius, *Apologia Contra Arianos* 6), but it is notable that in his own works and particularly in his later accounts of Nicaea, Athanasius never attributes to himself any prominent part in the council.

15 For surveys of the difficult evidence for Athanasius' election see Barnard (1975*b*) 329–36, who argues that the widely varied source material suggests that there were serious questions at stake, and the more panegyrical account of Arnold (1991) 25–48, who defends Athanasius' legitimate ordination.

16 On the origins and nature of the Melitian schism, see Bell (1924) 38–99, Barnard (1973), Martin (1974) and (1996) 219–389, and Hauben (1998).

in 365–6. By the 360s, however, Athanasius' position within Egypt was increasingly secure, and after his final return in 366 he remained in firm possession of his see until his death in 373.[17]

An awareness of the outline of Athanasius' turbulent episcopate is essential, for like the works of every author, the polemical writings of Athanasius can only be understood within the context in which they were composed, and it is those writings which comprise my subject. Not only has Athanasius' presentation of the fourth-century Christian controversies and their participants been hugely influential on later generations, but his writings represent the only extensive contemporary account of this critical period in the development of the Christian Church. Although it has long been recognized that Athanasius' works are highly polemical and tendentious, even to the extent that 'Athanasius consistently misrepresented central facts about his ecclesiastical career',[18] no modern scholar has yet fully explored the nature and implications of that polemic and its potential distortions.[19] The purpose of this monograph is to provide such an analysis, focusing upon Athanasius' construction of himself and of his opponents, the continuity and development of his polemic across the thirty-year span of his writings, and the evaluation of his presentation of the fourth-century Church and its ecclesiastical and theological controversies.

Athanasius was not a historian.[20] He wrote as a bishop and theologian engaged in a life or death struggle for his own conception

[17] More detailed outlines of Athanasius' career can be found in (among others) Tetz (1979*a*), Barnes (1993), and Martin (1996). Both the chronology and the interpretation of many of the events of Athanasius' life remain controversial, and I will return to the period 330–46 in particular in much greater detail in Chs 2–4.

[18] Barnes (1993) 2.

[19] Given Athanasius' importance as a source for the fourth-century Church, it is surprising that the only recent scholarly analysis concerned specifically with the polemical nature of Athanasius' writings is that of Christopher Stead (1976). The best explanation for that silence is perhaps to be found in Stead's own conclusion, in which he felt the need to justify his argument. 'To an extraordinary degree the faith of Athanasius has become the faith of the Church, and to criticize him must look as if we wished to shatter the rock from which we were hewn. Nevertheless I have come to think that the methods used by Athanasius in defending his faith will not serve to commend eternal truths to the present age; and it is for the Church's ultimate good that we seek to show where their weakness lies' (136–7).

[20] See Warmington (1986).

of the Christian religion, and at the same time as an accused man who needed to justify himself against the charges on which he had been convicted and exiled. It is against this background that we must approach his many polemical writings. Throughout those works, Athanasius presents a polarized vision of the fourth-century Church divided into two distinct factions, the 'orthodox' whom he represents, and 'the advocates of the Arian heresy'. This vision of the 'Arian Controversy' forms the framework for his construction of himself and of his foes. Athanasius depicts himself as the champion of 'orthodoxy', innocent of the charges levelled against him and assaulted at every turn by 'Arians', whose sole purpose was the elimination of the 'orthodox' in order to establish their 'heresy'. That depiction rests in turn upon Athanasius' presentation of his opponents as a collective 'heretical party', threatening not only himself but the Christian Church as a whole. It is this Athanasian construction of those he condemned as 'Arian' that this monograph will examine in detail, and specifically the presentation in Athanasius' polemical writings of the men whom he branded as '*hoi peri Eusebion*', 'those around Eusebius' or 'the Eusebians'.[21]

These so-called 'Eusebians', named not after the Church historian Eusebius of Caesarea but his contemporary and namesake Eusebius, bishop of Nicomedia, are presented in all Athanasius' polemical writings as an ecclesiastical and above all heretical 'party'. For Athanasius, and for the later historians who followed his lead, the 'Eusebians' represented the leading supporters of Arius and his theology both before and after the Council of Nicaea. They are the men who sought to impose 'Arianism' upon the Church in the years after 325, and who persecuted and expelled all those 'orthodox' bishops who resisted their 'heresy', most notably of course Athanasius himself. As we shall see in subsequent chapters, the identification of the individual members of this 'Eusebian party' is often difficult, for Athanasius rarely names the men whom he collectively condemns. But the title '*hoi peri Eusebion*', and the polarized contrast that Athanasius draws between the 'Arianism' of the 'Eusebians' and his own 'orthodoxy',

[21] I have translated '*hoi peri Eusebion*' throughout this monograph as 'the Eusebians'. I will return to the textual significance of this characteristic Athanasian expression in Ch. 5.

recurs consistently from Athanasius' earliest extant polemical works after his condemnation in 335 to the later writings of his third exile (356–62), by the end of which Eusebius of Nicomedia had been dead for some twenty years.

There has been much recent revisionist scholarship concerning the fourth-century Church and the 'Arian Controversy'. The relative insignificance of Arius himself within the debates has been amply demonstrated, notably by Maurice Wiles,[22] while Hanson among others has emphasized that the traditional image of a conflict between established 'orthodoxy' and manifest 'heresy' cannot be maintained. 'On the subject which was primarily under discussion there was not as yet any orthodox doctrine... [the controversy] is not the story of a defence of orthodoxy, but a search for orthodoxy, a search conducted by the method of trial and error'.[23] Furthermore, the distortion inherent in Athanasius' presentation of his foes has likewise been acknowledged, for 'it was Athanasius' great polemical success to cast his opponents as "Arians"'.[24] No modern student of the so-called 'Arian Controversy' is now unaware of these problems of terminology and categorization.[25] As Rowan Williams declared in his review of Hanson, 'the time has probably come to relegate the term "Arianism" at least to inverted commas, and preferably to oblivion'.[26]

Yet the legacy of the polarized polemic of Athanasius, and to a lesser extent that of other 'orthodox' writers, has not proved so easy to avoid. The assumption that it is possible to identify a theological position that can in some sense be described as 'Arian' remains highly pervasive, and no-one has yet fully taken up the challenge that Williams laid down. Few modern writers have thus ever seen fit to question Athanasius' presentation of the 'Eusebians' as an ecclesiastical and heretical 'party', or to deny that Eusebius of Nicomedia was the leader of that 'party', and in some sense an 'Arian'.[27] Hanson indeed refers explicitly to 'the kind of Arianism professed by Arius,

22 Wiles (1996). 23 Hanson (1988*b*) xviii–xx; see also id. (1989).

24 M. R. Barnes and D. H. Williams (eds.) (1993), 'Introduction', xv; see also M. R. Barnes (1998) 53–8.

25 See the recent remarks of Ayres (2004*b*) 2–3, 13–14, and Behr (2004) 21–36.

26 R. D. Williams (1992) 102.

27 To my knowledge, the only exceptions that reject this traditional assessment of Eusebius of Nicomedia are the articles of Luibheid (1976) and Gwynn (1999).

and among his followers by Eusebius of Nicomedia/Constantinople',[28] and declares 'that Eusebius was the leader of a party, and that he was recognized as such by his contemporaries, there can be no doubt at all'.[29] Williams prefers to speak of the 'Eusebians' as a 'loose and uneasy coalition', organized around the pupils of Lucian of Antioch,[30] and a similarly broad definition of 'Eusebian theology' has been adopted recently by Lienhard,[31] followed in turn by Ayres.[32] But none of these writers question the existence in some shape or form of a 'Eusebian party', and few would challenge the verdict of T. D. Barnes, that 'ecclesiastical politics after Nicaea are party politics'.[33]

All of these scholars rightly emphasize that the writings of Athanasius are highly tendentious and potentially distorted. Yet I believe that it is necessary to look more closely at the nature of Athanasius' polemic and the construction of the 'Eusebians' that his works create. Athanasius represents his opponents as an organized 'heretical party', who employ both ecclesiastical patronage and secular power to achieve their collective aims and above all to promote their shared 'Arian' theology. But can we accept Athanasius' presentation of the actions, motives, and above all the theology of the men whom he described as 'Eusebians' at face value? Did the 'Arian party' that figures so prominently in Athanasius' works actually exist, or is it a polemical construct? And if the 'Eusebians' are such a construct, what might this imply for our understanding of Athanasius' own career and of the fourth-century doctrinal controversies as a whole?

Only the detailed analysis of the polemic of Athanasius can begin to provide answers to these questions. As we have already seen, Athanasius' writings comprise the only substantial contemporary account of the fourth-century controversies and their participants, while the works of the men whom he described as 'Eusebians', by contrast, have survived only in fragments. Those works would presumably have been no less biased and distorted than those of Athanasius himself, and it is important to emphasize that to question

[28] Hanson (1988*b*) 290. [29] Ibid. 275.

[30] Williams (1987) 166 (the same phrase is adopted by Behr (2004) 53). For a discussion of the controversial question of Lucian and his influence, see Ch. 7.

[31] Lienhard (1999) 34–5. [32] Ayres (2004*b*) 52. [33] Barnes (1981) 225.

the presentation of events and individuals in Athanasius is not simply to assume that any other presentation must therefore be true. But in the absence of such alternative evidence, Athanasius' construction of the 'Eusebians' must be approached through the examination of the content, methodology, and motivation of his polemic, and of the development of that polemical construction across his various works.

The main body of this monograph is divided into three sections. Part I identifies the corpus of writings within which Athanasius' construction of the 'Eusebians' is presented. Before turning to the actual content of his polemic, it is essential to establish the approximate chronology (if not necessarily the precise dates of composition) of the individual works that Athanasius wrote, for his construction of his opponents evolves markedly over time, while the context and intended audience of a given work must inevitably influence the arguments that Athanasius presents (Chapter 1). Only then will it become possible in Part II to define Athanasius' construction of the 'Eusebians' more precisely, and to trace the origins and development of that construct from its earliest appearance in Athanasius' works in the period surrounding his condemnation at the Council of Tyre in 335 (Chapters 2–4).

This definition then provides the foundation for the analysis of that construct in the light of Athanasius' own polemical methodology and by comparison with our fragmentary alternative evidence for the careers and theological writings of those whom he condemns. This is the subject of Part III. The analysis begins with a further consideration of the concept of a 'church party' and of the individuals whom in his different works Athanasius names as 'Eusebians' (Chapter 5). This is followed by an evaluation of Athanasius' depiction of the 'Eusebians' in action, particularly their alleged manipulation of ecclesiastical and imperial politics and the persecution that they are reported to have inspired against Athanasius and other 'orthodox' leaders (Chapter 6). The last and longest chapter then examines in detail the theological dimension so important to Athanasius' polemic, above all the polarization that he constructs between his own 'orthodoxy' and the 'Arianism' of his foes. The development of that polarization can be traced from his initial theological writings in the 330s and early 340s through to the later works in which Athanasius placed an ever-increasing emphasis upon the Council of

Nicaea and the Nicene Creed (Chapter 7). As we shall see, although Athanasius' presentation of the 'Eusebians' as 'Arian' has exerted great influence, it is this theological dimension of his polemic that reveals most explicitly the degree to which Athanasius has distorted our knowledge of the fourth-century Christian controversies, of the men he condemns, and of himself.

Part I

1

The Polemical Writings of Athanasius: Chronology and Context

Athanasius' construction of his opponents as the 'Eusebians' occurs throughout his numerous writings, in works that vary widely in form, purpose, and intended audience.[1] Athanasius was certainly an educated man, but the extent of that education remains uncertain,[2] and his writings rarely fall within the traditional models of classical rhetoric.[3] In any case, polemic is not a genre in its own right, and indeed there is no precise distinction between polemic and the related category of 'apologetic', for arguments composed in defence of oneself or others almost invariably contain (as in the writings of Athanasius) polemical elements against one's accusers.[4]. I have therefore defined 'polemic' here fairly loosely, as a general descriptive term for the works and arguments through which Athanasius constructs

[1] In this chapter I am concerned solely with Athanasius' extant written works. All of these works must at the time of their composition and distribution have been accompanied by oral messages, as indeed is explicitly stated at the end of the *Encyclical Letter* of the Council of Alexandria of 338 (quoted in *Apologia Contra Arianos* 19) and in Athanasius' own *Epistula Encyclica* (1).

[2] Gregory of Nazianzus (*Oration* XXI.6) declares that Athanasius studied non-Christian literature only to avoid complete ignorance. The report of Sozomen (II.17) that Athanasius was educated in grammar and rhetoric cannot be confirmed, for the ultimate source of this report, the Latin *Ecclesiastical History* of Rufinus (X.15), merely states that Athanasius was instructed by a *notarius* and *grammaticus*, without reference to a *rhetor*. For further discussion, see Stead (1976).

[3] Barnes (1993) 11.

[4] On the difficulty of classifying 'apologetic' texts as a literary genre, and the widely varied definitions that can be applied to terms like 'polemic' and 'apologetic', see the papers collected in Edwards, Goodman, and Price (eds.) (1999), and particularly the introductory discussion by the editors (1–13).

his presentation of himself and his opponents. Before we can turn to the content and development of that construction, it is necessary to examine briefly the individual works themselves from which that construct derives.

Athanasius composed his attacks upon the 'Eusebians' across a span of some three decades, during a period of great personal and ecclesiastical controversy. Every work was written in a different context for a different audience,[5] and Athanasius' presentation of himself and of his foes in a given text must therefore be assessed according to the events and motives that caused him to write. For the vast majority of Athanasius' works, it must be admitted, the specific context of composition is impossible to determine with absolute precision. Several of his works underwent multiple stages of editing and revision, while the traditional Athanasian authorship of a number of texts has been questioned in recent years. The dates, audiences, and purposes proposed for Athanasius' individual writings in the catalogue that follows thus cannot be definitive. But it is essential to establish at least the chronological sequence in which Athanasius' works were written, for only then may the relationships between the different texts and the development of Athanasius' polemic over time be identified.

Certain Athanasian (or traditionally Athanasian) works have been omitted from this catalogue, for reasons that perhaps require explanation.[6] A few texts in his corpus, while unquestionably of genuine authorship, are not directly relevant to the present study of Athanasius' polemic. This includes many of his letters (including the four *Letters to Serapion on the Holy Spirit*), the majority of Athanasius' ascetic writings,[7] and most importantly the treatise *Contra Gentes-De*

[5] The old assumption that polemical writings were invariably addressed to those against whom the polemic is directed has been increasingly abandoned as modern scholars have recognized that such texts are often actually intended for an internal audience already sympathetic to the author. The readership would have been largely but not exclusively ecclesiastic, including some of the monastic communities of Egypt. See Warmington (1986) 13–14.

[6] In addition to the works discussed below, I have also omitted here the *Encyclical Letter* of Alexander of Alexandria, which Stead (1988) has attributed to Athanasius. I will return to this argument in Ch. 3.

[7] For a recent assessment of these 'Ascetic Athanasiana' and their variable authenticity, see Brakke (1994).

Incarnatione, a much-debated work but one that contains no explicit reference to 'Arians' or 'Arian' theology.[8] Other texts, however, have been rejected as they are no longer believed to have been written by Athanasius at all. Thus the *Fourth Oration against the Arians*, different in argument and vocabulary to the other three *Orations* although sharing a number of similarities with Athanasian theology, has long been recognized as a pseudonymous work.[9] Charles Kannengiesser has also questioned the Athanasian authorship of the *Third Oration*,[10] but this argument has been widely criticized,[11] and the Athanasian authorship of all three *Orations* has here been upheld. I do believe, on the other hand, that Kannengiesser is correct to reject the Athanasian authorship of the *Epistula Ad Afros*, which would appear to have been composed by a later author familiar with Athanasius' earlier works.[12]

These exceptions having been omitted, the remaining polemical writings of Athanasius have been catalogued below in their

[8] My omission of the *Contra Gentes-De Incarnatione* here is certainly not to deny the importance of this work for Athanasius' own theology (see Ch. 7).

[9] For recent debates concerning the content, context, and provenance of this work, see Hanson (1988*a*), who places the *Fourth Oration* with the followers of Eustathius of Antioch in the 350s, and in particular Vinzent (1996), who argues more plausibly that the work was composed by an unknown author in the period immediately preceding the Council of Rome and the 'Dedication' Council of Antioch in 340–1.

[10] Kannengiesser (1982) 994–5. Kannengiesser later refined this argument (1993*a*), and argued that the *Third Oration* is divided into three distinct parts (a conclusion upheld in my discussion of the *Orations* below), and then more dubiously that in language and theology at least the first two sections (1–25, 26–58) are not Athanasian but Apollinarian.

[11] Stead (1985*b*) 227; Hanson (1988*b*) 418. In an earlier response, Stead (1981) observes that Kannengiesser's theory requires 'a totally slavish, though talented, imitator, who, moreover completely altered his vocabulary and argumentation later in life. Try believing that before breakfast.' In a paper given at the recent Oxford patristics conference (2003), Kannengiesser conceded that his attribution of the *Third Oration* to Apollinarius of Laodicea was 'over-adventurous'.

[12] Kannengiesser (1993*b*), an argument admittedly based in part on his questionable interpretation of the *Third Oration against the Arians*. Kannengiesser's argument has been challenged by Stockhausen (2002), who dates the *Ad Afros* to 367 and highlights the literary parallels between this text and Athanasius' authentic writings. However, such parallels are hardly surprising in a work that draws heavily upon earlier Athanasian writings, particularly the *De Decretis* and the *De Synodis*, and it still needs to be explained why the *Ad Afros* is the only 'Athanasian' work to refer to 318 bishops at Nicaea (*Ad Afros* 2) or to repeatedly praise the 'bishop of Great Rome' (1, 10). It thus still seems more probable that the *Ad Afros* is not by Athanasius, but is early evidence for the influence of his polemic on later generations.

approximate order of chronology and context, an order that has been the subject of much recent scholarly revision.[13]

THE *APOLOGIA CONTRA ARIANOS*

The *Apologia Contra Arianos*[14] demonstrates acutely the difficulties of date and context that Athanasius' works so often pose. This long and complex text, which represents the only detailed extant account of the events that surrounded Athanasius' condemnation at the Council of Tyre in 335, is not a single composition, but an assemblage of documents of varying dates and authorship connected by an Athanasian narrative. The documents themselves date from before Athanasius' accession in 328 to after the Western Council of Serdica in 343, and are collected into two chronological sections, the first half covering 338–47, and the second half (somewhat confusingly) covering the earlier period of 328–37. However, the narrative that surrounds these documents cannot be dated with certainty. The last section of the text (89–90) refers to the persecution and lapse of Liberius of Rome and Ossius of Cordova, conventionally placed in 358,[15] but while this reference has provided the traditional date for the entire work,[16] these passages appear to be a later addition and cannot provide a context for the *Apologia Contra Arianos* as a whole.[17] Moreover, the addition of this final section would seem to represent only one of a series of editorial phases that occurred before

[13] For a useful survey see Leemans (2000) 129–71.

[14] In the most recent Greek edition of the *Apologia Contra Arianos*, Opitz (1938*a*–1940*a*) follows the earlier manuscript editors who misnamed this work the *Apologia Secunda* (due to its placement after the *Apologia de Fuga*). As Barnes (1993) observes, this title 'is both inauthentic and seriously misleading' (6.n.30).

[15] For the revised date of 357 for this episode accepted throughout this chapter, see the discussion of the *Historia Arianorum* below.

[16] E.g. Opitz (1938*a*) 87; Young (1983) 76; Hanson (1988*b*) 420; Arnold (1991) 3.n.5.

[17] Likewise, the statement in *Apologia Contra Arianos* 59 that at the time when he wrote Athanasius was suffering from persecution, which has often been interpreted as a reference to the period of his third exile (356–62) and thus as confirmation for a composition date of 358, could equally refer to his second exile (339–46), and cannot be taken as evidence for the date of the overall work.

the work reached its final extant form. It is thus extremely difficult to determine accurately the date or dates when the documents that Athanasius cites were collected or when the interlocking narrative around them may have been composed.

The most plausible theory, albeit one that must be treated with caution, is that the *Apologia Contra Arianos* was composed in multiple stages. This argument was first proposed in a 1932 thesis by Seiler[18], and more recently was restated in a revised form by T. D. Barnes.[19] In Barnes' simplified model, which reduced the initial six 'stages' of Seiler to four, Athanasius first composed a defence against his conviction at Tyre, consisting of a narrative supported by but not integrated with a documentary archive, for the Council of Alexandria that he called in 338 on his return from his first exile.[20] This initial narrative and its associated documents were then combined into a single text, 'almost identical to the present second part (59.1–88.2)',[21] after Athanasius had fled Alexandria into his second exile in 339. It was this text that he presented to the Council of Rome in 340 and to the Western Council of Serdica in 343. The third stage of revision then took place after Athanasius' return to Egypt in 346, when, according to Barnes, 'Athanasius composed the first part (1–58) and a peroration (probably 88.3 and 90.1,3) to defend himself at the Council of Antioch which met and deposed him in 349 . . . he included the already existing second part to show that the charges brought against him had always been false'.[22] Finally, the *Apologia Contra Arianos* reached its present form through a series of additional phases of minor editing,[23] most notably of course the references to Liberius and Ossius.[24]

[18] R. Seiler, *Athanasius'* Apologia Contra Arianos *(Ihre Enstehung und Datierung)* (Diss. Tübingen, 1932).

[19] Barnes (1993), Appendix 2, 'The Composition of the *Defence against the Arians*' (192–5).

[20] Ibid. 194. According to Seiler, this initial account comprised the narrative sketch that later became *Apologia Contra Arianos* 59.1–5, 60.1–3, 63.1–5, 65.1–4, 71.1–2, 72.2–6, 82, 86.1, 87.1–2, and 88.1, and he proposed that Athanasius may already have produced such an account in preparation for his appeal to Constantine after the Council of Tyre in 335. For reasons that will emerge later in this monograph, however, it is highly unlikely that Athanasius' polemical narrative could have been composed this early.

[21] Barnes (1993) 194. [22] Ibid. 194–5. [23] Ibid. 195.

[24] According to Jones (1954) 224–7, changes were still being made after 370, for the manuscript text of *Apologia Contra Arianos* 83.4 refers to a certain Rufus, who had

The primary weakness of this 'stage model' is the lack of evidence for the precise dates and contexts to which Barnes assigns the different stages of editing that he has identified. That some form of text must have existed by 338 can be taken as established, for the synodal letter of the Council of Alexandria in that year (quoted in *Apologia Contra Arianos* 3–19) drew upon parts of the narrative and some of the documents later incorporated into the second half of the work. A further phase of composition between 338 and 340 would likewise seem to be highly probable, for Julius of Rome's *Letter to the Eastern Bishops* (*Apologia Contra Arianos* 20–35) reflects the influence of that second section of Athanasius' work in something resembling its present form. However, there is no evidence in the *Apologia Contra Arianos* or elsewhere to suggest that Athanasius felt the need to revise the text in order to defend himself at the Council of Antioch in 349. Barnes' reconstruction is not impossible, but it is purely a hypothesis. All that can actually be said with confidence is that the first half of the *Apologia Contra Arianos* was almost certainly composed between the beginning of 347, when the 'Eusebians' Ursacius and Valens wrote their so-called 'Recantation' of the charges against Athanasius (*Apologia Contra Arianos* 58), and *c.*350/1 when their statement was withdrawn. Athanasius places great emphasis upon the 'Recantation' in both the introduction (1–2) and the peroration (58) of the first half of his work, but he shows no awareness of its subsequent withdrawal.[25] This silence is not decisive, but it would seem that the *Apologia Contra Arianos* thus reached approximately its final shape (with the exception of minor later additions) in the period 347–51,[26]

been a secretary with the Mareotis Commission, having later become Augustal Prefect. Opitz amended the text to remove this reference, as no such Prefect was known before 382, but Jones argues that the first such Prefect took office *c.*367–70, and thus that the text must have been edited after this date.

[25] In particular, Athanasius declares near the end of the *Apologia Contra Arianos* that by their recantation Ursacius and Valens chose 'rather to suffer shame for a little time, than to undergo the punishment of false accusers for eternity' (88; Opitz (1940*a*) 167, 9–10). It seems unlikely that Athanasius would have written such a statement after the two bishops had resumed their accusations against him.

[26] This conclusion rejects the argument of Orlandi (1975), who placed the main phase of the composition of the *Apologia Contra Arianos* after 351. As Barnes (1993) 194 observes, this argument underestimates the central role that the recantation of Ursacius and Valens plays in the first half of the *Apologia Contra Arianos*.

although not necessarily in the specific context that Barnes would propose.

We may therefore conclude that the narrative and documentary archive of the second half of this work was essentially completed in the period 338–40, and that of the first half in 347–51. Contrary to those who still argue that the *Apologia Contra Arianos* is a unitary whole,[27] the different sections of this Athanasian work were thus written at different times for different immediate contexts and audiences. For the purposes of this monograph, more specific dates of composition for those sections are not necessarily required. Rather, what is important to emphasize is that whatever chronology we adopt, the Athanasian narrative of the *Apologia Contra Arianos* must post-date his condemnation and exile in 335, whereas a number of the documents preserved in the second half of the *Apologia Contra Arianos* pre-date the Council of Tyre. Athanasius' narrative must thus be distinguished from the documents that he quotes, for the narrative represents Athanasius' later polemical interpretation of the events that led to his first exile. As we shall see in Chapter 3, there are significant discrepancies between the narrative account and the evidence of the documents themselves.[28] The primary purpose of the *Apologia Contra Arianos* in all its incarnations was to vindicate Athanasius against the charges on which he was convicted in 335, and to present his construction of the 'Eusebians', the men whom he held responsible for his condemnation. The contrast between the narrative and the documents of this defence will prove crucial when we come to examine the origins and development of that polemical presentation in detail.

[27] To those who follow the conclusion of Opitz that the work was composed entirely in 357/8, one should add the arguments of Twomey (1982) 292–305, who restated the theory of unitary composition but with a date of 356, when he believed Athanasius received a copy of the recantation of Ursacius and Valens, and of Warmington (1986) 8, who placed the *Apologia Contra Arianos* in *c.*350, inspired by Athanasius' need to defend himself on Constans' death.

[28] These discrepancies also represent a powerful argument against the older assertion of Otto Seeck (already refuted by Baynes (1925) 61–5) that Athanasius was an 'arch-forger' who fabricated the documents that he cites for his own purposes. This is not to deny, however, that Athanasius' documentary archives still require careful handling (see Young (1983) 76, Warmington (1986) 9), for the documents that we possess are those that he chose to preserve, and either defend his own presentation of events or are interpreted through his polemical narrative.

THE *EPISTULA ENCYCLICA*

The *Apologia Contra Arianos* has been placed at the head of this catalogue of Athanasian writings because it had already begun to take shape by the time of the Council of Alexandria in 338. However, the earliest complete polemical work that can be ascribed with certainty to Athanasius is in fact the *Epistula Encyclica* (also known as the *Epistula ad Episcopos*), a short letter written approximately one year after that council. Athanasius had returned from his first exile on Constantine's death, arriving in Alexandria on 23 November 337. He was then condemned once more by a Council of Antioch attended by the new eastern emperor Constantius in late 338, and Gregory of Cappadocia was appointed to take control of his see. The *Epistula Encyclica* describes the recent entrance of Gregory into the city of Alexandria on 22 March 339, and Athanasius' own subsequent flight back into exile on 16 April of that same year.[29] The letter can therefore be dated with confidence to mid-339.

The traditional view of the composition and immediate audience of the *Epistula Encyclica* is that the letter was written shortly before Athanasius arrived in Rome during his second exile, possibly while the bishop was hiding in the Egyptian desert.[30] The most important intended recipient of the letter was thus the Bishop of Rome himself. Athanasius, it is argued, sought to prepare his position in the west in advance of his own arrival, and to proclaim his innocence despite his renewed exile. This view has been challenged by Barnes, who argues that Athanasius would not have delayed to write such a letter while in Constantius' territory, and therefore that he wrote the *Epistula Encyclica* immediately upon reaching Rome,[31] with the primary

[29] The precise dates for the events of 337–8 given here derive from *Festal Index* X–XI. A number of older scholars have argued that the years given in the *Festal Index* for this period are one year too early, and thus place Athanasius' return from his first exile in 338, the Council of Alexandria in 339 (Baynes (1925) 65–9, Nordberg (1964) 34, Barnard (1975*b*) 338 and (1983) 26–7), and the arrival of Gregory and the second flight of Athanasius in 340 (Bright (1881) ix). The chronology adopted here, which accepts the *Festal Index* dates as accurate, is that constructed by Schneemelcher (1974*a*) 309–15 and followed by Hanson (1988*b*) 266–7 and Barnes (1993) 36.

[30] E.g. Schneemelcher (1977) 322; Hanson (1988*b*) 419.

[31] Barnes (1993) 50.

audience being 'eastern bishops who had taken no part in Athanasius' deposition'.[32] However, Barnes can cite no evidence for either of these assertions, and there seems no reason to assume that Athanasius intended the letter for a specifically eastern or western audience. As Barnes indeed observes, Athanasius' purpose in the *Epistula Encyclica* was 'to persuade the bishops who received the letter not to recognize his successor as bishop of Alexandria',[33] a threat to Athanasius' own position that he had not faced during his first exile when Constantine refused to allow such a replacement to be installed. It was therefore essential to Athanasius that his own polemical interpretation of these events reached as wide an audience as possible in both east and west, whether he wrote from the Egyptian desert or in Rome itself. As we shall see in the next chapter, the *Epistula Encyclica* of 339 represents the earliest concise statement of Athanasius' construction of his foes as an 'Arian party', presenting Gregory as nothing more than the nominee of the 'Eusebians'.

THE THREE *ORATIONS AGAINST THE ARIANS*

To an even greater extent than any other Athanasian work, the three authentic *Orations against the Arians* have been the subject of scholarly controversy. The date and context of their composition and their intended audience and purpose all remain uncertain, and indeed it is probable that the three *Orations* themselves were not originally written as a unified whole, and that different *Orations*, and even individual sections within a given *Oration*, may have been written at different times and for different audiences and motives. The following argument does not claim to be conclusive, but certain questions must be raised before the *Orations* can be studied as a source of Athanasian polemic, and in particular it is necessary to justify their placement in this chronological catalogue immediately following the *Epistula Encyclica* of 339.

The *Nicene and Post-Nicene Fathers* translation of Athanasius' writings followed the conventional chronology of his works and

[32] Ibid. 49. [33] Ibid. 48.

placed the *Orations against the Arians* in 356–60, among the works of Athanasius' third exile.[34] Yet there is very little explicit evidence for date of composition within the *Orations* themselves, and what evidence does exist suggests a date considerably earlier than *c.*356. The statements that Arius is dead (I.3) and that Constantius is emperor (I.10, III.28) merely confirm that the *Orations* were written between 337 and 361, but far more significant, as has long been recognized, is that in all the long and repetitive arguments of the three *Orations*, the term *homoousios* occurs only once (I.9). This silence, which also extends to the Council of Nicaea itself, stands in stark contrast to every known theological work composed by Athanasius in the period of his third exile, for by 356 at the latest and probably from some years earlier Athanasius had already begun to represent himself as the champion of the Nicene Creed against the 'Arian heresy'.[35] There is thus considerable justification for the argument, presented most strongly by Charles Kannengiesser, that the *Orations against the Arians* should not be dated to the 350s, but to the period of Athanasius' second exile, 339–46.[36]

Kannengiesser's reinterpretation of the *Orations* is much more complex than merely an argument over chronology. Not only does he deny that the *Third Oration* is Athanasian at all, an argument rejected earlier in this chapter, but Kannengiesser also proposes that the extant texts of the *First* and *Second Orations* were not originally composed in anything resembling their present form, but are instead later revisions of an earlier and simpler treatise.[37] That treatise, according to his theory, included neither the introduction to the *First Oration* (I.1–10), which incorporates the summary of Arius' *Thalia* and the sole use of *homoousios*, nor the detailed exegesis of Proverbs 8:22 in the *Second Oration*. Instead, 'the two treatises, *C.Ar.* 1–2, were completed in their original form, as one single treatise, in 339–340 when the exiled Athanasius secured himself in Rome. They

[34] Robertson (1892) 303–4.

[35] This Athanasian self-presentation first appears in the *De Decretis Nicanae Synodi*, another work difficult to date precisely (see below), but which was certainly composed between 350 and 356.

[36] Kannengiesser (1982) and (1983*a*).

[37] That original draft apparently consisted of *Orations* I.11–28, I.35–64, II.2–18a, and II.44–72 (Kannengiesser (1982) 983–4; see also id. (1983*a*) 373–4).

were reworked by him with more documentary evidence about the Arian doctrine, including the *Thalia* fragments, before his return from the West in October 346, or just after it'.[38] Furthermore, Kannengiesser believes that this original treatise is the 'short account (*di' oligōn*) concerning what we have suffered ourselves . . . [and] refuting as far as I may the abominable heresy of the Ariomaniacs', that Athanasius states that he has sent to his correspondents in his *Ad Monachos* 1.1 (Opitz (1940*a*) 181, 6–7), a letter which Kannengiesser dates to *c*.339. The 'short account' in question has traditionally been identified as Athanasius' later *Historia Arianorum*, to which the *Ad Monachos* had been attached as a preface. But Kannengiesser asserts that his reduced 'Treatise' 'corresponds perfectly'[39] to the text that Athanasius describes, and thus he concludes that the *Ad Monachos* provides both the context and the audience for the original '*Oration against the Arians*'.[40]

There are certain weaknesses in this argument, both in Kannengiesser's interpretation of the *Ad Monachos* and in his overall conception of a reduced original 'Treatise'. The separation of the *Ad Monachos* from the *Historia Arianorum* is highly persuasive,[41] but Kannengiesser's proposed 'Oration' can hardly be said to 'perfectly correspond' to the text referred to in that letter. Athanasius declares that the work he has sent is not purely a theological treatise but also describes his own suffering, which the *Orations* certainly do not, while Kannengiesser's reduced 'Treatise' is still a substantial work, and is no easier to reconcile with Athanasius' reference to a 'short account' than the *Historia Arianorum*.[42] More significantly,

[38] Kannengiesser (1985*a*) 62. Kannengiesser repeated this argument in 1993*a* (377–8), and again at the Oxford patristics conference (2003), suggesting that the first draft was possibly begun as early as 337.

[39] Kannengiesser (1982) 992.

[40] In his 1993*a* article, Kannengiesser further develops this argument, suggesting that the same Egyptian audience also received the *Contra Gentes-De Incarnatione*, which he placed in 335, and that this audience then requested the refutation of Arianism that was absent from that double treatise (376).

[41] The manuscript connection between these two works had already been questioned by Robertson (1892) 267–8.

[42] Like Robertson (1892) 268 and Brakke (1995) 131, my own belief is that the work or works referred to in the *Ad Monachos* have not survived, in keeping with Athanasius' instructions to the monks to neither copy the texts in question nor to allow them to be copied.

no explicit evidence supports the existence of Kannengiesser's hypothetical 'Treatise',[43] and although it is true that some sections of the extant *Orations* may have originated as individual compositions, his argument underestimates the underlying unity of the *Three Orations* in their present form. In particular, as I will seek to demonstrate in the final Part of this monograph, Athanasius' introductory presentation of 'Arianism' and the *Thalia* in *Oration* I.1–10 is not a later addition, but lays the rhetorical and theological foundation for Athanasius' construction of his 'Arian' foes. For this reason, in an analysis of the polemic of Athanasius the three *Orations against the Arians* must still be treated as a coherent whole.[44]

Despite these criticisms, Kannengiesser's revised chronology for the *Orations* should be broadly accepted, for the period of Athanasius' second exile (339–46) remains the most plausible context for their composition. These years were crucial to the development of Athanasius' construction of himself and of the 'Eusebians', as the *Epistula Encyclica* and the *Apologia Contra Arianos* also demonstrate. The *Orations against the Arians* represent the theological expression of that construction, proclaiming both Athanasius' own 'orthodoxy' and the condemnation of the 'Arianism' that he attributes to his foes.[45] At the same time, this earlier date for the *Orations* also renders Athanasius' theological arguments more immediately relevant to the period in which he wrote. The primary subjects of his polemic, namely Arius (d.336), Eusebius of Nicomedia (d.341/2), and their associate Asterius 'the Sophist' (d.*c*.343), are no longer figures of the past but prominent contemporary 'heretics', and the theology

[43] As emphasized by Stead (1985*b*) 226, (1994) 29.

[44] This is not to deny that there are visible differences particularly between the first two *Orations* and the third, which appears to have been written slightly later (perhaps *c*.342–5), and is not as tightly structured, being comprised of three largely distinct blocs (1–25, 26–58, 59–67). Among a number of recent studies of this *Third Oration*, see in particular Abramowski (1991), Kannengiesser (1995), and above all Meijering (1996–8), whose three volume study follows the tripartite division of the work itself. However, as all three *Orations* do share the same polemical framework and theological terminology (including the silence on *homoousios*), the differences between them are not directly relevant to the argument presented here.

[45] This conclusion agrees with the increasingly popular model of the 'construction of Arianism' during the period when Athanasius and Marcellus of Ancyra were both in exile in Rome: see M. R. Barnes (1998) 55; Ayres (2004*b*) 106; Behr (2004) 76; and Parvis (2004).

expressed in the *Orations* is likewise more appropriate to the context of the early 340s than the later 350s. Although no argument for the exact chronology of the *Orations* can be decisive, I would therefore agree with Hanson that 'we should place the composition of the *Orationes contra Arianos* between 339 and 345, perhaps envisaging their production as a fairly long drawn-out process over that time'.[46]

This earlier date of composition assigned to the *Orations* must in turn alter our understanding of the intended audience and purpose for which these works were written, a complex question for which no single explanation will suffice.[47] In the Introduction to the *First Oration*, Athanasius declares that he wrote in response to the requests of individuals who held theological positions akin to his own (I.1; Tetz (1998) 110, 16–17). There is an element of rhetoric in this statement, for Athanasius invariably insists that he composed his works not on his own behalf but in reaction to the errors of 'heretics' and to the pleas of others. But it is also true that apologetic and polemical writings are often intended less to convince their ostensible targets than to provide material and encouragement for those who already share the beliefs of the writer.[48] Certain sections of the *Orations* would seem to have been written for just such an audience. Thus Athanasius concludes his detailed exegesis of Proverbs 8:22 with the explicit statement that his purpose was 'to furnish these arguments as a reason (*prophasin*) for those more learned to construct further arguments in refutation of the Arian heresy' (II.72; Tetz (1998) 250, 24–5). Such a statement would suggest that Athanasius was writing less to convince his 'Arian' foes than to rally

[46] Hanson (1988*b*) 419.

[47] Thus neither the argument of Robertson (1892) 303 that the *Orations* were written against the 'Arians' Valens and Eudoxius in the later 350s nor that of Kannengiesser (1982) 992 that the intended audience for his original 'Treatise' were the Egyptian recipients of the *Ad Monachos* is entirely satisfactory, although both these approaches have elements of truth.

[48] This interpretation, which can equally be applied to the *Contra Gentes-De Incarnatione* (as it was by Meijering (1968) 107–8) and to Athanasius' other anti-Arian writings, particularly the *De Decretis*, finds an interesting parallel in Theodoret's description of the later theologian Diodore of Tarsus. According to Theodoret, Diodore 'did not himself preach at the services of the Church, but furnished a great abundant supply of arguments and scriptural thoughts to preachers, who were thus able to aim their shafts at the blasphemy of Arius' (IV.25.4–5; Parmentier (1998) 264, 8–11).

his own supporters in east and west, and to reinforce both their opposition to 'Arianism' and their association with himself.

At the same time, Athanasius also insists in his introduction that he wrote 'so that those who are far from it [the Arian heresy] may continue to flee it [and] those who have been deceived by it may repent' (I.1; Tetz (1998) 110, 18–19). Here again there is a strong element of rhetoric, and Athanasius' repeated appeals to his 'Arian' opponents to heed his words and cease to struggle against the truth cannot be taken at face value as evidence that Eusebius of Nicomedia and other alleged 'Arians' were truly the intended audience for the *Orations*. Yet it is probable that Athanasius did compose the *Orations* not only to reassure those who already shared his theology, but also to convince others, particularly in the east, to acknowledge both his own 'orthodoxy' and the 'Arianism' of those he wished to condemn. From the outset, the congregations and above all the bishops of the wider Christian body, particularly in the east, comprised an essential audience for Athanasius' polemical works. Like all of those works, the *Orations against the Arians* thus had a dual audience and a dual purpose, to reinforce Athanasius' position among his own supporters and to persuade others to uphold his presentation both of himself and of his opponents.

THE *DE MORTE ARII* (LETTER LIV, 'THE LETTER TO SERAPION (BISHOP OF THUMIS) ON THE DEATH OF ARIUS')

In his reconstruction of the *Orations against the Arians* and the *Ad Monachos* that we have just considered above, Charles Kannengiesser also proposed a new interpretation for the date and purpose of another much-debated Athanasian polemical text, the *Letter to Serapion* that describes the death of Arius, usually known as the *De Morte Arii*. This work has traditionally been dated to 358, for the opening paragraph of the letter states that 'I have despatched to your piety what I wrote to the monks' (1; Opitz (1940*a*) 178, 5–6). Thus the *De Morte Arii* must have been written shortly after the *Ad Monachos*, which in turn was placed in 358 alongside the *Historia*

Arianorum.[49] When Kannengiesser reassigned the *Ad Monachos* to the earlier period of Athanasius' second exile, therefore, he also reassessed the *De Morte Arii*, and declared that this work too must date from 'the first part of Athanasius' Roman exile', between 339 and 342.[50]

For the *De Morte Arii*, as for the *Orations against the Arians*, the argument that the date of composition was earlier than traditionally believed is highly compelling, although once again there is insufficient evidence to identify the exact year in which the work was written. As Kannengiesser observes, the *De Morte Arii* must have been composed before 356, for Athanasius gives a nearly identical account of the death of Arius in the *Encyclical Letter to the Bishops of Egypt and Libya* that he wrote in that year.[51] Serapion, the bishop of Thumis, would presumably have received a copy of that *Encyclical Letter*, and the *De Morte Arii* must logically therefore have been written before the 356 text was circulated. However, the only certain *terminus post quem* for the *De Morte Arii* is the death of Arius himself, which occurred in Constantinople shortly after Athanasius' first exile in 335, and most probably in 336.[52] Within the period

[49] E.g. Robertson (1892) 563–4. I will return to the question of the actual date of composition of the *Historia Arianorum*, in 357 rather than 358, later in this chapter.

[50] Kannengiesser (1982) 992–4. This date was approved by Stead (1985*b*) 222, and accepted without comment by Barnes (1993) 278.n.8. Hanson, however, although aware of Kannengiesser's argument, does not judge between the latter's theory and the traditional date ((1988*b*) 419), while Brakke (1995) 131.n.229 agrees that the *Ad Monachos* and the *De Morte Arii* must be dated together, but rejects the revised chronology, arguing instead that the *De Morte Arii* was part of Athanasius' campaign to win the support of the Egyptian monks in the 350s, alongside the *Life of Antony* and the *Historia Arianorum* (131–3).

[51] Kannengiesser (1982) 993. This *Encyclical Letter* too will be discussed further below.

[52] According to Athanasius, Arius died after the Council of Tyre (335), in the episcopate of Alexander of Byzantium/Constantinople, and before the death of Constantine in 337 (*De Morte Arii* 2). Hanson (1988*b*) 280, following the argument of Opitz (1940*a*), rejects this account because the *Encyclical Letter* of the eastern bishops at the Council of Serdica reports that Alexander's successor Paul of Constantinople approved Athanasius' condemnation, presumably at the Council of Tyre, and if Paul was already bishop in 335 then Arius could not have died during Alexander's episcopate. However, Barnes (1993) 213 has suggested that Paul attended Tyre not as bishop but as the delegate of the aged Alexander (according to Socrates, II.6, Alexander was 96 years old in 335), and although unproven, 336 thus remains the most probable date for Arius' death.

336–56, neither the *De Morte Arii* nor the *Ad Monachos* can be fixed with precision. Nevertheless, an approximate date of 339–46 for the *De Morte Arii* is not implausible, and two observations, although not conclusive, do favour such a context.

Athanasius composed the *De Morte Arii* in response to a written request from Serapion for a report on 'present events concerning ourselves' (1; Opitz (1940*a*) 178, 2–3). This request might be taken to imply that at that time Athanasius was in exile outside Egypt, hence Serapion's particular desire for recent information, and this is also suggested by Athanasius' complaint later in the letter that 'the Emperor Constantius now uses violence against the bishops on behalf of it [the Arian heresy]' (4; Opitz (1940*a*) 180, 6). Such open hostility to Constantius in Athanasius' writings otherwise first appears only in the *Historia Arianorum* of the later 350s. If the *De Morte Arii* was indeed composed before Athanasius' third exile began in 356, it seems more probable that Athanasius would express such a view before his return to Egypt in 346, rather than during his period of reconciliation with that emperor (346–56).[53]

Secondly, and more importantly, in the introduction to the *De Morte Arii*, Athanasius declares that 'since there was a debate among you . . . about whether Arius died in communion with the Church, for this reason, so that the enquiry may be resolved, I necessarily desired to give an account about his death' (1; Opitz (1940*a*) 178, 9–11). Athanasius here states explicitly the purpose for which the *De Morte Arii* was composed, and Kannengiesser makes a valid point that the natural context for such a debate over Arius' status would be the period immediately following his death in 336.[54] Whether earlier composition improves the credibility of the *De Morte Arii* is open to question,[55] for Athanasius' account was written for a favourable and specifically Egyptian audience whom he expected to accept his presentation of Arius and of Arius' 'Eusebian' allies at face value.

[53] A similar reference to Constantius' patronage of Athanasius' opponents (although less explicitly hostile) occurs in *Oration* I.10, a work that on this chronology was approximately contemporary to the *De Morte Arii*. It is possible that at this time Athanasius was prepared to express such a sentiment more openly in a private letter to a close friend than in a work intended for wider circulation.

[54] Kannengiesser (1982) 993.

[55] As was suggested by Stead (1985*b*) 226.

But a date of *c*.339–46 places the *De Morte Arii* roughly contemporary with the *Orations against the Arians* and the bulk of the narrative of the *Apologia Contra Arianos*, and therefore this work too plays an important role in the early development of Athanasius' polemical construction of his foes.

THE *DE DECRETIS NICAENAE SYNODI*

The letter or treatise[56] traditionally entitled the *De Decretis* is another Athanasian work whose date and context has been the subject of much controversy, yet whose chronology is vital to our understanding of both the polemic of Athanasius and his theological development. For it was in the *De Decretis* that Athanasius first began explicitly to uphold the unique authority of the Council of Nicaea, and to present the Nicene Creed as the sole bastion of 'orthodoxy' against the 'Arian heresy'. Unfortunately, although the *De Decretis* can be attributed to the period *c*.350–6 with relative confidence, the exact date of composition within those years remains open to debate. Athanasius' statement in his introduction to the work that the 'Arians' are presently inactive but 'in a little while (*met' oligon*) will turn to outrage' (2; Opitz (1935) 2, 15–16) suggests that at the time of writing persecution was imminent (exactly how imminent is impossible to determine) but had not yet occurred. Recent scholarship has been divided between those who associate this reference with the beginning of Constantius' sole rule after Constans' murder in 350 and the Battle of Mursa (28 September 351),[57] and those who believe that such a statement can only have been written in 356 itself, shortly before Athanasius' third exile.[58] Neither argument can be taken as

[56] The *De Decretis* 'opens like a letter' (Barnes (1993) 111), but then becomes a theological treatise.

[57] E.g. Opitz (1935) 2; Kopecek (1979) 116; Kannengiesser (1982) 988; Young (1983) 76.

[58] E.g. Hanson (1988*b*) 419. Brennecke (1984) 110 went further than Hanson in arguing that the *De Decretis* must have been composed after the ban upon the use of the term *ousia* at Sirmium in 357, as until that year Nicaea and *homoousios* had not been directly attacked and so would not have required defence, while Twomey (1982) 313.n.100 went still further and places the *De Decretis* in the reign of Jovian in 363.

established, and recently T. D. Barnes has proposed a new alternative, that the *De Decretis* was 'probably written in 352 in response to a letter from Liberius, the bishop of Rome, and addressed to him'.[59]

According to Barnes, Liberius of Rome, shortly after his accession to the episcopate in 352, was asked to endorse the synodal letter of the Council of Sirmium in 351 that contained both a creed and a condemnation of Marcellus of Ancyra, Photinus of Sirmium, and Athanasius. Liberius sent an embassy to invite Athanasius to Rome for his case to be re-examined, but Athanasius declined to come, and, in Barnes' reconstruction, despatched the *De Decretis* to defend himself and to place the Council of Nicaea and the Nicene Creed at the centre of debate.[60] 'It is a reasonable hypothesis that he addressed the work to a prominent western bishop, but one with whom he had yet had no personal dealings.' Barnes identifies this addressee as Liberius. 'If Liberius' name has disappeared from the title of *On the Council of Nicaea*, it could be because in 357 he finally subscribed to the synodical letter of the Council of Sirmium of 351—precisely the document which *On the Council of Nicaea* asked him to reject'.[61]

As Barnes himself admits, however, if Athanasius wrote the *De Decretis* to persuade his audience to reject the Council of Sirmium in 351, it seems peculiar that 'Athanasius nowhere refers explicitly to the council'.[62] Nor is there any indication in the work that Athanasius is writing to a bishop of Rome. Although the *De Decretis* is presented as a letter to a friend, that friend is not named, only addressed as 'a learned man' (*logios anēr*) (1; Opitz (1935) 1, 11) who has been involved in disputations with 'Arians' and has requested from Athanasius an account of the Council of Nicaea. Barnes does suggest that 'one detail fits a bishop of Rome particularly well',[63] but the 'detail' in

However, Athanasius is evidently writing before he was expelled from his see in 356, and nor does the *De Decretis* show any apparent awareness of the theological debates of the later 350s.

[59] Barnes (1993) 6. This hypothesis is presented in full in ibid., Appendix 4, 'The Date of *On The Council of Nicaea*' (198–9).

[60] Ibid. 109–11. Barnes derives his argument that the Council of Sirmium issued such a condemnation of these three bishops from the *Chronicle* of Sulpicius Severus (II.37.5), while the evidence for Liberius' invitation to Athanasius in 352 is found in the bishop of Rome's letter to the eastern bishops in 357 justifying his previous actions (CSEL 65.155).

[61] Ibid. 199. [62] Ibid. 111. [63] Ibid. 199.

question is Athanasius' concluding instruction to the recipient to 'read [the *De Decretis*] by yourself when you receive it; and if you judge it to have merit, let it be read also to the brethren who are present at that time' (32; Opitz (1935) 28, 20–1). This request could equally have been written to Serapion, or to any other bishop favourable to Athanasius' cause. As in the case of the *De Morte Arii*, the intended audience of the *De Decretis* would seem to have been expected to welcome Athanasius' words, but this can hardly be taken as evidence that the audience in question was Liberius of Rome in 352. Barnes' proposed chronology is therefore no more than plausible speculation, and the date of composition of the *De Decretis* remains undefined within the period 350–6.

Nevertheless, Barnes' hypothesis does raise important questions regarding the intended purpose, possible audience, and initial circulation of this Athanasian work. These questions have also been raised by Thomas Kopecek in his *History of Neo-Arianism*. Kopecek, who dates the *De Decretis* to *c.*350, argues that in his theological arguments Athanasius 'had the Macrostich Creed of AD 344 primarily in mind'.[64] This 'Long-Lined Creed' refers to the Son as 'like' the Father, and describes God as 'unbegotten' (*agennētos*) in a manner that Athanasius in the *De Decretis* was particularly concerned to refute. Perhaps more significantly, Kopecek also asserts that Athanasius' arguments deeply influenced Aetius, the founder of 'Neo-Arianism'. 'The publication of Athanasius' *De Decretis* affected Aetius profoundly and stimulated him to formulate out of earlier Arian positions to which he had long subscribed the distinctive theological emphases for which Neo-Arianism became famous.'[65] Not only does Kopecek cite this conclusion as further evidence that the *De Decretis* was written in *c.*350,[66] but he assumes that the *De Decretis* must therefore have spread sufficiently widely to reach Aetius within a year of 'publication'. He further argues that this Athanasian work also influenced other eastern theologians, notably the so-called 'Homoiousians' Basil of Ancyra and Eustathius of Sebaste.[67]

[64] Kopecek (1979) 119–20. [65] Ibid. 127.

[66] According to Gregory of Nyssa (*Contra Eunomium* I.37–8) and Philostorgius (III.17), Aetius first began to teach his 'distinctive doctrines' in *c.*351. If the *De Decretis* did help to inspire those doctrines, therefore, it must have been written and circulated before that date (Kopecek (1979) 127). [67] Kopecek (1979) 158.

Kopecek's conclusions have received considerable support, even from those scholars who reject his proposed date of composition.[68] Yet his hypothesis, like that of Barnes, cannot be proven from the evidence that we possess. Aetius (unsurprisingly) never refers explicitly to Athanasius as an influence upon his thought, nor does Athanasius himself in the *De Decretis* ever refer to the Macrostich Creed. While it is true that Athanasius does reject the 'Arian' use of the term 'unbegotten', this was a theme that he had already emphasized in the *First Oration against the Arians*, which as we have seen was probably written before the Creed of 344. Most importantly, Kopecek speaks repeatedly of the 'publication' of the *De Decretis*, but at no stage does he define what this term might mean in a fourth-century context. The *De Decretis* is framed as a letter to a single recipient, and although it seems highly likely that Athanasius intended his presentation of Nicaea and the Nicene Creed to reach a wider audience, we cannot assume that this or any other Athanasian work was 'published' in the modern sense of the word, with numerous copies and widespread distribution. However widely the *De Decretis* may have eventually become known, its immediate circulation and influence are very difficult to judge. We do not know if Aetius ever even read the work, and if Basil of Ancyra and his 'Homoiousian' colleagues were familiar with the *De Decretis* then Athanasius' arguments seem to have had very little effect, for none of these bishops saw any need to raise the subject of Nicaea at the great Council of Seleucia in 359.[69]

The composition and audience of the *De Decretis* must thus remain to a certain extent an open question. Written in the form of a letter to an unknown recipient, the *De Decretis* could easily have been intended from the beginning to have a wider audience in both east and west, while within the years 350–6 no precise time of

[68] Thus Barnes (1993) 199 follows without comment Kopecek's model for the relationship between the *De Decretis*, the Macrostich Creed, and Aetius, and the influence of the *De Decretis* upon Aetius at least was also accepted by Hanson (1988*b*) 606–7.

[69] This lack of Athanasian influence would appear to have been equally marked in the west in the light of Hilary of Poitiers' famous statement (*De Synodis* 91) that he only read the Nicene Creed when he was about to go into exile in 356, and the emergence of widespread western awareness of Nicaea only after the Council of Ariminum in 359 (see Ulrich (1997), esp. 20–1).

authorship can be determined (although my own inclination leans towards an earlier date of *c*.350–3). Whatever date we assign to the text, however, the *De Decretis* was the earliest of the many writings that Athanasius composed in the period before and during his third exile (356–62), and the first definitive statement of Athanasius' conception of Nicaea and the Nicene Creed. The *De Decretis* thus laid the foundation for the revised construction of himself, his foes, and the 'Arian Controversy' that Athanasius developed in his later works, and represents the essential link joining the *Apologia Contra Arianos* narrative and the *Orations against the Arians* to the great polemical writings of the second half of Athanasius' episcopate.

THE *DE SENTENTIA DIONYSII*

The preceding discussion of the *De Decretis* in turn dictates to a significant extent our interpretation of the date and intended audience of the *De Sententia Dionysii*.[70] This work represents Athanasius' defence of his predecessor Dionysius of Alexandria (bishop 247/8–64/5) against allegations that his theology was 'Arian' and that he had refused to describe the Son as *homoousios* to the Father. The debate between Dionysius of Alexandria and his namesake the bishop of Rome in *c*.259–60 had already been cited by Athanasius in *De Decretis* 25–6 as part of his defence of *homoousios* as a term approved by the earlier fathers, and the *De Sententia Dionysii* would appear to be a further refinement of that *De Decretis* presentation. Indeed, it has

[70] This Athanasian text has been the subject of much scholarly debate in recent years, following the argument of Luise Abramowski (1982) that almost all the material attributed to the third century bishops of Rome and Alexandria in the *De Sententia Dionysii* actually derives from works first composed and falsely attributed to those bishops in *c*.339/40 and then further revised (possibly by Athanasius himself) with the addition of *homoousios* in the 350s. This theory has since been upheld and further developed by Uta Heil (1999) 22–71 and 210–31, although the difficulty remains that such a hypothesis requires Athanasius to show no apparent awareness that the material he quotes first appeared less than two decades earlier. For the purposes of my monograph it is Athanasius' presentation of his material that is important, and in the argument that follows I will assume (tentatively) that the statements attributed to the Dionysii are genuine.

been argued that the anonymous recipient of that earlier work also received the *De Sententia Dionysii*,[71] and while this cannot be proven the similarities in content and argument do suggest that the latter was written only shortly after the *De Decretis*, possibly in response to those who challenged Athanasius' original presentation of Dionysius of Alexandria.[72] If we accept an estimated date of *c.*350–3 for the *De Decretis*, therefore, then a date of *c.*354 for the *De Sententia Dionysii* should not be too far amiss.[73] The *De Sententia Dionysii* thus represents a further statement of Athanasius' construction of 'Arianism' composed shortly before his third exile in 356, and also provides a demonstration of how Athanasius struggled to defend an earlier father of the Church whose alleged theological views did overlap to an embarrassing degree with a position that Athanasius condemned.[74]

THE *LIFE OF ANTONY*

The *Life of Antony* has been the subject of vast debate concerning its authorship, its date, and even its original language of composition, and I have no intention of even attempting to do justice to these scholarly controversies here.[75] My own preference is to accept the traditional Athanasian authorship of the *Life*, but for the purposes of this monograph all that is important is that what polemical content this work contains is entirely compatible with Athanasius' construction

[71] Robertson (1892) 173.

[72] Thus Kopecek (1979) suggests that 'Athanasius' citation of Dionysius of Alexandria in his *De Decretis* did not sit well with some of Athanasius' opponents, for they protested that Dionysius supported their view rather than Athanasius'. This led the bishop to pen his *De Sententia Dionysii* in defence of his judgement' (119).

[73] Kannengiesser (1982) 988. Heil (1999) dates the *De Sententia Dionysii* to *c.*359/60 (22–35), but this is the consequence of her acceptance of the argument of Brennecke that the *De Decretis* must date to 357–60, an argument that I have already rejected above.

[74] In the words of Hanson (1988*b*) 243, the *De Sententia Dionysii* demonstrates how Athanasius 'tries to buttress a weak case by more than usually ferocious language against his opponents'.

[75] See Leemans (2000) 153–9.

of the 'Arians' and 'Arianism' elsewhere in his corpus.[76] As the date of the *Life of Antony* can only be fixed approximately in the years 356–62,[77] it has been placed at this point in my catalogue in order to separate the *Life* from the far more explicitly polemical works of that period that must now be considered.

THE *ENCYCLICAL LETTER TO THE BISHOPS OF EGYPT AND LIBYA*

In striking contrast to the vast majority of the Athanasian works described in this catalogue, the date and context of composition and the audience of the *Encyclical Letter to Egypt and Libya*, the first great work of Athanasius' third exile, can be identified with almost complete certainty. The *Encyclical Letter* was addressed to 'the churches of Egypt and Libya and Alexandria' (9; Tetz (1996) 49, 8–9), and was written shortly after Athanasius' expulsion from Alexandria in February 356, when George of Cappadocia's appointment to replace Athanasius was already known (7), but before George's delayed arrival into the city in February 357. The dual purpose of the *Encyclical Letter*, which was written from within Egypt where Athanasius remained throughout his third exile, was to exhort his Egyptian supporters to renounce the claim of the 'Arian' George to act as the

[76] Thus Antony is said to have refused all communion with Melitians or Arians (68); he is famously reported to have come to Alexandria to denounce Arianism (69); and on his death-bed he instructs his disciples to maintain the 'true faith' and avoid the 'Arian heresy' in precisely the same polarized terms that Athanasius employs throughout his works (89, 91). For further discussion of such polemical parallels between the *Life of Antony* and Athanasius' known works, see in particular Brakke (1995) 135–7.

[77] Barnard (1974*b*) summarizes the evidence for these chronological parameters (170–1), and then attempts to place the work more precisely by arguing that the 'decidedly cool' reference to Constantine and his sons (*Vita Antonii* 81) suggests that the *Life of Antony* was composed between the *Apologia ad Constantium*, which is respectful towards Constantius, and the violently hostile *Historia Arianorum* (172–5). This view is repeated in the recent edition of the *Life* by Bartelink (1994) 27–35, but as Brennan (1977) notes in his reply to Barnard, such an argument pays insufficient attention to the differences in context, audience, and purpose of the three works in question. We thus cannot date the *Life* more precisely than 356–62.

legitimate bishop of Alexandria and to encourage them to continue to uphold the 'orthodox' faith.

There is one crucial passage in the *Encyclical Letter*, however, that appears at first sight to contradict the established date of 356. Near the end of *Encyclical Letter* 21, Athanasius suddenly introduces into his polemic the Melitian schismatics, frequently condemned in his earlier writings but otherwise entirely absent from this text. After condemning the 'new alliance' that the Melitians and the 'Arians' have now formed, he declares that the existence of these two evils has long been manifest to all. 'For it is not a little time [that they have existed], but the former became schismatics 55 years ago; [while] the latter were proclaimed heretics 36 years ago and were expelled from the Church by the judgement of the whole ecumenical synod' (22; Tetz (1996) 63, 14–17). If we calculate these figures from 306, the traditional date for the origin of the Melitian schism, and from the condemnation of the 'Arians' at the Council of Nicaea in 325, it immediately becomes apparent that Athanasius could only have written this passage in 361, not in 356. It was on the basis of this exact calculation that Hanson declared that 'it is now accepted that Athanasius' *Letter to the Bishops* was written in 361'.[78]

Yet the vast bulk of the *Encyclical Letter* simply cannot be made to fit this late a date. The public politeness towards Constantius (5) and the open condemnation of Basil of Ancyra as an 'Arian heretic' (7) both stand in direct contrast to the *De Synodis* of 359, and the emphasis upon the impending arrival of George (7) and the persecution that has already ensued (19) almost certainly refers not to George's return to Alexandria in 361, but to the period before his first entrance into the city in 357. Thus the passage quoted above (22) should be interpreted as a later addition, inserted by Athanasius in 361 into a work that had already been composed and presumably circulated to an essentially favourable audience within Egypt in the first half of 356.

[78] Hanson (1988*b*) 130. Unfortunately, Hanson directly contradicts this statement later in his book, when he states that 'the *Encyclical Letter to the Bishops of Egypt*, protesting against his ejection in 356, must be placed early in that year' (420). It is possible that his first statement was intended to indicate only that *Encyclical Letter* 22 must date to 361, but if this is true then his argument is extremely unclear.

THE *APOLOGIA AD CONSTANTIUM*

Another work that underwent multiple stages of revision within Athanasius' own lifetime, and thus is difficult to fix within a chronological corpus of his writings, is the defence against charges of treason that Athanasius addressed to the emperor Constantius. In the present catalogue, the *Apologia ad Constantium* has been placed immediately after the *Encyclical Letter* of 356, for the final touches to the work can be dated to the approximate time of George's entrance into Alexandria in February 357.[79] Yet the bulk of the 'Defence before Constantius' would seem to have been written earlier. As has long been recognized, the description of the persecution of Athanasius after February 356 in the *Apologia ad Constantium* is a later composition that does not entirely follow from the refutation of the treason charges that comprises the main body of the work. Scholarly debate has therefore focused upon the date of Athanasius' original defence, and upon the point of division between that original text and the continuation that was added in early 357.

Archibald Robertson in the *Nicene and Post-Nicene Fathers* volume of Athanasius' works concluded that the original *Apologia ad Constantium* was written before the arrival of George into Alexandria, possibly at the same time as the *Encyclical Letter* in early 356. He placed the division between that initial defence and the continuation between sections 26 and 27, where Athanasius begins to describe the events of late 356 and early 357.[80] However, this traditional conclusion has since been challenged by J.-M. Szymusiak,[81] who dates the original composition of the *Apologia ad Constantium* to 354–5, and fixes the division within the work at the end of Athanasius' refutation of the four treason charges levelled against him (21), and before

[79] Athanasius does not explicitly refer to George's arrival in Alexandria in the *Apologia ad Constantium*, in contrast to the *Apologia de Fuga* discussed below, but near the end he quotes from two letters of Constantius (30, 31) which both imply that George is either already established in Alexandria or that he will shortly take up that position. The *Apologia ad Constantium* cannot have been re-edited significantly later than February 357, for Athanasius refers to the exile of Liberius of Rome and Ossius of Cordova (27) but not to their 'lapse', which occurred in mid-357.

[80] Robertson (1892) 236; Hanson (1988*b*) 419.

[81] J.-M. Szymusiak (1987) 30, 55, 59–63.

Athanasius turns to the attacks upon his position in Alexandria, which began in late 355 (22). Szymusiak rightly emphasizes that this division rather than that of Robertson follows the most obvious break in the *Apologia ad Constantium* narrative, for section 22 begins Athanasius' account of his persecution with the words 'after twenty-six months' (Szymusiak (1987) 136, 2). More recently, Barnes has proposed a further revision of Szymusiak's hypothesis,[82] placing the date of initial composition firmly in 353,[83] and shifting the point of division to between the third (18) and fourth (19) charges. However, this assumption that Athanasius wrote a refutation of the first three charges before the fourth charge had even been raised rests in turn upon Barnes' assertion that the three charges in question were the product of the Council of Sirmium in 351, and that Athanasius' original defence was written in response to that council. No explicit evidence supports those assertions,[84] and it seems more likely that Szymusiak is correct that the *Apologia ad Constantium* was originally composed in 21 sections in *c.*354, then extended into its present form early in 357.

Wherever we may place the division between the two distinct phases in the production of the *Apologia ad Constantium*, this debate raises the further question of whether the purpose and intended audience of the work differ between the first composition and the later continuation. As the title suggests, the original 'Defence' was addressed to Constantius (1), and Athanasius writes as if the emperor were himself the audience (16). Both Szymusiak[85] and Barnes[86]

[82] Barnes (1993), Appendix 3, 'The *Defence before Constantius*' (196–7).

[83] Barnes observes that both the *Historia Akephala* (1.7) and the *Festal Index* (XXV) state that on 19 May 353 Athanasius sent an embassy to the court with a gift for the emperor, and argues that 'the original *Defence before Constantius* is probably identical with the communication from Athanasius to the emperor which his envoys who set out from Alexandria on 19 May 353 must have taken with them' (ibid., 197).

[84] See ibid. 109–14. As Barnes himself acknowledges (112), the *Apologia ad Constantium* never actually refers to the Sirmium Council of 351, nor is there any explicit evidence that this council even condemned Athanasius, and Barnes' argument is essentially circular: 'A condemnation of Athanasius by the council is a necessary hypothesis...for it was to controvert his condemnation by a council of hostile bishops shortly after 350 that Athanasius originally composed his *Defence before Constantius*' (110).

[85] Szymusiak (1987) 60–1.

[86] Barnes (1993) 63. See also Setton (1941) 73.

accept that Athanasius did indeed intend his initial text for presentation to Constantius, but this cannot be confirmed. The rhetorical framework of an address to the emperor was a common device in this period for speeches and writings never intended for a physical imperial audience,[87] and Athanasius extends that rhetoric throughout the later chapters of the *Apologia ad Constantium* (27, 34), chapters which all agree were never brought to Constantius' court. Although it is not impossible that the emperor was a recipient of the original edition of this work, it therefore seems probable that Athanasius also intended his defence to reach a wider audience. I would conjecture that Athanasius wrote the continuation of the *Apologia ad Constantium* precisely because his initial attempt to convince both Constantius and others that the charges against him were false had failed, and those charges were still being used to justify his expulsion in 356. In this scenario, the audience for at least the later chapters of the *Apologia ad Constantium* would once again have been primarily Egyptian and favourable to Athanasius, with the work intended to encourage his followers to continue to protest his innocence and support his legitimacy as the rightful bishop of Alexandria.

THE *APOLOGIA DE FUGA*

The *Apologia de Fuga*, which continues and develops the justification of his flight from his see in 356 that Athanasius had already begun in the final chapters of the *Apologia ad Constantium* (32–5), was written in the second half of 357.[88] Athanasius had heard of the lapse of Ossius (*Apologia de Fuga* 5), which should be dated to approximately August in that year, but he did not know of the death of Leontius of Antioch (who died in *c.*October 357,[89] yet is still assumed to be

[87] For one example among many, see Libanius, *Oration* XXX (The *Pro Templiis*).

[88] Hanson (1988*b*) 419; Barnes (1993) 124. For a discussion of the context and particularly the theological justification of Athanasius' defence of his flight from Alexandria, which I will not examine here, see Tetz (1979*b*) 40–6 and Pettersen (1984).

[89] News of Leontius' ultimately fatal illness had already reached his eventual successor Eudoxius in Rome by May 357 (Socrates, II.37).

alive in *Apologia de Fuga* 1 and 26). The intended audience of the work is less straightforward. Athanasius only reveals that he wrote the *Apologia de Fuga* against the 'Arians' who are 'spreading reports and slanders about me' (1; Szymusiak (1987) 176, 3–4). This statement gives no indication of exactly where these rumours were being spread, or of who he wished to convince that the 'slanders' were false. While it is possible that the original audience was Egyptian, the work would eventually circulate far more widely,[90] and a definite conclusion is thus impossible. However, it is highly probable that the *Apologia de Fuga*, like so many of Athanasius' polemical works, was initially written not to convince those who actually condemned him but to reassure his supporters, and so was intended once again for an audience who already accepted Athanasius' presentation of contemporary events and individuals.

THE *HISTORIA ARIANORUM*

The most explicitly polemical of all his extant works, the *Historia Arianorum* represents the culmination of Athanasius' apologetic writings, and has been hugely influential upon later reconstructions of his career and of the 'Arian Controversy'. Athanasius' highly selective summary of the events of 335–57 draws upon and elaborates arguments that he had previously presented in the *Apologia Contra Arianos*, the *Apologia ad Constantium*, and the *Apologia de Fuga*, and he composed the *Historia Arianorum* shortly after the completion and final revision of those earlier writings.[91] The traditional attribution

[90] Pettersen (1984) 39 observes that Athanasius needed to defend himself both against the actual opponents who were apparently accusing him of cowardice and to those within his own diocese for whom his flight might compromise his authority as bishop of Alexandria. I would emphasize an internal Egyptian audience as the most important initial recipients of this work, but the *Apologia de Fuga* ultimately spread sufficiently to be quoted by both Socrates (II.28, III.8) and Theodoret (II.15), and according to the former (III.8), Athanasius read the work publicly at the Council of Alexandria in 362.

[91] Like the *Apologia Contra Arianos*, the *Historia Arianorum* narrative is structured around a series of documents and statements attributed to his opponents. However, in this latter work a number of these alleged 'quotations' are manifestly Athanasius'

of this work to 358,[92] however, cannot be accepted, for as we have already seen this date derives from the old chronology of the 'lapse' of Liberius and Ossius (described in *Historia Arianorum* 41, 45), which actually occurred in August 357.[93] Barnes' conclusion that the composition of the *Historia Arianorum* 'may be assigned to the closing months of 357'[94] has therefore been adopted here, a date that also accords with the content of the work itself, which focuses upon the period 351–7.

The intended audience of the *Historia Arianorum* is again a matter of conjecture. The old argument that this work was written primarily for the Egyptian monks[95] derives from the alleged connection between the *Historia Arianorum* and the *Ad Monachos*, which is often attached to the former work in the manuscript tradition as a 'preface'.[96] As we saw earlier, this connection cannot be maintained, and no evidence within the text suggests that Athanasius' intended audience was primarily monastic.[97] Instead, Athanasius would seem to have written for a wider but still Egyptian audience, denouncing his 'Arian' successor George and calling upon his supporters to endure this 'heretical persecution' and to continue to uphold his own legitimacy and 'orthodoxy'. The *Historia Arianorum* too was thus primarily

own compositions, notably the repeated appeals of the 'Arians' to Constantius to 'persecute' and 'spare the heresy' (9, 30, 42). Such passages were evidently not intended to deceive Athanasius' audience, but rather to present Athanasius' own arguments through the mouths of his foes (see Barnes (1993) 130–1), and they must be distinguished carefully from the authentic documents that he quotes elsewhere.

92 Robertson (1892) 266.

93 For a detailed discussion of the fall of Ossius see Ulrich (1994), esp. 153–5 on the controversial chronology of this episode.

94 Barnes (1993) 126. This revised date also resolves the difficulty (noted by Robertson (1892) 266–7, but ignored by Hanson (1988*b*) 420) that the *Historia Arianorum*, like the *Apologia de Fuga* above, was written at a time when Athanasius believed that Leontius of Antioch (d.*c.*October 357) was still alive (*Historia Arianorum* 4).

95 Robertson (1892) 267.

96 It is true that the *Historia Arianorum* in its extant form opens very abruptly (one reason that the *Ad Monachos* was placed at the beginning of this work). It is possible that the original introduction to the *Historia Arianorum* has been lost, but it seems more likely that Robertson (1892) 266 is correct that Athanasius wrote the latter work as a continuation of the narrative of the second half of the *Apologia Contra Arianos*, resuming his account from Arius' admission to communion at Jerusalem in 335.

97 *Pace* Barnes (1993) 126.

written for an audience already sympathetic to his cause, and appeals to that audience to endorse his interpretation of the 'Arian Controversy' and also of the Emperor Constantius, who is now condemned as the leader of the 'Arians' and the 'forerunner of Antichrist'.

THE *DE SYNODIS ARIMINI ET SELEUCIAE*

If the *Historia Arianorum* represents Athanasius' definitive interpretation of the ecclesiastical framework of the fourth-century controversies, then the *De Synodis* represents the theological culmination of his polemic, upholding the Nicene Creed as the only symbol of 'orthodoxy' against the diverse writings and councils of the 'Ariomaniacs'. However, both the date and the intended audience of this work, the last of the great writings of Athanasius' third exile, require careful analysis, for the *De Synodis* is another Athanasian text that was re-edited at least once after its initial composition. The bulk of the work was written in October 359, after the eastern Council of Seleucia had broken up (1 October), but before Athanasius had heard that Constantius had forced the western envoys of Ariminum to accept a new creed (10 October). According to the postscript that Athanasius added at the end of the *De Synodis*, 'after I had written my account of the Councils, I learnt that the most irreligious Constantius had sent letters to the bishops remaining at Ariminum; and I have hastened to obtain copies of them from true brethren and to despatch them to you, and also what the bishops answered' (55; Opitz (1941) 277, 24–7). This would suggest that Athanasius was writing while these events were still proceeding, and also reveals that Athanasius was in close contact with the western bishops at Ariminum and presumably received these letters fairly swiftly.[98] The composition of the main body of the *De Synodis* can thus be placed fairly securely in early to mid-October 359.

[98] Kopecek (1979), however, is too precise when he states that the *De Synodis* was written 'between October 1, 359, and October 10, 359' (216), for we should still allow for some delay in the transmission of information regarding these councils to Athanasius in Egypt.

Yet this date cannot hold true for the entire extant text. Chapters 30–1 of the *De Synodis* were by necessity written later than 359, as they refer respectively to the creed produced in Constantinople in 359–60 and to the death-bed baptism of Constantius in 361. This has led some scholars to view the entire work as a unitary composition of late 361–2.[99] However, not only does the postscript quoted above confirm that Athanasius was still receiving information on Ariminum's progress when he originally wrote the *De Synodis*, but Athanasius' theological arguments in *De Synodis* 32–54 contain no reference to the material in chapters 30–1, and begin instead with Athanasius' refutation of the creed of Acacius of Caesarea at Seleucia which he quoted in chapter 29. The logical conclusion is that chapters 30–1 were inserted into a work that had already been composed, and that the *De Synodis* was written in two unequal phases, with the majority of the work completed by the end of October 359, and sections 30–1 added approximately two years later.

The original *De Synodis* of 359 is usually understood to have been written by Athanasius for the immediate aim of making a common cause against the 'Arians' with the eastern 'Homoiousians' who dominated the Council of Seleucia.[100] It is certainly true that in the later chapters of the *De Synodis* Athanasius accepts that those who teach that the Son is *homoiousios* to the Father are 'orthodox', although he continues to maintain the superiority of *homoousios* to define the relationship of the Father and the Son. This argument is highly significant in the development of Athanasius' polemic, as for the first time he acknowledges the possibility that a Christian might hold a different theology to his own, and yet not be 'Arian'. But does this mean that the 'Homoiousians' themselves were the immediate

[99] Opitz (1940*b*) 231. This argument was rejected by Barnes (1993) 280.n.48, but Hanson (1988*b*) seems to contradict himself on this question, declaring at one point that the *De Synodis* 'was written, not in 359 but in 361' (376.n.112), but elsewhere recognizing that at least a 'first draft' of the text must have been completed by the end of 359 (421). Hanson supports his 361 date by asserting that Athanasius' description of George of Alexandria as 'driven from the earth' (12; Opitz (1940*b*) 239, 17) refers to his death in December 361 rather than to his departure from the city in 358 (376.n.112). This is possible, but elsewhere in the *De Synodis* Athanasius states explicitly that George was 'expelled from Alexandria' (37; Opitz (1941) 263, 30–264, 1), and the earlier text may also refer to that same episode.

[100] Robertson (1892) 449; Kopecek (1979) 226–7; Barnes (1993) 133.

audience of the *De Synodis*, or that the work was directly intended to convince the former that the Nicene Creed alone represented the 'orthodox faith'? Like the *De Decretis*, the *De Synodis* would eventually circulate widely, yet would seem to have had little if any immediate impact.[101] And there is some evidence to suggest that the *De Synodis*' original intended audience was not the 'Homoiousians', nor the eastern Church in general, but once again the supporters of Athanasius himself and particularly those within Egypt.

In the opening words of the *De Synodis*, Athanasius declares that he has written in order to provide his audience with an account of Ariminum and Seleucia, for 'perhaps news has reached even yourselves concerning the Council, which is at this time the subject of general conversation' (1; Opitz (1940*b*) 231, 3). Whoever those addressed in this passage might be, it is evident that they did not attend the councils themselves, and so cannot be identified with the eastern bishops at Seleucia. Nor is Athanasius' theological argument that the 'Homoiousians' should be reconciled with those who follow Nicaea actually addressed to the former directly.[102] Rather, Athanasius declares that 'those who accept everything else that was defined at Nicaea, and doubt only about the *homoousion*, must not be treated as enemies. For indeed we do not attack them here as Ariomaniacs... but we discuss the matter with them as brothers with brothers, who share our meaning and dispute only about the word' (41; Opitz (1941) 266, 28–32). Athanasius' purpose is not to convince the 'Homoiousians' of the superiority of Nicaea, so much as to appeal to those who already uphold the Nicene Creed to receive the latter as friends and not as enemies. The intended audience of the *De Synodis* is therefore most probably the monks, clergy, and laity of the Egyptian Church. The *De Synodis* did eventually reach a wider eastern audience, but first and foremost this work too was written

[101] Perhaps most significantly, there is little evidence that Athanasius' theological arguments directly influenced the Cappadocian Fathers, and this is equally true of his polemical model of the fourth century controversies (on the latter point, see M. R. Barnes (1998) 58–61).

[102] Although there are exceptions to this rule, notably in the conclusion of the *De Synodis* when Athanasius does address certain passages to the 'Homoiousians', and declares that 'this [argument] is sufficient to persuade you not to accuse those who have said that the Son is *homoousios* to the Father' (53; Opitz (1941) 276, 21–2).

to inspire and reassure Athanasius' own supporters, who already endorsed his construction of the 'Arian Controversy'.

THE *TOMUS AD ANTIOCHENOS*

The last individual text traditionally assigned to the Athanasian corpus that will be included in this chronological catalogue was not in fact written by Athanasius himself. The *Tomus ad Antiochenos* was the letter sent to the divided Christians of Antioch by the Council of Alexandria that Athanasius summoned after his return from his third exile in February 362, and before his expulsion by Julian 'the Apostate' on October 23 of that year.[103] The Antiochene context that provoked this letter was highly complex, but for our present purposes all that it is necessary to observe is that the *Tomus ad Antiochenos*, although the product of a council, almost certainly does reflect 'the influence (if not the actual pen) of Athanasius'.[104] The letter may therefore be cited as evidence for the ongoing development of Athanasius' own theology, and as we shall have cause to observe in the final chapter of this monograph, the *Tomus ad Antiochenos* represents a significant shift in Athanasius' theological terminology.[105]

THE *FESTAL LETTERS* AND THE *FESTAL INDEX*

The *Festal Letters* of Athanasius and the *Festal Index* stand at the end of this catalogue and outside the chronological sequence of his works, for these texts differ in nature and content from those that

[103] On the content of this Athanasian work, which I do not intend to discuss in detail, see Tetz (1975) and Hanson (1988*b*) 642–52. In a later article, Tetz (1988) goes on to argue that the Council of Alexandria in 362 that produced the *Tomus ad Antiochenos* also composed an encyclical letter, of which the conclusion survives as the so-called pseudo-Athanasius *Epistula Catholica*.

[104] Hanson (1988*b*) 639.

[105] For a recent reconsideration of both the Antiochene schism and the theological context of the *Tomus ad Antiochenos*, emphasizing that the primary concern of the Council of 362 was 'Arianism' and not 'Apollinarianism', see Pettersen (1990) and also Hall (1991) 151–3.

we have considered above, and pose their own special problems.[106] Following the custom of earlier bishops of Alexandria,[107] each year Athanasius wrote two letters concerning the Easter celebration for circulation to all the bishops subordinate to his see.[108] The first letter, a brief note, was despatched shortly after each Easter, and announced the date of Easter for the following year. The *Festal Letter* proper, a much longer work, was then sent out in January or February of the year itself, to confirm that date and to transmit Athanasius' Easter message to his churches. These *Festal Letters* have rarely been studied in depth for their polemical content, for their primary purpose was to promote the proper celebration of Easter. In the words of Frances Young, the letters 'are full of scriptural quotations, traditional typology and simple piety. They make up, to some extent, for the loss of his sermons'.[109] Yet the *Festal Letters* also gave Athanasius an ideal vehicle through which to transmit his interpretation of events to the bishops and people of his region. These texts thus offer a unique opportunity to trace the development of Athanasius' polemical presentation of himself and his foes year by year. The great obstacle to such an analysis is the difficulties posed by the organisation and chronology of the *Festal Letters* themselves.

Most modern scholarly work on Athanasius' *Festal Letters* has concerned their manuscript transmission and order, a highly complex subject that can only briefly be summarized here.[110] With

[106] A new edition of the *Festal Letters* is currently being prepared by Alberto Camplani. The *Festal Index* was edited by Albert in Martin (1985).

[107] This custom existed at the very latest by the time of Dionysius in the mid-third century AD (Eusebius of Caesarea, *Historia Ecclesiastica* VII.20; see Camplani (2003) 25–7).

[108] See Barnes (1993), Appendix 1, 'The *Festal Letters*' (183–91).

[109] Young (1983) 80. There is a detailed study of the *Festal Letters* as a source for Athanasius' pastoral activities in Kannengiesser (1989), who emphasizes that our understanding of Athanasius as a preacher and pastor is seriously compromised if we focus only upon his polemical works. There is much force in this argument (which is certainly applicable to the present study), but at the same time I would question Kannengiesser's assertion that the polemical content that does occur in the *Festal Letters*, against Jews, heretics, and schismatics, is largely conventional rhetoric and is 'much less motivated by polemics than by spirituality' (82). There *is* important polemical content within these texts, as I will seek to demonstrate through the use of that material in Ch. 3.

[110] See Camplani (1989) 17–196 and (2003); Lorenz (1986) 8–37; Barnes (1993) 183–91.

the exception of a few fragments, the original Greek texts of the letters are lost, and the extant *Festal Letters* derive instead from two main sources, a Syriac manuscript edited by Cureton in 1848,[111] and a number of Coptic fragments edited by Lefort in 1955.[112] There is some degree of overlap between these two editions, but the Coptic fragments provide little additional material for the early letters of 329–42, and these are the most important texts for the development of Athanasius' polemic. My primary source is therefore the Syriac manuscript which in turn provided the basis for the *Nicene and Post-Nicene Fathers* translation of the *Festal Letters.*

Far more problematic than the sources of the letters, however, is the question of their chronological order. The traditional numeration of the *Festal Letters* from I to XLV (which includes numbers for years in which no letter appears to have been written) derives from the *Festal Index* which was found with the Syriac manuscript and was followed by Cureton and by the *Nicene and Post-Nicene Fathers* volume. But that *Index* was not created by Athanasius. It was intended to accompany an edition of the letters compiled after his death,[113] and as scholars have realized since the late nineteenth century, the transmitted order of the *Festal Letters* cannot be accepted at face value. For the ancient editors of the *Index*, just as for modern scholars, the reconstruction of the original order of the *Festal Letters* depended almost entirely on the internal content of the letters themselves. The letters do not record the year in which they were written, but the day and month of the Easter in question could be compared against existing tables of Easter dates for fourth-century Egypt, and a letter with a unique Easter date (i.e. a date that occurred only once in Athanasius' episcopate) could thus be fixed with certainty, as with *Festal Letters* I and IV. Unfortunately, many of the Easter dates recorded in Athanasius' *Festal Letters* were attributable to more than

[111] Cureton (1848); revised with two additional manuscript leaves by Burgess (1854).

[112] Lefort (1955).

[113] As an additional complication, the *Festal Index* that we possess does not in fact parallel the Syriac manuscript to which it has been attached. Instead, it appears to have been written for another collection, possibly that of Alexandria, and to have become attached to our existing Syriac corpus at some point in the transmission process. See Camplani (1989) 115–29.

one year, and modern analyses have demonstrated the flaws in the attempts of the ancient editors to classify these difficult texts. In particular, it has been observed that the letters transmitted as I, IV, V, and XIV all speak of only a 6-day pre-Easter fast, whereas the other letters all refer instead to a 40-day Lenten fast.[114] At some time between 334 and 338 the Egyptian practice evidently shifted from a fast of a single week to one of forty days,[115] and therefore *Letters* II and III which refer to the longer fast must in fact date to 352 and 342 respectively, while the fragmentary *Letter* XXIV (assigned to 352) should in fact be dated to 330, and *Letter* XIV (assigned to 342) to 331. *Letters* I (329), IV (332), and V (333) retain their transmitted dates, but the attribution of *Letters* VI and VII to 334 and 335 respectively remains uncertain.[116] I will return to these chronological questions in Part II, for these early *Festal Letters* are an essential source for understanding the original purpose and development of Athanasius' construction of himself and of his opponents in the years surrounding his condemnation at the Council of Tyre.

[114] Schwartz (1935).

[115] The precise moment at which this shift occurred is impossible to determine with certainty, but a tentative date of 334 has plausibly been proposed. Scholars once argued that the change occurred in *c.*336–7, after Athanasius was influenced by practices in the west (e.g. Cross (1945) 17), but I would agree with Barnes (1993) 190 that it is unlikely that Athanasius would have introduced such a change while he was in exile. This leaves a date of either 334 or 337–8, and both Brakke (2001) 457–61 and Camplani (2003) 178–81 have argued that the shift most probably occurred in 334, for *Festal Letter* VI (if this letter is correctly placed in that year) includes a special justification of the 40-day fast which suggests that this practice was a new development at that time.

[116] For a list of currently accepted dates, and those still under debate, see Barnes (1993) 188–9 and Camplani (2003) 613–20.

Part II

2

Athanasius' Earliest Polemical Work: the 'Eusebians' in the *Epistula Encyclica* of 339

On 16 April 339, Athanasius fled Alexandria and departed for a second time into exile in the west, following the entrance into the city of his newly designated replacement Gregory on 22 March. In order to vindicate himself against this renewed condemnation and to proclaim his legitimacy as the true bishop of Alexandria, Athanasius wrote an encyclical letter to clergy in both the east and the west. Throughout the letter, he contrasts his own innocence and piety to the violence and malice of his opponents, denouncing the actions against him as an 'Arian conspiracy' and calling upon all 'orthodox Christians' to unite in his defence.[1] This short *Epistula Encyclica* is the earliest polemical work that can be ascribed with certainty to Athanasius himself,[2] and represents the first detailed expression of Athanasius' construction of the 'heretical party' that he holds responsible for his exile: '*hoi peri Eusebion*'.

Two inseparable themes that dominate the *Epistula Encyclica* are introduced immediately in the opening paragraphs of the letter: Athanasius' own suffering and the 'Arian conspiracy' that threatens not only himself but the entire Church. Invoking the Scriptural account of the Levite who called upon all Israel to avenge the defilement of his wife (Judges 19:29), Athanasius declares that 'the calamity of the Levite was but small, when compared with the enormities which have now been committed against the Church . . . [for] now

[1] For a full survey of Athanasius' arguments in this letter see Schneemelcher (1974*a*), esp. 325–37.

[2] Both the *Encyclical Letter* of Alexandria, which has been attributed to Athanasius by Stead (1988), and the *Encyclical Letter* composed by the Council of Alexandria over which Athanasius presided in 338 will be considered in the next chapter.

the whole Church is wronged, the sanctuary is insulted, and worse, piety is persecuted by impiety' (1; Opitz (1940*a*) 170, 2–6). Every Christian must therefore rally to his defence, 'considering that these wrongs are done unto you no less than unto us' (1; Opitz (1940*a*) 170, 9). Athanasius proceeds to describe the violence against himself and against the Church which has accompanied the intrusion of Gregory into Alexandria, denouncing Gregory as no more than the 'hireling' of those notorious 'Arians', the 'Eusebians'.

According to Athanasius, all was customary and at peace when suddenly the Prefect of Alexandria declared that 'a certain Gregory from Cappadocia was coming as my successor from the court (*apo tou komitatou*)' (2; Opitz (1940*a*) 170, 28–9). This confounded everyone, for 'neither the people themselves, nor a bishop, nor a presbyter, nor altogether anyone had ever complained against us' (2; Opitz (1940*a*) 171, 2–3). Yet immediately it was recognized that Gregory

> was an Arian himself, being sent out to the Arians by the Eusebians. For you know, brothers, that the Eusebians have always been patrons (*prostatas*) and partakers (*koinōnous*) of the impious heresy of the Ariomaniacs, and that through them they were always plotting against us, and were the cause of our exile into Gaul.... This novel and iniquitous attempt was now made against the Church not on the grounds of any charge brought against me by ecclesiastical persons, but through the assault of the Arian heretics alone... [so that] a person brought from outside by the Arians, as if trafficking (*emporeuomenon*) in the name of 'bishop', should through the patronage and force of magistrates thrust himself from outside upon those who neither asked for nor desired his presence, nor indeed knew anything of what had occurred. (2; Opitz (1940*a*) 171, 3–7; 8–10; 15–18)

Following Gregory's arrival, a persecution of the Church was begun in Alexandria by Philagrius the Prefect, 'who had indeed the Eusebians as his patrons (*prostatas*), and was therefore full of zeal against the Church' (3; Opitz (1940*a*) 172, 1–2). A church was burnt, virgins were stripped, and monks were trampled underfoot and killed, while sacrifices were offered in the churches, and Jews and pagans polluted the sacred Baptistery (3). During the season of Lent, 'presbyters and laymen were lacerated; virgins were stripped of their veils, led away to the tribunal of the governor, and cast into prison; others had their goods confiscated and were scourged; the bread of the ministers and virgins was cut off' (4; Opitz (1940*a*) 9–12).

Athanasius himself escaped only through divine grace, while Gregory handed over the churches to the 'Ariomaniacs', 'perhaps (*isōs*) following the orders of the Eusebians' (5; Opitz (1940*a*) 174, 9–10). Thus 'the people of God and the clerics of the catholic church were forced either to have communion with the impiety of the Arian heretics or not to enter into the churches . . . there is persecution here, and such a persecution as was never before raised against the Church' (5; Opitz (1940*a*) 174, 13–15; 25–6).

There are a number of evident distortions inherent in the presentation of both Athanasius and Gregory in these highly rhetorical and polemical passages. It is hardly true in the light of his condemnation at the Council of Tyre in 335 that no charge had ever been levelled against Athanasius by 'ecclesiastical persons', nor that Gregory, whose ordination was also ratified by a formal council, came to Alexandria directly 'from the court' and through the patronage of secular power.[3] The account of the alleged 'persecution' in Alexandria is also suspiciously vague, neither naming any of the individuals who suffered nor identifying the church that is said to have been burnt.[4] As we will see in greater detail in Chapter 6, all of the crimes that are here attributed to the 'Arian' 'persecutors' are motifs that recur in every Athanasian denunciation of his foes. The destruction of churches; the abuse of monks, virgins, and clergy; the alliance of the 'heretics' with pagans and Jews; and the confiscation of goods and of charitable bread are all rhetorical *topoi*, and their historical truth cannot easily be assessed.

Most importantly, in these *Epistula Encyclica* passages we are able to identify all the essential elements of Athanasius' construction of his opponents as '*hoi peri Eusebion*'. Here, as throughout Athanasius' works, the 'Eusebians' inspire persecution and violence, and are patrons of both secular power (Philagrius) and episcopal office (Gregory). They are men who 'traffic in the name of bishop', and are the cause of Athanasius' original exile into Gaul. Above all, the 'Eusebians' are 'Arians', 'partakers' of the doctrines of Arius, and it is

[3] This point was well-emphasized by Barnes (1993) 50.

[4] See ibid. 49. Interestingly, the *Encyclical Letter* of the Eastern Council of Serdica in 343 that condemned Athanasius (CSEL 65.55.5–7) declares that it was he who hired the pagans to burn the church in question!

their support for this 'heresy' that motivates their actions. Not only is Gregory discredited and dismissed as an 'Arian' and the nominee of an 'Arian party', but as the victim of this conspiracy, Athanasius' own innocence and 'orthodoxy' are confirmed. He has been exiled not because of any personal guilt, but because he represents the 'true faith' against 'heretics' who threaten the entire Church. Through this polarization, Athanasius is able to appeal to the wider Christian body, insisting that all who renounce 'Arianism' must also support him against the impiety and violence of the 'Arian' Gregory. That polarized interpretation in turn is only made possible through Athanasius' construction of the 'Eusebians' as an 'Arian party', whose influence lies behind the intrusion of Gregory into Alexandria, and the persecution of the 'orthodox' that is even now taking place.[5]

The concluding paragraphs of the *Epistula Encyclica* repeat and elaborate this polarized Athanasian construction in still more explicit form. 'Gregory is an Arian, and to the Arians he has been despatched', for he is nothing more than a hireling (*misthōtos*) of the 'Eusebians' (6; Opitz (1940*a*) 175, 7–8). Indeed, Gregory is not even the first such 'Eusebian' nominee to be imposed upon the see of Alexandria.

But since, after we wrote concerning Pistus, whom the Eusebians formerly appointed over the Arians, all of you the catholic bishops of the Church justly anathematized and excommunicated him because of his impiety, they have now in like manner despatched this Gregory to the Arians. And lest indeed they should bring on themselves a second shame by our writing against them once more, for this reason they have used external force against us, so that, having obtained possession of the churches, they may think to escape the suspicion of being Arians.... This then is the plot (*dramatourgēma*) of the Eusebians, these things the Eusebians have long been rehearsing and composing, and now have succeeded in performing because of the false

[5] It is true (see Wiles (1993*b*) 35–6 and Behr (2004) 23–5) that Athanasius both in these passages and elsewhere in the *Epistula Encyclica* and the *Apologia Contra Arianos* appears to make a distinction between the 'Arians' in Egypt and their external patrons, '*hoi peri Eusebion*' (the same distinction also occurs in the *Encyclical Letter* of Alexander, see Ch. 3). However, the 'Eusebians' are nevertheless described in the *Epistula Encyclica* as 'partakers of the Arian heresy' and as sharing 'the same heresy' as the 'Ariomaniacs', and here as elsewhere Athanasius thus constructs a polarization of 'orthodoxy' and 'heresy' through the presentation of the 'Eusebians' as themselves 'Arian'.

charges which they have made against us to the emperor. (6; Opitz (1940*a*) 175, 10–15; 18–20)

It is necessary for everyone to avenge the suffering of so great a Church as though he were himself suffering the deed. For we have a common Saviour, who is blasphemed by them, and canons belonging to us all, which are transgressed by them. (6; Opitz (1940*a*) 176, 2–5)

Let all declare their opposition to these men and condemn them.

You know well all that concerns the Ariomaniacs, beloved, for many times both individually and in common you have all condemned their impiety. And you know also that the Eusebians, as I have said before, are of the same heresy (*tēs autēs haireseōs*) as them, because of which indeed for a long time they have plotted against us. (7; Opitz (1940*a*) 176, 11–13)

If it happens that Gregory may write to you, or some other concerning him, do not receive his writings, brothers, but reject [them] and put to shame those who bring [them] as ministers of impiety and evil. (7; Opitz (1940*a*) 176, 25–7)

Since [it is] also likely that the Eusebians will write to you concerning him . . . drive out from before you those that come from them; because for the sake of the Ariomaniacs they have caused at such a time persecutions, rape of virgins, murders, plundering of the property of the churches, burnings, and blasphemies in the churches to be committed by the pagans and Jews. . . . Send a reply to us, and condemn these impious men. (7; Opitz (1940*a*) 176, 29–177, 3; 177, 7–8)

In this final condemnation of the 'Eusebians', the persecution of the 'orthodox' and patronage of the 'Arians' are again prominent themes, although the mysterious figure of Pistus here precedes Gregory as the first 'Eusebian' nominee to challenge Athanasius for the see of Alexandria.[6] Certain additional motifs also now appear

[6] For what little is known of Pistus and his career, see Schneemelcher (1974*a*) 313–15 and Klein (1977) 68–71. The letter of Athanasius on this subject is lost, and all that remains are brief references here and in the letter of Julius of Rome quoted in the *Apologia Contra Arianos* (there is also possibly a reference to Pistus in the Egyptian *Encyclical Letter* of 338 quoted in the same work, but this only alludes to 'a bishop' whom the 'Eusebians' have appointed over the 'Arians' (19; Opitz (1938*a*) 101, 12–13)). According to Julius, Pistus was ordained by the Libyan bishop Secundus of Ptolemais (24), and there is no other evidence that the eastern bishops whom Athanasius calls 'Eusebians' played any role in Pistus' appointment as bishop of Alexandria at all. Barnes has argued that Pistus was only ordained a priest by

that will likewise recur throughout Athanasius' polemic. The allegation that his opponents have aroused the hostility of the emperor against him through slander and deception is one such *topos* (denounced here as a '*dramatourgēma*' in language that we will encounter again in the next chapter), as too is the warning against the letters that the 'Eusebians' circulate to support their conspiracy. Here as before, however, these additional elements are again subordinated to the 'heresy' that Athanasius ascribes to his foes. All of the actions of the 'Eusebians' are performed 'for the sake of the Ariomaniacs', and their assault upon Athanasius is purely to avoid their own condemnation as 'Arians'. Athanasius' final appeal to all Christians to renounce the 'Eusebians' and to rally to his own defence is in effect an appeal to his audience to recognize the distinction that he has drawn between the 'true Church' and the 'Eusebian heretics', and so to endorse the polarization upon which his polemical construction rests.[7]

The men whom Athanasius brands as '*hoi peri Eusebion*' appear in the *Epistula Encyclica*, as they do in all Athanasius' polemical writings, as a single 'Arian party', united in theology and motivation, and collectively responsible for the actions that Athanasius has attributed to them. In Part III, I will take up and examine in detail the individual components of this Athanasian construction of the 'Eusebians'. But the brief analysis of the *Epistula Encyclica* in this chapter has already demonstrated the principal elements of that construction, and also the degree to which Athanasius' presentation of the 'Eusebians' in a specific work may be shaped by the immediate context and purposes for which he wrote. As he began his second exile in 339, Athanasius for the first time faced the challenge of a rival whom it was necessary to discredit, as well as the need to vindicate

Secundus, and that he was made a bishop either at the Council of Tyre in 335 ((1981) 239) or at the Council of Antioch in 337/8 that repeated Athanasius' condemnation ((1993) 36). Neither of these hypotheses can be proven, however, while after this brief appearance, Pistus vanishes entirely from history.

[7] [Thus in the words of Schneemelcher (1974*a*) 326: 'der Brief an alle Bischöfe gerichtet ist, die nicht zu der Gruppe um Eusebios von Nikomedien gehören'. Yet this distinction between 'the bishops' and the 'Eusebians', so widespread within modern studies of this period, is itself a product of Athanasius' polemic. This is an argument which I will develop more fully in ch. 3.

his own innocence and legitimacy as the true and 'orthodox' bishop of Alexandria. These twin pressures inevitably influenced the image that he created of his foes as the patrons of the 'usurper' Gregory and as 'Arians' who represented a threat not only to himself but to the entire Christian Church. To better understand Athanasius' construction of the 'Eusebians', we must now identify the original context and motivation which led him to thus present his opponents as an 'Arian party'. Already in the *Epistula Encyclica*, Athanasius declares that 'for a long time' the 'Eusebians' have conspired against him, and he evidently expected his audience to recognize the title '*hoi peri Eusebion*' and the individuals within that 'party', whom he saw no reason to name. When do the 'Eusebians' first appear in the writings of Athanasius? This is the question that the next chapter will seek to resolve.

3

The Origin of the 'Eusebians' in the Polemic of Athanasius

The *Epistula Encyclica* of 339 is Athanasius' earliest complete polemical work, but it is not his earliest extant writing, and nor does the letter represent the earliest Athanasian construction of his opponents as the 'Eusebians'. Through the documents preserved in the *Apologia Contra Arianos* and the *Festal Letters* of the opening years of his episcopate, we can reconstruct the development of Athanasius' presentation of himself and of his foes in the period between his accession in 328 and the beginning of his second exile (339–46). From that evidence it is possible to identify the exact context and purpose for which Athanasius first began to depict his opponents as a 'Eusebian party', at the very Council of Tyre in 335 at which he was originally condemned.

The earliest extant reference to '*hoi peri Eusebion*' in fourth-century Christian writing, however, does not occur in the works of Athanasius, but in the *Encyclical Letter* of his predecessor Alexander of Alexandria. To trace the origins of Athanasius' polemic against the 'Eusebians', it is therefore necessary first to determine the date and context in which Alexander's letter was composed, and the influence that this letter may have exerted upon Athanasius.

THE *ENCYCLICAL LETTER* (*HENOS SOMATOS*) OF ALEXANDER OF ALEXANDRIA AND THE CHRONOLOGY OF THE EARLY 'ARIAN CONTROVERSY'

The *Encyclical Letter* attributed to Alexander of Alexandria is a crucial source for the theological and ecclesiastical controversies that preceded the Council of Nicaea.[1] Yet both the authorship and the traditional date of this letter have been challenged in recent years. The issue of authorship will be discussed later in this chapter, but first we must confront the highly complex question of the context in which the letter was written, a question that inevitably leads into the wider and much-debated subject of the chronology of the early 'Arian Controversy'.

Alexander's *Encyclical Letter* is just one of a number of documents preserved from the years between the initial conflict of Alexander with his presbyter Arius and the commencement of the Nicene Council. These documents include Alexander's only other extant writing, his *Letter to Alexander of Byzantium/Thessalonica*,[2] and certain texts extremely important for the purposes of this monograph, notably Arius' *Letter to Eusebius of Nicomedia*,[3] the bishop of Nicomedia's fragmentary reply,[4] and the same bishop's *Letter to Paulinus of Tyre*,[5] the only extant theological statement by Athanasius' greatest foe. None of these documents can easily be dated, and as their respective contents provide the only immediate evidence for their chronology and their relationship to each other, they must be considered as a collective whole. The analysis of the date and context of the *Encyclical Letter* of Alexander will therefore involve a consideration of the chronological order of all of these documents, and will also shed light on the position of Eusebius of Nicomedia in the early years of the controversy.

The most commonly accepted chronology for the 'Arian Controversy' before the Council of Nicaea is that laid down in the magisterial study of the German scholar Hans-Georg Opitz.[6] According to Opitz, the controversy began in AD 318, with the condemnation of Arius by Alexander at a Council of Alexandria. This condemnation

[1] The *Encyclical Letter* of Alexander (Opitz, *Urkunde* IV) is quoted in Socrates, I.6. The alternative title, *Henos Somatos*, derives from the letter's opening words.

[2] This letter is quoted in Theodoret, I.4 (Opitz, *Urkunde* XIV), and according to Theodoret was addressed to Alexander of Byzantium (I.3). This identification was accepted by Williams (1987) 48.n.3, but is rejected by Hanson (1988*b*) 136.n.24, who favoured the bishop of Thessalonica as recipient. My own preference is that of Hanson, for reasons that will become apparent later in this chapter, but no decisive conclusion is possible.

[3] Quoted in Theodoret, I.5, and Epiphanius, *Panarion* 69.6 (Opitz, *Urkunde* I).

[4] Preserved in Athanasius, *De Synodis* 17 (Opitz, *Urkunde* II).

[5] Quoted in Theodoret, I.6 (Opitz, *Urkunde* VIII).

[6] Opitz (1934).

led Arius in the same year to write his *Letter to Eusebius of Nicomedia*, which brought Eusebius' now fragmentary reply, and it was in response to this activity, and particularly to the involvement of Eusebius of Nicomedia, that Alexander wrote his *Encyclical Letter* in 319. Opitz places considerable emphasis upon Eusebius' participation in the early stages of the controversy, and proposes that Arius' conciliatory *Letter to Alexander*[7] was composed in Nicomedia in *c.*320 under Eusebius' influence, an argument that has also been made for Arius' *Thalia*,[8] which Opitz dated to *c.*321. Eusebius' own *Letter to Paulinus of Tyre* he also assigned to 321. At that point the eastern emperor Licinius allegedly ordered a ban on Church councils as he prepared for his final war with Constantine,[9] a ban that Opitz dated to 322, and the controversy therefore only resumed with Licinius' defeat in September 324. To this period Opitz assigned Alexander's *Letter to Alexander*, which refers to the 'Arians' now stirring trouble. Constantine's *Letter to Alexander and Arius*[10] must then be placed in late 324 or early 325, and this was followed in turn by the Councils of Antioch and finally Nicaea in 325.[11]

[7] Quoted in Athanasius, *De Synodis* 16, and Epiphanius, *Panarion* 69.7 (Opitz, *Urkunde* VI).

[8] This argument derives from the statement of Athanasius, *De Synodis* 15, that Arius wrote the *Thalia* '*para*' the 'Eusebians' (Opitz (1941) 242, 5). Athanasius' statement is difficult to evaluate, for it is a product of his construction of his opponents as united by a single 'heresy', and both Telfer (1936) 61–2 and Lorenz (1979) 52 have rejected any alleged 'Eusebian' influence upon the composition of the *Thalia*.

[9] This ban, whose nature and extent remains uncertain, is reported by Eusebius of Caesarea, *Vita Constantini* I.51–6.

[10] Quoted in Eusebius, *Vita Constantini* II.64–72 (Opitz, *Urkunde* XVII). This famous letter has recently been the subject of much debate, for it has been plausibly argued that Constantine's *Letter to Arius and Alexander* was not in fact written to those two men themselves but to a council, quite possibly that held in Antioch in early 325 (Hall (1998); the more recent attempt of Woods (2002) 214–21 to date the council in question (and thus the letter) to 327 is unconvincing). The traditional identification of the bearer of the letter as Ossius of Cordova (Socrates, I.7) has also been challenged by Warmington (1985) 95–6, who proposes that the actual messenger was Marianos, an imperial *notarius*.

[11] The date of Nicaea in June–July 325 is relatively secure. The Council of Antioch that preceded it is only known from a Syriac letter first published by Schwartz in 1905, the authenticity of which was long questioned. For surveys of this debate see Chadwick (1958), Nyman (1961), Abramowski (1975), and Logan (1992) 428–32. In recent decades scholarly acceptance of this Council has been almost unanimous (one of the few exceptions is Holland (1970)).

The first major challenge to Opitz's model was that of Telfer,[12] who argued that the entire controversy only began in June 323. Telfer's thesis has received little support, for his efforts to reduce all the known documents and events that precede Nicaea to this very short period pose a number of problems.[13] However, his arguments do raise important questions, notably his emphasis that the chronology of the early controversy presented in Sozomen (I.15), upon which Opitz had in part relied, in fact has no validity as a source independent of the documents themselves.[14] Although he rejected Telfer's conclusions, Rowan Williams was thus in part building upon the former's observations when he produced a much more important reappraisal of the work of Opitz in his book *Arius*. Like Telfer, Williams emphasizes that almost all of the documents involved provide no precise evidence for their own date,[15] and he also supported Telfer's argument that Licinius' ban on councils, if it actually occurred, seems to have been very limited in effect and duration.[16] Most crucially, Williams also raises serious questions against Opitz's interpretation of the two letters of Alexander of Alexandria. Why does Alexander emphasize the role of Eusebius of Nicomedia in the *Encyclical Letter*, dated by Opitz to 321, and indeed declare that the latter is now resuming hostilities, but then make no

[12] Telfer (1946). See also id. (1949), an article that he wrote in response to criticism of his thesis by Baynes (1948). A defence of Opitz's chronology against Telfer was published by Schneemelcher (1954).

[13] Telfer's assertion that Alexander first showed hostility to Arius because of Constantine's victory over the Sarmartians in July 323 ((1946) 139–40), is particularly dubious. The need to reject any evidence that conflicted with his emphasis on the speed of the debates also forced Telfer to argue that the account of the slow development of the controversy in Eusebius, *Vita Constantini* II.61, describes the situation after Constantine's *Letter to Alexander and Arius* ((1949) 188), even though Eusebius' statement directly precedes the letter in question.

[14] Telfer (1946) 133–5. As Baynes (1948) 167 observes, Telfer goes rather too far in his argument. However, Baynes is wrong to question Telfer's essential criticism of Sozomen's chronology. The ecclesiastical historians, like modern scholars, could only construct their chronologies of the early controversy from the documents they possessed.

[15] As Williams observes, the great difficultly with judging Opitz's approach is that 'we possess virtually no external fixed points by which to check the plausibility of this reconstruction' ((1987) 49).

[16] Telfer (1946) 135. However, Baynes (1948) 165 would seem to be correct that Telfer's own dating of the ban to only April–November 324 is probably too short, and that the ban possibly began in late 323.

reference at all to Eusebius in his *Letter to Alexander* in 324, which was sent (whether to Thessalonica or Byzantium) to a bishop whose see was not too distant from Nicomedia?[17] And why, as Stead also notes, does only the allegedly earlier *Encyclical Letter* seem to show any knowledge of Arius' *Thalia*?[18]

To answer these questions, Williams constructed a new model for the chronology of the period before Nicaea, placing the formal beginning of the controversy, the Council of Alexandria that condemned Arius, in *c*.321.[19] According to Williams, Arius withdrew to Palestine, where he steadily gained support in 321–2, and Alexander thus wrote his *Letter to Alexander* at this time, warning his namesake of the danger in Syria but making no reference to Eusebius of Nicomedia, who had as yet played no part in the controversy. It was this activity by Alexander that then led Arius to write his *Letter to Eusebius of Nicomedia*, seeking the patronage of the bishop of the eastern capital.[20] Arius may not in fact have ever gone to Nicomedia in person,[21] and Eusebius therefore finally entered the controversy perhaps only in late 322, long after his namesake of Caesarea who played a much more prominent early role.[22] Williams places

17 Williams (1987) 51.

18 Stead (1988) 86–91, Williams (1987) 51. As we shall see below, Stead explains this difference on the grounds of authorship, Williams on the grounds of chronology.

19 Williams (1987) 56 also suggests that Arius' *Letter to Alexander* was considered and dismissed at this council, although there is no direct evidence to support this claim.

20 'The likeliest reason for this search for a new ally is a new offensive by Alexander' (Williams (1987) 54). Arius possibly approached Eusebius of Nicomedia particularly because he believed that Eusebius would know of him as a '*sulloukianista*', a 'fellow-Lucianist', although the exact meaning of this term remains uncertain (see Ch. 7). Williams also observes that Arius may have been encouraged to write by his Syrian supporters, who would have known Eusebius of Nicomedia as the latter had originally been bishop of Berytus, modern Beirut (for an outline of Eusebius' career, see Ch. 5).

21 Williams (1987) 54, taking up the argument of Telfer (1936) 63. The only ancient source that suggests that Arius did go to Nicomedia is Epiphanius, *Panarion* 69.4–7.

22 Williams (1987) 61. The role of Eusebius of Caesarea is in fact recognized by Eusebius of Nicomedia in his *Letter to Paulinus*. It should also be observed, as Williams again notes (54), that at this time Eusebius of Nicomedia was not only more distant from affairs than his namesake, but his position as the bishop of Licinius' capital, while a potential source of strength, must have become increasingly ambivalent as tensions grew between Licinius and Constantine and between Licinius and the Church.

Eusebius of Nicomedia's *Letter to Paulinus of Tyre* as part of a general letter-writing campaign by the supporters of Arius in 322–3, seeking to secure Arius' restoration to Alexandria,[23] before the conciliar ban of Licinius, which Williams places roughly in 323, brought formal disputes to an end. The victory of Constantine, however, opened new possibilities for all those involved in the controversy, and Williams argues that it was to exploit this new situation that Eusebius of Nicomedia called his Council of Bithynia to support Arius in 324.[24] This council may in turn have influenced Constantine's *Letter to Alexander and Arius* in 324/5,[25] and it is as a response to both this letter and the Bithynian Council that Williams finally places Alexander's *Encyclical Letter* in early 325.

Williams' proposed chronology is in general highly persuasive,[26] for the reversal of the traditional order of Alexander's letters readily explains why only the *Encyclical Letter* reveals knowledge of the *Thalia* or refers to Eusebius of Nicomedia as the 'Arian leader'.[27]

[23] Ibid. 54–5. Aside from the *Letter to Paulinus*, Williams also assigns to this period several other letters written by men later linked by Athanasius to the 'Eusebians': Eusebius of Caesarea's *Letter to Euphration* (a letter preserved in the *Acta* of the Second Council of Nicaea in AD 787; Opitz, *Urkunde* III), the two *Letters* of the Alexandrian presbyter George (later bishop of Laodicea), and the *Letter to Alexander* of Athanasius of Anazarbus (fragments from these letters are quoted in Athanasius, *De Synodis* 17; Opitz, *Urkunden* XI–XIII).

[24] Williams thus rejects the chronology of Sozomen, I.15 (followed by Opitz), who placed this council much earlier in the controversy.

[25] This was the view of Telfer (1946), who argued that 'the assumptions of the Emperor's letter to Alexander and Arius, defensive of the latter and insulting to the former, can hardly have emanated from any brain but that of Eusebius of Nicomedia' (129.n.2). Such an interpretation, although widely followed (e.g. De Clercq (1954) 197–9, Nyman (1961) 483, Kopecek (1979) 43–4), depends more upon the prevailing stereotype of Eusebius of Nicomedia than the actual contents of Constantine's letter.

[26] Surprisingly, Williams' argument seems to have received little detailed scholarly attention. The only direct response of which I am aware is the short article of Loose (1990) in defence of Opitz's original model, to which Williams replies in (2001) 252–4.

[27] Williams (1987) 50 acknowledges that an important factor in determining Opitz's original chronology of the two letters of Alexander was that the *Letter to Alexander* refers to the condemnation not only of Arius but of another Alexandrian presbyter, Colluthus, yet the same Colluthus signed the *Encyclical Letter* at the head of the other Alexandrian clergy. However, whereas Opitz thus assumed that Colluthus must have been condemned as an 'Arian' in the period between the two letters (an argument restated by Stead (1988) 91 and Loose (1990) 89–91 in their rejections of Williams' proposed model), Williams suggests that the condemnation of Colluthus in the *Letter to Alexander* was not because of 'Arianism', but because he was one of those

But there is one slight yet significant adjustment that I would suggest should be made to his model. Williams places the *Encyclical Letter* after Eusebius' Council of Bithynia and Constantine's *Letter to Alexander and Arius*,[28] yet Alexander makes no explicit reference to either the council or the letter.[29] Rather than place the *Encyclical Letter* after the epistle of Constantine, therefore, we should return to Williams' emphasis upon the new opportunities that the victory of Constantine over Licinius opened for the eastern Church. Constantine's *Letter to Alexander and Arius* is itself evidence that by early 325 the controversy had burst into renewed life. I would thus place both Alexander's *Encyclical Letter* and Eusebius' Council of Bithynia in late 324, shortly before that Constantinian letter, as two approximately simultaneous attempts by leading bishops to exploit the new situation created by the emergence of a Christian emperor.

Whether we date the *Encyclical Letter* of Alexander to late 324 or early 325, this revised reconstruction of the early 'Arian Controversy' has important implications for our understanding of the letter itself and of Eusebius of Nicomedia's role in the years before the Council of Nicaea. The earliest documents of the controversy, particularly Alexander's *Letter to Alexander* of *c.*321–2, are now strikingly silent concerning Eusebius, who would seem to have entered the debates late in 322, and whose *Letter to Paulinus of Tyre* is now dated to 323.[30]

who (according to Sozomen, I.15) criticized Alexander's initial reluctance to condemn Arius himself (55). Colluthus was therefore temporarily condemned early in the controversy for opposing his bishop, but by the time of the later *Encyclical Letter* he and Alexander had been reconciled, and Colluthus' position at the head of the signature list may have been intended as a statement of that renewed loyalty.

[28] Building upon his interpretation of the career of Colluthus (see n. 27), Williams (1987) 55 argues that the reconciliation of Colluthus and Alexander occurred at a council summoned when Ossius of Cordova came to Alexandria with Constantine's *Letter to Alexander and Arius.* Williams believes that it was this council that also produced the *Encyclical Letter*, which must therefore post-date the epistle of Constantine. However, we have already seen that it is far from certain that Constantine's letter either came to Alexandria or was carried by Ossius, and there is no evidence that Ossius was present when the *Encyclical Letter* (which is signed only by Alexandrian clergy) was composed.

[29] Loose (1990) 90.

[30] It was in fact precisely this reinterpretation of Eusebius of Nicomedia's role which (along with the question of Colluthus) led Loose (1990) to question Williams' chronology. She prefers to place Eusebius' interference on behalf of Arius much nearer the start of the controversy, and argues that Alexander does not mention the earlier activities of the bishop of Nicomedia in the *Letter to Alexander* because in that

Only towards the end of 324, after the victory of Constantine over Licinius had drastically increased both the status of the Church and the stakes involved in Christian theological and ecclesiastical conflict, did Alexander write the *Encyclical Letter*, presenting to his 'fellow-ministers everywhere' his own interpretation of the controversy and its participants. It is therefore all the more significant that it is in this letter that we find the earliest extant polemic against Eusebius of Nicomedia and the 'Eusebians'.

But did Alexander write the *Encyclical Letter*? This apparently straightforward question is in fact of considerable importance here, for the traditional authorship of the letter has been challenged by Christopher Stead, who has asserted that this work was composed not by Alexander but by Athanasius.[31] Stead observes both that the *Encyclical Letter* differs markedly from Alexander's *Letter to Alexander*, for whereas the latter is a long and rambling document the *Encyclical Letter* is formal and concise, and that there are considerable parallels in content, style, and vocabulary between the *Encyclical Letter* and the later writings of Athanasius.[32] Thus he concludes that Athanasius, who was Alexander's deacon before Nicaea, must have drafted this work. This conclusion is far from impossible, but the question must remain open. The differences between the two letters of Alexander might equally be explained by the different audiences and purposes for which they were written, and although there are certainly striking parallels between the *Encyclical Letter* and Athanasius' known writings, those parallels could equally represent the influence that his predecessor and mentor inevitably exerted upon Athanasius' language and thought. The *Encyclical Letter* will therefore be accepted here as representative of Alexander's own vision of the controversy and in particular of Eusebius of Nicomedia and the 'Eusebians', a vision which we will then compare to the later polemic of Athanasius himself.

The *Encyclical Letter* opens with a condemnation of the *Christomachoi* ('fighters against Christ') who have disturbed the

epistle he only discusses 'die jüngsten Ereignisse' (91). This argument is unconvincing, not least because it is hardly polemical practice to omit past events in this manner, as we shall see throughout Athanasius' highly repetitive condemnation of his 'Eusebian' foes.

[31] Stead (1988) 76–91, restated in (1994) 27.

[32] Stead (1988) 82.

Alexandrian church. But after this introduction, Alexander immediately focuses his polemic against the man whom he believes is primarily responsible for the escalation of that conflict.

Eusebius, who is now in Nicomedia, thinking the affairs of the Church to be in his possession because he has forsaken Berytus and cast envious eyes (*epophthalmisas*) on the church of the Nicomedians... appointed himself leader (*proistatai*) of these apostates and endeavoured to write everywhere supporting them, if by any means he could drag some ignorant people into this last and Christ-fighting heresy. (Hansen (1995) 7, 3–8)

Alexander declares that it was in response to Eusebius' activities that he felt bound to write the *Encyclical Letter*, in order to warn all bishops against this man and his support for the 'Arian heresy'. And he cautions his audience that

if Eusebius should write [to you], pay no attention. For now through these affairs he wishes to renew his former malevolence (*tēn palai kakonoian*),[33] which seemed to have been silenced by time, [and] he has feigned (*schēmatizetai*) to write as if on behalf of them [the Arians], when in fact it is clear that he does this for the promotion of his own purposes. (Hansen (1995) 7, 11–14)

After a long and detailed theological description of the 'Arian heresy' (to which I will return in my final chapter), Alexander resumes his attack upon Eusebius with the assertion that it was these 'Arians' whom 'the Eusebians received, endeavouring to blend falsehood with truth, impiety with piety' (Hansen (1995) 8, 18–20). The *Encyclical Letter* then concludes with a further repetition that all those whom Alexander condemns share the 'errors' that he has attributed to Arius, and that the bishops to whom he writes must pay no heed to the arguments of his foes.

Neither receive any of them, if they should presume to approach you, nor put faith in Eusebius or in anyone else writing [to you] concerning them. For it is fitting for those of us who are Christians to turn away from all who say

[33] As Williams (1987) 51 notes, this reference to Eusebius' 'former malevolence' has long puzzled scholars who place the *Encyclical Letter* near the start of the controversy. But it fits well with a date of composition of late 324, when Eusebius' earlier letters and appeals in support of Arius in 323 were resumed after the period of inactivity imposed by Licinius' ban on councils and the war with Constantine.

these things against Christ and who think like those who are fighters against God. (Hansen (1995) 10, 20–4)

Certain elements within Alexander's representation of Eusebius of Nicomedia and the 'Eusebians' in these passages bear obvious similarities to the later polemical construction of Athanasius that we have already observed in his *Epistula Encyclica* of 339. Again there is the repeated emphasis that the letters that such men might compose must be rejected, and the condemnation of their manipulation of episcopal positions, a charge that in the *Encyclical Letter* is levelled directly against Eusebius himself and his translation from Berytus to Nicomedia. Above all, Eusebius and the 'Eusebians' once more are 'Arians'. Not only has Eusebius appointed himself the 'leader of the apostates', and so must share their 'heresy', but Alexander's invocation of '*hoi peri Eusebion*', the earliest known occurrence of that phrase, is made in the specific context of their association with '*hoi peri Areion*'.[34] The immediate emphasis is that the 'Eusebians' share in full the 'errors' that Alexander attributes to Arius himself, and as we shall see in Chapter 7, the construction of 'Arianism' in Alexander's letter closely parallels that presented in Athanasius' theological works. Like Athanasius fifteen years later, Alexander in 324 thus constructs a polarized contrast between the 'Arian heresy' of the 'Eusebians' and his own status as the representative of the 'orthodox' faith. Through that contrast he seeks, with considerable success in the light of the Council of Nicaea, to rally the Church to receive his own interpretation of the controversy and to reject the arguments of his foes.

Yet there is also a significant difference between the polemic of the respective *Encyclical Letters* of Alexander and Athanasius. Alexander places far greater emphasis on Eusebius of Nicomedia as an individual, and less upon the 'Eusebians' as a collective 'party'. His condemnation is primarily reserved for Eusebius' own career and actions, culminating in the explicit assertion that Eusebius is motivated more by his own ambition than his zeal for 'Arianism'. This is in contrast to

[34] Here we see again the distinction, likewise drawn in the *Epistula Encyclica*, between the 'Arians' within Egypt and the 'Eusebians' who interfere from outside. As in the later argument of Athanasius, however, this does not alter Alexander's insistence that all his foes share the same 'heresy'.

Athanasius, who invariably presents the 'heresy' of his foes as the true inspiration for their 'conspiracies'. Although Alexander unquestionably exerted great influence both upon Athanasius' own theology and upon his attitude to 'Arians' and 'Arianism', Athanasius' construction of the 'Eusebians' cannot be understood simply as the continuation of the polemic of his predecessor. Alexander never developed his image of his opponents in the systematic manner of Athanasius himself, and it was only in 335, over a decade after Alexander's depiction of Eusebius of Nicomedia as 'Arian' and as the leader of an 'Arian party' in his *Encyclical Letter*, that Athanasius first began his own attack upon the 'Eusebians'. To understand the polemic of Athanasius we must therefore look beyond the influence of Alexander, and examine the context and motivation that first led Athanasius to adopt this construction of a 'Eusebian party'. This examination will centre upon Athanasius' presentation of the controversial early years of his episcopate from his accession in 328 to the aftermath of his condemnation at the Council of Tyre in 335.

THE *APOLOGIA CONTRA ARIANOS*, THE *FESTAL LETTERS*, AND THE COUNCIL OF TYRE

The pages that follow first examine Athanasius' own presentation of the period 328–35 as described in the narrative of the *Apologia Contra Arianos* that he began to compose after his return from his original exile in 337. That later narrative will then be compared with the contemporary documents that Athanasius cites in the same work, and with his own *Festal Letters* from the years before the Council of Tyre. Through that comparison, it will be shown that the narrative of the *Apologia Contra Arianos*, which places great emphasis on the 'Eusebians' and their 'conspiracies', represents Athanasius' later reinterpretation of the events that surrounded his condemnation in 335. The 'Eusebians' are in fact entirely absent from either the documentary evidence or the *Festal Letters* until the time of the Council of Tyre itself. It is therefore possible to identify both the context and motivation which first led Athanasius to present his foes as an 'Arian party', and the extent to which in his later narrative he retrojected this image of the 'Eusebians' onto the earlier events that preceded his exile.[35]

It is emphatically *not* my intention to return here to the much-debated question of Athanasius' guilt or innocence. In reality, even the exact charges on which he was condemned in 335 remain uncertain.[36] Athanasius' own account focuses upon two charges—that he murdered a Melitian bishop named Arsenius (which it seems true that Athanasius disproved, as he produced Arsenius alive)[37] and that he was responsible for a certain Macarius breaking a sacred chalice in a Melitian church (a charge that is not clear even in the *Apologia Contra Arianos*, as Athanasius both argues that nothing happened and that, if it did happen, it did not matter). There were certainly other charges of violence that Athanasius does not mention, charges that would seem to have had a basis of truth on the evidence of *Papyrus London 1914*, a rare contemporary Melitian letter that refers to the imprisonment and abuse of Melitian clergy by Athanasius' supporters.[38] But neither those additional charges nor the precise legal proceedings of the Council of Tyre can be reconstructed with any degree of confidence.[39]

In the context of this monograph, no such reconstruction is necessary. My subject is Athanasius' presentation of his condemnation, and in that presentation it is not the actual charges that matter, but the image of himself and of his foes that Athanasius constructs.

35 A modified version of this argument that follows was published as Gwynn (2003).

36 For the fullest extant ancient account of those charges, though still not complete see Sozomen, II.25.

37 The famous story that Athanasius actually identified Arsenius as among those present at the Council of Tyre does not appear in any Athanasian work, only in Sozomen, II.25.10.

38 The importance of this document (first pub. by H. I. Bell (1924) 53–71) to our understanding of Athanasius' career has been much emphasized in recent scholarship (see Hanson (1988*b*) 252–4; Barnes (1993) 32). As Bell observed, 'it was always suspicious that Athanasius, while dwelling on the charges concerning the chalice and Arsenius, which he could refute, says nothing of those which accused him of violence and oppression towards the Meletians. The reason is now clear: these charges were in part true' (57). An attempt to reject this interpretation of *Papyrus London 1914* has been made by Arnold ((1989); (1991) 62–89), but his argument is unconvincing (see DiMaio (1996); Hauben (2001) 612–4).

39 The difficulties posed by such a reconstruction are clearly visible in the markedly disparate interpretations of Tyre that have been proposed by Drake (1986) 193–204, Arnold (1991) 143–63, and Barnes (1993) 22–5. For a survey of the sources and chronology of the events surrounding the Council, see also Schneemelcher (1974*a*) 297–309.

I was the hindrance to the admittance of the Arians (*hoi peri Areion*) into the Church . . . all the proceedings against me, and the fabricated stories about the breaking of the chalice and the murder of Arsenius, were for the sole purpose of introducing impiety into the Church and of preventing their being condemned as heretics. (*Apologia Contra Arianos* 85; Opitz (1940*a*) 163, 12–16)

This passage encapsulates Athanasius' interpretation of his trial and of his accusers as an 'Arian party'. Not only is he innocent of the charges that have been fabricated against him, but those charges themselves (charges which one should note were concerned entirely with Athanasius' behaviour, *not* theology) are nothing more than a smoke-screen to conceal the 'impiety' of his opponents. Athanasius is innocent because his accusers are 'heretics', 'Arians' who threaten the entire Church and against whom every Christian must rally to his defence. We have already seen Athanasius construct this image of himself and of his foes in his *Epistula Encyclica* of 339, in which the 'Eusebians' were represented as the driving force behind the 'Arian conspiracy' that drove Athanasius into exile. It is the development of this image that we must now trace through the narrative of the second half of the *Apologia Contra Arianos.*

The opening paragraph of that narrative provides an immediate statement of the polemical framework within which Athanasius will present the sequence of events that culminated in his condemnation at Tyre. After a very brief history of the Melitian schism down to his own election as bishop, Athanasius declares that, after Alexander's death

the Melitians . . . like dogs unable to forget their vomit, began again to trouble the churches. Upon learning this, Eusebius, who was the leader (*proistamenos*) of the Arian heresy, sent and bought the Melitians with many promises. He became their secret friend (*krupha philos*), and made compact with them for the time (*kairon*) he wished. (59; Opitz (1938*b*) 139, 16–20)

Eusebius of Nicomedia is thus introduced immediately as the leader of the 'Arian heresy',[40] and Athanasius here establishes what will become a constantly recurring theme, that of a 'secret alliance'

[40] In the opening passages of the *Apologia Contra Arianos* narrative (59–60), Athanasius first condemns 'Eusebius' as an individual, and then shifts to the plural '*hoi peri Eusebion*'. The reason for this shift is unclear (on the precise significance of '*hoi peri*' terminology, see Ch. 5).

between the 'Eusebians' and the Melitians. The charges against him may have originated from the Egyptian schismatics, but their true source lies with the 'heretics' who threaten not only Athanasius himself but the wider Christian Church. So in turn, Athanasius reports that in 330–1

> Eusebius, availing himself of the occasion (*ton kairon*) which he had agreed upon with the Melitians, wrote and persuaded them to invent some pretext, so that, as they had practised against Peter and Achillas and Alexander, thus also they might devise and spread reports against us. Accordingly, after seeking for a long time and finding nothing, they at last, with the advice of the Eusebians, came to an agreement and fabricated their first accusation ... concerning the linen vestments. (60; Opitz (1938*b*) 140, 12–17)

The exact significance of these 'linen vestments' remains unclear,[41] and the charge itself was soon dropped. But when Athanasius was summoned to court in 332 to answer the complaints that had been levelled against him, this same conspiracy reared its head again. For

> Eusebius persuaded them [the Melitians] to wait; and when I arrived, they next accused Macarius regarding the chalice, and brought against me not any chance accusation but the most wicked charge possible, that, as an enemy of the Emperor, I had sent a purse of gold to one Philumenus. (60; Opitz (1938*b*) 140, 22–141, 1).

As before, the charges are Melitian, but the motivation derives from Eusebius and his fellow 'Arians', for the schismatics acted only 'with the aim of pleasing those who had hired them (*tois misthōsamenois autous*)' (63; Opitz (1938*b*) 142, 25–6). When even these charges were in turn dismissed, the Melitians once more 'communicated with the Eusebians, and at last that calumny was invented by them that indeed Macarius broke a chalice, [and that] a certain bishop Arsenius was murdered by us' (63; Opitz (1938*b*) 143, 6–8).

Constantine now ordered Athanasius to face an enquiry, but when Athanasius informed the emperor that Arsenius had been found alive, the trial was abandoned.[42]

[41] For one interpretation, that the vestments were linked to the imperial grants of supplies to the Alexandrian Church for liturgy or charity, see Barnes (1989) 394.

[42] At no point in the *Apologia Contra Arianos* or elsewhere does Athanasius admit that Constantine in fact ordered an ecclesiastical council to be held at Palestinian

Thus the conspiracy had an end, and the Melitians were repulsed and covered with shame. But the Eusebians still did not remain quiet. For they did not care for the Melitians, but for the Arians (*tōn peri Areion*), and they were afraid lest, if the proceedings of the former should be stopped, they should no longer find persons to play the parts (*tous hupokrinomenous*), through whom they might be able to introduce those men [into the Church]. Therefore again they incited the Melitians, and persuaded the Emperor to give orders that a Council should be held afresh at Tyre. (71; Opitz (1938*b*) 148, 25–149, 1)

Athanasius presents the Council of Tyre as a direct continuation of the earlier accusations, a product of the ongoing 'conspiracy' of the 'Eusebians', who exploit the Melitians and mislead the Emperor in order to spread their 'Arian heresy'. The same two charges concerning the broken chalice and the fate of Arsenius are thus once more the focus of Athanasius' account of the Council itself, and when those charges apparently failed to produce a decisive result, it was again the 'Eusebians' who conspired to pervert justice and bring about Athanasius' fall.

the Eusebians were aggrieved that they had lost the prey of which they had been in pursuit, and they persuaded the Count Dionysius [the secular official appointed by Constantine to supervise the council],[43] who was one with them (*ton sun autois*), to send [a commission] to the Mareotis in order to see whether they might not be able to find something there against the Presbyter [Macarius], or rather, so that at a distance they might plot as they wished when we were absent. (72; Opitz (1938*b*) 151, 16–19)

In fact, Athanasius asserts that not only did the 'Eusebians' organize this commission of enquiry, but they assigned themselves to that commission,[44] and fabricated its findings through violence and

Caesarea to investigate his behaviour (although Barnes (1978) 61–2 would seem to be correct to see an allusion to this episode in Athanasius' reference to the 'court of Dalmatius the censor' in *Apologia Contra Arianos* 65). The existence of the abortive council is known from *Festal Index* VI, *Papyrus London 1913* (Bell (1924) 45–53), and from the later historians Sozomen, II.25, and Theodoret, I.28.

[43] 'I have sent Dionysius, a man of consular rank... who will be present to observe the proceedings, with a particular eye to good order' (Constantine's first letter to the bishops at Tyre, *Vita Constantini* IV.42.3; Cameron and Hall (1999) 169).

[44] I will discuss the specific identification of the individuals whom Athanasius names as 'Eusebians' here and elsewhere in his *Apologia Contra Arianos* narrative in Ch. 5.

corruption. 'Who then from these things does not behold the conspiracy? Who does not see clearly the wretchedness of the Eusebians?' (72; Opitz (1938*b*) 151, 29–30).

With the verdict of the Council inevitable,[45] Athanasius fled and appealed to Constantine, who then wrote his famous letter to the bishops at Tyre (86).[46] After describing his encounter with a dishevelled Athanasius at the gates of Constantinople, Constantine expressed concern that there may have been impropriety at the council, and ordered that all of the bishops who constituted the synod should come to court and explain their judgement. However, again according to Athanasius

> when the Eusebians learnt this, knowing what they had done, they prevented the other bishops from going up and only went themselves... [And] they no longer said anything about the chalice and Arsenius, for they did not have the boldness, but, inventing another accusation which concerned the Emperor directly, they declared before the Emperor himself that 'Athanasius has threatened to withhold the corn being sent from Alexandria to your country'. (87; Opitz (1940*a*) 165, 36–166, 4)

Losing his temper, Constantine exiled Athanasius to Trier, although Athanasius would later explain that 'this being the reason why I was sent away into Gaul, who again does not perceive the intention of the Emperor and the murderous spirit of the Eusebians, and that the Emperor had done this lest they resolve on some more desperate scheme?' (88; Opitz (1940*a*) 167, 1–3).

Athanasius' account of the circumstances surrounding his final condemnation and subsequent exile in 335 is highly controversial. No external evidence can be found to support the assertion that the immediate cause of his banishment was the charge that he had

[45] Although Athanasius himself never explicitly acknowledges that the council did indeed condemn him *in absentia* after his flight, nor does he ever identify the specific charges on which he was convicted.

[46] There is a longer version of the letter that Athanasius quotes here preserved in Gelasius of Cyzicus, *Historia Ecclesiastica* III.18. As the Gelasius version includes a further section in praise of Athanasius' piety, which it is difficult to believe that Athanasius would have removed (Baynes (1925) 63, Drake (1986) 195.n.4), it seems highly likely that Athanasius' text is the original and that of Gelasius reflects later additions, probably made by Gelasius himself (Ehrhardt (1980) 55–6). However, Barnes (1993) 30–2 rejects this conclusion, while Elliott (1996) 308–16 proposes that the letter in both forms is an Athanasian forgery.

threatened to withhold grain from Constantinople.[47] Nor is it apparent whether Constantine, in ordering this sentence, enforced the Council of Tyre or pronounced his own judgement.[48] Whatever the precise legal status of Athanasius' exile, however, the entire *Apologia Contra Arianos* testifies to the need that he and his supporters felt to undermine the Council of Tyre and its verdict.[49] Athanasius achieves this end through his construction of his accusers as an 'Arian party'. The allegation that the 'Eusebians' manipulated Constantine's summons to court and compelled the 'other bishops' to remain behind is almost certainly false,[50] but through this presentation, and through his construction of the charges against him as the product of an 'Arian conspiracy', Athanasius separates '*hoi peri*

47 The silence of the eastern bishops at Serdica in 343 regarding this charge, which was taken by Barnard (1983) as 'an indication that it could not be proved' (83), could equally be interpreted as evidence that the entire grain episode is no more than an Athanasian invention (Elliott (1996) 316.n.92).

48 The older conclusion that Constantine's judgement represented the confirmation of the verdict of the Council of Tyre (Nordberg (1964) 31, Drake (1986) 204) has been challenged by Barnes ((1981) 240, (1993) 24 and (1998) 14–15), who asserts that when Constantine summoned the bishops at Tyre to court he implicitly annulled the decision of the Council. Barnes rightly emphasizes that Athanasius' exile was not a straightforward ecclesiastical deposition, for Constantine refused to allow a new bishop of Alexandria to be established in Athanasius' place, yet according to Sozomen (II.31), the emperor also refused to allow Athanasius to return specifically because he was condemned by a Church council.

49 The argument of Barnes (1993) 28, that 'Athanasius needed to discredit the Council of Tyre, not because its verdict was the legal basis of his exile in either 335 or 339, but lest Christians everywhere regarded the sacrilege of which the Council of Tyre found him guilty as automatically disqualifying him from discharging the functions of a bishop', is unconvincing. The *Encyclical Letter* of Athanasius' own Council of Alexandria in 338 (see below) explicitly complains that the 'Eusebians' 'put forward the name of a Council and ground its proceedings upon the authority of the Emperor' (*Apologia Contra Arianos* 10; Opitz (1938*a*) 95, 27) to justify Athanasius' exile. This suggests that the eastern bishops did uphold Tyre's verdict as the basis of Athanasius' deposition, and asserted (rightly or wrongly) that Constantine had enforced that judgement.

50 Quite aside from the doubt that the bishops at Tyre would really have disobeyed an imperial command in this manner, *Festal Index* VIII states that Athanasius was in Constantinople for only 9 days. This does not allow enough time for Constantine to meet Athanasius and despatch his letter and then for that letter to reach Tyre and for the 'Eusebians' to set out (Peeters (1945)). It seems more probable that the bishops who arrived in Constantinople from Tyre were already en route to the court as representatives of the synod when Constantine first met Athanasius (Drake (1986) esp. 196).

Eusebion' from the wider body of bishops who were present at Tyre. The 'Eusebians' are no more than a small minority, a 'heretical faction', and as such their judgement against him cannot represent the verdict of a true council of the Christian Church.

The precise date at which Athanasius composed the narrative of his condemnation in the *Apologia Contra Arianos* cannot be determined, for reasons that were discussed in Chapter 1. Yet it is apparent that the essential elements of Athanasius' presentation of the 'Eusebians' and their role had already become established by 338. At that time a Council of Alexandria was held, presided over by Athanasius himself, to justify his return to his see on Constantine's death the previous year. The *Encyclical Letter* of this Council is quoted in *Apologia Contra Arianos* 3–19 and provides important confirmation that the interpretation of the events of 328–35 described above (and indeed many of the documents around which that interpretation is presented)[51] was already being put forward in Athanasius' defence within barely three years of the Council of Tyre.[52]

The stated purpose of the Alexandrian *Encyclical Letter* is to reveal to every Christian bishop the 'conspiracy' which the 'Eusebians' have fabricated against Athanasius (3). That conspiracy is described in exactly the same terms as we have already traced in the narrative of the second half of the *Apologia Contra Arianos*. Only the charges regarding the chalice and Arsenius are acknowledged, and such accusations must be false, for everything that is said against Athanasius 'is nothing but calumny and a plot of our enemies... an impiety on behalf of the Ariomaniacs, which rages against piety so that, when the orthodox are out of the way, the advocates of impiety

[51] The vast majority of the documentary dossier preserved by Athanasius in the second half of the *Apologia Contra Arianos* would appear to have already existed in 338 (see Barnes (1993) 39). Among the documents cited in the Alexandrian *Encyclical Letter* are the '*Recantation*' of Ischyras (*Apologia Contra Arianos* 64), the letters of Alexander of Thessalonica (66) and Constantine (68) to Athanasius in 334, the list of Melitian clergy in 325 (71.6), and the undated letter ordering a church to be built for Ischyras (85).

[52] The Alexandrian *Encyclical Letter* was certainly written with Athanasius' approval and under his influence (Barnard (1975*b*) 338; Warmington (1986) 7; Arnold (1991) 33), and therefore may be assumed to reflect his own polemical position in 338. However, the evidence does not allow us to confirm the assertion of Barnes (1993) 39 that Athanasius wrote the letter himself.

may preach whatever they wish without fear' (5; Opitz (1938*a*) 91, 28–31).

Moreover, this 'conspiracy' is once again the product of a 'secret alliance' of the Melitians and the 'Eusebians', within which the schismatics play very much a subordinate role. 'The Melitians who are the accusers on no account ought to be believed, for they are schismatics and enemies of the Church' (11; Opitz (1938*a*) 96, 14–15). In any case, 'their slander and false accusations have never prevailed [against Athanasius] until now, that they have gained the Eusebians as their supporters (*sunergous*) and patrons (*prostatas*)' (11; Opitz (1938*a*) 96, 19–21). The Melitians are merely the pawns in a 'Eusebian' drama.

> When he [John Arcaph, the Melitian leader] saw the Eusebians zealously supporting the Ariomaniacs, though they did not dare to cooperate with them openly but were seeking for others to use as masks (*prosōpois*), he submitted himself, like an actor (*hypokritēn*) in the pagan theatres. The subject (*hypothesis*) was a contest (*agōn*) of Arians, and the real design was their success, but John and those with him were put forward and played these parts, in order that through their pretext, the supporters of the Arians who were in the guise of judges might drive away the enemies of their impiety, establish that impiety, and bring the Arians into the Church. (17; Opitz (1938*a*) 99, 33–40)

Just as in the *Apologia Contra Arianos* narrative, the Melitians who actually brought forward the accusations against Athanasius are nothing more than 'actors', for it is the 'Eusebians' who are the true source of Athanasius' suffering. So the judgement of Tyre is itself dismissed, for it is merely the product of this 'Arian conspiracy'.

> What credit does that council or trial have of which they boast? . . . What kind of a council of bishops was then held? . . . Who of the majority among them was not our enemy? Did not the Eusebians hasten against us because of the Arian mania? . . . How can they dare to call that a council, at which a Count presided, which an executioner attended, and where an usher instead of the deacons of the Church led us in? He alone spoke, and all present were silent, or rather were obedient to the Count, and the removal of those bishops who seemed to deserve it was prevented by his will. When he ordered we were dragged about by soldiers, or rather the Eusebians ordered, and he was subservient to their wishes. (8; Opitz (1938*a*) 94, 1; 4–5; 11–16)

The verdict of such a trial cannot be valid, nor can such a 'heretical' gathering represent a true council of the Christian Church. Moreover, because he is the victim of such a 'conspiracy', Athanasius is not merely innocent of the charges that have been fabricated against him, but the very fact that he is attacked in this manner is itself proof of his status as the 'representative of orthodoxy', the champion who will not yield to the 'Arian heresy'.

It was not then the chalice nor the murder nor any of their marvellous tales that led them to act in this way, but the aforementioned impiety of the Arians, because of which they have conspired against Athanasius and other bishops, and still now wage war against the Church. (17; Opitz (1938*a*) 100, 10–13)

The *Encyclical Letter* then concludes with a further appeal to every bishop

to welcome this our declaration, to share in the suffering of our fellow bishop Athanasius, and to show your indignation against the Eusebians . . . for truly wretched are the deeds that they have done, and unworthy of your communion. (19; Opitz (1938*a*) 101, 21–3; 26–7)

The Alexandrian *Encyclical Letter* of 338, the narrative of the *Apologia Contra Arianos*, and Athanasius' own *Epistula Encyclica* of 339 all present the events surrounding the Council of Tyre in a manner that goes far beyond merely proclaiming Athanasius' innocence. The Council of Tyre is rejected as invalid, and the alleged charges levelled against him are denied, but in a sense even those charges have become irrelevant. In the polemic of Athanasius the true issue at stake is not his own behaviour, correct or otherwise, but the greater theological controversy against which he has set his trial. He has achieved this presentation, and with it his image of himself as the 'champion' of the Church, through his construction of his opponents not as a local schismatic sect but as the 'Eusebians', a 'heretical party' who represent a threat to the Church as a whole.

This polemical construction of his opponents serves an obvious function in Athanasius' presentation of his own innocence, legitimacy, and 'orthodoxy'. To better understand the nature and potential distortions of Athanasius' presentation of the 'Eusebians', however, we must determine the context in which he first brought forward this construction of his opponents, why he did so, and what effect that initial polemic had. To achieve this, it is necessary to return to the

Apologia Contra Arianos, and compare the Athanasian presentation of the events of 328–35 described above with the documents preserved in that same work and with the *Festal Letters* that Athanasius composed for the Easter celebrations of those years. Whereas the *Apologia Contra Arianos* narrative and the Alexandrian *Encyclical Letter* of 338 post-date the Council of Tyre, many of the documents that Athanasius quotes and his earliest *Festal Letters* pre-date 335, and thus provide a glimpse of how Athanasius and others represented those events in the years before his condemnation and exile. In stark contrast to the later Athanasian narrative, what we find in these texts is a complete silence regarding the 'Eusebians'.

The chronology of the *Festal Letters* of Athanasius is a highly controversial subject, but as I discussed in Chapter 1 the letters that date from the very early years of his episcopate can be identified with relative certainty. Athanasius' first three *Festal Letters* (*Letters* I, XXIV, and XIV) contain no relevant polemical material, but in *Letter* IV of 332 Athanasius apologizes for the lateness of his epistle, for 'I am at the court, having been summoned by the emperor Constantine to see him' (IV.5; Robertson (1892) 517). No mention is made of what the charges may have been that provoked this summons, but Athanasius writes in a tone of triumph, 'our enemies having been put to shame... because they persecuted us without cause' (IV.1; Robertson (1892) 516). Crucially, Athanasius explicitly identifies those 'enemies'. 'The Melitians... sought our ruin before the Emperor. But they were put to shame and driven away thence as calumniators' (IV.5; Robertson (1892) 517). Whereas in the *Apologia Contra Arianos* narrative Athanasius specifically asserts that Eusebius of Nicomedia was the 'secret friend' who inspired the schismatics to bring forward these charges, in the *Festal Letter* actually written in 332, and written indeed from court where Eusebius is usually presumed to have been a significant figure, Athanasius' only concern is with the Melitians themselves. This is also true of the documents cited in the *Apologia Contra Arianos* in relation to the events of this year. Neither Constantine's Letter to the Church of Alexandria in 332 (61–2)[53] nor the documents relating to the

[53] In this letter, Constantine denounces 'the fools (*hoi mōroi*)' (62; Opitz (1938*a*) 141, 29) and 'the wretches (*hoi ponēroi*)' (62; Opitz (1938*a*) 142, 12) who have slandered Athanasius, but he does not identify the slanderers in question.

Ischyras and Arsenius charges that Athanasius quotes (64, 67) leave any trace of 'Eusebian' involvement.

This silence continues in the *Festal Letter* that can be assigned with confidence to 333 (V),[54] and in the *Letters* that have been placed, without the same certainty, in 334 and 335 (VI and VII).[55] There are no known *Festal Letters* for 336 or 337, and the first explicit reference to the 'Arians' in Athanasius' writings only occurs in *Festal Letter* X (338), when the Melitians are described merely as the allies of the 'heretics' and the sharers of their 'impiety'.[56] The sole invocation of the 'Eusebians' in the extant *Festal Letters* then appears in *Letter* XI (339), by which time the Melitians have entirely disappeared.[57] Thus only after his condemnation in 335, and specifically after his return from his first exile in 337, did Athanasius in his Easter communications to the Egyptian churches present the construction of his opponents that we have seen expressed in the narrative of the *Apologia Contra Arianos* and in the Alexandrian *Encyclical Letter* of 338.

[54] *Festal Letter* V does refer to 'the heretics and schismatics of the present time' (V.4; Robertson (1892) 518), but Athanasius does not elaborate on this statement, which is part of a rhetorical denunciation of all those, including also pagans and Jews, who cannot celebrate the true Easter. A similar general denunciation likewise appears in *Festal Letters* VI and VII (Wiles (1993*b*) 33–4).

[55] Although Camplani (1989) and (2003) places *Festal Letters* VI and VII in the years given here, Lorenz (1986) argues in favour of the dates 345–6, while Schwartz (1935) had originally proposed 356 and 340 respectively. This debate reflects the problems posed by the chronology of Athanasius' *Festal Letters* in general, for there is no decisive evidence to allow a judgement to be made between these alternative dates.

[56] *Festal Letter* X, written immediately following Athanasius' return from his first exile when his position was far from secure, is one of the longest and certainly the most polemical of Athanasius' Easter epistles, and demonstrates that Athanasius did not hesitate to incorporate such material into the *Festal Letters* when he desired to do so. For a detailed study of this letter see Lorenz (1986), particularly 82–6 on Athanasius' presentation of 'Arianism' (which closely follows that of Alexander's *Encyclical Letter*). There is no reference to the 'Eusebians', but Athanasius emphasizes that his foes are 'Ariomaniacs' (X.9, although this characteristic Athanasian phrase is miscopied in the Syriac manuscript as 'Arius and Manetes', Robertson (1892) 531.n.11), while the schismatics allied with them play a clearly subordinate role (X.9–11).

[57] 'Let no one of us fail of his duty... counting as nothing the affliction or the trials which, especially at this time, have been enviously directed against us by the party of Eusebius [i.e. "*hoi peri Eusebion*" in the Syriac]. Even now they wish to injure us and by their accusations to compass our death, because of that godliness, whose helper is the Lord' (XI.12; Robertson (1892) 537). A slightly different translation of this passage is offered by Anatolios (2004) 17.

At this stage, it is to the documents preserved in the *Apologia Contra Arianos* that we must turn. A number of the texts that Athanasius cites here are dated to 334 and 335, and it is in these documents that the precise origins of the Athanasian construction of the 'Eusebians' may finally be found. After his description of the abortive trial of 334, Athanasius cites a letter that he received from Bishop Alexander of Thessalonica (66),[58] a letter that Athanasius in his narrative declares will 'show that they [the Eusebians, named in the previous sentence] accused me of having destroyed Arsenius' (65; Opitz (1938*b*) 144, 21–2). Yet Alexander says nothing of the 'Eusebians', or indeed of 'Arians' at all. His focus is purely upon John Arcaph and the Melitians, and this is all the more significant for Alexander states that he received his information from an envoy of Athanasius named Macarius (presumably the same man involved in the chalice charge). It is therefore at least possible that Alexander reflects Athanasius' own representation of these charges at that time. This hypothesis receives further support from the letter that Athanasius then proceeds to quote (68), sent to him by Constantine in the same year (334). In this letter, the emperor explicitly acknowledges that he has read the letters he received from Athanasius, and then condemns once more those who bring false accusations against the bishop, namely 'the most wicked and lawless Melitians' (68; Opitz (1938*b*) 146, 10).

Despite the claims of Athanasius' narrative, the documents that he cites from 334 thus do not support his later construction of the 'Eusebians' and their actions. Moreover, there is reason to believe that in the years before the Council of Tyre Athanasius himself did not present the charges against him in terms of a 'Eusebian conspiracy'. His sole concern was with the Melitians, the men who actually brought the charges forward. It is of course possible that Athanasius' initial silence concerning the 'Eusebians' indicates that he had not yet

[58] As we saw in the previous chapter, the bishop of Thessalonica may have been the recipient of Alexander of Alexandria's *Letter to Alexander*, in which case he was a longstanding ally of the Alexandrian see. Athanasius declares in his narrative that he quotes this letter of Alexander of Thessalonica merely as one example of the many such letters he received, 'from which it is possible to know the tenor of the rest (*tas tōn allōn*)' (65; Opitz (1938*b*) 144, 23–4). As Athanasius provides no other information, however, it is impossible to evaluate his claim.

recognized their 'secret alliance' with his Egyptian foes.[59] But I believe that at this time Athanasius had simply not yet begun to represent himself and his opponents according to the polemical model that he would later construct. The alleged involvement of the 'Eusebians' in the events preceding Tyre and their 'alliance' with the Melitians that figure so prominently in modern scholarship are the product of a retrojection upon the years before 335 of Athanasius' later construction of his foes, a construction for which no contemporary evidence exists.

So when did Athanasius first begin his polemic against the 'Eusebians'? The answer is at the Council of Tyre itself. Athanasius presents a series of documents in relation to the Council in the *Apologia Contra Arianos*. The first two are written by clergy in Alexandria (73) and in the Mareotis (74–5), and only speak vaguely of a 'conspiracy' against Athanasius without reference to the 'Eusebians' as an 'Arian party'.[60] Far more important are three letters written at Tyre by the bishops who had accompanied Athanasius to the Council,[61] letters which Athanasius presumably influenced, and which therefore reflect Athanasius' own presentation of the proceedings against him. The first and longest of those letters was written as an 'Encyclical' to 'the bishops assembled at Tyre' (77; Opitz (1938*b*) 156, 22), and represents the earliest extant reference to the 'Eusebian party' as the source of the charges against Athanasius.

> We believe that the conspiracy is no longer secret which is being formed against us by Eusebius and Theognis and Maris and Narcissus and Theodore and Patrophilus... you yourselves know their enmity, which they entertain

[59] This was the argument of Arnold (1991) 64.n.282: 'Athanasius was far more concerned with the Melitian threat and only later became aware of their links with the Eusebian or pro-Arian party'. Twomey (1982) 346–7 too argues that Athanasius only identified the alliance against him at Tyre, while Kannengiesser (1970) 414–16 suggests that Athanasius' earlier silence (especially in the *Festal Letters*) has a political explanation, that Athanasius could not attack the 'Arians' openly while Constantine lived.

[60] The letter of the Mareotis Clergy (74–5) does include a very rare reference to '*hoi peri Theognion*' (75; Opitz (1938*b*) 154, 23), signifying Theognis of Nicaea as the leader of the Mareotis Commission, and also asserts that the Commission in question had the support of the 'Arians'. But neither letter refers to the 'Eusebians', or describes Athanasius' foes at Tyre specifically as 'Arian'.

[61] According to Sozomen, II.25.16–19, the violent conduct of these Egyptian bishops at Tyre became one of the final charges levelled against Athanasius.

not only towards us but indeed towards all the orthodox, [and] that for the sake of the mania of Arius and his impious doctrines they persecute all and conspire against all. (77; Opitz (1938*b*) 156, 24–5; 28–31)

Here for the first time the charges against Athanasius are denounced as the product of a 'heretical conspiracy', which represents a threat not merely to Athanasius himself but to the entire Church. This was the polemical construction that the Egyptians appealed to the other bishops at Tyre to endorse, to recognize the accusers of Athanasius as an 'Arian party', and so to denounce them and reject their charges against the 'orthodox' bishop of Alexandria.

The other two letters from the Egyptian bishops at Tyre cited by Athanasius in the *Apologia Contra Arianos* are both addressed to Dionysius, the Count appointed by Constantine to oversee the Council. As we saw earlier, both Athanasius in his later narrative and the Alexandrian *Encyclical Letter* of 338 accused Dionysius of being 'one' with the 'Eusebians'. However, in 335 Athanasius' Egyptian bishops petitioned the Count as a neutral and independent adjudicator whom they evidently hoped to win over to their side. The first of the two letters (78) is nearly identical to that sent to the other bishops at Tyre, and appeals to Dionysius to recognize that Athanasius is the victim of a 'Eusebian conspiracy', although the reference to the 'Eusebians' as 'Arian' is omitted, possibly because the theological argument was seen as inappropriate in a letter to a secular official. The second letter to Dionysius (79), written when the verdict of Tyre was apparently inevitable, again repeats that 'many conspiracies and plots are being formed against us through the machinations of Eusebius and Narcissus and Flacillus and Theognis and Maris and Theodore and Patrophilus' (79; Opitz (1938*b*) 159, 28–160, 2).[62] On the basis of these 'conspiracies', the Egyptian bishops request that Dionysius 'reserve the hearing of the affairs which concern us for the most pious Emperor himself' (79; (Opitz (1938*b*) 160, 7–8). This letter may have been written to prepare the ground for Athanasius' flight to Constantine from Tyre,[63] although

[62] Note that in the list of 'Eusebians' in this later Egyptian letter the name of Flacillus of Antioch (who appears to have been the president of the Council) has been added to those condemned in their first letter above. See Ch. 5.

[63] Like the earlier pair of letters written by Athanasius' supporters at Tyre, this second letter to Dionysius would seem to have been part of a systematic polemical

as we have seen this did not enable the bishop of Alexandria to avoid exile.

In the letters of the Egyptian bishops who attended the Council of Tyre, it is thus possible to isolate the exact date, context, and intended audience which first led Athanasius and his supporters to present the accusations against him as the product of an 'Arian party' identified by the title '*hoi peri Eusebion*'. Why? What was the intended purpose of this polemic, which goes so much further than the mere assertion of Athanasius' innocence? It was the other eastern bishops who were gathered at Tyre to whom the first and most important Egyptian letter was sent; these are the men whom Athanasius and his supporters most wished to convince. And one passage in that Egyptian letter to the bishops reveals both the circumstances that inspired the Egyptian appeal and the effect that they hoped their polemic would have.

> After they [the Eusebians] had made what preparations they pleased and had sent these suspected persons [on the commission to the Mareotis], we heard that they were going about to each of you and requiring a subscription (*hypographēn*), in order that it might appear as if this had been done by the design (*tē skepsei*) of you all. For this reason we were obliged to write to you and to present this our testimony, witnessing that we are the victims of a conspiracy, suffering by them and through them, and expecting that, having the fear of God in your minds and condemning their conduct in sending whom they pleased without our consent, you would not subscribe (*mē hypograpsēte*), lest they should claim that those things are done by you, which they are contriving only among themselves.... As you will have to give an account on the Day of Judgement, receive this testimony, recognize the conspiracy which has been framed against us, and be on your guard that if you are requested [by them] you do nothing against us and that you do not take part in the design (*tē skepsei*) of the Eusebians. (77; Opitz (1938*b*) 157, 14–21; 30–4)

In this Egyptian appeal to the bishops at Tyre to defend Athanasius against the 'conspiracy' of the 'Eusebian party', we see the imposition upon that Council of the polarization between 'Arian' and 'orthodox'

campaign addressed both to the Count and to the bishops of the Council. Although in this instance Athanasius does not quote the parallel letter, the second epistle to Dionysius ends with a statement that 'we have also explained concerning the same things to our Lords the orthodox Bishops' (79; Opitz (1938*b*) 160, 17–18).

on which the polemic of Athanasius is based. According to this polarized vision, the Council of Tyre is divided into three distinct blocs. There are the Egyptian bishops themselves; there are the men who have been branded as '*hoi peri Eusebion*'; and there are 'the rest'. It is this final bloc, the wider body of bishops present at Tyre, to whom the letter has been addressed. They must now join with the Egyptians in support of Athanasius and reject the 'Eusebians', who as a 'heretical party' cannot be representative of the Council as a whole. Hence in the paragraph quoted above there is the repeated emphasis that the bishops at Tyre must not sign the alleged 'subscriptions' of the 'Eusebians', nor act in any way as if in support of the 'Eusebian conspiracy'. To do so would suggest that they too were part of that 'heretical party' and imply that they stood with the 'Arians' in opposition to the 'true Church'.[64]

Thus the Council of Tyre is divided into 'parties', and ecclesiastical politics after Nicaea are indeed 'party politics'. But this polarized opposition of the 'Eusebians' and the 'catholic Church', between which the bishops to whom the Egyptian letter is addressed must choose, is itself a product of the polemic, not the reflection of reality that it is all too often taken to be. By addressing the eastern bishops gathered at Tyre as in some sense distinct from the 'Eusebians', the Egyptian bishops have imposed their own polemical polarization upon the Council, and separated the alleged 'Eusebian party' from the wider body of the eastern Church.

Only once this imposition has been recognized can the full purpose of the polemic be understood. In appealing to the 'bishops assembled at Tyre' to disassociate themselves from the 'Eusebians', the Egyptian bishops have attempted to turn their polarized construction into reality. They ask their audience to accept the existence of the 'Eusebians', as they are described in the letter that they had just received, and so in turn to define themselves as 'other' than that

[64] There is a useful discussion of the significance of 'subscription' in the fourth-century Church in Amidon (2002), esp. 53–60. Amidon emphasizes that a subscription was not just a name like a modern signature, but often a brief sentence or sentences endorsing the contents of the documents subscribed (as in the appeal of the *Encyclical Letter* of Western Serdica (*Apologia Contra Arianos* 47.6) asking absent bishops to further subscribe to their decisions). It was this endorsement of his condemnation by those at Tyre that Athanasius and his bishops hoped to avert.

'heretical party'. This, according to the polarized model of the polemic, must dictate that they support Athanasius. The letter of the Egyptian Bishops is therefore not a description of the Council of Tyre as it was, but an image of the Council that Athanasius and the authors of that letter wished the members of that Council to accept. The clearest indication that this image of the Council of Tyre and of the so-called 'Eusebians' is one that the majority of the bishops who gathered in that city did not share, is that in 335 at least, the polemic failed to avert Athanasius' condemnation.[65]

In his later writings from 338 onwards, Athanasius would react to the failure of his initial polemical presentation at Tyre by denouncing the entire Council as the vehicle of his enemies. Yet, although Athanasius brought some 48 bishops with him from Egypt when he came to Tyre, throughout the proceedings of the Council his supporters would seem to have been a minority.[66] The condemnation of Athanasius, upheld by some 60 or more eastern bishops, was therefore not the product of the manipulation of a small 'faction', but the verdict of a considerable bloc of the eastern Church.[67] In the words of Hanson, '[Athanasius] represents the Council of Tyre, which was a properly

[65] This is not to suggest that the Athanasian polemical campaign in 335 had no effect at all. The appeals of the Egyptian bishops did convince at least one individual, Alexander of Thessalonica (whose support for Athanasius in 334 we have already observed). Alexander appears to have attended the Council of Tyre, and he wrote his own letter to Count Dionysius (quoted in *Apologia Contra Arianos* 80), in which he states that he has heard the appeals of the Egyptian bishops, and repeats their condemnation of the 'conspiracy' of the Melitians and 'Arians' against Athanasius.

[66] The exact number of bishops who attended the Council cannot be precisely determined. Hanson (1988*b*) 259 speaks of 'about 60 bishops present', citing Socrates, I.28, but Socrates' estimate cannot include the Egyptian contingent of 48 bishops (whose names are attached to the letters that they wrote at Tyre quoted in the *Apologia Contra Arianos* (Opitz (1938*b*) 159)). As the Egyptians were clearly unable to sway the verdict of the assembly, the overall number of bishops present must have been greater than this, and the estimate of between 110 and 150 bishops proposed by Arnold (1991) 153 is probably closer to the truth.

[67] The bishops who attended the Council of Tyre then travelled onwards to Jerusalem to attend the dedication of the Church of the Holy Sepulchre. Athanasius again condemns that Council of Jerusalem as the vehicle of a 'heretical faction', for the synod ordered the restoration of Arius to communion (*Apologia Contra Arianos* 84–5; *Historia Arianorum* 1; *De Synodis* 21–2). But the description of the Jerusalem celebrations by Eusebius of Caesarea (*Vita Constantini* IV.43.4), although probably exaggerated in turn (see Cameron and Hall (1999) 330–2), suggests a large episcopal gathering, including bishops from almost all the eastern provinces of the empire.

constituted and entirely respectable gathering of churchmen, some of whom had been confessors . . . as a gang of disreputable conspirators, and brands all his opponents as favourers of heresy'.[68] This does not imply that Athanasius was necessarily guilty of the charges on which he was condemned, nor that the Council of Tyre should be seen as a model of legal justice. But the bishops who rejected the pleas of Athanasius' supporters evidently did not accept the polemical image of the 'Eusebians' that the Egyptian bishops attempted to impose upon them. The condemnation of Athanasius is thus evidence both for the degree of hostility to the bishop of Alexandria that existed within the eastern Church in 335 and that some 60 contemporary bishops at least saw no reason to believe the Athanasian construction of the 'Eusebians' as an 'Arian party'.

It is striking that this polemical construction, although rejected by the Council of Tyre that it was first intended to persuade, would nevertheless ultimately gain widespread acceptance and until recently dominate modern interpretations of the opening decades of the 'Arian Controversy'. And it is all the more ironic that many scholars who do not accept the proclamation of innocence that was Athanasius' original intention[69] nevertheless continue to accept the presentation of the 'Eusebians' and their role in the events preceding the Council of Tyre which derives exclusively from the unsupported later polemical narrative of Athanasius himself. I will not attempt to explain the triumph of Athanasius' polemic here. But in the next chapter I will examine the influence that the polemic did exert at least upon the western Church in the period immediately following Athanasius' second exile, for this influence sheds further light upon the effect that Athanasius desired his presentation of himself and of his opponents to have.

[68] Hanson (1988*b*) 262.

[69] Thus Hanson (1988*b*) describes the Council of Tyre as possessing 'an air of nemesis' (262), while Barnes (1981) famously said of Athanasius that 'like a modern gangster, he evoked widespread mistrust, proclaimed total innocence—and usually succeeded in evading conviction on specific charges' (230).

4

The Influence of Athanasius' Polemic 339–46

The arguments of Athanasius and his supporters at Tyre failed to avert his condemnation, and nor was the Alexandrian *Encyclical Letter* of 338 sufficient to prevent his second exile (339–46). The eastern bishops who received these writings evidently did not accept Athanasius' construction of the 'Eusebians' and their alleged 'Arian conspiracy', and indeed there is little indication that the polemic of Athanasius had any immediate effect upon eastern opinion in these years. However, the *Apologia Contra Arianos* preserves several documents that testify to the support that Athanasius did receive in the west during his second exile, specifically the letter of Julius of Rome to the eastern bishops at Antioch (20–35) and the letters of the Western Council of Serdica (36–50). In this chapter I will look briefly at these letters, for the nature of the influence that Athanasius' polemic exerted upon his western audience provides an important insight into the intended purposes of the polemic itself. As we shall see, for both Julius and the western bishops at Serdica the defence of Athanasius' innocence became inseparable from the condemnation of a 'Eusebian party' set apart from the main body of the eastern Church.

THE LETTER OF JULIUS OF ROME TO THE BISHOPS AT ANTIOCH (*APOLOGIA CONTRA ARIANOS* 20–35)

The letter of Julius to the eastern bishops assembled at Antioch has received considerable attention from scholars as an important source for the position of the see of Rome in the fourth-century Church.[1] For my current purposes, however, the primary significance of this text lies in Julius' presentation of Athanasius and of those he addresses, following Athanasius' lead, as '*hoi peri Eusebion*'. Unfortunately, the precise context of Julius' letter, and of the Council of Rome whose judgement that letter represents, is once again difficult to establish with certainty. According to both Athanasius in the *Apologia Contra Arianos* narrative (1, 20) and Julius himself in his letter (22, 25), after Athanasius arrived in Rome following his flight from Alexandria in April 339, the 'Eusebians' first requested that Julius summon a council to reconsider Athanasius' case, but then took fright and refused to attend. This account is open to question, for the eastern bishops saw no need to revise the verdict of Tyre, and indeed rejected Rome's authority to hear an appeal. It is possible that Julius was actually asked to endorse Tyre's verdict and renounce Athanasius, a request that he interpreted as a call for a new council.[2] Whatever the truth, the Council of Rome then met, and Julius composed his letter vindicating Athanasius, either in late 340 or in 341. Although this letter is addressed to the eastern bishops 'who have written to us from Antioch' (21; Opitz (1938*a*) 102, 14), the eastern letter in question is lost.[3] Thus it is impossible to establish conclusively either the nature of the Antiochene assembly to which

[1] Most famously, Julius concludes his letter with the much-debated claim that he should have been informed earlier of the trial of Athanasius, for regarding the Church of Alexandria, 'the custom (*ēthos*) has been for word to be written first to us, and then for just decisions to be defined from here' (35; Opitz (1938*a*) 113, 6–7). Despite the arguments of the Catholic scholars Twomey (1982) 382–6 and Nichols (1992) 159–60, however, there is little evidence to support Julius' appeal to 'custom'. Certainly the bishops to whom he wrote did not accept the right of Rome to judge the verdict of an eastern council (on this issue see most recently Hess (2002) 184–90 and Chadwick (2003) 15–16).

[2] Hanson (1988*b*) 267 proposes that the eastern delegates in Rome 'let fall a remark which Julius was able to interpret as a request to him to call a Council', a view shared by Barnes (1993) 40.

[3] From Julius' references it is possible to reconstruct certain elements of the letter of the eastern bishops, including their rejection of Roman interference (25), the complaint that Julius has preferred the communion of Athanasius to their own (34), and their charge that by his actions Julius has 'lit the flame of discord', a phrase that Julius quotes several times (25, 34). There is also a summary of the contents of the letter of the eastern bishops in Sozomen, III.8.4–8, but this summary would appear to derive from Sozomen's own reading of Julius' letter, and adds little to an attempted reconstruction.

Julius wrote,[4] or the exact relationship between the council and letter of Julius and the great gathering of eastern bishops at the 'Dedication' Council of Antioch in 341.[5]

These questions of date and context, although important, fortunately do not directly affect the analysis of Julius' defence of Athanasius, a defence that draws extensively from the latter's own polemical arguments and documentary dossier.[6] Athanasius, Julius declares, has twice been the victim of a conspiracy (27). The letters of the Egyptian clergy in 335, the letter of Alexander of Thessalonica to Count Dionysius, and the Alexandrian *Encyclical Letter* of 338 all testify that the judgement of Tyre was false, for Arsenius is still alive, the commission that was sent to the Mareotis was composed of 'suspicious individuals', and the charge that a chalice was broken has not been proved (27–8). Likewise, the imposition of Gregory into Alexandria is uncanonical, for he depended on patronage and military aid, and Julius denounces the reported persecution of Egyptian virgins, monks, and clergy (29–30), which he has copied from the *Epistula Encyclica* of 339. Julius' account thus derives entirely from the polemic of Athanasius and his supporters, and possesses no independent

[4] The names that Julius gives for the authors of the eastern letter to which he replies will be discussed in Ch. 5.

[5] In addition to Julius' own letter, the only other document to survive from the exchange between the bishop of Rome and the eastern bishops in Antioch is the so-called 'First Creed' of this 'Dedication' Council, which was in fact a letter addressed to Julius himself (see Ch. 7). The great difficulty is to determine which of the extant letters was composed first, a difficulty compounded by the loss of much of the correspondence, and by the confusion in the ecclesiastical histories of Socrates (II.8) and Sozomen (III.5) regarding the various councils held in Antioch 338–41. Scholars remain divided between those who would place Julius' letter in late 340 or early 341, and argue that the 'Dedication' Council met in part in response to this Roman epistle (Barnard (1971) 341–8, Hanson (1988*b*) 284–5, Vinzent (1994) 295–6), and those who would place Julius' letter later in 341, as itself a 'riposte' to the eastern council (Schneemelcher (1977) 330, Barnes (1993) 57–9, Seibt (1994) 138–9). No evidence exists to decisively settle this question, not least because the chronology of the 'Dedication' Council is itself a matter of debate between those who maintain the traditional date of May–September 341 (e.g. Hanson (1988*b*) 284–5), and those who follow the argument of Eltester (1937) 254–6 that the Council met on 6 January (Epiphany) in that year, a date supported by the Syriac Chronicle of 724 (Schneemelcher (1977) 330, Barnes (1993) 57, Burgess (1999) 239).

[6] For a detailed discussion of the contents of the letter, albeit one that accepts the historicity of Julius' presentation of the 'Eusebians' throughout, see Twomey (1982) 398–425.

historical value. But for this very reason, the letter of Julius is important evidence both for the influence that this polemic could exert upon a contemporary, and for the development by 340–1 of the Athanasian narrative and dossier of the second half of the *Apologia Contra Arianos.*

Less immediately apparent, but more significant for the purposes of this monograph, is the degree to which Julius' attitude to the eastern bishops to whom he writes has been shaped by Athanasius' construction of the 'Eusebians', and by the Athanasian separation of that 'Eusebian party' from the wider eastern Church. Throughout his letter, Julius repeatedly implies that those bishops who have written to him condemning Athanasius do not represent the eastern Church, or even a Christian council, but comprise a distinct 'faction', '*hoi peri Eusebion*'. Thus he complains that the eastern letter was written 'because certain persons (*tinōn*) have been aggrieved because of their meanness of spirit towards one another (for I will not impute this judgement to all)' (21; Opitz (1938*a*) 103, 14–15). More specifically, Julius dismisses the protest of those eastern bishops who say that he wrote 'not to all of you, but only to the Eusebians'. According to Julius, in that case, 'it was necessary either for the Eusebians alone not to have written separately from all of you, or else you, to whom I did not write, should not be offended, if I wrote to those who had written to me. For if it was indeed necessary that I should address [my letter] to you all, you also ought to have written with them' (26; Opitz (1938*a*) 106, 23; 26–8).

Julius presents this protest as trivial, but the actual issue at stake in this passage is the very image of the 'Eusebians' and the eastern Church that Athanasius' polemic has constructed, and Julius has here endorsed. In asserting that Julius should have written to them all, and not to '*hoi peri Eusebion*', the eastern bishops deny the existence of any such 'Eusebian party'. Instead they insist, with considerable justice, that the condemnation of Athanasius was the representative judgement of those who gathered at Tyre and have now assembled in Antioch. Julius' dismissal of their 'trivial protest' thus sidesteps a question of great importance,[7] and enables him to

[7] At the same time, Julius insists that he himself did not write on his own behalf, but that 'although I alone wrote, yet this judgement was not only that of myself, but

continue to impose Athanasius' polarized model of the 'Eusebians' upon the very eastern bishops who have consistently rejected its validity. This imposition is apparent in Julius' repeated description of those to whom he writes as the 'Eusebians', and is made most explicit in the final paragraphs of his letter.

I thought it necessary to write these things to you, so that you might at length put to shame those who because of their hatred towards each other have thus treated the churches. For I have heard that a certain few (*tines oligoi*) are the authors of all these things. (34; Opitz (1938*a*) 112, 13–16)

It is against them rather than against Julius himself that the eastern bishops should now write (35).[8]

Julius' assertion that only 'a certain few' are responsible for the crimes and conspiracies that he has described once again reduces the opponents of Athanasius to a small minority 'faction'. Just as the Egyptian bishops in 335 appealed to the Council of Tyre to denounce the 'Eusebians', so Julius now calls upon the bishops who have gathered at Antioch to reject those 'persons' who have inspired this persecution, and therefore by implication to recognize Athanasius' construction of a distinct 'Eusebian party'. In direct contrast to the Council of Tyre, Julius thus explicitly endorses the image of his opponents that lies at the heart of Athanasius' polemic, and so in turn he upholds Athanasius' presentation of his own innocence and legitimacy that the eastern bishops have repeatedly denied.[9]

of all the bishops throughout Italy and in these parts' (26; Opitz (1938*a*) 106, 32–4). Julius thus attributes to himself the very representative status that he has denied the eastern bishops.

[8] I see no evidence for the argument of Barnard (1971) 343–4 that this section of Julius' letter reveals 'a more independent and conciliatory line on Julius' part' (343), and that the anti-Eusebian tone of the bulk of the letter is primarily to satisfy the other bishops at the Council of Rome. This passage is in fact a direct continuation of the polemic against the 'Eusebians' earlier in Julius' letter.

[9] One of the few scholars to recognize this point is Lienhard (1999): 'Julius' letter changed the situation between East and West. He defined two parties, 'the Eusebians' and 'the Athanasians', and identified himself with Athanasius and Marcellus as orthodox. The Eusebians themselves had promoted the definition of two parties by writing to Julius that he preferred communion with Marcellus and Athanasius to communion with them, thus sharpening the division and trying to force a choice on Julius' (140). There is considerable truth in the argument that the eastern demands to Julius sharpened the growing division between east and west in this period, although I would question Lienhard's acceptance of the existence of a 'Eusebian party' clearly distinct from the wider eastern Church.

Yet there is one striking exception to Julius' otherwise unquestioning acceptance of Athanasius' construction of his foes. Although Julius openly addresses '*hoi peri Eusebion*' as a distinct 'party', at no point in his letter does he ever explicitly repeat Athanasius' condemnation of the 'Eusebians' as 'Arian'.[10] Julius does declare that the 'heretics' who were condemned at Nicaea 'are said now to have been received [into communion], which I think you also ought to hear with indignation' (23; Opitz (1938*a*) 104, 29), and he warns his audience to renounce such an 'error', 'so that none of you should receive such heresy, but abominate it as foreign to sound teaching' (32; Opitz (1938*a*) 110, 28–9). But Julius does not directly accuse the 'Eusebians' themselves of 'Arianism', or of sharing the 'heresy' that he here condemns. Julius surely knew that Athanasius had presented these men as 'followers of Arius', and indeed had attributed to them the restoration of Arius to communion at the Council of Jerusalem in 335 (*Apologia Contra Arianos* 84–5). His silence is therefore difficult to explain, for it appears unlikely that Julius endorsed Athanasius' general polemical model only to reject this one essential element. It is possible that to this degree at least Julius desired to be conciliatory, and also to avoid actual theological debate. But it is equally possible that Julius wrote his letter before Athanasius' construction of the 'Arianism' of his opponents had received its fullest expression, in the *Orations against the Arians* that Athanasius was composing at precisely this time. In any case, as we shall now see, Julius' silence on the 'Arianism' of the 'Eusebians' is certainly not shared by the Western Council of Serdica, which met just a few years later.

THE LETTERS OF THE WESTERN COUNCIL OF SERDICA (*APOLOGIA CONTRA ARIANOS* 36–50)

The Council of Serdica, which Athanasius describes immediately following the letter of Julius in the *Apologia Contra Arianos*, was

[10] Lienhard (1987) 417–8 and (1999) 140 argues that Julius condemns the 'Eusebians' as 'Arian' because of their support for Pistus, and that it was in response to this charge that the 'First Creed' of the 'Dedication' Council rejected the name of 'Arian'. I will return to that Antiochene statement in my final chapter, but *contra* Lienhard, although Julius does condemn Pistus himself as an Arian, he does not extend that label explicitly to the 'Eusebians'.

called by the emperors Constans and Constantius as a joint gathering of eastern and western bishops in 343.[11] Intended to settle the ongoing controversies concerning both theological doctrine and the status of the eastern bishops then exiled in the west (particularly Athanasius and Marcellus of Ancyra), the full synod never actually met, for the eastern bishops refused to allow the presence of the exiles whom the western contingent insisted must attend.[12] The eastern 'half' of the council is dismissed by Athanasius as the vehicle of 'the associates (*tous koinōnous*) of the Eusebians' (36; Opitz (1938*a*) 114, 5), although Eusebius of Nicomedia had died over a year before, and he makes no mention of their proceedings or of the *Encyclical Letter* that the eastern bishops composed.[13] Athanasius' sole concern is with the 'holy synod' (36) of the western bishops at Serdica. From this council, which he attended, Athanasius quotes several documents: a *Letter to the Church of Alexandria* (37–40), a nearly identical *Letter to the Bishops of Egypt and Libya* (41), and the *Encyclical Letter* (42–50).[14] All these letters, like that of Julius above, vividly attest to the influence exerted upon the western bishops by Athanasius' polemical construction of himself and his foes.

The letter of Western Serdica to the Church of Alexandria presents a defence of Athanasius against both his condemnation in 335 and his expulsion by Gregory in 339 that differs little in detail from that recorded in the letter of Julius. Indeed, Julius' letter is now cited by the western bishops in 343 as further evidence to support the arguments and documents of Athanasius himself. Once again the

[11] The chronology of the Council of Serdica was long the subject of great controversy, but although some scholars still maintain the older date of 342 (notably Brennecke (1984) 25–9 and Elliott (1988) 65–72), an increasing consensus of modern studies has favoured the year 343 (see among others De Clercq (1954) 313–24, Barnes (1978) 67–9, Barnard (1983) 49–55, Burgess (1999) 241–3, and Hess (2002) vii–viii), and this is the date that I have adopted here.

[12] For a discussion of the course of the two councils of Serdica and their texts see De Clercq (1954) 334–62, Barnard (1983) 63–118, and Hess (2002) 93–111. All these accounts are unfortunately rather uncritical of the 'orthodox' tradition that dominates our sources for these events.

[13] This *Eastern Letter of Serdica*, which represents a rare and important (although again highly polemical) statement of the accusers of Athanasius, is only preserved in Latin by Hilary of Poitiers, *Collectanea Antiariana Parisina* IV.1–3 (CSEL 65, 48–67).

[14] The above numbering of the *Apologia Contra Arianos* sections in which these letters are quoted is that of Opitz (1938*a*–*b*), which differs from the numbering followed by Robertson (1892) in the *Nicene and Post-Nicene Fathers* translation.

conspiracy against Athanasius is denounced. The charges concerning Arsenius and the broken chalice are false, and the Mareotis Commission was a biased and *ex parte* proceeding (37–8). 'As for Gregory, who is said to have been illegally appointed by the heretics, he has been deposed by the judgement of the whole sacred synod, although indeed he has never at any time been considered to be a bishop at all' (39; Opitz (1938*a*) 117, 31–118, 2). Unlike Julius, moreover, the bishops of Serdica do explicitly uphold Athanasius' presentation of his accusers as 'Arians', whose actions are motivated solely by their desire to spread their 'heresy'. 'It was manifest to us that the patrons (*prostatai*) of the abominated heresy of the Arians were practising many and dangerous machinations ... for this has always been their deadly purpose, to expel and to persecute all who are to be found anywhere of orthodox beliefs' (37; Opitz (1938*a*) 115, 20–5). Athanasius is thus both innocent and 'orthodox', and the conclusion of the letter again affirms his status and condemns his 'Eusebian' foes. For 'everything that has been done by the Eusebians against the orthodox has redounded to the glory and support of those who have been attacked by them' (40; Opitz (1938*a*) 118, 12–14).[15]

This *Letter to the Church of Alexandria* was written specifically for the clergy and people of Athanasius' own diocese, and we might therefore expect that letter to provide a more explicitly 'Athanasian' presentation than the Western Serdica *Encyclical Letter* intended for a much broader audience. In fact, the only significant difference visible in the latter document is that the western bishops are here concerned to defend not only Athanasius, but also Marcellus of Ancyra and other eastern exiles. Even so, the case of Athanasius still receives markedly greater attention, and it is his polemical framework that again shapes the arguments that the western bishops present. The 'Arianism' of those who have accused the exiles is restated in even more emphatic form, for 'the Ariomaniacs have dared repeatedly to attack the servants of God who maintain the orthodox faith ... and sought to substitute a false doctrine' (42; Opitz (1938*a*) 119, 7–9). The *Encyclical Letter* restates the defence of Athanasius already presented in the *Letter to*

[15] This conclusion is the only section of the Serdican *Letter to the Church of Alexandria* not repeated in the otherwise identical *Letter to the Bishops of Egypt and Libya* quoted in *Apologia Contra Arianos* 41.

the Church of Alexandria above, while in their conclusion the western bishops justify their support for the eastern exiles with a statement that incorporates all the elements that we have already identified as characteristic of Athanasius' presentation of the 'Eusebians'.

It was necessary for us not to remain silent, nor to pass over unnoticed their calumnies, imprisonments, murders, woundings, conspiracies by means of false letters, outrages, stripping of virgins, banishments, destruction of churches, burnings, translations from small cities to larger dioceses, and above all, the insurrection of the ill-named Arian heresy by their means against the orthodox faith. (47; Opitz (1938*b*) 122, 32–7)

The *Encyclical Letter* of Western Serdica, like the letter of Julius, not only endorses Athanasius' defence of his own innocence, but also Athanasius' construction of the 'Eusebians' as a distinct 'party'. According to the western bishops, when the eastern contingent first approached Serdica, 'the leaders (*exarchoi*) after the Eusebians[16] ... would not permit those who came with them from the East to enter into the holy council' (46; Opitz (1938*b*) 122, 14; 18–19). Rather, they compelled the other eastern bishops to join with them and flee the judgement of a united synod. The western bishops declare that they have learnt this from Macarius and Asterius, two eastern ministers who escaped the 'Eusebians' to attend the 'holy council'. These two men are reported to have revealed that 'there might be many [among the eastern bishops] who upheld orthodox beliefs, and who were being prevented from entering here by those men [the Eusebians], because of their threats and promises against those who wished to separate from them' (46; Opitz (1938*b*) 122, 27–9). The 'Eusebians' therefore cannot represent the main body of eastern Christians, for those who associate with them do so only from compulsion or deception, and do not share their 'heresy'. The rigid distinction between the 'Eusebians' and the eastern Church that Athanasius and his supporters first attempted in vain to impose upon the Council of Tyre is thus upheld in the *Encyclical Letter* of Western Serdica, as it was in the letter of Julius of Rome. This is the true measure of the influence that Athanasius' polemic exerted upon the west in these years.

16 I will discuss the interpretation of this phrase '*meta tous peri Eusebion*', as well as the individual 'Eusebian' names cited in the documents of Western Serdica, in the next chapter.

Conclusion to Part II

When Athanasius came to stand before the Western Council of Serdica in 343, the polemical construction of himself and of his opponents that he presented to his audience was already well-established. In the letters of the Egyptian bishops at Tyre in 335 and the Alexandrian *Encyclical Letter* of 338, just as in his own *Epistula Encyclica* in 339 and the narrative of the *Apologia Contra Arianos*, Athanasius and his supporters depict his condemnation and successive exiles as the consequence of a single 'Arian conspiracy'. The charges brought against him from the beginning of his episcopate were raised openly by the Melitian schismatics, but the Melitians were nothing more than 'actors', playing a role on behalf of their 'secret friends' Eusebius of Nicomedia and the 'Eusebians'. It was this 'heretical party' who inspired the assaults upon Athanasius that culminated in the Council of Tyre and Athanasius' exile. When Athanasius returned, the 'Eusebians' then caused his expulsion once more, through the enforced intrusion of the uncanonical Gregory and the persecution that he and his soldiers unleashed upon the Alexandrian Church.

In his later works, Athanasius would never significantly deviate from this interpretation of his early episcopal career, an interpretation that would exert great influence first upon Julius of Rome and the western bishops at Serdica, and eventually upon the eastern Church and later Christian generations. Yet that construction of the 'Eusebians' and their conspiracy only developed gradually within Athanasius' own polemical writings. Although the association between Eusebius of Nicomedia and Arius and the title '*hoi peri Eusebion*' had already been invoked by his predecessor Alexander in the latter's *Encyclical Letter* in 324, there is little direct continuity between that letter and Athanasius' initial presentation of his foes. On the contrary, once a distinction has been drawn between the *Apologia Contra Arianos* narrative that post-dates Athanasius' exile and the documents and *Festal Letters* that survive from the years before the Council of Tyre, it becomes apparent that until 335

Athanasius' sole concern was with the Melitians. In marked contrast to the later narrative, the contemporary evidence of 330–4 contains not a single reference either to 'Arians' or to the 'Eusebians' as the source of a conspiracy against Athanasius. Only in 335 itself do the 'Eusebians' finally appear, in the appeals of Athanasius' Egyptian supporters to rally the bishops at Tyre and the Count Dionysius in his defence against this 'Arian party'. And only after the condemnation of Athanasius, and indeed after his return from his first exile, in the Alexandrian *Encyclical Letter* of 338 and then in the *Epistula Encyclica* and the *Apologia Contra Arianos* narrative of Athanasius himself, do the 'Eusebians' emerge not only as the controlling force at the Council of Tyre, but also as the true inspiration behind the earlier Melitian accusations.

This chronological analysis of the development of Athanasius' presentation of himself and of his foes is not intended to prove (or disprove) that a 'Eusebian party' did or did not exist. Athanasius and his Egyptian bishops at Tyre evidently believed that their audience might accept the existence of such a 'party', and despite the failure of the polemic in 335, the later influence that Athanasius exerted upon Julius and the Western Council of Serdica suggests that this belief was not entirely unfounded. Nor does my study necessarily imply that Athanasius was guilty of the charges on which he was condemned. What I have sought to demonstrate is that the presentation of the 'Eusebians' in Athanasius' earliest extant writings is a polemical construct, whose origins, motivation, and subsequent development can be precisely defined. Through that construction of the 'Eusebians' as an 'Arian party', set apart from the wider body of the Church, Athanasius in turn vindicated his own innocence and 'orthodoxy' as the victim of their 'heretical conspiracy'. It was this interpretation of his own career and of the activities of his opponents that Athanasius and his supporters attempted to impose first upon the Council of Tyre in 335, and then more widely through the *Encyclical Letters* of 338 and 339 and the *Apologia Contra Arianos.* We must remember the polemical and subjective nature of that interpretation as we now turn in the last part of this monograph to assess in detail the content of Athanasius' construction of the 'Eusebians' and its potential distortions.

Part III

5

Who were the 'Eusebians'?

INTRODUCTION

The fundamental elements that comprise Athanasius' construction of the 'Eusebians' remain essentially consistent throughout his polemical writings, from the early works that I examined in Part II to the great works of the 350s upon which I will draw heavily in the pages that follow. The purpose of the third and final part of this monograph is to assess both Athanasius' collective presentation of these men as a 'heretical party' and the specific actions and theological doctrines that he attributes to them. Through such an assessment it is possible not only to shed further light upon the motivation and development of Athanasius' polemic, but also to examine in some detail the actual content of that construction and its distortions. The two longest chapters of this part will focus respectively upon Athanasius' presentation of the 'Eusebians' 'in action' and upon his condemnation of their alleged 'Arianism'. But before such analyses can begin, certain important questions must first be resolved. How are we to understand the title '*hoi peri Eusebion*'? What does it mean to refer to the 'Eusebians' as in some sense a 'church party'? Who are the individuals who comprise that 'party', and what is known regarding their careers and theological writings?

'*HOI PERI EUSEBION*' AS A 'CHURCH PARTY'

Translated literally, '*hoi peri*' is an entirely neutral phrase, denoting 'the ones around' a certain individual or on occasion solely that individual alone.[1] Such terminology is employed repeatedly in fourth-century and earlier Christian and non-Christian Greek writings without any necessarily polemical intent. Magistrates and their entourages and philosophical teachers and their schools might both be described in this manner,[2] and even within the documents quoted in Athanasius' own works we find a number of non-polemical instances of '*hoi peri*' terminology,[3] including several references to '*hoi peri Athanasion*' made by men undoubtedly favourable towards Athanasius himself.[4]

Yet there can be no doubt that '*hoi peri Eusebion*', in every text in which that expression is known to occur, is a title with explicitly polemical connotations. This is true, as we have already seen, in the earliest extant appearance of 'the ones around' Eusebius of Nicomedia, in the *Encyclical Letter* of Alexander of Alexandria. It is equally true, although addressed in this instance against '*tōn amphi*

[1] For a general discussion of the meaning of '*hoi peri* + accusative', see the articles of Radt (1980, 1988), and for the 'individual' use of '*hoi peri*', see Turner (1963) 16. Barnes (1993) 248–9.n.22 rejects the argument of Müller (1952) 1169 that Athanasius himself ever employs '*hoi peri Eusebion*' in this individual sense, although there is one possible exception which will be discussed below.

[2] The use of '*hoi peri*' terminology for the 'followers' of a philosopher and his teachings is well demonstrated in Diogenes Laertius' *Lives of Eminent Philosophers* (e.g. VII.68; VII.76; VII.92; VII.128). For a comparison between Diogenes' account of the *diadoche* (succession) of the philosophical schools and early Christian concepts of apostolic and heretical succession, see Brent (1993).

[3] Thus Count Dionysius, in a letter described by Athanasius as written to '*hoi peri Eusebion*' but which in fact appears to have been sent to the Mareotis Commission during the Council of Tyre (*Apologia Contra Arianos* 81), informs the bishops on that Commission that Dionysius has already discussed the issues at stake with '*tois kuriois mou tois peri Phlakillon*' (Opitz (1940*a*) 161, 6), an evidently respectful reference to the bishops still at Tyre (who are led, notably, by Flacillus of Antioch and not Eusebius of Nicomedia).

[4] In the letter of Julius of Rome, Julius dismisses the complaints that '*hoi peri Eusebion* formerly wrote against *tōn peri Athanasion*' (*Apologia Contra Arianos* 27; Opitz (1938*a*) 107, 3–4), and '*hoi peri Athanasion*' also occurs in a speech attributed by Athanasius to the Western Council of Serdica (*Apologia Contra Arianos* 36; Opitz (1938*a*) 114, 15). In the former instance, it is possible that Julius has taken up the phrase '*hoi peri Athanasion*' from the eastern letter to which he replies, which would indicate that the polemical terminology that Athanasius employed against the 'Eusebians' was also in use by the eastern bishops against Athanasius. But Julius gives no indication that he considered the title polemical in itself.

ton Eusebion' (Parmentier (1998) 34, 8),[5] in the fragmentary account of the Council of Nicaea of another contemporary, Eustathius of Antioch.[6] And in the writings of Athanasius, who above all systematically employs this phrase,[7] '*hoi peri Eusebion*' always designates the polemical construct that he has imposed upon his foes. Whether we translate this expression as 'Eusebius and his fellows',[8] 'Eusebius and his supporters',[9] or, as throughout this monograph, simply as 'the Eusebians', the individual identities of Athanasius' opponents have been subordinated to their collective presentation as a single uniform 'party'. Before we attempt to examine those individuals and their careers and writings in more detail, therefore, it is first necessary to consider further this collective construction of the 'Eusebians' as a 'church party' and its implications.

When T. D. Barnes declared that 'ecclesiastical politics after Nicaea are party politics',[10] he gave concise expression to a conception of the fourth-century Church that has been highly influential on modern interpretations of the 'Arian Controversy'. Yet only a few scholars have attempted to define precisely what is meant by this concept of

[5] Although Athanasius himself only ever speaks of '*hoi peri Eusebion*', the terms '*hoi peri*' and '*hoi amphi*' appear to have been used synonymously in Greek Christian literature of this period. Of the fifth-century ecclesiastical historians, Socrates only applies the phrase '*hoi peri*' to heretics, but Sozomen can also speak of both '*hoi peri Athanasion*' (III.11.3; Hansen (2004) 366, 21–2) and '*tous amphi ton Athanasion*' (III.11.4; Hansen (2004) 368, 1), and Theodoret likewise employs both constructions indifferently.

[6] Eustathius' account (preserved in Theodoret, I.8, from a lost *Homily on Proverbs 8:22*) is highly controversial, but the description of the 'Eusebius' named here as the leader of a 'party' suggests that Eustathius' subject is the bishop of Nicomedia, and not his namesake of Caesarea. Despite this parallel to the polemic of Athanasius, however, Eustathius would appear to have written entirely independently, and neither man shows any awareness of the other's works.

[7] It has already become apparent that the title '*hoi peri Eusebion*' is ubiquitous in Athanasius' polemic (for a catalogue of such references, see Müller (1952) 1169–70). More rarely, he does also speak of '*hoi peri Areion*' (as in *Apologia Contra Arianos* 85; see also the *Encyclical Letter* of Alexander), while the letter of the Egyptian clergy from the Mareotis in 335 (quoted in *Apologia Contra Arianos* 74–5) also refers to '*hoi peri Theognion*'. Intriguingly, Athanasius at no time describes the Melitian schismatics in this manner, preferring to designate them simply as '*Melitianoi*' (a title the 'Melitians' themselves originally avoided but did eventually adopt, see Hauben (1998) 331–3).

[8] The translation used by Robertson (1892).

[9] The preferred translation of Barnes (1993) 249.n.22.

[10] Barnes (1981) 225.

a 'church party'.[11] Barnes himself draws explicitly the frequently implied parallel between such ecclesiastical factions and modern political organizations. He asserts that this period 'encouraged the formation within the church of coalitions of bishops which functioned much like modern political parties—a broad ideological (or theological) cohesiveness furthered and sometimes hindered by personal ambitions'.[12] Other scholars conceive of 'parties' formed around specific councils and their creeds, a view well-expressed by Winrich Löhr: 'the existence of definite theological alignments, centred around and named after credal documents, cannot and need not be doubted'.[13] There are certainly elements of truth within these arguments, for associations between bishops did exist, and councils did compose creeds around which individuals could unite, particularly as doctrinal debates developed in the 350s and 360s.[14] But to envisage the fourth-century Church in terms of organized ecclesiastical and theological 'parties' is to underestimate the polemical nature of the sources from which this interpretation of the 'Arian Controversy' and its divisions has derived.[15]

None of the participants of the fourth-century controversies ever identified themselves as a 'church party',[16] for within Christian heresiology, a 'party' by definition stood apart from the 'true Church'.

[11] Thus Gwatkin (1882) argued that in the 340s 'Arians and Nicenes were still parties inside the church rather than distinct sects' (134), while Kopecek (1979) 359 can declare that 'Neo-Arianism' was transformed 'from an ecclesiastical party within Catholic Christianity into an independent sect'. Neither scholar explains precisely what he means by 'party' or by 'sect', but their shared conception of 'parties' *within* Christianity (a conception also expressed in Barnes' statement quoted above) directly contradicts Athanasius' polemical construction of the 'Eusebians' as a 'faction' set apart from the 'true Church'.

[12] Barnes (1993) 174, (1998) 17. This 'political' interpretation of the alleged 'factions' within Constantinian Christianity had already been expounded in the discussion of 'church parties' in the fourth century by Vogt (1973) 37–8, and is particularly emphasized by Drake (2000), esp. 29.

[13] Löhr (1993) 81. The same conception of a 'church party' was specifically applied to the 'Eusebians' by Hanson (1988*b*), who defined this 'party' as a coalition united around a single theology that they desired to impose upon the Church as a whole (284).

[14] For this slightly later period see Vogt (1973) 39–43 and Löhr (1991) 81.

[15] See also Ayres (2004*b*) 13.

[16] *Pace* Löhr (1993) 83, who speaks of 'Homoiousian' 'self-definition as a church party'.

Already in the writings of St Paul,[17] and in the works of the early fathers (notably the *Adversus Haereses* of Irenaeus of Lyons),[18] those who are alleged to follow and take their name from a chosen leader cannot be followers of Christ. To be branded in those terms was a condemnation of heresy.[19] A 'church party' therefore could not exist, for to be a 'party' was to be outside the Church,[20] and it is within this heresiological tradition that Athanasius' polemic must be understood. We have already seen in the previous section how in the *Apologia Contra Arianos* Athanasius and his supporters separate the 'Eusebians' from the wider eastern Church. But by far Athanasius' most emphatic statement of this construction of his foes stands at the beginning of the first great *Oration against the Arians*, when Athanasius states explicitly what is implied by his definition of the 'Eusebians' as an 'Arian party':

Instead of Christ for them is Arius, as for the Manichees Manichaeus (I.2; Tetz (1998) 110, 7–8).

[For] 'while all of us are and are called Christians after Christ, Marcion broached a heresy a long time ago and was cast out; and those who stood by the one who rejected him remained Christians; but those who followed

17 'I appeal to you, brothers and sisters, by the name of our Lord Jesus Christ, that all of you should be in agreement and that there should be no divisions among you.... For it has been reported to me by Chloe's people that there are quarrels among you, my brothers and sisters. What I mean is that each of you says, "I belong to Paul", or "I belong to Apollos", or "I belong to Cephas", or "I belong to Christ". Has Christ been divided?' (1Corinthians 1:10–13, NRSV).

18 On the life and polemical writings of Irenaeus, especially the *Adversus Haereses*, see most recently Minns (1994) and Grant (1997), and on his possible influence upon Athanasius (primarily concerned with theology rather than heresiology) see Anatolios (2001). For Irenaeus' conception of 'heresies' as named for their founders, just as 'true Christians' are named for Christ, see *Adversus Haereses* I.23.

19 'Names locate: they fix a thing as good or bad, friend or foe. When something is given a name, that thing is also given an identity, and with identity significance. Names can dignify, and they can also debase' (Drake (2000) 436). See also Lyman (1993*b*) and Ch. 7 below.

20 Thus Sozomen could declare that in the immediate aftermath of the Council of Nicaea there were no 'parties', for 'although the dogma of Arius was zealously supported by many persons in disputations, there had not yet been a division into a distinctive people (*idion laon*) with the name of the founder (i.e. Arius), for all assembled together and held communion with each other' (II.32.1; Hansen (1994) 322, 9–12). See also Theodoret (I.21), who is at pains to emphasize that although the followers of his hero Eustathius of Antioch took the name 'Eustathians', they nevertheless remained devoted to the 'orthodox faith'.

Marcion henceforth were no longer called Christians, but Marcionites. Thus also Valentinus and Basilides and Manichaeus and Simon Magus have imparted their own names to their followers... and so also when the blessed Alexander cast out Arius, those who remained with Alexander remained Christians; but those who went out with Arius abandoned the Saviour's Name to us who were with Alexander, and they were henceforth called Arians. (I.3; Tetz (1998) 111, 1–6; 112, 10–13)

And let them not excuse themselves nor upon being reproached falsely accuse those who are not as they are, thus calling those who are indeed Christians after their teachers... [for] after the death of Alexander, those who are in communion with his successor Athanasius, and with whom the same Athanasius communicates, are instances of the same rule (*tupon*);[21] neither do any of them bear his name, nor is he named from them, but all again and customarily are called Christians. For though we have a succession of teachers and become their disciples, yet, because we are taught by them the teachings of Christ, we are and are called Christians and nothing else. But those who follow the heretics, though they have countless successors, yet in every respect they bear the name of the founder of their heresy. While Arius is dead, and many of his followers have succeeded him, nevertheless those who hold the doctrines of that man, as being known from Arius, are called Arians. (I.2–3; Tetz (1998) 111, 16–18; 112, 13–22)

This introduction to the first *Oration against the Arians* encapsulates Athanasius' polarized presentation of the 'Arian Controversy'. According to Athanasius, the 'Eusebians' are 'Arian' because they collectively follow the teachings of Arius, and abandon the traditional faith of Christ. Thus they have separated themselves from the 'true Church', just as the Marcionites, Manichees, and Valentinians had done before them. This model of a collective 'heretical party' (a model, it should be observed, that Athanasius insists must not be imposed upon himself and his own supporters)[22] underlies

[21] Rusch (1985) interprets '*tupon*' here as a reference to the shared 'standard' or 'rule of faith' that all Christians hold. I would argue that Athanasius is referring to the rule of students bearing the names of their teachers. See also Brakke (1995) 66–8, who sees Athanasius' rejection of 'teachers' in this passage as part of an attack on academic Christianity, especially within Egypt.

[22] That Athanasius' contemporary opponents did in fact speak of '*hoi peri Athanasion*' is probable but cannot be proven. Aside from the possible reference in the letter of Julius already noted above, the only explicit statement that 'Arians called Catholics "Athanasians"' occurs in a much later text, Augustine, *Contra Julianum (Opus Imperfectum)* 1.75.2 (CSEL 85, 91, 36–7).

Athanasius' presentation of the 'Eusebians' throughout his polemical works. It is because the 'Eusebians' are constructed in this collective fashion that the alleged membership of '*hoi peri Eusebion*' in Athanasius' writings is so difficult to define, for their individual identities are subordinated to their image as a uniform 'party'. Indeed, as we shall see, even when Athanasius does identify specific foes by name, those names can vary significantly according to the context and purpose of a given work. Most importantly, this polemical model makes it possible for Athanasius to present all his opponents, from his initial foes in the 330s to the contemporaries who he condemned in the late 350s (almost twenty years after Eusebius of Nicomedia's death) as representatives of a single ongoing 'Arian party'.

The earliest extant Athanasian references to the individuals who comprise the 'Eusebians', rather than to the collective (and essentially faceless) 'party' which dominates the vast majority of Athanasius' polemic, occur in the documents and narrative of the *Apologia Contra Arianos*. The letter of the Egyptian bishops in 335 to 'the bishops assembled at Tyre', in which the 'Eusebians' appear for the first time in Athanasius' works, condemns the conspiracy of 'Eusebius and Theognis and Maris and Narcissus and Theodore and Patrophilus' (77; Opitz (1938*b*) 156, 24–5).[23] The Mareotis Commission, according to Athanasius' own later narrative, consisted of 'the very persons whom we rejected on account of the Arian heresy... Diognius [Theognis], Maris, Theodore, Macedonius, Ursacius, and Valens' (72; Opitz (1938*b*) 151, 25–6).[24] And in his highly dubious allegation that when Constantine summoned the Council of Tyre to court the 'Eusebians' 'prevented the other bishops from going up and only went themselves', Athanasius identifies those who then

23 These six names also occur in the letter that the Egyptian bishops simultaneously wrote to Count Dionysius (*Apologia Contra Arianos* 78). However, as I noted in Ch. 3, in their second letter to Dionysius, written later in the proceedings of the Council (87), the bishops add Flacillus of Antioch to the members of the 'conspiracy'. Little is known of Flacillus, although he was probably president both at Tyre and at the 'Dedication' Council of Antioch, and was the dedicatee of Eusebius of Caesarea's *De Ecclesiastica Theologia*.

24 The same men are named as the members of the Mareotis Commission by the Alexandrian *Encyclical Letter* of 338 (*Apologia Contra Arianos* 13).

came to Constantinople as 'Eusebius, Theognis, Patrophilus, the other Eusebius, Ursacius, and Valens' (87; Opitz (1940*a*) 165, 36–166, 1).[25]

These three passages define a solid core of 'Eusebian' bishops who consistently recur whenever Athanasius singles out specific individuals among his foes. In addition to Eusebius of Nicomedia himself, the names of Theognis of Nicaea, Maris of Chalcedon, Narcissus of Neronias, Theodore of Heraclea, Patrophilus of Scythopolis, and the Balkan bishops Ursacius of Singidunum and Valens of Mursa are prominent throughout Athanasius' polemic. It is their careers and theological writings I will examine later in this chapter. Yet the passages quoted above also highlight the potential difficulties that the identification of such individuals within the 'Eusebian party' can involve. Neither Macedonius (bishop of Mopsuestia) in the Mareotis Commission nor Eusebius of Caesarea (the 'other Eusebius') among the bishops who came to Constantinople from Tyre ever appear elsewhere in an Athanasian catalogue of those he condemns. Little is known of this Macedonius, whose only other appearance in the writings of Athanasius is at the head of Julius' letter to the eastern bishops, which is formally addressed to 'Danius, Flacillus, Narcissus, Eusebius, Maris, Macedonius, Theodore, and the ones with them, who have written to me from Antioch' (*Apologia Contra Arianos* 21; Opitz (1938*a*) 102, 13–14).[26] The status of the 'other Eusebius' in Athanasius' writings, on the other hand, is extremely ambiguous, and whenever possible Athanasius seems to have preferred to avoid direct

[25] Intriguingly, Socrates in his account of the delegation to Constantinople adds Maris of Chalcedon to Athanasius' list of the bishops who came to court from Tyre, but removes Eusebius of Caesarea (I.35), whom he defends against charges of 'Arianism' (II.21). Sozomen follows Socrates' lead on the Tyre delegation (II.28), but can also speak elsewhere of the 'party' of the two Eusebii (II.25).

[26] The order of the names given here is peculiar, for Danius (either the bishop of Cappadocian Caesarea or a corrupt reference to Theognis (Diognius) of Nicaea) precedes Flacillus of Antioch (the bishop of the see to which Julius wrote), while Eusebius of Nicomedia (now Constantinople) appears only in the middle of the list. This suggests that the order is that of the original eastern letter to which Julius replies, given that Julius (as we have seen) nevertheless addresses the authors of the letter consistently as the 'Eusebians'.

criticism of the respected bishop of Caesarea.[27] But Athanasius wishes to present both the Mareotis Commission and the deputation to Constantinople after Tyre as entirely the vehicles of an 'Arian conspiracy', and so not representative of the wider eastern Church. Thus the pressures of his own polemical argument require that he incorporates all those involved in these events within his collective construction of the 'Eusebians'.

Eusebius of Nicomedia-Constantinople died before the Council of Serdica met, but as we have already seen, Athanasius nevertheless continues to describe his foes in 343 in the narrative of the *Apologia Contra Arianos* as 'the associates (*tous koinōnous*) of the Eusebians' (36; Opitz (1938*a*) 114, 5). Moreover, the *Encyclical Letter* of Western Serdica concludes with a denunciation of the men whose 'leaders are now, *meta tous peri Eusebion*, Theodore of Heraclea, Narcissus of Neronias in Cilicia, Stephen of Antioch, George of Laodicea, Acacius of Caesarea in Palestine, Menophantus of Ephesus in Asia, Ursacius of Singidunum in Moesia, and Valens of Mursa in Pannonia' (*Apologia Contra Arianos* 46; Opitz (1938*b*) 122, 14–18).[28] The exact significance of *meta* ('after') the 'Eusebians' in this passage is not entirely clear, for the western bishops elsewhere in the *Encyclical Letter* refer to their eastern opponents simply as 'Eusebians'. '*Tous peri Eusebion*' may in this instance denote only the two Eusebii themselves, both of whom were dead by 343. In any case, Athanasius and his supporters have here once again reduced the men whom they condemn to a minority faction, a construction made possible through the collective presentation of both Athanasius' older opponents like Theodore and Narcissus and newly appointed bishops Acacius of Caesarea and Stephen of Antioch as representatives of one and the same 'Arian party'. This continuation of the polemic

[27] In his later works, Athanasius twice invokes Eusebius' letter to his see after the Council of Nicaea as representative of his own interpretation of the Nicene Creed (*De Decretis* 3, *De Synodis* 13), see Ch. 7 below. In his earlier writings, Athanasius only explicitly attacks 'the other Eusebius' in the context of the abortive council of Caesarea in 334 (*Apologia Contra Arianos* 77) and the account of the Tyre delegation quoted above (there is no evidence for the assertion of Walker (1990) 27 that Eusebius of Caesarea was the president at Tyre).

[28] An identical list of the supporters of the 'Arian heresy' also appears in the letters of Western Serdica to the Church of Alexandria (*Apologia Contra Arianos* 40) and to the bishops of Egypt and Libya (41).

against the 'Eusebians' to embrace not only his original accusers but also his later contemporary opponents can be traced throughout Athanasius' great writings of 350–61.

In the later works of Athanasius, just as in his earlier polemic, the identification of his individual opponents is often difficult, for only rarely does Athanasius specifically name his foes. In all these later works, however, Athanasius continues to draw a direct line of 'succession' from the 'Eusebians' of the 330s and early 340s to their subsequent 'heirs'. The introduction to the *De Decretis* of 350–6 refers to 'the advocates (*presbeuontas*) of the doctrines of Arius ... [who include] certain of the companions (*tines tōn hetairōn*) of Eusebius' (1; Opitz (1935) 1, 1–2), but Athanasius identifies only one of these men by name: Acacius of Caesarea (4). The *Apologia de Fuga* in 357 specifically names three contemporary 'Arians', 'Leontius, now at Antioch, and Narcissus of the city of Nero, and George, now of Laodicea' (1; Szymusiak (1987) 177, 1–3).[29] In this work no immediate connection is drawn between these men and the earlier 'Eusebians', but in the *Historia Arianorum*[30] written a few months later that connection is made explicit. Athanasius condemns 'the inheritors (*klēronomoi*) of the opinions and impiety of the 'Eusebians': the eunuch Leontius ... and George and Acacius and Theodore and Narcissus' (28; Opitz (1940*a*) 198, 1–5), to whom Ursacius and Valens are shortly added (29; Opitz (1940*a*) 198, 17). These men represent a coherent 'Arian' tradition in continuous succession from the original 'Eusebians', with whom Athanasius had of course already associated all these men (except Leontius) in the *Apologia Contra Arianos*.

Before either the *Apologia de Fuga* or the *Historia Arianorum* were written, Athanasius had already composed a far more detailed

[29] The same three men are condemned in some detail at the end of the *Apologia de Fuga* (26–7), Leontius for castrating himself in order to live together with a virgin, and both Narcissus and George for their deposition by councils and their immoral lives. However, Athanasius here again focuses upon his opponents as a collective 'Arian party' rather than as individuals. 'Each man surpasses the others in his own peculiar evils, but there is a common stain that attaches to them, that through their heresy they are fighters against Christ, and are no longer called Christians, but rather Arians' (27; Szymusiak (1987) 242, 1–4).

[30] The traditional title of this work, the '*History of the Arians*', is itself of course a reflection of Athanasius' construction of those he condemns throughout the period 335–57 as a single 'Arian party'.

statement of his construction of his contemporary opponents as the 'heirs' and 'associates' of the 'Arian party'. In his *Encyclical Letter to the Bishops of Egypt and Libya* in 356, the first work that he composed during his third exile, Athanasius presents a roll call of 'the men who have been promoted (*proachthentes*) by the Eusebians for advocating this Christ-fighting heresy' (7; Tetz (1996) 46, 6–7): Secundus of Ptolemais, George of Laodicea, Stephen and Leontius of Antioch, Theodore, Ursacius, Valens, Acacius, Patrophilus, Narcissus, Eustathius of Sebasteia, Demophilus of Thracian Beroea, Germinius of Sirmium, Eudoxius of Germanicia (later of Antioch and then Constantinople), Basil of Ancyra, Cecropius of Nicomedia, Auxentius of Milan, Epictetus of Centumcellae, and George of Alexandria. I will return to Athanasius' presentation of the 'Eusebians' as ecclesiastical patrons in the next chapter, but what is immediately striking here is the sheer diversity of individuals whom Athanasius has named. The bishops included in this catalogue range from early 'Arians' like Secundus and old enemies Theodore, Patrophilus, and Narcissus, to the recently appointed Eudoxius, Auxentius, and of course George of Alexandria, whose ordination provided the immediate context of the *Encyclical Letter* itself. All of these men are now alleged to owe their sees to their 'heresy' and to the patronage of the 'Eusebians', reducing them once more to a single uniform 'Arian party' and representing the 'Eusebians' as the 'fathers' of every contemporary whom Athanasius in 356 wished to condemn.

The culmination of Athanasius' monolithic conception of his opponents, however, lies in the *De Synodis*. The very polemical structure and arguments of this work are founded upon his construction of an 'Arian party' united across some thirty years by their 'heresy' and by their shared association with the 'Eusebians'. Athanasius presents his account of the Councils of Ariminum and Seleucia in 359 against the background of this 'Arian tradition', tracing a direct line of theological succession from the *Thalia* of Arius and the writings of the original 'Eusebians', through the eastern credal statements of the 330s and 340s, to the dual councils themselves. Just as in the years preceding the Council of Nicaea 'the Arian heresy rose up against the catholic Church, and found patrons (*prostatas*) in the Eusebians' (5; Opitz (1940*b*) 234, 1–3), so in 359 the men who controlled Ariminum and Seleucia were those who 'always championed the Arian heresy... and eagerly received those who taught the doctrines of Arius' (7; Opitz (1940*b*) 235, 6–7). Athanasius' 'heretical genealogy' thus binds together the alleged leaders of the 'Eusebians' before 325 with the contemporaries whom he now condemned: Germinius, Auxentius, Valens, and Ursacius at Ariminum (8); and Acacius, Patrophilus, Eudoxius (now of Antioch), and George of Alexandria at Seleucia (12).

It is in the *De Synodis* that the degree of distortion inherent in this Athanasian construction of a single 'Arian party' is most immediately apparent. The precise theological content of Athanasius' arguments form the subject of my final chapter, but even a brief glance is sufficient to reveal that the men whom he collectively condemns as 'Arian' did not all hold a single shared 'heresy', nor are the diverse creeds he quotes all statements of the same theological position. The highly subjective nature of Athanasius' construction of his foes is made particularly self-evident by his treatment of Basil of Ancyra. Basil, whom we saw condemned in the *Encyclical Letter* of 356 alongside Germinius and Eudoxius as one of the men 'promoted' by the 'Eusebians' for his 'heresy', now less than three years later is declared to be 'orthodox', and separated completely from his former 'associates'. This abrupt shift is not due to any sudden change in Basil's own theology in the period 356–9,[31] but is purely the product of Athanasius' now favourable attitude towards Basil, and the 'Homoiousian' position in general, when he wrote the *De Synodis*. Within the confines of Athanasius' rigidly polarized vision of the fourth-century controversies, every individual must be defined either as 'orthodox' or as 'Arian'. The construction of his foes as a uniform 'heretical party' uniting the original 'Eusebians' to his contemporary opponents of the late 350s is an essential component of that polarized vision.

Two important conclusions for the study of the 'Eusebians' in the polemic of Athanasius need to be drawn from the analysis of the preceding pages. Firstly, not only does Athanasius subordinate the individual identities of those he condemns beneath his collective construction of his foes as a single 'party', but, despite his repeated references to the contemporary 'Arians' of the mid- and late-350s as the 'heirs' of the 'Eusebians', a precise distinction between the

[31] On the theology of Basil at this time, and specifically his attitude to the term *homoousios*, see Steenson (1985).

original men he branded as '*hoi peri Eusebion*' and their 'successors' cannot actually be drawn. As we have seen, Athanasius names among those later 'heirs' a number of bishops, including Theodore of Heraclea, Narcissus of Neronias, and others, whom he and his supporters had already condemned in their writings at the time of the Councils of Tyre and Serdica. For this reason, the analysis of Athanasius' construction of the 'Eusebians' must examine his presentation of his opponents throughout the entire corpus of his polemical works. Just as the men whom Athanasius condemns in the 350s are represented as a continuation of those whose 'conspiracy' caused his initial exile in 335, so in his later works Athanasius continues to develop and reinterpret his presentation of previous events and their participants. In my study of the actions and theology that Athanasius attributes to his opponents in the next two chapters, I will thus draw heavily upon the works that Athanasius composed in the period 350–61, for to a very marked extent it is these works that have shaped later interpretations of the 'Eusebians'.

Secondly, and no less importantly, it is precisely because they are subordinated to Athanasius' collective construction of an 'Arian party' that it is essential to identify and to study the so-called 'Eusebians' as individuals in their own right. For an analysis of Athanasius' polemical presentation of the 'Eusebians' to have any historical value, it is necessary to set against that presentation whatever evidence we may have for the actual careers and writings of the men whom he condemned. I cannot attempt to trace in detail here all of the men declared to be 'Arian' in the Athanasian passages cited above (not least because many of those men are indeed no more than names to us). However, sufficient evidence exists to allow at least a brief reconstruction of the careers and extremely fragmentary writings of certain individuals who appear repeatedly in Athanasius' construction of the 'Eusebians': Eusebius of Nicomedia, Asterius 'the Sophist', Theognis of Nicaea, Athanasius of Anazarbus, Maris of Chalcedon, Patrophilus of Scythopolis, Theodore of Heraclea, Narcissus of Neronias, Ursacius of Singidunum, Valens of Mursa, and George of Laodicea.[32]

[32] A number of these men also figure prominently in the study of Bardy (1936) of the so-called 'school' of Lucian of Antioch. See Ch. 7.

WHO WERE THE 'EUSEBIANS'?

Eusebius of Nicomedia and Constantinople, whose presentation within the polemic of Athanasius has been followed without question in the vast majority of modern accounts of the 'Arian Controversy', has nevertheless received surprisingly little detailed scholarly attention.[33] The traditional image of Eusebius is of an archetypal ecclesiastical politician,[34] and the known details of his career do provide some justification for that image. Originally the bishop of Berytus, Eusebius was related to Julius Julianus, praetorian prefect to the eastern emperor Licinius 315–24, and so to the later emperor Julian 'the Apostate'.[35] This connection may have influenced his translation to Nicomedia, the capital of Licinius, after 314.[36] He is also reported

[33] The only two modern studies specifically concerned with Eusebius' career and theology written since the first decade of the twentieth century are the articles of Luibheid (1976) and Gwynn (1999), although there are also brief surveys of his career and known writings in Bardy (1936) 296–315 and Lienhard (1999) 77–83. This limited scholarly emphasis is primarily due to the lack of evidence for Eusebius outside the polemic of his 'orthodox' foes. In the words of Gwatkin (1882) 71: 'Eusebius is a man of whom we should like to know more. His influence in his own time was second to none, his part in history for many years hardly less than that of Athanasius; yet we have to estimate him almost entirely from the allusions of his enemies.'

[34] There is a concise summary of this negative interpretation of the career of the bishop of Nicomedia in his entry by Reynolds in the *Dictionary of Christian Biography* (1880). Fifty years previously, Newman (1833) had described Eusebius as 'the most dexterous politician of the age' (270), and recently Drake (2000) repeats this image when he declares that 'Eusebius was a great manipulator, a master of what today would be called insider politics', who after the Council of Nicaea 'never again let principle keep him from access to power' (395).

[35] The evidence for this relationship, which receives no mention in Athanasius or the later ecclesiastical historians, derives from Ammianus Marcellinus (*Res Gestae* XXII.9.4), who reports that Eusebius once tutored the future emperor Julian. Vanderspoel (1999) 410–11, in his study of Julius Julianus, argues that Eusebius is most likely to have been a relative of Julianus' unnamed Christian wife, possibly her brother, and observes that Julianus remained at Constantine's court after Licinius' defeat and so would have continued to be a possible source of patronage for Eusebius.

[36] The precise chronology of Eusebius' early career (including his date of birth) cannot be reconstructed, but his move from Berytus to Nicomedia (which as we have seen was condemned in Alexander's *Encyclical Letter* of 324) must post-date 314, when a certain Eustolus signed the acts of the Council of Ancyra as bishop of Nicomedia.

to have been a favourite of Constantia,[37] Licinius' wife and Constantine's half-sister, and it has been suggested that Eusebius interceded on Licinius' behalf after his defeat by Constantine in 324, for Constantine would later denounce Eusebius in one letter as a supporter of the 'tyrant'.[38] Eusebius attended the Council of Nicaea, where it is probable that he gave the initial address,[39] and he signed the Nicene Creed, although not the anathemas.[40] Shortly after the Council, however, in September–October 325, he and Theognis of Nicaea

[37] On the life of Constantia see Pohlsander (1993). Unfortunately, although Pohlsander accepts without question the much repeated assertion of a connection between Constantia and the 'Arians' (162–3), this alleged connection receives no support from Athanasius or any other contemporary. Our sole evidence is the unsupported narratives of the later ecclesiastical historians, who describe her relationship with an unnamed 'Arian presbyter' (Rufinus, X.12; Socrates, I.25; Sozomen, II.27) and report that she aided Eusebius and Theognis of Nicaea to return from exile after the Nicene Council (Sozomen, III.19).

[38] Chadwick (1958) 302; Grant (1975) 3. The denunciation of Eusebius by Constantine occurs in the latter's *Letter to the Church of Nicomedia* (quoted in Theodoret, I.20, and Gelasius of Cyzicus, Appendix I.1–17), in which the emperor explains why he exiled Eusebius shortly after the Council of Nicaea. Constantine's language is highly rhetorical and difficult to assess, for he not only accuses Eusebius of having been 'the participator (*summustēs*) in the tyrant's savagery' (Parmentier (1998) 66, 20), but alleges that Eusebius spied for Licinius and 'almost afforded armed assistance to the tyrant' (Parmentier (1998) 67, 3). However, this letter does support Chadwick's argument that due to his connection to the court of Licinius, Eusebius' position may have been somewhat tenuous immediately following Constantine's triumph.

[39] The *kephalaion* (chapter-heading) of Eusebius of Caesarea, *Vita Constantini* III.1, merely says that 'the bishop Eusebius' delivered this opening address. Sozomen (I.19) identified this as a reference to the bishop of Caesarea himself, while Theodoret (I.7) asserted that the speaker was actually his own hero Eustathius of Antioch. As the ranking metropolitan and the bishop of the then imperial capital, however, Eusebius of Nicomedia would appear to have the strongest claim (although he was not the president, for this role fell to Ossius of Cordova (see De Clercq (1954) 228–38 and Barnes (1978) 57)).

[40] There is some confusion over this important question, for although Athanasius (*De Decretis* 2–3) and Sozomen (I.21) both state that Eusebius and his colleague Theognis of Nicaea signed the Nicene Creed, Socrates (I.8) believed that they refused to do so, while Philostorgius (I.9) recounts the almost certainly fictitious legend that the two men signed a creed on which *homoousios* had been replaced by *homoiousios*. The so-called '*Letter of Recantation*' that Eusebius and Theognis wrote to secure their return from exile (quoted in Socrates, I.14) suggests that they did sign the Creed, for their primary concern is to explain their refusal to sign the anathemas, which they assert misrepresented Arius' theology. For a possible reconstruction of the signature lists of Nicaea see Honigmann (1939) 44–8, according to whom the bishops signed by region, with Eusebius signing first for Bithynia, followed by Theognis and Maris of Chalcedon.

were banished, apparently for receiving friends of Arius.[41] Both men were only restored in late 327/early 328,[42] but from this time onwards Eusebius is usually assumed to have been a prominent figure in or near the court of Constantine.[43] In 337 it was Eusebius who baptized the first Christian emperor,[44] and shortly after Constantine's death,

[41] The date (approximately three months after the Council of Nicaea) is given by Philostorgius (I.10). In his *Letter to the Church of Nicomedia*, Constantine declares that Eusebius and Theognis were exiled because they had received 'certain Alexandrians (*tinas Alexandreas*) who had left our faith' (Parmentier (1998) 68, 20–1) Although Barnes (1981) 226 suggests that these 'Alexandrians' were Melitians or Colluthians, Elliot (1996) 170–1, 231–2 must be correct that they were men accused of 'Arianism' (though not, as has sometimes been suggested, Arius himself). For Constantine wrote at the same time to another bishop, Theodotus of Laodicea (Opitz, *Urkunde* XXVIII), warning him explicitly that he too will be exiled if he follows Eusebius and Theognis who by their actions 'defiled the name of the Saviour God' (Opitz (1934–5) 63, 3–4).

[42] The circumstances of this return have also been debated, for the '*Letter of Recantation*' of Eusebius and Theognis is addressed not to Constantine but to a council of bishops, a council that apparently had already restored Arius after his exile at Nicaea. This fact led Martin (1989) 311–19 to argue that the letter in question was actually written to the Council of Jerusalem in 335, and is not in fact by Eusebius and Theognis at all, but by the Libyan bishops Secundus and Theonas. Others have argued that the council in question was the so-called 'Second Session' of Nicaea, reassembled in late 327. However, Martin's thesis remains unproven, and there is no explicit reference to any 'Second Session' either in our contemporary sources or in the later ecclesiastical histories (see Luibheid (1983)). If the attribution of the letter by Socrates is genuine, Barnes (1978) 60–1 would seem to be correct that the council that restored Eusebius and Theognis was a provincial Bithynian synod (albeit possibly on a considerable scale).

[43] Eusebius 'virtually took charge of the affairs of the Greek speaking Eastern Church from 328 until his death' (Hanson (1988*b*) 29). However, although many scholars have described Eusebius as Constantine's 'ecclesiastical adviser' (Barnes (1981) 226) or 'spiritual father' (Drake (2000) 394), the exact relationship between these two men is difficult to assess from our hostile sources. Warmington (1989) and Woods (2002) 222–3 both reject the idea of a bishop attached to the court in any formal capacity in this period, while Hunt (1989) also emphasizes the need to look beyond the 'orthodox' polemic against 'heretical court bishops' (89). Elliott (1992) 192–3 (repeated in (1996) 325) speaks of Eusebius and Constantine sharing 'a modest working relationship, or cautious friendship', a conclusion that may not be far from the truth, although Elliott here as elsewhere is primarily concerned to protect Constantine from too close contact with an alleged 'Arian'.

[44] Eusebius, *Vita Constantini* IV.62, does not name 'the bishops' (plural) who performed Constantine's baptism, nor do Socrates (I.39), Sozomen (II.34), or Theodoret (I.32). Eusebius of Nicomedia *is* named, however, by Jerome (*Chronicon* 2353 for AD 337). On the many legends that later developed around the baptism of Constantine, particularly that he was baptized in Rome by the Pope Sylvester, see Fowden (1994) and S. Lieu (1998) 136–57.

Eusebius was translated once more to the imperial see of Constantinople by the new eastern emperor Constantius.[45] He died in late 341/early 342.

The social and political prominence of Eusebius' life and career is sadly not reflected in the extremely fragmentary survival of his writings and doctrines. Sozomen (II.15) describes him as a man of considerable learning, yet aside from a single sentence from his *Letter to Arius* in late 322 (quoted in *De Synodis* 17; Opitz, *Urkunde* II), the only Eusebian works to survive are his *Letter to Paulinus of Tyre* in *c.*323 (Theodoret, I.6; Opitz, *Urkunde* VIII) and the '*Letter of Recantation*' (Socrates, I.14; Sozomen, II.16; Opitz, *Urkunde* XXXI) that Eusebius and Theognis of Nicaea wrote in 327 to request their restoration from exile. In addition, statements of uncertain authenticity attributed to Eusebius are preserved in later sources, notably Ambrose of Milan (*De Fide* III.15; Opitz, *Urkunde* XXI)[46] and Sozomen (II.21), and we also possess the letters and creeds composed by the 'Dedication' Council of Antioch in 341, which was attended by Eusebius and by almost all the alleged members of his 'Eusebian party'. All of the above texts will be cited in some detail in the two chapters that follow, but it must be acknowledged that the nature of this evidence cannot permit a full

[45] Socrates, II.7; Sozomen, III.4 (Theodoret, I.19, misdates Eusebius' second translation to the reign of Constantine). The exact chronology of Eusebius' move to Constantinople is uncertain, but it was known to the authors of the Alexandrian *Encyclical Letter* of 338 (*Apologia Contra Arianos* 6). Barnes (1978) 66 makes a plausible case that the statement in Eusebius of Caesarea's *Contra Marcellum*, written within a year or so of the council that condemned Marcellus in 336, that 'very many distinguished provinces and cities' (I.4.9; Klostermann (1972) 19, 9–10) have laid claim to his namesake, suggests that Eusebius had already been translated to his third see by late 337. DiMaio and Arnold (1992) suggest that Eusebius received the see of Constantinople in reward for forging or doctoring a document found at the time of Constantine's death to aid the succession of Constantius and the subsequent purge of the imperial family, but even Athanasius does not accuse Eusebius of this.

[46] For a recent assessment of this Ambrosian work, and specifically the context and purpose of *De Fide* III–V, which were later additions to Books I–II, see Williams (1995*a*), esp. 524–31, and (1995*b*) 128–53. Ambrose's attribution of this fragment to Eusebius of Nicomedia has been challenged by Tetz (1993) 235–7, who argues that the author was actually Eusebius of Caesarea, but no evidence supports this claim.

reconstruction of the role that Eusebius played in the controversies of his lifetime.[47]

Frequently associated with Eusebius of Nicomedia in the polemic of Athanasius, although not himself a bishop nor ever specifically named as a member of the 'Eusebians', is Asterius 'the Sophist'.[48] Little is known of his career.[49] A Christian who compromised and offered pagan sacrifice during the Great Persecution, Asterius could not be ordained, but he was an important theologian and preacher who is said by Athanasius to have travelled the eastern Church with 'introductions' from the 'Eusebians' (*De Synodis* 18) to teach from his treatise, the *Syntagmation*.[50] Thus Asterius is a significant figure in his own right, for through quotations from that lost work by Athanasius, and also from fragments of Asterius' defence of Eusebius of Nicomedia when the latter was in exile (quoted by Marcellus of Ancyra and preserved in turn in Eusebius of Caesarea's *Contra Marcellum*), there is more surviving evidence for the theology of 'the Sophist' than for any of his alleged 'Eusebian' allies.[51] Of course, this evidence ultimately

[47] The *Letter to Constantia* rejecting the legitimacy of creating an image of Christ (quoted by the Iconoclasts in the *horos* of the council of 754 as the work of Eusebius of Caesarea, and preserved in turn only in the *Acta* of the Iconophile Council of 787) might in fact have been composed by the bishop of Nicomedia (Schäferdiek (1980) 184–6). This hypothesis is attractive, for Eusebius of Nicomedia's relationship to the imperial house does appear to have been considerably closer than that of his namesake, but no decisive conclusion is possible. The authenticity of this letter as a fourth-century composition has been called into question (Murray (1997) 326–36), while the traditional attribution of the letter to Eusebius of Caesarea has been defended by Gero (1981).

[48] Until recently, scholarship on the life and writings of Asterius had been very limited, with the main exceptions being Bardy (1936) 316–57; Richard (1956); and Wiles (1985). Since the late 1980s, however, Asterius has begun to receive much greater attention, particularly in the various studies of Kinzig and Vinzent (see their entries in the Bibliography), and also Lienhard (1999) 89–101.

[49] On Asterius' life see Bardy (1936) 317–28, Kinzig (1990) 14–20, and Vinzent (1993*a*) 20–32. Asterius was presumably born *c.*260–80 if he was an adult at the time of the Diocletianic persecution. He is said by various later sources to have attended the councils of Nicaea (Epiphanius, *Panarion* 69.4), Jerusalem (Socrates, I.36), and Antioch in 341 (*Libellus Synodicus*), and he probably died soon after the latter date.

[50] The date of composition of this work cannot be established, although Bardy (1936) 322 and Lienhard (1999) 91 have argued that the *Syntagmation* was probably written before 325.

[51] The fragments of Asterius' works were collected by Bardy (1936) 339–54, and have now been re-edited with considerable further additions by Vinzent (1993*a*) 82–141. The attribution of many of these fragments is not entirely secure, however (see Ch. 7).

derives primarily from hostile sources and cannot be assumed to represent a complete statement of his theological position (the one other possible source for Asterius' theology, the *Homilies on the Psalms* attributed to him by Marcel Richard, cannot in fact be ascribed to the 'Eusebian' Asterius).[52] But from the material that does survive a relatively detailed model of Asterius' thought can be reconstructed, which reveals that there are indeed important parallels between the extant theological writings of Asterius and Eusebius of Nicomedia.

If our evidence for the careers and writings of Eusebius of Nicomedia and Asterius might be thought inadequate, that evidence dwarfs the extant material from which we derive our knowledge of the other 'Eusebians' prominent within Athanasius' polemic. Although a number of these bishops were metropolitans in their own right and presumably significant figures within the fourth-century Church, their lives and theological doctrines may be reconstructed only from isolated fragments retrieved from sources of widely variable quality. Thus Theognis of Nicaea, whose episcopal position suggests that he was an important player in 325 and whose exile and restoration after the Council of Nicaea alongside Eusebius of Nicomedia we have traced above, is otherwise remarkably little known. He apparently led the Mareotis Commission in 335, and also attended the Council of

52 The edition and attribution to Asterius of these *Homilies* by Richard (1956) opened great new opportunities for the study of Asterius' theology (see most notably the article of Wiles (1985)), but in 1990 Wolfram Kinzig published a full study of the manuscript transmission and content of the *Homilies* in which he emphatically rejected Richard's proposed attribution. Kinzig accepts that the *Homilies* (which survive under the name of John Chrysostom) were indeed written by an Asterius, but he concludes that they were actually written *c.*385–410 and cannot be by the 'Sophist', attributing these works instead to an otherwise unidentified 'Asterius Ignotus'. Through computer analysis, Kinzig demonstrates that the *Homilies* edited by Richard form a unitary whole, and therefore that the attempts of Richard and Wiles to reject certain passages which would contradict authorship by Asterius 'the Sophist' (notably the use of *homoousios* (XVIII.14, XXI.5) and the explicit reference to the later 'Neo-Arian' Eunomius in Homily XXVI) cannot be sustained. Although Kinzig's argument was rejected by Uthemann (1991, to whom Kinzig replied in the same year), it has otherwise been widely accepted (as by Vinzent (1993*a*) 37), and without further detailed textual studies the *Homilies on the Psalms* thus cannot be attributed to the 'Eusebian' Asterius. However, I am less convinced by Kinzig's secondary argument (against Wiles (1985)) that the theology of the *Homilies* is entirely incompatible with the known fragments of Asterius. For this reason, I will still refer to the *Homilies* in my discussion of Asterius' theology in the last chapter, even though I do not intend to try to defend his authorship of these works.

Serdica in 343, but Athanasius provides no insight into Theognis' own theology. The only surviving doctrinal statements attributed to this bishop are preserved in a late and fragmentary Latin translation of alleged 'Arian' quotations.[53] That same source also preserves a fragment from the writings of Athanasius of Anazarbus (metropolitan see of Cilicia II),[54] a bishop whom Athanasius of Alexandria entirely ignores in his earliest polemical works but who appears in *De Synodis* 17, where a fragment is quoted from his *Letter to Alexander* (Opitz, *Urkunde* XI).[55] This Athanasius is also said by Philostorgius (III.15) to have been a teacher of the 'Neo-Arian' Aetius, and a *Homily* wrongly ascribed to Athanasius of Alexandria may have been composed by the bishop of Anazarbus.[56] But this is the limit to our knowledge of his career or teachings.

No evidence even of this fragmentary quality illuminates the individual theological positions of Maris of Chalcedon, Patrophilus of Scythopolis, or Theodore of Heraclea. All three were prominent members of a number of eastern councils in the years following 325, and in his old age Maris, now blind, is said to have rebuked the Emperor Julian (Socrates, III.12; Sozomen, V.4), but no personal statements attributed to any of these three men survive.[57] The theology of Narcissus of Neronias[58] is known only from a few fragments, most famously his statement to Ossius of Cordova that there were three *ousiai* in the Trinity.[59] The two Balkan bishops Ursacius and

[53] This text was edited by de Bruyne (1928). See also Bardy (1936) 210–14.

[54] De Bruyne (1928) 110. A full collection of Athanasius' extant fragments appears in Bardy (1936) 204–10.

[55] This letter would appear to date to approximately the same period as Eusebius of Nicomedia's *Letter to Paulinus of Tyre*, in *c.*323.

[56] The text of this *Homily* was originally edited by Casey (1935), who rejected authorship by Athanasius of Alexandria but did not propose an alternative. The attribution to the bishop of Anazarbus is that of Tetz (1952–3) 304.n.26.

[57] Bardy (1936) 214–6.

[58] Lienhard (1999) 88–9 outlines what little is known of the career of Narcissus. After attending the councils of Nicaea, Tyre, and then Antioch in 341, he was one of the four bishops who brought the 'Fourth Creed' of Antioch to the west in 342, and he later attended the Councils of Serdica in 343 and Sirmium in 351.

[59] This passage is quoted by Eusebius of Caesarea, who in turn is quoting Marcellus, in *Contra Marcellum* I.4.39 (Opitz, *Urkunde* 19). Opitz (1934) 152–3 observes that the most plausible occasion for this episode was the Council of Antioch in 325 where Narcissus, along with Eusebius of Caesarea and Theodotus of Laodicea, was provisionally excommunicated.

Valens, despite their importance in the period of Constantius' sole rule after 350, likewise remain largely shadowy figures and little understood.[60] We do, however, know slightly more of George of Laodicea. Two fragments from letters that he wrote while a presbyter in Alexandria before the Council of Nicaea are quoted by Athanasius (*De Synodis* 17; Opitz, *Urkunden* XII, XIII),[61] and George is also reported to have been one of the 'Arians' whom Eustathius of Antioch refused to admit to communion after 325, an episode that helped provoke Eustathius' exile.[62] Later, George reappears in association with Basil of Ancyra in opposition to the so-called 'Neo-Arians' in 358–9 (Sozomen, IV.13), and in this context Epiphanius (*Panarion* 73.12–22) quotes a letter that appears to be composed by George,[63] and which represents the last personal theological statement that can be attributed with confidence to an alleged representative of the 'Eusebians'.

For all of the men considered in this brief survey, the most important source for their careers, writings, and theology ultimately lies in the polemic of Athanasius himself. It is his construction of the 'Eusebians', their 'conspiracies', and their 'Arianism' that creates the background for any study of the individuals whom he condemns. Thus the analysis of the origins, nature, and development of that construction which we have so far undertaken must now provide the foundation for the re-assessment of the alleged actions and theology

[60] According to Athanasius, writing in 356, Ursacius and Valens 'were instructed by Arius as young men' (*Encyclical Letter* 7; Tetz (1996) 46, 15), possibly during Arius' exile in the Balkans after the Council of Nicaea. In *Apologia Contra Arianos* 58, he also quotes their 'Recantation' admitting his own innocence of the charges they had helped bring against him. However, although Ursacius and Valens are particularly associated with the 'Dated Creed' of Sirmium in 359 (*De Synodis* 8), nothing is known of their personal writings, and the prevailing scholarly attitude towards their careers is nicely encapsulated by Hanson (1989), who describes them as 'no more than theological weathercocks, responding to every wind of imperial favour' (147).

[61] Again, these letters would appear to have been written in *c.*323, although like all the 'Eusebian' writings from before the Council of Nicaea they cannot be dated with precision.

[62] *Historia Arianorum* 4 (see Ch. 6 below).

[63] On the difficulties of date and authorship caused by the style of Epiphanius' presentation of this document, see Hanson (1988*b*) 365–6.

of the 'Eusebians' that follows. Through the comparison of the polemic of Athanasius to the fragmentary evidence for the careers and teachings of his opponents, important conclusions can be drawn regarding the nature and potential distortions of Athanasius' construction of the men he branded as '*hoi peri Eusebion*'.

6

The 'Eusebians' in Action

Who are the men who cause the murders and banishments? Is it not them? Who are the men who, exploiting external patronage, conspire against the bishops? Are not the Eusebians the men, and not Athanasius as they have written? . . . Is it not them . . . who do not refrain from all manner of falsehood, so that they may destroy a bishop who will not give way to their impious heresy? This was the reason for the enmity of the Eusebians; this was the reason for what was contrived at Tyre; this was the reason for the pretended trials; this was the reason also now for the letters written by them without a trial as if with full assurance; this was the reason for their calumnies before the father of the Emperors, and before the most pious Emperors themselves. (*Encyclical Letter* of the Council of Alexandria 338, *Apologia Contra Arianos* 17; Opitz (1938*a*) 100, 13–15; 18–24)

Throughout the polemical writings of Athanasius, from the Alexandrian *Encyclical Letter* of 338 and the *Epistula Encyclica* of 339 to the great works of his third exile, certain elements consistently recur in his construction of the 'Eusebians': the writing of letters; the manipulation of episcopal office; dependence upon secular power; violence and persecution; and above all the promotion of the 'Arian heresy'. The last and longest chapter of this monograph focuses on the most important of these elements, the repeated assertion that the 'Eusebians' are 'Arian', for according to Athanasius it is always the alleged 'heresy' of his foes that motivates their actions. Yet Athanasius' presentation of the actions of the 'Eusebian party' is highly significant in its own right, both for our understanding of Athanasius' polemic, and because of the influence that his writings have exerted on ancient and modern interpretations of the fourth-century Church.

Unlike the analysis of the theological doctrines of the men whom Athanasius condemns, however, an examination of the 'Eusebians' 'in action' cannot rely upon external evidence against which Athanasius' presentation may be compared. For the vast majority of the events which he describes, particularly in the 340s and 350s, Athanasius is the only extant contemporary source. We are therefore limited to a close study of his own writings, notably the *Apologia ad Constantium*, the *Apologia de Fuga*, and the *Historia Arianorum*. Athanasius' presentation of the actions of his opponents in these works is extremely repetitive in detail, and is dominated by certain recurring *topoi*. By tracing those *topoi* and their development, and highlighting the important differences in emphasis visible between Athanasius' individual works, it is possible to shed considerable light upon the motivation and rhetorical methodology of Athanasius' polemic. We are then also better able to understand the potential distortions that this polemic may create, most significantly through Athanasius' construction of an 'Arian' 'purge' against the 'orthodox' in the years after Nicaea and his repeated emphasis upon the alleged dependence of his foes upon secular power and persecution.

LETTER WRITING

Before we turn to the more prominent elements of Athanasius' presentation of the 'Eusebians' as a source of ecclesiastical patronage and violence, it is necessary to comment briefly upon another dimension of his polemic that appears repeatedly in his earlier writings: his condemnation of the 'Eusebians' for composing and circulating letters in order to promote their 'conspiracy'.[1] As we saw in Part II, not only Athanasius himself (*Epistula Encyclica* 7)

[1] There has been much recent interest in letter writing and epistolary networks in Late Antiquity: see esp. Clark (1993) 16–42 on the Origenist controversy. A comparable reconstruction of a 'Eusebian' network is simply not possible from the limited evidence we have.

but also his predecessor Alexander, the Alexandrian Council of 338 (*Apologia Contra Arianos* 19), and the Western Council of Serdica (*Apologia Contra Arianos* 49) all conclude their *Encyclical Letters* by appealing to their audience not to receive or heed the letters of the 'Eusebians'. The content of those letters is never described in detail, but the implication is that the 'Eusebians' circulated their epistles not unlike a political party distributing polemical pamphlets. 'They do not cease from writing destructive letters (*olethrou grammata*) for the ruin of the Bishop who is the enemy of their impiety' (*Encyclical Letter* of the Alexandrian Council of 338, *Apologia Contra Arianos* 3; Opitz (1938*a*) 89, 20–1).

That the men whom Athanasius condemns as 'Eusebians' did indeed write letters is not in question. Eusebius of Nicomedia's *Letter to Paulinus of Tyre* from before the Council of Nicaea survives, and although no similar evidence exists for the period after 325, it is virtually certain that some such correspondence continued to take place, and probably included letters to publicize and justify Athanasius' condemnation at the Council of Tyre. More problematic is the Athanasian assertion that those letters represent the 'conspiracy' of an organized 'party'. It has often been ignored that this interpretation of the letters of the 'Eusebians' is itself expressed through *Encyclical Letters* composed and circulated by Athanasius and his supporters, whose denunciations of the 'Eusebians' are no different in polemical tone and purpose from the hostile correspondence that they attribute to their foes. Yet Athanasius presents the letters written on his own behalf not as the product of a 'heretical conspiracy', but as representative statements of the 'true Church'.[2] In reality, the writing of Christian letters in the fourth century was hardly a specifically 'party' or 'Eusebian' activity. It is Athanasius' presentation that has created this distortion, attributing all writings hostile to himself to the 'Eusebians' and so discrediting those letters that he did not wish his audience to read.

2 E.g. the letters of Julius and Western Serdica, and the letter of Alexander of Thessalonica to Alexandria in 334, which Athanasius claims to have been representative of a number of such letters of support that he received at that time (*Apologia Contra Arianos* 65).

ECCLESIASTICAL POLITICS, PATRONAGE, AND THE 'ANTI-NICENE PURGE'

The man who is their friend and associate in impiety, although he is responsible for other crimes and is open to ten thousand accusations, although the evidence and proofs against him are most clear; this man is approved by them, and immediately he becomes the friend of the emperor, having a recommendation from his impiety, and having acquired great powers, he is given freedom before the magistrates to do whatever he wishes. But he who exposes their impiety, and honestly advocates the cause of Christ; this man, although he is pure in all respects, although he is conscious of no faults, although he has no accuser, yet on the pretexts which they have framed against him, he is immediately seized and sent into exile by the judgement of the emperor... while he who advocates the cause of their heresy is sought for, and immediately despatched into the other's church. (*Historia Arianorum* 2; Opitz (1940*a*) 183, 18–184, 4)

Fundamental to Athanasius' construction of the 'Eusebians' as an 'Arian party' is the control and manipulation of ecclesiastical politics and patronage through which they promote those who will favour their 'impiety' and eliminate those who uphold 'the cause of Christ'. This again is a theme that recurs throughout Athanasius' various polemical works, and thus Athanasius defends himself against the 'Arians' whom the 'Eusebians' have imposed upon his own see of Alexandria, first Gregory (339–45) and then George (356–61). In his later writings, however, and particularly in the *Historia Arianorum*, this polemical presentation of 'Eusebian' patronage undergoes a subtle but crucial shift of emphasis. Athanasius increasingly comes to present his own condemnation and exile as only one (albeit significant) consequence of a wider persecution carried out by the 'Arians' against the 'orthodox Church'. This is the so-called 'anti-Nicene purge', which has played an extremely influential role in both ancient and modern interpretations of the fourth-century controversies.

Certain aspects of Athanasius' presentation of the ecclesiastical patronage and manipulation of the 'Eusebians' have already become apparent in earlier chapters. As we have seen, Eusebius of Nicomedia himself was condemned by Alexander in his *Encyclical Letter* in 324 for his translation from his original see of Berytus to Nicomedia. This charge was repeated in almost identical language in the Alexandrian *Encyclical Letter* of 338,[3] where Eusebius' 'illegal' advancement is contrasted to the 'unanimous and legitimate' ordination of Athanasius,[4] and the Egyptian bishops then further denounce Eusebius' subsequent shift from Nicomedia to Constantinople. Thus they conclude that Eusebius must 'think that piety consists in wealth and in the greatness of cities' (*Apologia Contra Arianos* 6; Opitz (1938*a*) 93, 7), a charge that was also levelled against the 'Eusebians' more generally by Julius of Rome and by Western Serdica.[5] Whatever the exact circumstances of Eusebius' translations may have been, there is no doubt that he did twice move towards sees of greater political power and influence, although such behaviour in the fourth-century Church was hardly restricted to Eusebius alone.[6]

More difficult to assess is another recurring theme of Athanasius' polemic against 'Eusebian' patronage that we encountered repeatedly in Part II, the alleged 'alliance' of the 'Eusebians' with the Melitian schismatics in Egypt. In gratitude for their assistance against Athanasius, which culminated at the Council of Tyre, the Melitians are said to have received in turn 'Eusebian' support. In the Alexandrian *Encyclical Letter* of 338, the aforementioned letters allegedly being circulated by Athanasius' foes are further denounced because 'though they may subscribe to their letters the names of Egyptian Bishops, it is clear that we are not the ones who write, but the Melitians' (*Apologia Contra Arianos* 19; Opitz (1938*a*) 101, 28–30). Yet after

[3] In particular, both letters describe Eusebius as 'casting envious eyes (*epophthalmiōn*)' upon the sees of others, an unusual expression that suggests that the Alexandrian *Encyclical Letter* of 338 was directly influenced by the earlier letter of Alexander.

[4] As I briefly commented in my Introduction, the ordination of Athanasius was itself highly controversial, and the condemnation of Eusebius in the *Encyclical Letter* of 338 was certainly influenced by the Egyptian bishops' corresponding attempts to vindicate Athanasius' own position.

[5] It is intriguing that the letter of Julius (*Apologia Contra Arianos* 25) is the only contemporary source attacking the translation of allegedly 'Eusebian' bishops to invoke (in somewhat veiled fashion) Nicene canon 15 which condemns such episcopal movements. The Alexandrian *Encyclical Letter* is conspicuously silent on this question, as is Western Serdica. For a discussion of the legal status of episcopal translations in this period, see Hess (2002) 162–8.

[6] Other well-known translations from around this time include that of Eustathius of Beroea (the ally of Alexander and Athanasius) to Antioch in 324–5, and that of Eudoxius of Germanicia first to Antioch and later to Constantinople under Constantius.

their prominent role in Athanasius' presentation of his trial and exile in 335, the Melitians then disappear entirely from Athanasius' polemic, and play no apparent part in the events of the 340s and early 350s.[7] The 'alliance' of the 'heretics' and the 'schismatics' only reappears in two important and difficult passages late in Athanasius' works. The first is near the end of the *Historia Arianorum* in 357, and the second is in that section of the Athanasian *Encyclical Letter* of 356 that was added to that work in 361.

According to the *Historia Arianorum*, at the time when George was installed in Alexandria during Athanasius' third exile, the 'Arians' would only ordain into the clergy those who adopted their 'heresy'. This was welcomed by the Melitians, for 'their ignorance of true piety quickly brings them to submit to whatever folly is now customary.... It is nothing to them to be carried about by every wind and tempest, if only they are exempt from duty and obtain human patronage' (78; Opitz (1940*a*) 227, 2–5). 'They are hirelings (*misthōtoi*) of any who will make use of them' (79; Opitz (1940*a*) 227, 24–5). This reference to the Melitians as 'hirelings' directly echoes the *Apologia Contra Arianos*, but no allusion is made to that earlier 'alliance'. The only motive of the schismatics is now the desire for patronage, their subservience merely one element within Athanasius' wider condemnation of the men whom the 'Arians' made 'bishops' in place of true Christians like himself.

The appearance of the Melitians in the *Encyclical Letter to Egypt and Libya* is still more problematic. In this later passage, Athanasius does return explicitly to the 'Arian–Melitian alliance', but his presentation of that 'alliance' in 361 seems to directly contradict the argument of the *Apologia Contra Arianos*. 'For behold, though before they were fighting amongst themselves (*to proteron machomenoi pros heautous*), now like Herod and Pontius [Pilate] they have conspired together in order to blaspheme against our Lord Jesus Christ... the Melitians for the sake of patronage and the madness of love of

[7] The one exception to this silence is Athanasius' declaration in the *Life of Antony* that the great monk never held communion with such schismatics (68; 89). But there is no allusion to an 'Arian–Melitian alliance', and this reference was probably intended to oppose Melitian influence among the ascetic communities for whom the *Life* was originally written.

money, the Ariomaniacs for the sake of their own impiety' (22; Tetz (1996) 62, 1–2; 62, 6–63, 1). The motives attributed to the two factions here echo those in the *Historia Arianorum* above. But their alleged previous enmity has no parallel in Athanasius' earlier works, and cannot be easily reconciled with Athanasius' emphasis elsewhere upon the cooperation of the 'Eusebians' with the Melitians throughout the 330s. It is possible that in this passage Athanasius is reacting to otherwise unknown events that occurred in Egypt between 357 and 361.[8] But without additional evidence, it is difficult to treat any of the accounts of alleged 'Arian–Melitian' interaction in the polemic of Athanasius as historical. Rather, the inherent contradictions between these accounts demonstrate the degree to which a given theme can be presented in significantly different ways in Athanasius' different works, according to his own needs and motives at the time of writing.

Nowhere are these difficulties of historicity and presentation more apparent than in Athanasius' depiction of the relationship between the 'Eusebians' and Arius himself. Unlike the alleged 'alliance' of the 'Eusebians' and the Melitians, for which no contemporary evidence exists outside Athanasius' polemic, a connection between Arius and at least Eusebius of Nicomedia is readily confirmed by their exchange of letters before Nicaea. After Alexander's death, Athanasius asserts that Eusebius 'first sent to me, urging me to receive *tous peri Areion*, and he threatened me verbally (*agraphōs*), while in his writings he made a request. When I refused... he caused the Emperor also, the blessed Constantine, to write to me, threatening me, if I should not receive *tous peri Areion*' (*Apologia Contra Arianos* 59; Opitz (1938*b*) 139, 20–140, 3). However, despite the willingness of many scholars to accept this claim that Eusebius secretly threatened Athanasius and caused Constantine to oppose him, no evidence exists to substantiate

[8] It has been argued (Camplani (1989) 262–82) that there was a Melitian resurgence in Upper Egypt in the 360s and 370s, reflected in this passage from the *Encyclical Letter to Egypt and Libya* and in the re-emergence of polemic against the Melitians in Athanasius' *Festal Letters* during this period. Thus *Festal Letter* XXXVII, probably written in 364, also condemns 'the Arians and their parasites the Melitians' (trans. from the Coptic by Brakke (2001) 477), and there is a similar attack upon the association of 'Arians' and Melitians in *Festal Letter* XLI for AD 369 (trans. in Brakke (1998) 474–8).

either assertion.[9] Athanasius presents Eusebius' patronage of Arius and his companions in this passage within his wider construction of the 'Eusebians', who compose letters and mislead the emperor in order to favour their 'heresy'. Once again, it is difficult to distinguish possible fact from polemical rhetoric, a dilemma that becomes still more acute when we turn to Athanasius' famous accounts of Arius' death.

Athanasius first described the death of Arius in the *De Morte Arii* of *c.*339–46, and then again in slightly modified form in the *Encyclical Letter* of 356.[10] According to his narrative, 'Arius was summoned by the emperor Constantine through the zeal (*spoudēs*) of the Eusebians' (*De Morte Arii* 2; Opitz (1940*a*) 179, 1–2; see also *Encyclical Letter* 18) to come to the imperial court and present his statement of faith. Arius did so, concealing his impiety and feigning to hold the Scriptural truth, and when he swore that this was the theology that he had always held, Constantine accepted Arius as orthodox, warning him that God would judge him, if he had sworn falsely.[11] Triumphant, the 'Eusebians' then demanded that Arius be admitted into the church in Constantinople, but they were opposed by Alexander, the bishop of that city. 'The Eusebians threatened that "just as against your [Alexander's] wishes we have caused him to be summoned by the emperor, thus tomorrow, even if it shall happen against your judgement, Arius shall be admitted to communion with us in this church"' (*De Morte Arii* 2; Opitz (1940*a*) 179, 11–14).[12] Alexander, however, prayed

[9] Both Barnes (1981) 231 and Hanson (1988*b*) 258 repeat Athanasius' presentation of these events as entirely historical, but the charge that Eusebius threatened him *agraphōs* obviously cannot be proven. Constantine certainly did write to Athanasius demanding that he admit Arius back into communion (part of this letter is quoted in *Apologia Contra Arianos* 59), but here as elsewhere the document that Athanasius cites provides no support for his narrative interpretation of an alleged 'Eusebian' role.

[10] See Martin (1989) 320–33.

[11] The precise content of Constantine's 'speech' varies between Athanasius' two accounts (*De Morte Arii* 2; *Encyclical Letter* 18), a fact which heightens the probability that Constantine's words (and indeed all the 'quotations' attributed to the participants in these events) were composed by Athanasius himself to fit the tone of his own presentation.

[12] Neither this alleged 'Eusebian' speech, nor Alexander's prayer that God must 'behold the words of the Eusebians, and not give Your inheritance into destruction and disgrace' (*De Morte Arii* 3; Opitz (1940*a*) 179, 20–1), appear in the *Encyclical Letter.*

that no heretic should be permitted to share communion with the pious, and God punished the perjury and impiety of Arius. Before the latter could enter the church, he came to a privy, and there ' "falling headlong he burst asunder [Acts 1:18]"... [and] he was deprived of both communion and his life' (*De Morte Arii* 3; Opitz (1940*a*) 179, 26–8; see also *Encyclical Letter* 19).

The uncertain veracity of this Athanasian account has long been recognized, particularly the physical description of Arius' death which is explicitly modelled on the Scriptural fate of Judas. But the involvement of the 'Eusebians' in these events has too rarely been questioned.[13] Athanasius' presentation of this 'Eusebian' role follows the same polemical model as Eusebius' alleged demand for Arius' restoration in the *Apologia Contra Arianos* above. Constantine's acceptance of Arius as orthodox is attributed once more to the 'zeal' of the 'Eusebians', and their threats and impiety are contrasted to the prayers and piety of the bishop Alexander. Athanasius' account of Arius' death, like his presentation of Eusebius' support for Arius in life, thus must be understood against the background of Athanasius' wider construction of the 'Eusebians' and their patronage of the 'Arian heresy'.

Arius himself is only one of the men whom the 'Eusebians' are alleged to have patronized for the sake of their 'impiety'. In the previous chapter, I listed in full the roster of those who according to Athanasius 'have been promoted by the Eusebians for advocating this Christ-fighting heresy' (*Encyclical Letter* 7; Tetz (1996) 46, 6–7). That list, as we saw, includes a number of men whose known theological positions differed sharply from one another, such as Secundus of Ptolemais, Acacius of Caesarea, and Basil of Ancyra. The 'Eusebian patronage' that all these men are said to have received is once again a product of Athanasius' presentation of his foes as a collective 'Arian party'. The degree of distortion possible in that presentation is clearly visible in the particular emphasis that Athanasius places upon the two men whom he accuses the 'Arians' of

[13] Thus Hanson (1988*b*) acknowledges that the *De Morte Arii* 'cannot be regarded as historically trustworthy' (265), yet accepts at face value the involvement of 'the Eusebian bishops' in the events surrounding Arius' death (264). See also Barnes (1993) 127. The later church historians Rufinus (X.13), Socrates (I.37–8), Sozomen (II.29), and Theodoret (I.13–14) all cite Athanasius' own description of Arius' death.

having imposed into his own see of Alexandria, first Gregory and then George.

In Part II we traced Athanasius' condemnation of the installation of Gregory in his *Epistula Encyclica* of 339, a condemnation subsequently taken up by Julius of Rome and by the Western Council of Serdica. Athanasius accused the 'Eusebians' of patronising Gregory's ordination, which he declared to be invalid, and which he attributed not to legitimate bishops but to secular power. In the *Historia Arianorum* Athanasius returns to this theme, asserting again that Gregory 'had not received his ordination according to ecclesiastical canon, nor had been called to be a bishop by apostolical tradition, but had been sent out from court (*ek palatiou*) with military power and pomp, as one entrusted with secular government' (14; Opitz (1940*a*) 189, 30–2). Yet by the time of this later work, one significant change has taken place in Athanasius' polemical presentation. In 339, although Gregory came 'from court', it was the 'Eusebians' who were held directly responsible for his imposition into Alexandria. In the *Historia Arianorum*, the emperor Constantius has become the primary patron of Gregory,[14] and in turn of George. For first the impious emperor 'sent Gregory from Cappadocia to Alexandria (74)...and now again George, a certain Cappadocian who was contractor of stores at Constantinople and having embezzled everything for this reason had to flee, he commanded to enter Alexandria with military pomp and with the authority of the general' (75; Opitz (1940*a*) 224, 23–4; 224, 29–225, 3).

Athanasius' repeated insistence that Gregory and George were appointed and imposed upon Alexandria through external patronage and secular power is of course tendentious. Athanasius at no stage acknowledges that both his rivals could indeed claim legitimate ordination through formally sanctioned Church councils, just as he never acknowledges the authority of those councils which ordered his own deposition.[15] On the contrary, by thus condemning

[14] The role of the 'Eusebians' in Gregory's ordination is not entirely omitted in the *Historia Arianorum*, for Athanasius 'quotes' the alleged request of the 'Arians' to Constantius that he 'send Gregory as bishop to Alexandria, for he is able to strengthen our heresy' (9; Opitz (1940*a*) 188, 17–19). But the role of these 'Arians' is now explicitly subordinated to the involvement of the emperor himself (see below).

[15] Barnes (1993) 128.

his rivals and asserting their dependence upon external power, Athanasius denies their claim to the title of 'bishop', and so maintains his own authority and legitimacy as the true holder of the see of Alexandria. Yet the shift in Athanasius' presentation of the source of the 'patronage' that he alleges Gregory and George received is striking. In the *Epistula Encyclica* of 339, Athanasius denounced Gregory as 'Arian' and the nominee of the 'Eusebians'. It was to them that he attributed Gregory's ordination, in which 'the most pious Emperor Constantius' (5; Opitz (1940*a*) 174, 21) played no role. But in the *Historia Arianorum* of 357, the central theme is rather the denunciation of Constantius as the 'precursor of the Antichrist'. Athanasius therefore reinterprets the earlier career of Gregory, as well as the ordination of his contemporary opponent George, in the light of this new imperial role. I will return to Athanasius' emphasis upon the secular dependence of the 'Arians' and the drastic transformation in his public attitude towards Constantius later in this chapter. Here what should be recognized is that Athanasius' presentation of the 'patronage' of his foes has not only been distorted by his construction of their 'uncanonical' actions, but has also again been shaped according to the context and purposes of his different works.

The argument of the preceding pages has not been intended to deny the importance of patronage within the fourth-century Church, or to suggest that Eusebius of Nicomedia, George of Alexandria, or indeed Athanasius himself did not appoint or ordain bishops and other clergy who shared similar theological beliefs to their own.[16] However, even to attempt to reconstruct such a patronage network from Athanasius' presentation of the 'Eusebians' is impossible, unless we first recognize the nature of the polemical construction upon which that presentation is founded. All the Athanasian accounts of 'Eusebian' benefaction towards fellow 'Arians' or Melitians serve

[16] Among the more important instances of ecclesiastical patronage attributed to the 'Eusebians' are the ordination of Basil of Ancyra to replace Marcellus (Athanasius, *Encyclical Letter* 7; Socrates, I.35; Sozomen, II.33), of Ulfila the 'Apostle to the Goths' (Philostorgius, II.5; see Barnes (1990) and Sivan (1996)), and of Eusebius of Emesa who was the original choice to replace Athanasius in 339 but who declined that role (Socrates, II.9; Sozomen, III.6; and see Wiles (1989*a*) 269–70). Yet the existence of patronage networks should not be taken to imply that 'patrons' and 'clients' must share the same theology.

Athanasius' polemic by discrediting his opponents, particularly Gregory and George, his rivals for the see of Alexandria. The interpretation offered for each individual episode is determined by the motives that inspired that particular Athanasian work, but those interpretations are in turn shaped by the underlying construction of a single 'Arian party' that runs throughout Athanasius' writings. Moreover, in the polarized polemic of Athanasius the 'patronage' of the 'Eusebians' is inseparable from their 'persecution' of himself and of the other 'true' bishops whom their own nominees would replace. From the Council of Nicaea onwards, the 'Eusebians' 'began to plot against the bishops who spoke against them, and instead of these men to appoint into the churches men of their own heresy' (*De Synodis* 21; Opitz (1941) 247, 18–19).

There seems little need to repeat here Athanasius' presentation of the 'Eusebians' as the cause of his own exile, first in 335 and then again in 339, that we examined in detail in Part II. Just as he had in his earlier works, so in his later apologetic writings Athanasius continued to denounce the accusations that he had faced in those years as the product of an 'Arian conspiracy'. Indeed, Athanasius now extended that earlier denunciation of his original condemnation to refute the new charges that were levelled against him in the 350s. 'If the same men who fabricated the former [charges] also devised these latter [charges], how is it not reasonably shown from the former that the latter also have been fabricated?' (*Apologia ad Constantium* 2; Szymusiak (1987) 88, 7–9). This continuity of Athanasius' polemic is for our present purposes more significant than the specific content of those later charges, which focused primarily upon treason to the emperor (in the *Apologia ad Constantium*) and cowardice (the *Apologia de Fuga*).[17] The accusers of Athanasius are still the 'same men' and their slanders are still motivated by the desire to spread their 'impiety',[18] while Athanasius himself thus remains in turn the 'champion of orthodoxy' against whom the 'heretics' conspire.

[17] See Barnes (1993) 113–26.

[18] 'The absence of the shepherd offers the wolves an opportunity to attack the flock. This was what the Arians and all the other heretics desired, that during our absence they might find an opportunity to deceive the people into impiety' (*Apologia ad Constantium* 26; Szymusiak (1987) 144, 10–13). See ibid. 13; *Apologia de Fuga* 2.

Alongside this continuity, however, an important further dimension to Athanasius' construction of the 'Eusebians' develops within his later polemical works. For Athanasius now begins to present himself as only one of a number of bishops who suffered under the 'persecution' of his foes. In the earliest writings of his first and second exile, of which the *Apologia Contra Arianos* narrative is the most extensive, Athanasius focuses almost exclusively upon his own suffering as the victim of a 'Eusebian conspiracy'. Only gradually does the concept of a wider 'Arian purge' against the 'orthodox' take shape in his writings. The Alexandrian *Encyclical Letter* of 338 speaks of how 'the Eusebians... conspire against many bishops, and thus also against Athanasius' (*Apologia Contra Arianos* 11; Opitz (1938*a*) 96, 20–2), but the Egyptian bishops provide no names for Athanasius' fellow victims. Julius of Rome likewise defends Athanasius alongside 'many other bishops also from Thrace, from Coele-Syria, from Phoenicia and Palestine' (*Apologia Contra Arianos* 33; Opitz (1938*a*) 111, 11–12), but the sole fellow-exile specifically identified is Marcellus of Ancyra. The *Encyclical Letter* of Western Serdica in 343 in turn adds just the name of Asclepas of Gaza to Athanasius and Marcellus as a fellow alleged victim of the 'Eusebians'. It was only in the later 350s, as he reinterpreted the decades that followed the Council of Nicaea in the light of contemporary events and his own developing construction of the 'Arian Controversy', that Athanasius began to present in full his highly influential vision of a systematic 'Arian purge' against the 'orthodox', led, inevitably, by the 'Eusebians'.

The earliest Athanasian statement of such a general 'purge' occurs in the *Apologia de Fuga* of 357, in which Athanasius for the first time presents an extensive enumeration of the alleged victims of this 'Arian conspiracy':

> Where is there a church that does not now lament because of their plots against her bishop? Antioch [is mourning] for the orthodox confessor Eustathius; Balanae for the most admirable Euphration; Paltus and Antaradus for Kymatius and Carterius; Adrianople for the lover of Christ Eutropius and his successor Lucius, who many times was loaded with chains by them and thus perished. Ancyra [mourns] for Marcellus, Beroea for Cyrus, Gaza for Asclepas. For after insulting these men many times previously, the treacherous ones (*hoi dolioi*) have caused them to be exiled. But Theodulus and Olympius, bishops of Thrace, and ourselves and our presbyters, they

caused to be sought in such a manner that, if we were found, we should suffer capital punishment... for having pursued and found Paul, bishop of Constantinople, they caused him to be openly strangled at a place called Cucusus in Cappadocia. (3; Szymusiak (1987) 182, 10–23; 184, 27–30)

The *Apologia de Fuga* narrative gives no explanation for the circumstances in which these individual bishops were banished or killed, beyond the repeated emphasis that all their fates were the product of the intrigues of the 'Arians'. For such detail, we must look instead to the *Historia Arianorum*, written later in the same year of 357.

Eustathius was bishop of Antioch, a confessor and pious in the faith. Because he was very zealous on behalf of the truth and hated the Arian heresy, and because he would not receive those who held its doctrines, he was falsely accused before the Emperor Constantine, and a pretext invented that he had insulted his mother [Helena]. Immediately he was banished... and after the bishop was exiled, then those whom he would not admit into the clergy because of their impiety were not only received into the Church, but indeed the majority were even appointed to be bishops, so that they might have accomplices in their impiety. Among these was Leontius the eunuch, now of Antioch, and his predecessor Stephen, George of Laodicea, and Theodosius who was of Tripolis, Eudoxius of Germanicia, and Eustathius now of Sebasteia. (4; Opitz (1940*a*) 184, 31–185, 9)

Did they therefore stop with these? No. For Eutropius, who was bishop of Adrianople, a good man and excellent in all respects, since he had many times convicted Eusebius and advised those who came that way not to be persuaded by Eusebius' impious words, he suffered the same fate as Eustathius, and was cast out of his city and his Church... Euphration of Balanae, Kymatius of Paltus, Carterius of Antaradus, Asclepas of Gaza, Cyrus of Beroea in Syria, Diodore of Asia, Domnion of Sirmium, and Hellanicus of Tripolis were only known to hate the heresy. Some of them on one pretext or another, some without any, they removed by imperial letters and expelled from their cities, and they appointed others instead of them whom they knew to be impious into their churches. (5; Opitz (1940*a*) 185, 10–19)

Concerning Marcellus, the bishop of Galatia, it is perhaps superfluous to speak, for all men know how the Eusebians, who had been first accused of impiety by him, brought a counter-accusation against him, and themselves caused the old man to be banished. He went to Rome, and there made his defence, and at their request, he gave a written declaration of his faith, which the Council of Serdica also approved. But the Eusebians did not defend themselves, nor when they were convicted of impiety out of their own writings were they put to shame, but rather acted more boldly against all. (6; Opitz (1940*a*) 186, 1–7)

I suppose no one is ignorant concerning Paul, bishop of Constantinople . . . for a pretext was fabricated against him also. Macedonius his accuser, who has now become bishop in his stead (we were present ourselves at the accusation) held communion with him and was a presbyter under Paul himself.[19] And yet when Eusebius with an envious eye (*epōphthalmia*) wished to seize upon the bishopric of that city (for he had been translated in the same manner from Berytus to Nicomedia),[20] the pretext was revived against Paul; and they did not give up their plot, but persisted in falsely accusing [him]. He was banished first into Pontus by Constantine, and a second time by Constantius . . . and a fourth time he was banished to Cucusus in Cappadocia, near the deserts of Mount Taurus; where, as those who were with him have declared, he died by strangulation at their hands.[21] (7; Opitz (1940*a*) 186, 9–20)

It is difficult to exaggerate the influence that these Athanasian passages have exerted upon later reconstructions of the period following the Council of Nicaea. Athanasius represents every bishop known to have been exiled or otherwise condemned in the years after 325 as the victims of a single persecution, for whatever the varied charges upon which these men were individually condemned, their true 'crime' was their hatred of the 'Arian heresy'. The 'Eusebians' themselves are only invoked once, in reference to the exile of Marcellus, but Eusebius of Nicomedia appears twice elsewhere, and

[19] Barnes (1993) 216 has proposed that this complex sentence should be rendered: 'Macedonius, the one who accused him and who is now the present bishop in his place, when we were present, communicated with him on the occasion of the accusation and was a priest under Paul'. This would suggest that Macedonius actually supported Paul when he was first accused, and only attacked him at a later time.

[20] The 'envious eye' that Eusebius cast upon the sees of others in Alexander's *Encyclical Letter* in 324 and the Alexandrian *Encyclical Letter* of 338 is here invoked by Athanasius himself.

[21] For a possible reconstruction of the difficult career of Paul of Constantinople, see Barnes (1993), Appendix 8 (212–17), significantly revising the older model of Telfer (1950). Barnes plausibly argues that the reference to Paul first being exiled by Constantine is a manuscript error for Constantius (215). However, I disagree with his statement that the account of Paul quoted in the passage here 'interrupts . . . both logically and chronologically' (128) the structure of the *Historia Arianorum*, for in my opinion the inclusion of Paul is entirely consistent with Athanasius' overall presentation of an 'Arian purge'.

throughout Athanasius' presentation all those who have suffered are the victims of one and the same 'Arian party'. This is the 'anti-Nicene purge' that features so prominently in the fifth-century ecclesiastical historians,[22] and in modern scholarship. Barnes writes that 'the Arian party, cowed and defeated in 325, suddenly recovered its power two years later and proceeded to dislodge its main opponents from their sees'.[23] Hanson, it is true, rejects the idea of 'a systematic campaign by the Eusebian party against known opponents of Arianism'.[24] Yet he can still declare that we know that 'a number of bishops were deposed between 328 and 336 for various reasons, and that Eusebius of Nicomedia or some of his party had a hand in most, or all, of these depositions. They were perhaps controlling events, but not controlling them in the interests of forwarding Arianism'.[25] A similar judgement has now also been expressed by Lewis Ayres.[26] Ayres, like Hanson, denies Athanasius' fundamental premise, that those he condemned were 'Arian', but he nevertheless continues to endorse Athanasius' presentation of the alleged conspiracy of a 'Eusebian party'.

Athanasius' presentation of this 'anti-Nicene purge', although at first sight impressive, on closer examination raises a number of serious questions. This is especially true, as has been emphasized by Thomas Elliott,[27] for the final decade of the reign of Constantine (327–37), in which period the power of Eusebius of Nicomedia is commonly assumed to have been at its peak. Of the individuals named by Athanasius whose exile can be dated, only the depositions of Eustathius of Antioch and Asclepas of Gaza in 327,[28] Athanasius himself in 335, and Marcellus of Ancyra in 336 can be placed with confidence within these years. The date of the first exile of Paul of Constantinople is very uncertain,[29] while a number of the other bishops named by Athanasius appear to have been exiled at various

[22] See Socrates, I.23–4, 27–38, II.2–3, 6–7; Sozomen, I.18–23, 25, 28, 33, II.1–7, III.7; Theodoret, 1.20–1, 1.24–9, 1.31, 2.2–5.

[23] Barnes (1981) 225.

[24] Hanson (1988*b*) 279.

[25] Ibid. 279.

[26] See Ayres (2004*b*) 105–6.

[27] Elliott (1992), (1996) 245–53.

[28] See below.

[29] See Barnes (1993) 215, who places Paul's first exile in 337 under Constantius, and Telfer (1950) 70–7, who favours 336, arguing that Paul was condemned by the same council that deposed Marcellus.

times during the reign of Constantius. Even if those individuals of whom nothing definite is known (Euphration, the Cymatii, Carterius, and Cyrus)[30] are added to the four men above, this still leaves only 'a suspiciously small number of victims for the Arians in a ten-year period',[31] particularly for a decade in which the 'Eusebians' are alleged to have been especially active. Moreover, to ascribe the exile of all of these bishops under both Constantine and Constantius to a single 'Arian conspiracy', led by Eusebius of Nicomedia, is extremely tendentious. Many of those whom Athanasius brings forward are nothing more than names, but the distortions inherent in his presentation can be demonstrated even by a very brief analysis of the four best known 'victims' of this so-called 'Arian purge': Eustathius and Asclepas, Athanasius himself, and Marcellus.

The chronology and context of the exile of Eustathius of Antioch has been the subject of much scholarly debate. The date of 327 that I have adopted here accepts the conclusion of Barnes[32] (who was in turn adapting the earlier argument of Chadwick)[33] that Eustathius was exiled not at the traditional date of 330–1,[34] but at the same time as Asclepas of Gaza, who is reported to have been condemned seventeen years before the Council of Serdica in 343.[35] The actual

[30] Both Barnes (1978) 60 and Elliott (1992) 178 suggest that these five bishops may have been exiled by the same council that deposed Eustathius and Asclepas.

[31] Elliott (1992) 178.

[32] Barnes (1978) 60.

[33] Chadwick (1948).

[34] This traditional date is still upheld by Hanson (1984), (1988*b*) 209–11, but ultimately rests almost entirely on the unanimous assertion of the fifth-century ecclesiastical historians (Socrates, I.23–4; Sozomen, II.16–19; Theodoret, I.21; Philostorgius, II.7) that Eustathius was condemned after Eusebius of Nicomedia returned from exile in 327/8. In fact, it would seem that these narratives have been influenced by Athanasius' construction of Eusebius, and that it was only because they assumed that Eustathius' exile must have been caused by Eusebius of Nicomedia that the fifth-century historians placed this episode after his return (an assumption shared by Hanson (1984) 170–1). Burgess ((1999) 191–6, (2000) 153–4) has again argued that Eustathius was exiled after Eusebius' return, but places that exile in late 328 on the evidence of his own reconstruction of a lost Greek continuation of Eusebius of Caesarea's *Chronicle*, completed in Antioch in 350. However, Woods (2001) 902 has observed that the sources Burgess cites show a repeated pattern for post-dating events by 2 years in the period 327–37 (as Burgess himself notes, (1999) 202, this is even true of the Council of Nicaea). Thus his evidence actually supports a date for Eustathius' exile of 326/7, before Eusebius of Nicomedia's restoration.

charges that were levelled against Eustathius remain difficult to define,[36] but apparently included causing disturbances in Antioch (Eusebius of Caesarea, *Vita Constantini* III.59–62),[37] 'Sabellian' heresy (Socrates, I.24),[38] and (as in the *Historia Arianorum* above) insulting Helena the mother of Constantine, presumably at the time of the latter's famous journey to the Holy Land, which has also now been dated to 327.[39] The significance of this earlier date, as Chadwick has emphasized, is that contrary to the fifth-century ecclesiastical historians, Eustathius was therefore condemned *before* Eusebius of Nicomedia returned from his own exile in early 328.[40] Whereas Chadwick was prepared to argue that the fate of Eustathius was nevertheless the work of 'the Eusebian party, although their leaders were still in exile',[41] no evidence outside the polemic of

[35] This statement was made in the *Encyclical Letter* of the eastern bishops at Serdica. The same letter also declares that Asclepas was condemned by a council at Antioch that apparently met under the presidency of Eusebius of Caesarea, which would seem impossible unless Eustathius had already been deposed, or was deposed by that same council (Chadwick (1948) 31–2). However, Chadwick dated the Council of Serdica to 342, hence his proposed date for Eustathius' exile of 326, whereas I, like Barnes, would place that Council in 343. In either case, it should be noted that we have no certain evidence for the causes of Asclepas' own exile (Burgess (2000) 158–60).

[36] Some of the charges alleged to have been brought against Eustathius are impossible to verify, notably the claim of Theodoret (on whose presentation of Eustathius see Allen (1990) 273–5) that the 'Eusebians' bribed a prostitute to testify against the bishop of Antioch (I.21). Such an accusation is a *topos* of hagiography, and although Sellers (1928) accepted the attribution of this charge to 'the vile intrigues of the Eusebian party' (47), it was rightly rejected by Chadwick (1948) 28.

[37] Chadwick (1948) 29–30 argues that the disturbances described in the *Vita Constantini* occurred after Eustathius' deposition, and it is true that the only explicit reference to Eustathius in this section of that work occurs in the *kephalaion* (chapter heading) of III.59, which was added by a later editor. But the account of Eusebius would suggest that these disturbances occurred during Eustathius' episcopate (possibly connected with his enforced exclusion of alleged 'Arians' from the churches as described by Athanasius), and were one of the grounds for his dismissal (see Sellers (1928) 42–5, Elliott (1992) 174–7).

[38] According to Socrates, George of Laodicea's lost *Panegyric* on Eusebius of Emesa included the claim that Eustathius was accused of Sabellianism by Cyrus of Beroea. Socrates himself rejected this account, on the grounds that Cyrus too was later deposed on exactly that charge, but such an accusation is not impossible. Eustathius' theology does bear certain similarities to that of Marcellus (see Hanson (1988*b*) 208–35), who was indeed seen as Sabellian by many bishops in the east.

[39] See Hunt (1982) 35; Drijvers (1992) 62–3.

[40] Chadwick (1948) 30.

Athanasius suggests that such a 'party' played any role in Eustathius' fall. Nor can we justify the conclusion of Hanson that the charges in question are irrelevant, for while 'the immediate reason or reasons for Eustathius' deposition are difficult to determine . . . the real motive was of course his championing of the Nicene formula and his opposition to those who disliked it'.[42]

The condemnations of Athanasius in 335 and Marcellus in 336 did unquestionably occur after Eusebius had returned to Nicomedia and been reconciled with Constantine. But in these instances too it is far from self-evident that either bishop was condemned through an 'Arian conspiracy'. The charges against Athanasius himself, as I have already emphasized in Chapter 3, were concerned purely with his behaviour in Egypt not theology, and his conviction at Tyre was not the verdict of a small 'heretical faction', but of a considerable body of eastern bishops. Marcellus of Ancyra, the only one of the individuals named by Athanasius who was explicitly condemned on theological grounds, was also convicted by a substantial Council, held at Constantinople in 336. In the *Historia Arianorum*, Athanasius still defends Marcellus as an 'orthodox champion',[43] and it is striking that it is here alone that Athanasius directly invokes the 'Eusebians' as the cause of Marcellus' fall. Yet Athanasius' polemic also contains at least one manifest distortion, in his assertion that the men whom Marcellus accused of heresy did not defend themselves, for both Asterius and Eusebius of Caesarea wrote to refute those accusations. I would suggest that the reputation for heresy that Marcellus acquired during this period first in the east and eventually in the west, although almost certainly exaggerated, provides an adequate explanation for his exile without requiring the involvement of an 'Arian conspiracy'.[44]

There is enough evidence even within this much abbreviated survey to question Athanasius' presentation both of the individual bishops whose exile he attributes to the 'Eusebians', and of the wider

[41] Ibid. 35. More recently, Behr (2004), who like Chadwick recognizes Eusebius of Nicomedia's absence at the time of Eustathius' exile, simply restates the traditional interpretation of the 'purge', but attributes the depositions of the supporters of Nicaea instead to 'the work of Eusebius of Caesarea' (131).

[42] Hanson (1988*b*) 210–11.

[43] On the relationship between Athanasius and Marcellus, see Lienhard (1993).

[44] For the controversial figure of Marcellus of Ancyra see Seibt (1994), Lienhard (1999), and Parvis (2006).

'Arian purge' that he constructs in the period after Nicaea. Rather than merely dismiss Athanasius' presentation out of hand, however, it is important to consider once more the nature of that polemical construction. Athanasius' conception of a single 'Arian conspiracy' against every 'orthodox' bishop was the logical culmination of his recurring assertion that the attacks upon himself were attacks upon the Church as a whole. Just as Athanasius from 338 onwards reinterprets the events preceding the Council of Tyre according to the image of the 'Eusebians' that was first expressed at the Council itself, so in the later passages quoted above Athanasius reinterprets the events of previous decades according to the polemical model of an 'Arian purge' that only develops within his works in the 350s. In the *Apologia Contra Arianos* and *Epistula Encyclica*, Athanasius' presentation of his original condemnation served to vindicate his own innocence and legitimacy to the audiences which those works addressed in the late 330s and early 340s. The interpretation of an 'Arian purge' that Athanasius now imposes upon that earlier period, particularly in the *Historia Arianorum*, must likewise be understood as a product of the construction of himself and of his foes that Athanasius wished to present to his contemporaries in the late 350s.

The *Historia Arianorum*, which takes up the account of the *Apologia Contra Arianos* from the Council of Jerusalem that restored Arius in 335, reinterprets a number of episodes from the 330s and 340s in the light of Athanasius' new emphasis that he was only one victim of a wider 'Arian purge'. The Council of Jerusalem itself is cited as confirmation of the 'Arianism' of his foes, as it was in *Apologia Contra Arianos* 84–5. But now those 'Arians' not only conspired against Athanasius for the sake of their 'heresy', but 'they also conspired thus against other bishops, fabricating pretexts against them likewise' (*Historia Arianorum* 1; Opitz (1940*a*) 183, 12–13). The letter of Constantine II approving Athanasius' return from exile in 337 is quoted (as in *Apologia Contra Arianos* 87), but now that letter is presented as one of many, for the sons of Constantine are said to have written to the churches of all the exiles (*Historia Arianorum* 8). And whereas in the *Apologia Contra Arianos* Athanasius' account passes directly from the Council of Serdica to Constantius' letters inviting him to return home, in the *Historia Arianorum* several additional paragraphs are inserted describing a 'purge' of the 'orthodox' in the aftermath of the council. The victims include the two eastern bishops who had joined the Western Council at Serdica (18), and the Thracian bishops Lucius of Adrianople, Olympius of Aeni, and Theodulus of Trajanople. 'This the Eusebians did first, and the Emperor Constantius wrote [against the exiled bishops], and second these men revived [the accusation] ... being instructed in such proceedings by the Eusebians and as heirs (*klēronomoi*) of their impiety and purpose' (19; Opitz (1940*a*) 192, 21–2; 25–6).

These discrepancies between the Athanasian narratives of the *Apologia Contra Arianos* and the *Historia Arianorum* could be explained by a difference in purpose, for the earlier apologetic was specifically composed in defence of Athanasius himself and might therefore have omitted wider details. Another explanation might be Athanasius' own increased knowledge of the events that he describes. Yet the systematic reinterpretation of these previous episodes in the *Historia Arianorum* serves a recognisable polemical function in Athanasius' presentation of his own position at the time he composed this later work. The construction of his foes remains consistent, for the restoration of Arius and the persecution that followed the Council of Serdica are still the products of a single 'conspiracy', in which the present 'Arians' merely complete the work begun by their 'Eusebian' teachers. But within that persecution Athanasius is now only one among many victims, and the false charges that he alleges were levelled against the other exiles are brought forward to vindicate his own innocence, and vice versa.

> Granted that they have accused Athanasius; yet what have the other bishops done? What pretexts do they have in their case? What dead Arsenius has been found there? What presbyter Macarius or broken chalice is there among them? What Melitian is there to play the hypocrite? But as it seems from these proceedings that the charges which they have brought against Athanasius are shown to be false; so from their charges against Athanasius, it is clear that their proceedings against those men are fabricated also. (*Historia Arianorum* 3 (Opitz (1940*a*) 184, 14–18); see also *Apologia de Fuga* 9)

Athanasius here reasserts once more that he was innocent of the charges on which he was originally condemned in 335, but his presentation of a widespread 'Arian purge' also vindicates Athanasius' position within the Church of the later 350s in which he now wrote. The 'purge' that Athanasius constructs is not confined to previous years, but is an ongoing 'persecution', and in the *Apologia de Fuga* and the *Historia Arianorum* Athanasius thus not only reinterprets the past, but also represents contemporary events as the continuation of the same 'conspiracy'. The *Apologia de Fuga* provides only a brief outline of the persecution of the western bishops Liberius of Rome and Ossius of Cordova in 353–7, but already attributes these outrages to the same 'Arian party' who caused the exile of the 'orthodox' bishops after Nicaea (*Apologia de Fuga* 3–5). The *Historia Arianorum* then expands upon the persecution of these western bishops in detail (33–45), and explicitly proclaims the continuity of the 'Arian conspiracy' under which they, Athanasius himself, and the earlier exiles all suffered.

> Who that saw when Liberius bishop of Rome was banished, and when the great Ossius, the father of bishops, suffered these things, or who saw so many bishops from Spain and from other regions exiled, does not perceive, however little sense he might possess, that the pretexts against Athanasius and the rest were false, and altogether mere calumny? . . . For not because of charges did these conspiracies take place, nor because of any accusation was each banished, but it was an insurrection of impiety against piety, and zeal on behalf of the Arian heresy. (46; Opitz (1940*b*) 210, 4–7; 12–14)

Two important conclusions can be drawn from this analysis of Athanasius' vision of an 'Arian purge' after Nicaea and his construction of the alleged role of the 'Eusebians' in those events. The first is to recognize the degree of distortion inherent in Athanasius' highly influential representation of every bishop exiled in this period as the victim of a single 'Arian conspiracy'. This interpretation is itself a polemical retrojection onto the events of the 330s and 340s of a concept that Athanasius only developed after 356. What evidence exists for the fates of those exiled bishops whom we are able to identify suggests that their individual depositions were neither for opposition to 'Arianism' nor the work of a specific 'party'. Indeed, many of the men named by Athanasius in the *Apologia de Fuga* and the *Historia Arianorum* as victims of this 'purge' do not even appear in his writings from the years in which they were banished. This could simply reflect the benefit of hindsight, but through his emphasis in these later works upon the 'Eusebians' as the cause not just of his own original condemnation but of a systematic 'Arian purge', Athanasius greatly reinforces his justification of his own position in both past and present. He reaffirms his innocence against the verdict of 335 and his emphasis that his condemnation at Tyre represented an attack upon the wider Church, and he forges a connection between the 'Eusebians' whom he holds responsible for those events and the 'Arians' who now exile his supporters both in Egypt and in the west.

The second conclusion derives from the first. By presenting the eastern bishops expelled in the 330s and 340s and the western exiles of the 350s as victims of the same 'Arian conspiracy', Athanasius reduces the entire period from the Council of Nicaea to his own third exile to a single ongoing conflict. To quote again from the passage inserted into Athanasius' *Encyclical Letter to Egypt and Libya* in 361:

> For no other reason than for the sake of their own impious heresy they have plotted against us and against all the orthodox bishops from the beginning. For behold, that which was intended long ago by the Eusebians has now come to pass, and they have caused the churches to be snatched away from us, they have banished the bishops and presbyters not in communion with themselves, as they wished, and the people who withdrew from them they have shut out of the churches, which they have handed over to the Arians who were condemned so long ago. (22; Tetz (1996) 63, 18–24)

Athanasius' presentation of the 'Arian purge' against the 'orthodox', and indeed his entire construction of the 'Eusebians', is inseparable from his conception of a monolithic 'Arian Controversy'. As I have emphasized throughout this monograph, at the heart of Athanasius' polemic lies the polarization of 'Arian' and 'orthodox'. It is through the imposition of that polarization upon the events that he describes that Athanasius constructs his interpretation of the 'Eusebians' and their role in fourth-century ecclesiastical politics.

CHURCH AND STATE: 'ARIANS', OFFICIALS, AND EMPERORS

Much has been written on the complex subject of Athanasius' attitude towards secular power and the relationship of the Church to the State.[45] The *Historia Arianorum* in particular expresses a strong emphasis on the separation of the Church from secular and imperial influence,[46] and in his polemic Athanasius repeatedly condemns the 'Arians' for their alleged dependence upon secular aid. Yet as has also long been recognized, Athanasius is far from consistent on this theme. Throughout his career, he frequently appealed to and welcomed imperial assistance on his own behalf,[47] and as Barnes rightly observed, '[Athanasius'] constant complaint that the emperor interferes in the affairs of the church is not in fact directed against interference as such, but against imperial actions of which he disapproves'.[48] It is in the context of this highly relative Athanasian attitude to the State that we must assess his construction of the 'Eusebians' as allied with, and dependent upon, secular power.

Athanasius' account of the Council of Tyre and its aftermath, which we considered in detail in Chapter 3, reflects all the characteristic elements of this aspect of his polemic, and also the tensions within his presentation of secular involvement in Church affairs. Throughout the *Apologia Contra Arianos* narrative and the Alexandrian *Encyclical Letter* of 338, the 'Eusebians' are repeatedly denounced for securing the condemnation of Athanasius through the aid of representatives of the State. The Mareotis Commission is said

[45] Setton (1941) 71–88, Nordberg (1964), Barnard (1974*a*), and Barnes (1993), esp. 165–75.

[46] The most famous statement of this theme of separation actually occurs in the letter of Ossius of Cordova quoted by Athanasius, in which that bishop warns the Emperor Constantius ' "Do not intrude yourself into ecclesiastical affairs, and do not give commands to us concerning them . . . God has put into your hands the kingdom; to us He has entrusted the affairs of His Church" ' (*Historia Arianorum* 44; Opitz (1940*b*) 208, 18–20). The authenticity of this letter has been questioned, notably by Klein (1977) 132–4 and (1982) 1002–9, and while I would reject his conclusion that this text is not the work of Ossius but of Athanasius, it is certainly true that Athanasius himself expresses precisely the same viewpoint elsewhere in his narrative. Thus, at the end of his account of the suffering of Ossius and Liberius, he asks 'when did a judgement of the Church receive its validity from the Emperor? Or altogether when was his decree ever recognized [by the Church]?' (52; Opitz (1940*b*) 213, 7–8). As Hanson (1988*b*) 244 observes, 'The answer was, of course, "ever since the Emperor Constantine began to favour the Church" '.

[47] In addition to the most famous such Athanasian appeal, his flight to Constantine after the Council of Tyre, Athanasius quotes the letters he received from Constantius supporting his return to Egypt in 345–6 (*Apologia Contra Arianos* 51, 54–6), and he wrote in person to Constantius (the *Apologia ad Constantium*), and again to Jovian (*Epistle* LVI) upon that emperor's succession in 363.

[48] Barnes (1993) 132.

to have depended upon the support of the Prefect of Egypt, just as at Tyre the Count Dionysius was 'one' with the 'Eusebians', and both in Egypt and at the Council soldiers are alleged to have persecuted Athanasius and his followers. Yet as we also saw, in 335 itself Athanasius' own supporters openly recognized Dionysius' authority at the Council, and indeed appealed for his assistance. Most importantly, at no stage does Athanasius ever attribute any blame for his condemnation to the Emperor Constantine. The arrival of Gregory into Alexandria in the *Epistula Encyclica* in 339 is likewise attributed to the assistance of magistrates and soldiers, but not to the 'most religious' Emperor Constantius, and even into Athanasius' third exile in the *Apologia ad Constantium* he continues to represent every imperial action hostile to himself as the product of 'Eusebian' deception. Only in the *Historia Arianorum* does Athanasius reverse this earlier presentation, and condemn Constantius not merely as under the influence of an 'Arian party', but as the 'precursor of Antichrist', and himself the leader and protector of the 'Arian heresy'.

Whether this remarkable shift in Athanasius' literary attitude towards Constantius actually represents an equally dramatic change in Athanasius' own feelings regarding that emperor is impossible to determine.[49] I do not intend to attempt to resolve this question, or to trace in full the development of Athanasius' attitude towards the State. However, the alleged dependence upon and exploitation of secular power by his opponents is an important component of Athanasius' wider polemical construction of the 'Eusebians'. For this reason, his shifting interpretation of imperial involvement in Church affairs, and particularly of Constantius' relationship with the 'Arians', inevitably has significant implications for Athanasius' presentation of his foes. Not only is that presentation itself extremely subjective, but in the *Historia Arianorum* Athanasius once again reinterprets the role in earlier events that he had

[49] Scholarly assessments of the relative sincerity of Athanasius' writings regarding Constantius have varied widely (Setton (1941) 80; Barnard (1974*a*) 323–4, (1975*b*) 340; Hanson (1988*b*) 243, 419; Barnes (1993) 123–4). The same shift from traditional flattery to vicious polemic against Constantius is also visible in the works of Hilary of Poitiers 359–61 (see Setton (1941) 98–103 and D. H. Williams (1992) 9–14).

previously attributed to the 'Eusebians' according to the new conception of imperial power that he now wished to present.

As I have already observed, throughout the works that Athanasius composed before and even to some extent during his third exile, the relationship that he constructs between the 'Eusebians' and secular power is essentially consistent. First and foremost, Athanasius presents the 'Eusebians' as dependent upon the assistance of civil magistrates and military force, and through that presentation reinforces his repeated insistence that the actions of his foes cannot represent the judgement of the Church. The role of Dionysius and his soldiers in 335 again reduces Tyre to the vehicle of an 'Arian conspiracy' and not a true council, and the same argument recurs in Athanasius' account of the Council of Serdica. When the 'associates' of the 'Eusebians' came to the Council from the east

> they again brought with them the Counts Musonianus and Hesychius the Castrensian, so that, as was their custom, they might do whatever they wished by their authority. But when the Council was without counts, and no soldiers were present, they were confounded and conscience-stricken. For they could no longer judge as they wished, but as the reason of truth required. (*Apologia Contra Arianos* 36; Opitz (1938*a*) 114, 7–11)

It was for this reason that the 'Arian party' fled in 343, for they were deprived of the secular assistance upon which their 'conspiracy' depended. By their flight, they proved once more the innocence of Athanasius himself, for those who act through counts and soldiers cannot judge by 'the reason of truth'.

In his later works, Athanasius continues to repeat this emphasis on the dependence of his opponents on the State. His primary focus is now on events within Egypt, and particularly the role of the magistrates and soldiers who he alleges aided the 'Arians' in the persecution that began with his own expulsion in 356. Before the outbreak of violence, Athanasius reports that he was suspicious of the Duke Syrianus and his officials in Alexandria, 'for there were many Arians about them, with whom they ate and with whom they took counsel. And while they attempted nothing openly, they were preparing to attack me by deceit and treachery' (*Apologia ad Constantium* 25;

Szymusiak (1987) 140, 8–11). Shortly thereafter, these men launched the famous assault upon Athanasius' own church that led to his flight into exile on the night of 8 February 356. Syrianus 'broke into the church with his soldiers . . . [and] the general brought them [the 'Arians'] with him; and they were the leaders (*exarchoi*) and advisors (*sumbouloi*) of this attack' (*Apologia ad Constantium* 25; Szymusiak (1987) 142, 20–1; 25–6; see also *Apologia de Fuga* 24).

I will examine the content of Athanasius' account of the assault of February 356 and the persecution that followed in more detail later in this chapter. Here I am concerned with Athanasius' condemnation of the 'Arians' for their alliance with secular power, which also recurs repeatedly in the *Apologia de Fuga* (6–7) and particularly in the *Historia Arianorum* (58–63). In the latter work, this condemnation is not only directed against Athanasius' contemporary opponent George, but is also projected back upon his earlier rival Gregory. Athanasius had already condemned Gregory's imposition into Alexandria as dependent upon secular power in the *Epistula Encyclica* in 339, as we saw in Chapter 2. But in the *Historia Arianorum*, Athanasius further develops this theme. Gregory 'boasted rather to be the friend of governors than of bishops and monks' (14; Opitz (1940*a*) 189, 33), and when the monk Antony wrote to him, Gregory 'caused Duke Balacius to spit upon the letter and to cast it away' (14; Opitz (1940*a*) 190, 1–2), a crime for which Balacius died soon afterwards when he was bitten and thrown by his horse. Intriguingly, a rather different account of the same episode appears in the *Life of Antony.* In this version, Antony foretold Balacius' death because of the latter's persecution of the Church on behalf of the 'Arians'. The horse that bit Balacius was not his own (*Vita Antonii* 86), and most significantly, in the *Life of Antony* Gregory is entirely absent. To condemn his former rival (and by implication his contemporary George), Athanasius in the *Historia Arianorum* has thus rewritten his earlier interpretation of this particular event in order to better serve his polemical purposes.

In Athanasius' presentation of all these events, past and present, neither Constantine nor Constantius is ever attacked or held responsible for the actions of the 'Arians' and their secular allies. Every imperial decree hostile to his own cause is the product of the 'conspiracy' of his opponents, whereas every decision in his favour reflects the true judgement of the pious emperor himself.[50] Despite the failure of his appeal to Constantine from Tyre, Athanasius thus still insists that the emperor only exiled him in 335 for his own protection from the machinations of the 'Eusebians' (*Apologia Contra Arianos* 87). Likewise, the Alexandrian *Encyclical Letter* of 338 contends that 'it was not the father of the Emperors, but their [the Eusebians'] calumnies, that sent him into exile' (*Apologia Contra Arianos* 9; Opitz (1938*a*) 95, 2–3). The Alexandrian letter also extends the same argument to counter further charges that Athanasius faced after his return in 337. Constantius too has now written against Athanasius, but in fact it is the 'Arians' 'who cause these letters which are said to have come from the Emperor' (18; Opitz (1938*a*) 100, 34–5).

This Athanasian interpretation of imperial involvement in the Church remains consistent in the works that Athanasius wrote before and during the early years of his third exile. I have already quoted previously in this chapter from Athanasius' description of the events surrounding the death of Arius, not only in the *De Morte Arii* (*c.*339–46) but also in the *Encyclical Letter* of 356, in which Athanasius asserts that Constantine received Arius at court due solely to the 'zeal' of the 'Eusebians'. The emperor accepted Arius as 'orthodox' only because of the latter's false representation of his 'heresy', and in his *Encyclical Letter* Athanasius explicitly reports that when he heard of Arius' death, 'the blessed Constantine was amazed to find him thus convicted of perjury' (19; Tetz (1996) 59, 10–60, 12). No blame therefore attaches to Constantine for Arius' recall, while earlier in the same letter Athanasius likewise exonerates Constantius from responsibility for the contemporary conspiracies of his foes. 'When the most God-worshipping emperor Constantius is being charitable, against his judgement (*para gnōmēn*) these men

[50] In the polemic of Athanasius 'intriguing bishops thus have the same role, as agents in a general conspiracy theory, as emperors' wives, freedmen, eunuchs or secretaries do in other writers. This, at least, is when the imperial decision is unfavourable to Athanasius. But when an emperor decides in his favour... the decision is his own, no question of the advice of friends or supporters of Athanasius at court' (Warmington (1986) 13).

[the Arians] keep talking about whatever they wish' (5; Tetz (1996) 44, 8–10). Even after his flight from Alexandria in 356, Athanasius continues to insist that if Constantius only realized the truth of the 'Arian conspiracy', then he would act immediately in defence of the Church.

This presentation culminates in the *Apologia ad Constantium*, both in the original text written in *c*.353–6 and also in the additional passages added in mid-357. Throughout this work, Athanasius addresses Constantius as 'the most pious and religious Augustus', and the 'Arians' are denounced because 'they thought themselves able to deceive your Piety' (2; Szymusiak (1987) 88, 10–11). Even in the later sections of the work, which are dominated by accounts of the persecution of Athanasius and his supporters, Athanasius' language and presentation does not change. It is possible that this continued tone of deference is deliberately ironic, for Athanasius quotes several letters written by Constantius against himself that contrast sharply to the image of the emperor that his own narrative constructs.[51] But in his actual words, Athanasius never ceases to insist that 'I was confident that these things occurred contrary to the judgement of your Piety, and that if your Charity should learn of what was done, you would prevent it happening in the future' (29; Szymusiak (1987) 152, 5–7). Though his persecutors invoke the authority of the emperor, Athanasius continues to proclaim Constantius' innocence, and to defend the guiltless emperor against the deception of the 'Arian party'.[52] It is this very consistency that makes the contrast between the *Apologia ad Constantium* and the

[51] This contrast was emphasized by Szymusiak (1987) 60–1. In particular, Athanasius quotes two letters of Constantius praising the 'venerable George' and condemning the 'pestilent' Athanasius, the first written to the people of Alexandria (30), and the second addressed to the rulers of Auxumis (Ethiopia) (31).

[52] Thus Athanasius asserts that the Duke Syrianus and the 'Arians' who attacked his church in 356 'did not act as if under imperial authority' (*Apologia ad Constantium* 25; Szymusiak (1987) 140, 11–12), and he complains that when the 'Arians' were convicted of persecuting clergy and virgins, 'instead of being ashamed, they pretended this to be the command of your Piety' (33; Szymusiak (1987) 168, 32–3). It must be said, however, that Athanasius' efforts to defend Constantius are at times somewhat strained, notably in his claim that Constantius himself only intended to threaten Athanasius, but that the 'Arians' who did not understand this might kill him by mistake (34).

Historia Arianorum, completed later in that same year, all the more startling.[53]

In the *Historia Arianorum*, Athanasius not only violently condemns Constantius as the precursor of the Antichrist; he rewrites his entire construction of the relationship between his 'Arian' opponents and secular power. This is not to say that he does not still present the 'Eusebians' as acting in alliance with such power, as we have seen above. But the nature of that alliance is now expressed in markedly different terms. Constantius has become the true source of the secular assistance upon which the 'heretics' depend, but more fundamentally, it is now he and not Eusebius of Nicomedia or any other bishop who is the 'leader' of the 'Arian party'.[54] Athanasius thus reinterprets the events both of the preceding decades and of the 350s, which in his other polemical writings were dominated by the role of the 'Eusebians' and their successors, in the light of this new model in which the primary protagonist is the Emperor Constantius himself.

There is one particular respect, it is true, in which Athanasius' construction of the relationship of the 'Eusebians' and imperial power does remain consistent in the *Historia Arianorum*. Even in this work, Athanasius still will not criticize the first Christian emperor.[55] This positive presentation of Constantine implicitly accepts his involvement in the Church, and so contradicts the condemnation of Constantius elsewhere in the *Historia Arianorum* as the first

[53] The only major work composed by Athanasius between the *Apologia ad Constantium* and the *Historia Arianorum* is the *Apologia de Fuga*, which contains no reference to Constantius except a single line added to the description of Leontius of Antioch, that 'the heretic Constantius by violence caused him to be named a bishop' (26; Szymusiak (1987) 240, 20–1). This passage is out of context with the rest of the *Apologia de Fuga* and does not appear in several manuscripts of that work (Robertson (1892) 264.n.7, Szymusiak (1987) 241), and it is therefore most likely an interpolation, probably added by a later editor rather than by Athanasius himself.

[54] 'Those who hold the doctrines of Arius have indeed no king but Caesar; for through him the fighters against Christ accomplish everything they wish' (*Historia Arianorum* 33; Opitz (1940*b*) 201, 27–9).

[55] Thus Athanasius repeats (from *Apologia Contra Arianos* 84) his denial that the 'Eusebian' bishops who restored Arius to communion at the Council of Jerusalem in 335 possessed the imperial support they claimed (*Historia Arianorum* 1). He likewise repeats his earlier assertion from the *Encyclical Letter* of 356 (19) that 'although his father [Constantine] received Arius, yet when Arius perjured himself and burst asunder he lost the charity of his father, who, on learning this, then condemned him as a heretic' (*Historia Arianorum* 51; Opitz (1940*b*) 212, 13–15).

emperor to interfere in Christian affairs. But through that presentation of Constantine, Athanasius contrasts Constantius' alleged actions against himself and the 'orthodox' with the pious decisions of his father. 'Due to the plot of the Eusebians, that man [Constantine] sent the bishop for a time into Gaul because of the cruelty of the conspirators . . . but he would not be persuaded by the Eusebians to send the person whom they desired as bishop' (50; Opitz (1940*b*) 212, 4–8). . . . 'Why therefore did he [Constantius] first send out Gregory, and now George the peculator?' (51; Opitz (1940*b*) 212, 10–11). Whereas Constantine only banished Athanasius due to the slanders of his enemies, and nevertheless still kept a check on the 'Eusebian conspiracy', Constantius alone is here responsible for the entrance of Gregory and George into Alexandria. The role of the 'Eusebians' in these events, so prominent in Athanasius' earlier polemical works, is now subordinated to the role of the emperor.

In the same manner, Athanasius' expulsion from Alexandria in 339 and the intrusion of Gregory into his see is now reported to have occurred only after the 'Eusebians' appealed to Constantius for aid (*Historia Arianorum* 9). The refusal of the 'Eusebians' to attend the Council called by Julius of Rome in 340–1 is attributed not just to their lack of confidence in the absence of magistrates and soldiers (as in the *Apologia Contra Arianos*), but because 'the proceedings of the synod would not be regulated by imperial order' (11; Opitz (1940*a*) 188, 34–5). And in 343, the eastern bishops are said to have justified their decision to abandon the Council of Serdica because 'if we flee, we shall still be able somehow to defend our heresy; and even if they condemn us for our flight, still we have the emperor as our patron (*prostatēn*)' (15; Opitz (1940*a*) 191, 4–6). In all these passages, Athanasius' recurring emphasis on the dependence of the 'heretics' upon secular power has become focused almost exclusively on their relationship with the emperor. Moreover, the entire 'Arian purge' against the 'orthodox' is in the *Historia Arianorum* only possible through the patronage of Constantius. For the 'Arians' 'summon some of the bishops before the Emperor, while they persecute others again by letters, inventing pretexts against them, so that the first might be overawed by the presence of Constantius, and the others . . . might be brought to renounce their orthodox and pious opinions' (32; Opitz (1940*a*) 200, 24–8).

Athanasius' presentation of the 'Arian party' and their actions in these extracts from the *Historia Arianorum* does not differ significantly in detail from his earlier polemical works. It is the nature of their relationship with secular power that has changed. The 'Eusebians' now do not deceive the emperor, but instead appeal for his aid, and their responsibility for the 'persecution' of the 'orthodox' is to some extent diminished by the subordination of their role to that of Constantius. 'Arius took it upon himself to dare to blaspheme openly, while Eusebius took upon himself the patronage (*prostasian*) of his blasphemy. But he [Eusebius] was not able earlier to support the heresy, until, as I said before, he found a patron (*prostatēn*) for it in the Emperor' (66; Opitz (1940*b*) 219, 14–17). Athanasius here conveniently ignores all the activities of the 'Eusebians' before Constantius' accession that in the *Apologia Contra Arianos* and elsewhere he repeatedly condemned. The emperor has superseded Eusebius of Nicomedia, and it is he whom the 'Arians' now follow, for the 'heresy' 'has enlisted Constantius, as if the Antichrist himself, to be the Christ-fighting leader of the impiety' (67; Opitz (1940*b*) 220, 4–5).

Yet the 'Eusebians' are not reduced merely to followers. Athanasius' image of Constantius fluctuates between strength and weakness according to his polemical needs, and while the 'Arians' depend upon the emperor's patronage and power in the passages quoted above, elsewhere in the *Historia Arianorum* it is once again they who corrupt and manipulate him. Thus, when Constantius began his persecution of the western bishops in 353, 'he acted entirely as the heretics counselled and suggested; or rather, they acted themselves, and having authority furiously attacked everyone' (31; Opitz (1940*a*) 199, 22–200, 1). The exile of Liberius is attributed primarily to the 'Arian' eunuchs at court, for 'they now exercise authority over ecclesiastical affairs, and in submission to them Constantius conspired against all' (38; Opitz (1940*a*) 204, 36–7).[56] In the midst of

[56] This claim that Constantius was dominated by the eunuchs of his court (repeated in *Historia Arianorum* 43, and also levelled against Constantius by Ammianus Marcellinus (*Res Gestae* XXI.16)) is a *topos* of anti-imperial invective in Late Antiquity. The only truly novel element of Athanasius' polemic here is his presentation of those eunuchs as 'Arian', and in a sense as the ultimate symbol of the alliance between the 'Arian party' and secular power. 'The Arian heresy, which denies the Son of God, has support from eunuchs, who, as they are thus by nature and their souls are barren of virtue, cannot bear to hear at all concerning a son' (*Historia Arianorum* 38; Opitz (1940*b*) 204, 23–5).

Athanasius' construction of Constantius as the precursor of the Antichrist, the emperor is declared to be nothing more than the puppet of the 'Arian party'.

How can he be able to think of anything just or reasonable, a man having been moulded by the iniquity of those with him, who bewitch [him] or rather who have trampled his brains under their heels?...Under the semblance and name of freedom he is the slave (*doulos*) of those who drag him on to gratify their own impious pleasure... at once doing whatever they wish, and gratifying them in their design against the bishops and their authority over the churches. (70; Opitz (1940*b*) 221, 12–14; 17–18; 20–2)

Between these extremes of imperial and episcopal dominance and subservience, there is also a third, median, dimension to Athanasius' presentation of Constantius and the 'Arians': that of mutual alliance.

Heretics have assembled together with the Emperor Constantius, in order that he, having the pretext of the authority of the bishops, may act against whomsoever he wishes, and persecuting may avoid the name of persecutor; and that they, having the power of the Emperor, may plot against whomsoever they will.... One might look upon this as a comedy performed by them on a stage (*epi skēnēs kōmōdoumenon*), and the so-called bishops are actors (*hypokrinomenous*), and Constantius carries out their behests. He again promises this, as Herod did to Herodias, and they again dance their false accusations for the banishment and death of the true believers in the Lord. (52; Opitz (1940*b*) 213, 13–21)

This imagery of actors and dancers on stage recalls Athanasius' presentation of the 'Eusebian–Melitian alliance' in the *Apologia Contra Arianos*, but here the relationship of Constantius and the 'Arians' is one of equals. The bishops of the 'Arian party' do not deceive the emperor, nor do they follow his commands, but all alike are responsible for the persecution of the 'orthodox' and the promotion of their 'heresy'.

I have quoted these different interpretations of the relationship between the 'Arians' and Constantius in the *Historia Arianorum* at some length, for they illustrate well the methodology and subjectivity of Athanasius' polemic. Here as elsewhere, we see how Athanasius' presentation of an individual or episode may vary significantly, both between his different works and even within a single text, according to the purpose that a given argument is intended to achieve. Not only does the marked hostility of the *Historia Arianorum* differ drastically from Athanasius' apologetic attitude towards Constantius in his earlier works, but Constantius is condemned in that narrative both as the leader of the 'heresy' and as a puppet of the 'Arian party'. Yet the role that the emperor is said to have played in the events described in the *Historia Arianorum* in fact differs very little from the imperial actions that in his earlier writings Athanasius went to such lengths to attribute to the deception of his foes. The dependence of the 'Arians' on secular power remains a constant theme throughout Athanasius' polemic. But the shifting presentation of their relationship with the State in Athanasius' different works ultimately rests not on any major shift in the involvement of secular power within the Church during the fourth-century controversies, but on the contrasting interpretations of that power that Athanasius has chosen to present.

VIOLENCE AND PERSECUTION

> The other heresies, when they are convicted by the evidence of Truth itself, become silent, being ashamed by nothing more than their conviction. But this new and accursed heresy of theirs, when it is overthrown by arguments, when it is cast down and covered with shame by the Truth itself, thereupon endeavours to coerce by violence and stripes and imprisonment those whom it has been unable to persuade by arguments, and thus acknowledges itself to be anything rather than godly. For it is proper to godliness not to compel, but to persuade. (*Historia Arianorum* 67; Opitz (1940*b*) 219, 35–220, 1)

The final element of Athanasius' construction of the 'Eusebians' that I will discuss in this chapter is the violence and persecution that the 'Arians' are alleged to have inspired against Athanasius and the 'orthodox' Church. This dimension of Athanasius' polemic will be examined here only in brief. There is a significant degree of overlap between Athanasius' narratives of persecution and his presentation of the 'anti-Nicene purge' and of his opponents' dependence on secular power that I have already discussed, and in any case the analysis of the violence that Athanasius attributes to his opponents faces its own very serious limitations. To an even greater degree than elsewhere in his polemic, the many episodes of persecution in the works of Athanasius are extremely stereotypical and repetitive. In every Athanasian account certain recurring *topoi* appear: attacks upon churches by 'heretics' and pagans;[57] the abuse and imprisonment of clergy, monks, and virgins; the denial of burial to the dead; and the deprivation of charity from the poor.[58] None of these motifs is self-evidently false or implausible in itself, but in the absence (with one significant exception, to which I shall return) of external evidence against which Athanasius' statements may be compared, the separation of fact from fiction within his narratives raises almost insoluble problems. Only certain very limited conclusions will thus be drawn from the following investigation of these *topoi* as they occur in Athanasius' presentation of the alleged persecution of the Egyptian Church during his first and second exile (335–46), and particularly during the episcopate of George (356–61).

Athanasius gives a number of different accounts of the violence that is reported to have taken place in Egypt in 335–46. According to the Alexandrian *Encyclical Letter* of 338, when the Mareotis Commission was sent to Egypt from Tyre in 335, 'naked swords were advanced against the holy virgins and brethren, and scourges were at work against their persons honoured before God... [while] the pagan people (*demoi*) were incited to strip them naked, to insult them, and to threaten them with their altars and sacrifices' (*Apologia Contra Arianos* 15; Opitz (1938*a*) 98, 30–1; 33–99, 1). Yet the letters of the contemporary Egyptian clergy who observed that Commission

57 On the rhetorical construction of this alleged 'alliance' between 'Arians' and pagans in fourth-century 'orthodox' polemic, see D. H. Williams (1997), esp. 181–4 on Athanasius.

58 Athanasius repeatedly presents the alleged interference of the 'Arians' in the distribution of bread and oil to widows and orphans as proof of their impiety and cruelty, but control of the charitable duties of the Church within a given see was both a means to rally support and an important official indication of episcopal legitimacy (Brown (1992) 90, Barnes (1993) 179, Haas (1997) 248–56). When Athanasius and his supporters complain that his opponents desire to take the distributions away from the 'orthodox' and give them instead to the 'Arians' (see *Apologia Contra Arianos* 18 (the Alexandrian *Encyclical Letter* of 338) and *Historia Arianorum* 13, 31, 61), such complaints may actually refer to challenges to Athanasius' own right to control that legitimate distribution, and to the inevitable reorganization of the supply of bread and oil in Alexandria that would have occurred during his periods of exile, particularly in the episcopates of Gregory and George (see Brakke (1995) 190–1).

and wrote in protest to the Council of Tyre (quoted in *Apologia Contra Arianos* 73–5) speak only vaguely of 'threats' being brought against the supporters of Athanasius, and give no suggestion of persecution on such a systematic scale. The description of the arrival of Gregory into Alexandria in Athanasius' own *Epistula Encyclica* in 339 follows a similar pattern. 'The church and the holy Baptistery were set on fire . . . holy and undefiled virgins were stripped naked . . . monks were trampled underfoot and perished . . . and Jews who killed the Lord and godless pagans entered irreverently into the holy Baptistery' (3; Opitz (1940*a*) 172, 7–8; 10; 11; 16–17). In this instance, Athanasius describes the same episode again later in the *Historia Arianorum*. Here the 'Arians' are further reported to have seized the charitable oil and wine from the poor, and also to have 'so persecuted the bishop's aunt, that even when she died he [Gregory] would not suffer her to be buried' (13; Opitz (1940*a*) 189, 21–2), a personal outrage that strangely Athanasius never even mentioned in his original version of those events.

The same recurring *topoi* that dominate these early Athanasian persecution narratives, and the progressive elaboration of detail that characterizes his presentation of such events, is visible to a still greater extent in Athanasius' accounts of the violence that he alleges followed the order that he be expelled from Alexandria in late 355.[59] These accounts focus upon the period between 8 February 356, when the Church of Theonas in which Athanasius was presiding over a vigil was seized by the Duke Syrianus and Athanasius was forced to flee, and 2 October 358, when George (who had only arrived in the city on 24 February 357) left Alexandria just over a month after having almost been lynched on 29 August of that year.

The closing chapters of the *Apologia ad Constantium*, added to that work in 357, provide the earliest Athanasian description of the initial outbreak of violence in 356. Athanasius immediately takes up the emphasis of his earlier polemic upon the expulsion of bishops and

[59] Haas (1991), (1997). However, Haas' unquestioning acceptance of Athanasius' account as evidence for the social composition and violence of the 'Arians', their regional power centres, and their alleged alliances with pagans and Jews, underestimates the potential distortions inherent in such polemical writings.

the stripping of virgins,[60] while the bodies of those killed 'were not immediately given up for burial, but were cast outside to the dogs, until their kinsmen, at great risk to themselves, came secretly and stole them away' (27; Szymusiak (1987) 150, 38–40). The *Apologia de Fuga* reports that the same crimes accompanied the arrival of George into Alexandria in early 357, with the addition that 'the houses and bread of orphans and widows were plundered' (6; Szymusiak (1987) 188, 9–10), and for the first time also presents a list of the names of Egyptian bishops who suffered under this persecution (7). This list is then repeated with additions in the *Historia Arianorum* (71–2), in which a number of new names and alleged incidents of violence appear, and episodes that were reported in the earlier two works are repeated with further elaboration.[61] Thus Athanasius can conclude that so terrible were the actions of the 'Arians' that they surpassed even the deeds of the pagan persecutors of previous centuries. 'This is a new iniquity. It is not simply persecution, but more than persecution, it is a prelude and preparation for the Antichrist' (71; Opitz (1940*b*) 222, 1–2).

In the absence of external evidence, no meaningful historical assessment can be made of the highly rhetorical persecution narratives of these three Athanasian works, or in turn of the role that the

[60] This emphasis is further expanded in the *Historia Arianorum*, in which it is reported that the 'Arians' 'gave permission to the women with them to insult whom they wished; and although the holy and faithful women stepped aside and gave them the way, yet they gathered around them like Maenads and Furies, and thought it a misfortune not to find a way to injure them' (59; Opitz (1940*b*) 216, 17–19). It is impossible to assess the truth of such allegations, but the women who are condemned here as 'Maenads' and 'Furies' were almost certainly virgins and holy women themselves, whose status Athanasius will not acknowledge. See Burrus (1991), esp. 248, and Brakke (1995) 63–75.

[61] There are certain exceptions to this rule, notably Athanasius' accounts of a number of virgins being exposed to fire and of the beating of forty members of the laity with the thorny branches of palm trees, both of which occur in most detail in the *Apologia de Fuga* (6–7), and only in a more abbreviated form in the *Historia Arianorum* (72). However, the great majority of Athanasius' detailed narrative descriptions of individual suffering appear only in the latter work, including the scourging and death of the sub-deacon Eutychius, the double flogging of four 'Christian citizens' (60), and the fate of a presbyter at Barka who was reportedly kicked to death by the 'Arian' Secundus of Ptolemais (65). In every instance, the victim is blameless, and suffered only because he refused to comply with the 'Arian impiety'.

'Arians' are reported to have played in these events. Yet there is one episode which does offer the possibility of a degree of analysis, and that is the attack upon the Church of Theonas that led directly to Athanasius' initial flight from Alexandria on the night of 8/9 February 356. Although the *Encyclical Letter to the Bishops of Egypt and Libya* that Athanasius wrote in that year contains no account of this event, two Athanasian descriptions of the attack and a contemporary document that he quotes do survive. Thus we possess a priceless opportunity not only to trace the development of Athanasius' own presentation of this episode across different works, but also to compare that presentation to the interpretation that others within Alexandria placed upon an experience that they and Athanasius apparently shared.

The first of Athanasius' two narratives, in the *Apologia ad Constantium*, describes the attack upon the Church of Theonas only briefly. The Duke Syrianus, accompanied by the 'Arians', 'broke into the church with his soldiers, while we were praying as was customary' (25; Szymusiak (1987) 142, 20–1). Athanasius therefore 'first exhorted the people to depart, and then withdrew myself after them, God concealing and guiding me, as indeed those who were with me then witnessed' (25; Szymusiak (1987) 142, 29–32). The *Apologia de Fuga* offers a much more elaborate description of the same event. The number of soldiers with the 'Arians' is indicated (over 5,000), armed with swords, bows, spears, and clubs, and Athanasius emphasizes still more emphatically that 'I considered that it would be unreasonable to desert the people during such a disturbance, and not rather to endanger myself on their behalf' (24; Szymusiak (1987) 234, 18–20). Therefore he remained within the Church until, 'when the greater part [of the people] had gone forth and the rest were following, the monks who were there with us and certain of the clergy came up and dragged us away' (24; Szymusiak (1987) 236, 32–4). Athanasius then further develops the theme of divine protection, that only through the guidance of God did he escape. He concludes that, 'when Providence had thus delivered us in such an extraordinary manner, who can justly lay any blame [upon us], that we did not give ourselves up to those who pursued us?... This would have been plainly to show ingratitude to the Lord' (25; Szymusiak (1987) 236, 1–238, 5).

Throughout these Athanasian accounts, two themes predominate: his denunciation of the 'Arians' as the true instigators of the attack, and his justification of his own escape. The *Apologia de Fuga* unsurprisingly develops these themes (and particularly the role of divine providence in aiding his flight) in greater detail than the *Apologia ad Constantium*, but overall the narratives of both texts are consistent in content and emphasis. The one other surviving contemporary account of this episode, however, provides a somewhat different perspective. The *Historia Arianorum* itself contains no detailed description of the assault, but at the end of that work Athanasius (as he states at *Historia Arianorum* 48) attached a letter written to Constantius by 'the people of the catholic Church in Alexandria, which is under the most reverend bishop Athanasius' (81; Opitz (1940*b*) 228, 29–30). This letter, which was written in protest against the violence of the Duke Syrianus,[62] is dated to 12 February 356, just a few days after the events took place, and so represents the earliest extant account of the expulsion of Athanasius, preceding his own narratives by almost a year.

Like Athanasius, the authors of this letter declare that Syrianus attacked the Church on the night of a vigil, but their account of the entrance of the soldiers into the Church is far more dramatic. 'Some of them were shooting, others shouting, and there was rattling of shields, and swords flashing in the light of the lamps. Forthwith, virgins were being slain, many men were trampled down and fell over one another as the soldiers attacked, and men were pierced with arrows and perished' (81; Opitz (1940*b*) 229, 20–3). Athanasius himself remained upon his episcopal throne, until 'the bishop was dragged away and almost torn to pieces; and having been greatly weakened and appearing as if dead, he disappeared from among them, and we do not know where he has gone' (81; Opitz (1940*b*) 229, 28–9). The bodies of those killed have been removed, but 'no little evidence for the hostility of this assault is that the shields and javelins and swords of those who entered

[62] In the letter, Syrianus is declared to have persecuted the Church against the wishes of the 'most gracious emperor'. Such respect for Constantius is somewhat ironic in a document attached to the *Historia Arianorum*, but is entirely in keeping with Athanasius' own position (as expressed in the *Apologia ad Constantium*) at the time this letter was written in early 356.

were left in the Lord's house. They have been hung up in the Church until this time, so that they might not be able to deny it' (81; Opitz (1940*b*) 230, 5–7).

The 'people of the catholic Church in Alexandria' who composed this letter unquestionably intended to defend Athanasius. They conclude their text with the demand that 'let them not attempt to bring in here some other bishop, for we have resisted until death, desiring to have the most reverend Athanasius, whom God gave to us from the beginning' (81; Opitz (1940*b*) 230, 12–14). Yet the description of Athanasius' behaviour and flight that they provide is less flattering than his own self-presentation in the *Apologia de Fuga.* Although he remained on his throne and encouraged the people to pray, there is no suggestion that Athanasius encouraged all others to leave ahead of himself, and he was then apparently seized and fainted, before vanishing from his supporters' view. At the same time, the Alexandrian letter places vivid emphasis upon the violence of the soldiers within the church. The assaults upon clergy and virgins are described in terms very like those that appear elsewhere in Athanasius' descriptions of persecution, with the additional unique assertion that the soldiers have left their weapons behind as proof of their crimes. Finally, and most significantly in the overall context of this monograph, the account of the 'people of the catholic Church' at no time suggests that the actions of the soldiers were inspired by 'heretics'. In his presentation of these events, as in every polemical work that he wrote denouncing the persecution of himself and his followers, Athanasius represents the 'Arians' as the true cause of his suffering. The complete omission of this theme from a letter written by his close supporters is therefore striking, and strongly suggests that it was above all Athanasius himself who insisted upon the characterization of those he opposed as 'Arian'.[63]

[63] It is possible that the authors of the Alexandrian letter omitted any reference to 'heresy' because their epistle was intended for a secular audience (the emperor), just as the Egyptian bishops at Tyre in 335 condemned the 'Arians' in their letter to their fellow bishops, but not in their address to Count Dionysius. However, Athanasius' own *Apologia ad Constantium*, addressed (at least in form) to the same audience, shows no such hesitation.

CONCLUSION

Severe limitations must circumscribe any final conclusions that may be drawn from the preceding pages, for an analysis of the different elements that comprise Athanasius' construction of the 'Eusebians' 'in action' must inevitably be largely inconclusive. As we have seen, all of the actions that Athanasius attributes to his foes as an 'Arian party'—the writing of letters, the manipulation of episcopal politics, the dependence upon secular power, and the instigation of violence and persecution—are *topoi*, repetitive motifs that recur in every Athanasian polemical work. These *topoi* are not to be dismissed as necessarily false, but nor can they be accepted at face value, and without external evidence against which Athanasius' narratives may be compared, no clear distinction can be drawn between the 'factual' and 'rhetorical' content of his accounts. On those rare occasions when external sources do exist (as for the bishops whose exile Athanasius interprets as an 'Arian purge') or when a significant comparison can be made between different Athanasian works (as for the alleged relationship between the 'Arians' and Constantius or for the persecution of 356), it is the subjectivity of Athanasius' polemic that is most immediately apparent. His construction of his foes as a 'heretical party' remains constant, but Athanasius' presentation and interpretation of the actions that he attributes to that 'party' can vary significantly according to the context, purposes, and emphases of a given work.

The accusations alleged by Athanasius against the 'Eusebians' are not *topoi* limited to Athanasius' own works. They represent charges that could be (and were) raised against any Christian bishop throughout the fourth-century controversies, including Athanasius himself.[64] Thus the complaints of Athanasius and his supporters condemning the hostile writings circulated by his foes are expressed

[64] In addition to the evidence of Athanasius' own works and the fifth-century ecclesiastical historians, the two main extant sources for accusations raised against Athanasius by his foes are the *Encyclical Letter* of the Eastern Council of Serdica in 343 and the (possibly fabricated) Appendix attached to Athanasius' own letter to the Emperor Jovian (*Letter* LVI) in 363, which purports to describe the petitions against Athanasius then brought by the 'Arians' to that emperor.

in polemical encyclical letters that perform an identical function. Likewise, Athanasius criticizes the 'Eusebians' for their manipulation of episcopal offices and patronage, yet he secured his own position in Egypt through the removal of those clergy he opposed and the installation of his own nominees.[65] His condemnation of his opponents for their willingness to turn to secular and above all imperial assistance contrasts vividly to his own famous appeal to Constantine in 335, or the respectful tone of the *Apologia ad Constantium*.[66] And despite his constantly repeated allegation that violence is only the resort of a 'heretical party', Athanasius' declaration that 'it is proper to godliness not to compel but to persuade' (*Historia Arianorum* 67; Opitz (1940*b*) 219, 39–220, 1) would have come as a considerable surprise to the Melitians who were being persecuted before the Council of Tyre.[67]

The point is that it is not the actions themselves attributed to Athanasius or his foes that matter, so much as the *presentation* of those actions in a particular source. Writing a letter or ordaining a bishop can reveal the corruption of a 'heretical faction' or represent

[65] Athanasius' control over Egyptian episcopal offices is best attested by *Festal Letter* XIX (for AD 347): 'I have thought it necessary to inform you of the appointment of bishops which has taken place in the stead of our blessed fellow-ministers, that you may know to whom to write, and from whom you should receive letters' (XIX.10; Robertson (1892) 548). A substantial list of names follows, which would seem to represent Athanasius' reorganization of the Egyptian episcopal order on his return from his second exile. Of course, through such an action Athanasius was performing the traditional role of the metropolitan bishop of Alexandria, although both the *Encyclical Letter* of Eastern Serdica and Sozomen (III.21) also refer to his alleged interference in ordinations outside the borders of Egypt.

[66] In particular, the explicit condemnation of the intrusion of the State into the Church in the *Historia Arianorum* directly contradicts Athanasius' emphasis on his own obedience to the State (as contrasted to the deception of the emperor by his foes) in the *Apologia ad Constantium*. 'I did not resist the commands of your Piety. I am not so great that I would resist even an official (*logistēs*) of the city, much less so great a Prince' (*Apologia ad Constantium* 19; Szymusiak (1987) 128, 9–11).

[67] The primary evidence for Athanasian violence against the Melitians in Egypt remains *Papyrus London 1914* (see Ch. 3). In addition, both the Eastern *Encyclical Letter* of Serdica and the alleged 'Arian' petitions to Jovian accuse Athanasius of causing persecution, and the Alexandrian *Encyclical Letter* of 338 not only defends Athanasius against the charges of violence and misbehaviour for which he was condemned at Tyre, but also reports that after his return from exile in 337 Athanasius was again accused of causing further murders and banishments through the aid of secular power (*Apologia Contra Arianos* 3–5).

the heroic defence of 'orthodoxy', depending entirely upon the author's point of view. Reliance upon secular power and the instigation of persecution are universal attributes of heresy, which could therefore be charged against anyone whom a given writer wished to condemn. To describe one's opponents as a 'party', as Athanasius does in his construction of the 'Eusebians', is one more element within this process of presentation. The image of the 'Eusebians' that Athanasius has constructed creates a framework through which the actions of the men he condemns can be presented (indeed, it is highly probable that Eusebius of Nicomedia, if his writings survived, described '*hoi peri Athanasion*' in exactly the same way). This does not deny that a 'Eusebian party' in some form might actually exist, for a number of the individuals whom Athanasius condemns certainly knew and corresponded with each other, just as the fact that the actions attributed to them are *topoi* does not prove that they did not really occur. But the rhetorical nature of the construct that underlies Athanasius' polemic must determine how we approach his presentation of those men, their actions, and most importantly their allegedly 'Arian' theology. As we have seen throughout this chapter, every action that Athanasius attributes to the 'Eusebian party' is motivated by their desire to impose their shared 'heresy' upon the Church. The 'Arianism' of the 'Eusebians' thus stands at the heart of Athanasius' construction of his foes, and it is to this theological dimension of his polemic that we must now finally turn.

7

The 'Arianism' of the 'Eusebians'

He who does not hold the doctrines of Arius (*ta Areiou*) necessarily holds and intends the doctrines of the [Nicene] Council (*ta tēs sunodou*). (*De Decretis* 20; Opitz (1935) 17, 26–7)

Throughout the polemic of Athanasius, the fundamental principle of his construction of the 'Eusebians' is that the men whom he condemns are 'Arian'. They are 'heretics', who threaten the faith of the entire Church. In this final chapter, it is necessary to examine in detail the methodology and content of Athanasius' theological presentation of his foes. Not only does the very nature of his polemic require that he justify his construction of the 'Eusebians' as an 'Arian party', but Athanasius without question sincerely believed that the 'heresy' that he attributed to his opponents compromised the salvation oered through the Incarnation of the divine Christ that lies at the heart of the Christian faith. Nevertheless, I will argue that it is Athanasius' construction of the 'Arianism' of the 'Eusebians' that reveals most explicitly the degree to which Athanasius has distorted our understanding of his foes, of himself, and of the fourth-century theological controversies.

Athanasius constructs a vision of the fourth-century Church dominated by a single 'Arian Controversy', an ongoing conflict polarized between the 'Arianism' of his opponents and the 'orthodoxy' which he himself claims to represent. Neither of those positions existed in reality in the form that Athanasius presents. The 'heresy' that he constructs, which I will term 'Athanasian Arianism', does not derive from the writings of Arius or of the individuals who allegedly comprise the 'Eusebians'. On the contrary, Athanasius' definition of 'Arianism' derives from the imposition of his own interpretations upon those he wishes to condemn.[1] When we come to analyse the fragmentary extant theological writings of the best known 'Eusebians', particularly Asterius 'the Sophist' and Eusebius of Nicomedia, we shall see that they differ markedly both from the position that Athanasius defines as 'Arian' and from the teachings of Arius himself. On the other hand, the theology that Athanasius proclaims as 'orthodox', and which in his later works at least he asserts is symbolized by the Nicene Creed, is no more (or less) than his own interpretation of the Christian truth. That interpretation would come in time to be upheld by the majority of Christians, but in the period in which he wrote Athanasius' doctrinal position was certainly not the traditional and universal faith of the Church that he wished to claim.

Athanasius' polarized vision of an 'Arian Controversy' was to exert great influence upon later generations. The fifth-century ecclesiastical historians, who upheld Athanasius' representation of himself as the 'champion of orthodoxy', likewise accepted his construction of opposing 'Nicene' and 'Arian' factions, and until quite recently this remained the prevailing basis for the interpretation of the fourth-century doctrinal controversies. Modern scholars are now fully aware of the difficulties that such categories raise for the analysis of this period. As R. P. C. Hanson observed, 'when we look at the participants themselves . . . we cannot neatly divide them into orthodox and heretical'.[2] Rowan Williams took up the same theme in his review of Hanson's work, where he wrote that in the fourth-century debates, 'we are not looking at rival theologies . . . but a wide spectrum of responses to a number of shared problems'.[3] The more recent studies of Ayres, Behr, and others have further reinforced these conclusions. The argument that follows is intended to be a contribution to this ongoing process of reinterpretation.

The purpose of this chapter is therefore to assess in detail Athanasius' theological construction of the 'Eusebians', the distortions inherent in that construction, and the implications of those distortions. The analysis will begin with the polarization of 'orthodoxy' and

[1] 'Athanasius is not only responsible for creating the concept of Arianism; he is also responsible for determining how the concept has been understood' (Wiles (1996) 6).

[2] Hanson (1989) 152.

[3] Williams (1992) 104.

'heresy' that underlies Athanasius' entire conception of the 'Arian Controversy', and with his own definition of the Athanasian Arianism that he attributes to his foes within that polarization. This definition must then be compared in turn to the actual theological writings of the men whom Athanasius condemns as 'Arian', first Arius himself and then the two so-called 'Eusebians' of whose doctrines we are best informed, Asterius 'the Sophist' and Eusebius of Nicomedia. Only through such a comparison is it possible to identify the distorted nature of Athanasius' construction of the theology of these men and the polemical methodology through which that construction has been created, notably the imposition of Athanasius' own doctrines and interpretations upon individuals and councils who held very different theological positions. For the polarized polemic of Athanasius both conceals the full complexity of the fourth-century controversies and significantly distorts the roles played in those controversies not only by his opponents but also by himself.

THE RHETORIC OF POLARIZATION

Instead of Christ for them is Arius, as for the Manichees Manichaeus. (*Oration* I.2; Tetz (1998) 110, 7–8)

As we saw in Chapter 5, Athanasius consistently condemns the 'Eusebians' as a single 'Arian party', representatives of an ongoing heretical tradition who take their name from the heresiarch whose teachings they are alleged to share. Against their 'Arianism', Athanasius contrasts the 'orthodox faith' of the Christian Church, which he himself represents. The exact definition of that 'orthodoxy' does not remain consistent within his polemic, for only in Athanasius' later writings does the emphasis upon the Council of Nicaea and the Nicene Creed for which he was remembered by subsequent generations emerge. But throughout his works, Athanasius never deviates from his essential construction of his foes as an 'Arian party' and of an 'Arian Controversy' polarized between 'heresy' and 'orthodoxy'. Before we turn to examine the theological content of Athanasius' polemic in detail, it is helpful first to trace briefly the framework of heresiological rhetoric through which that polarization is constructed.[4]

The opening paragraphs of the *First Oration against the Arians*, from which I have just quoted, set the 'Arianism' of the 'Eusebians' against the background of a wider 'genealogy of heresy'.[5] 'Arianism' is the 'last heresy' and 'something more than other heresies, that indeed it is called "Christ-fighting" (*Christomachos*) and is reckoned the forerunner of the Antichrist' (I.7; Tetz (1998) 116, 21–2). The 'Arians' are placed alongside the Marcionites, Manichees, and Valentinians (I.2), and with the Jews who denied Christ (I.8), for their errors, like every deviation from the truth, must ultimately derive from the devil. 'Thus he deceived Eve, thus he fashioned the other heresies, and thus at this time he persuaded Arius to speak' (I.8; Tetz (1998) 117, 9–10).[6] Like their diabolic father, the 'Arians' are deceitful and misuse Scripture for their own ends, misleading the ignorant and introducing novelties into the Church. Yet, being treacherous, 'they conceal [their teachings] under the bushel of their hypocrisy' (I.10; Tetz (1998) 119, 15).

[4] This is not the place to trace in full the long tradition of Christian heresiology within which Athanasius wrote, or his precise relationship to that tradition. In the following pages, I have therefore only highlighted certain themes which are particularly prominent in Athanasius' polemic. For some important discussions of the concept of 'heresy' and the development of heresiology in the Early Church, see Bauer (1971; first pub. 1934), Le Boulluec (1985), and Williams (2001*b*). On Athanasius' own rhetoric, see Stead (1976).

[5] This concept of a 'heretical genealogy' is from the beginning an essential component of Christian heresiology, already visible in Irenaeus, who traces all 'heresies' back to Simon Magus (*Adversus Haereses* I.22–3, 27) and contrasts that false lineage to the apostolic tradition maintained by the true Church (III.1–4, IV.33). Recent studies of the construction of such genealogies by different Christian authors and the difficulties that they pose for historical analysis include those of Young (1982) on Epiphanius, Edwards (1997) on the polemical role of Simon Magus, Elm (1997) on Jerome, and Buell (1999) on Clement of Alexandria. All these scholars rightly emphasize that the purpose of such a construct was not only to condemn one's opponents, but also to reinforce the author's own position.

[6] On the use of Eve as the archetypal foolish woman deceived by heresy in Athanasius' polemic, see Burrus (1991) 236–7, and on the alleged Athanasian parallel between the 'Arians' and the 'Manichees', see Lyman (1989) and (1993*b*) 54–8, who rightly characterizes this device as 'defamation by association'. Athanasius' particular emphasis upon the 'Arians' as the 'Jews of the present' has been discussed in some detail by Brakke (2001) 467–75, and especially by Lorenz (1979) 141–79, whose long comparative analysis of 'Arianism' and Judaism is more than the polemic merits, but who rightly dismisses the charge of *Arius Judaizans*.

Since all that remains to say is that they received their mania from the devil, for of such things he alone is the sower, we proceed to resist him ... so that they may be put to shame when they see that he who sowed this heresy in them is without resource, and they may learn, even if late, that being Arians they are not Christians (I.10; Tetz (1998) 120, 27–32).

In his characterization of the 'Arian heresy', Athanasius stands in a long rhetorical tradition. The condemnation of 'Arian' deceit and hypocrisy, the emphasis upon the devil as the origin of all error, and the corresponding connection drawn between the 'Arians' and both earlier 'heresies' and the Jews are all standard devices of Christian heresiology. All these motifs continue to recur throughout Athanasius' later works. The *De Decretis* and particularly the *De Sententia Dionysii* take up the insistence that 'both the Jews of the past and the new Jews of the present inherited their Christ-fighting mania from their father the devil' (*De Sententia Dionysii* 3; Opitz (1936) 48, 5–7; see also *De Decretis* 2). In the *De Sententia Dionysii*, this emphasis on the diabolic inspiration of the 'Arians' helps to lay the foundation for Athanasius' argument that such 'heretics' have no claim to the Christian tradition, represented here by his predecessor Dionysius of Alexandria.[7] The conclusion of this work rhetorically asks, 'who then can any longer name these men "Christians", whose teacher is the devil, and not rather "Diabolici"?' (*De Sententia Dionysii* 27; Opitz (1936) 66, 30–67, 1). Even in Athanasius' less specifically theological works, the diabolic origin of 'Arianism' remains a prominent theme (*Apologia de Fuga* 10; *Historia Arianorum* 66), and so too the presentation of the 'new heresy' as exceeding even the errors of earlier times. 'For these other heresies [the Hellenes, Jews, Manichees, and Valentinians] support their madness by persuasive arguments for the deception of the simple ... but the Arians are bolder than the other heresies ... and emulate them all, especially the Jews in their iniquity' (*Historia Arianorum* 66; Opitz (1940*b*) 219, 23–4; 28–31).

Perhaps the most emphatic statement of this heresiological framework forms the introduction to the *Encyclical Letter* of 356.

[7] 'Why is Dionysius to be named like Arius, when the difference between them is great? For the one is a teacher of the catholic Church, while the other has been the deviser of a new heresy' (*De Sententia Dionysii* 6; Opitz (1936) 49, 27–9).

Athanasius opens this letter with the declaration that Christ Himself foretold that 'there shall arise false prophets and false Christs' [Matt 24:24] (1). The polarization of 'orthodoxy' and 'heresy' is here again expressed through the opposition of Christ and the devil, who conceals his falsehoods and feigns to speak the truth, as do the 'heresies' which he has inspired (2–3). 'Such is the manner of the operations of the enemy, and such are the devices of the heresies, each of which has the devil for the father of its own thought' (3; Tetz (1996) 42, 19–22). The 'Arians' are then placed once more alongside the Marcionites, Manichees, and the followers of Paul of Samosata (4) within a 'genealogy of heresy', and like them they misuse the Scriptures and merely dissemble Scriptural language to mislead the simple. For what are the Scriptures to Marcion and Mani, or to the Jews, or to Paul of Samosata, 'and what are the Scriptures also to the Arians?' (4; Tetz (1996) 43, 16). Rather, these men 'pretend to study and to speak what is written, like their father the devil, so that from what they say they may seem to have the orthodox doctrine, and then they may persuade their wretched followers to believe what is contrary to the Scriptures' (4; Tetz (1996) 43, 23–5).

Having thus laid down the polarized framework for his construction of the 'Arian Controversy', Athanasius proceeds directly to impose this interpretation upon the specific theological context in which the *Encyclical Letter* of 356 was actually written. According to Athanasius, the 'Arians' have composed a creed that they intend to circulate within the Egyptian Church.[8]

This they do with great cunning and, it appears to me, for two particular reasons. One, so that when you subscribe (*hypograpsantōn*), they may seem to remove the evil repute of Arius, and to escape notice themselves as if not holding the doctrines of Arius; and on the other hand, so that by writing these things they might seem again to hide the Nicene Synod and the faith established there against the Arian heresy. But indeed, this rather exposes their malice and heterodoxy. For if they believed rightly, they would be satisfied by the faith established in Nicaea by the whole ecumenical synod. And if they thought themselves to be slandered and falsely to be called 'Arians', they should not have been so eager to pervert what was written

[8] The exact identity of the 'Arian' creed in question is uncertain, although Barnes (1993) 122 suggests that this is a reference to the Sirmium Creed of 351.

against Arius, lest what was written against him might seem also to be written against themselves. (5; Tetz (1996) 44, 10–45, 20)

To achieve these purposes they have already composed and then rejected many creeds, but their words are false (6). Indeed

even if they may write what is read from the Scriptures, do not accept their writings; even if they may utter the words of orthodoxy, do not thus pay attention to what they say. For they do not speak with an upright mind, but they put on the words like sheep's clothing, [while] inside they are thinking the doctrines of Arius, like the devil the author of the heresies. (8; Tetz (1996) 47, 7–48, 11)

Athanasius does in fact acknowledge that 'if these writings were from the orthodox . . . then nothing in their writings would be suspect' (8; Tetz (1996) 48, 15; 49, 27–8). However

since the writings are from those who are hired (*misthōthentōn*) to come together for the sake of the heresy . . . it is necessary to be watchful, brothers, as the Lord said . . . for these men conceal what they think and then use the language of the Scriptures in what they write themselves, so that through these writings they may entice the ignorant [and] drag them down into their own evil. (9; Tetz (1996) 49, 1–2; 3–4; 24–50, 26)

The 'heresy' and deceit of the 'Arians', who conceal their false teachings behind a cloak of Scripture in order to mislead the simple and avert their own condemnation, is here contrasted to the 'true faith' established at the Council of Nicaea. Athanasius' emphasis upon his opponents as 'hirelings' echoes the *Apologia Contra Arianos*, and so in particular does his concern that no one should 'subscribe' to the document that is being circulated by his foes, an argument that he presents in very similar terms to the appeal of his supporters to the bishops at Tyre in 335. Yet only if we accept Athanasius' own polarized contrast between an 'Arian party' united around the teachings of Arius and the 'orthodox faith' is it possible to accept Athanasius' assertion that only those who 'think with Arius' would question the faith of Nicaea, and so in turn to denounce the evidently Scriptural creed that the men whom he condemns have now composed.

As Athanasius admits, the creed in question is itself entirely 'orthodox'. It is only because the authors are 'Arian' that Athanasius can dismiss their actual statement as nothing but 'heretical deceit' and assert that 'if they do not have the confidence to speak openly, but rather conceal the words of their blasphemy, then it is clear that they know that their heresy is foreign and alien to the truth' (*Encyclical Letter* 11; Tetz (1996) 51, 25–7; see also *De Decretis* 2). Yet in thus denouncing the 'Arians' who 'conceal their blasphemy', Athanasius rejects as irrelevant hypocrisy the very theology that the men whom he condemns actually expressed. He has named them 'Arians', therefore 'Arians' they must be, and 'if they have written other words apart from the aforementioned doctrines of Arius, then condemn them as hypocrites who conceal the venom of their thought' (*Encyclical Letter* 19; Tetz (1996) 60, 23–4). The emphasis that Athanasius places on this theme suggests that he knew all too well that his various foes did not in fact express their respective doctrines in any such terms as those he defined as 'Arian'. But what is particularly manifest here is that the focus of the theological polemic of Athanasius in the *Encyclical Letter*, and indeed in all his writings, is not the doctrines that his foes actually taught or wrote, but the interpretation of their 'Arianism' that Athanasius himself has created and which they allegedly conceal. Thus he dismisses or reinterprets their own statements in order to force his opponents to fit the polarized model of an 'Arian party' and an 'Arian Controversy' that he constructs.

This process of polemical imposition culminates in the *De Synodis* of 359–61. As I have already observed in Chapter 5, in the *De Synodis* Athanasius represents every theological statement that he personally rejects, from the individual writings of the 'Eusebians' before the Council of Nicaea to the 'Dated Creed' presented to the Councils of Ariminum and Seleucia in 359, as the products of a single 'Arian tradition'. The content of a number of those statements will be considered in more detail later in this chapter, but Athanasius himself has no particular interest in the actual words that he quotes, except to assert that whenever the individual statements differ from each other the 'Arians' are evidently guilty of deceit and inconsistency. Instead, Athanasius interprets every theological fragment or creed as representative of the same 'heresy' and composed by the same 'Arian party'.

They will always be making conspiracies against the truth, until they return to themselves and say 'Let us rise and go to our fathers and say to them, we anathematize the Arian heresy and we acknowledge the Nicene Council', for against this they have their quarrel. Who then, even if having so little understanding, will endure them any longer? Who, on hearing in every council some things taken away and other added, does not perceive that their purpose is suspicious and treacherous against Christ . . . [and] that they write many things so that they might appear because of their unsuitable ostentation and so great abundance of words to seduce the simple and conceal what they are with regard to the heresy? (*De Synodis* 32; Opitz (1941) 260, 8–14; 16–18)

Here, as throughout his polemic, Athanasius presents the fourth-century theological controversies in terms of a polarization between the 'Arianism' of his opponents and the 'orthodoxy' that in his later writings at least is represented by the Council of Nicaea. Yet outside the works of Athanasius, there is in fact no evidence that either Arius or the Nicene Creed played a prominent role in the eastern doctrinal debates of the 340s and 350s. Moreover, the very material that Athanasius presents in the *De Synodis* reveals that the men whom he describes as the 'Eusebians' did not represent a monolithic or 'Arian' theological position. The diverse statements and creeds that he quotes are not evidence of 'deceit' or 'inconsistency', but rather of the widely varied doctrinal spectrum that existed within eastern Christianity at this time. In order to impose his polarized model of an 'Arian Controversy' upon his foes, Athanasius thus misrepresents both the complexity of the debates that took place in the decades surrounding the Council of Nicaea and the true theological positions of the different individuals whom he condemns. In the main body of this chapter, I will seek to demonstrate the nature and extent of these misrepresentations. To this end, we must now turn to the specific definition of 'Arianism' which Athanasius attributes to his foes within his polarized polemic, for only then can we assess in detail the distortions inherent in his construction of these men as 'Arian'.

ATHANASIAN ARIANISM

What does it actually mean to describe an individual or 'party' as 'Arian'? Recent scholarship has remained divided on this crucial question, a debate to which I will return later in this chapter. But for the purposes of the present study, it is first necessary to consider how Athanasius himself defines the 'Arianism' of those he condemns. Here we must look beyond the heresiological rhetoric against '*Christomachoi*' and 'modern day Jews', and likewise Athanasius' later condemnation of anyone who questions the Nicene Creed, and focus upon Athanasius' theological definition of the 'heresy' that he attributes to his foes. That definition, although extremely influential, is itself a polemical construct, which I have entitled 'Athanasian Arianism'.

The earliest systematic polemical description of the 'Arian heresy' is to be found not in Athanasius' own works, but in the *Encyclical Letter* of his predecessor Alexander in 324 (quoted in Socrates, I.6). This letter, which as we saw in Chapter 3 also represents the first condemnation of Eusebius of Nicomedia and the 'Eusebians' as an 'Arian party', depicts 'Arianism' in very similar terms to Athanasius' later and more extensive writings. Thus it is valuable to quote the relevant passages here:

What they have invented and assert, contrary to the Scriptures, are as follows: God was not always a father, but there was when (*hote*) God was not a father; the Word of God was not always (*aei*), but came to be out of nothing (*ex ouk ontōn*); for the ever-existing God has made Him who did not previously exist, out of the non-existent. Therefore indeed there was once when (*pote hote*) He was not. For the Son is a creature (*ktisma*) and a thing made (*poiēma*). He is neither like the Father according to essence (*kat' ousian*), nor true Word by nature (*physei*) of the Father, nor true Wisdom. He is one of the things made and one of the generated beings (*tōn poiēmatōn kai tōn genētōn*), being inaccurately called Word and Wisdom, since He came to be Himself through the proper (*idio*) Word of God and the Wisdom in God, in which indeed God made everything and also Him. Therefore indeed He is changeable and mutable (*treptos kai alloiōtos*) by nature, as are all rational beings, [and] the Word is foreign and alien and separate from the essence of the Father. And the Father is unintelligible (*arrētos*) to the Son, for the Word neither perfectly and exactly knows the Father, nor is He able to see Him perfectly. For indeed the Son does not know His own essence, for He was made because of us, in order that through Him as through an instrument (*di' organou*) God might create us; and He would not have existed, if God had not wished to make us. Accordingly, someone asked them if the Word of God is able to be changed, as the devil changed, and they were not ashamed to say that truly it is possible, for He is of changeable nature (*treptēs physeōs*), being generated and changeable from the beginning. (Hansen (1995) 7, 9–8, 15)

The Father was not always Father; the Son is neither eternal nor the true Word and Wisdom of God but was generated from non-existence as one of the created order; and the Son therefore is mutable and entirely separate from the essence (*ousia*) and nature (*physis*) of the Father. These are the fundamental elements of Alexander's interpretation of the 'Arian heresy', and the same elements immediately recur in Athanasius' earliest accounts of the theology of the men whom he condemns. In *Festal Letter* X of 338, three years after he had first branded the 'Eusebians' as 'Arians' at the Council of Tyre, Athanasius denounces the 'Ariomaniacs' as fighters against Christ, who 'have denied His essential Godhead... doubt His being truly the Son of God... deny His eternity... [and] do not believe in Him as the incorruptible Son from the incorruptible Father' (X.9; Robertson (1892) 531). A similar, though even more concise, description of the 'heretics', who say that 'He [the Son] is a creature and has His being from things which are not' (XI.10; Robertson (1892) 536), then appears in *Festal Letter* XI, written the very next year (339). This was followed, in *c.*339–46, by Athanasius' greatest exposition of 'Arian' theology, the three *Orations against the Arians.*

In the Introduction to the *First Oration against the Arians*, whose heresiological presentation of the 'Arian party' we have already considered, Athanasius lays down his interpretation of 'Arianism' in two famous passages that purport to represent a summary of the *Thalia* of Arius himself. Here he defines the teachings that all those who follow the heresiarch, including the 'Eusebians', must share:

Not always was God a father; but there was once (*hote*) when God was alone, and not yet a father; later He became a father. Not always was the Son; for since all things came to be out of nothing (*ex ouk ontōn*), and since all things are created (*ktismatōn*) and made (*poiēmatōn*) and came to be, thus also the Word of God Himself came to be out of nothing, and there was once when (*pote hote*) He was not. And He was not until He was generated, but He too had a beginning of creation. For he [Arius] says that God was alone, and not yet was the Word, nor the Wisdom. Then, wishing to fashion us, thereupon He made a certain one (*hena tina*) and named Him Word and Son and Wisdom, so that He might fashion us through Him. Thus he says that there are two Wisdoms, one proper (*idian*) and coexisting (*sunuparchousan*) in God, [and] that the Son was originated in this Wisdom, and only as partaking (*metechonta*) of this is named Wisdom and Word. For Wisdom, he says, came into existence in Wisdom by the will of the wise God. Thus also he said there was another Word than the Son in God, and the Son again as partaking (*metechonta*) of this is Himself named Word and Son according to grace (*kata charin*). And this too is a thought proper to their heresy, as is shown in other writings of theirs, that there are many powers. And the one in God is proper (*idia*) by nature (*physei*) and eternal (*aidios*); [but] Christ again is not the true (*alēthinē*) power of God, but He also is one of those who are called powers, one of which indeed, 'the locust' and 'the caterpillar', is called [in Scripture] not only the power, but the great power. [And] many others also are like the Son, concerning whom David also sang, saying 'Lord of the powers' [Psalm 24:10]. And just as everything else, thus the Word too is changeable (*treptos*) by nature (*physei*), and He remains good by His proper free will, while He wishes. Therefore when He wishes, He too is able to change, just as we are also, being of changeable nature (*treptēs physeōs*). For because of this, he [Arius] says, God who foreknew that He would be good, gave in advance to Him this glory, which He would have afterwards from virtue (*ek tēs aretēs*). Thus from His works, which God foreknew, He made Him such as He would come to be. (I.5; Tetz (1998) 114, 11–115, 34)

He [Arius] has dared to say again that the Word is not true (*alēthinos*) God. Although indeed He is called God, He is not true (*alēthinos*) [God], but by participation of grace (*metochē charitos*), [and] thus He, just as also all others, is called God only by name. And since everything is foreign (*xenōn*) and unlike (*anomoiōn*) to God according to essence (*kat' ousian*), thus also the Word is alien (*allotrios*) and unlike (*anomoios*) in everything to the essence and distinctive quality (*idiotētos*) of the Father, [but] He is proper to generated and created things (*tōn genētōn kai ktismatōn*) and is one of them. Afterwards, just as a successor to the recklessness of the devil, he [Arius] has laid down in the *Thalia* that therefore even to the Son the Father is unintelligible (*arrētos*), and the Word is able to neither see perfectly nor know precisely His own Father. But indeed what He knows and He sees, He knows and He sees according to His own measure (*analogōs tois idiois metrois*), just as also we know according to our own power. For the Son, too, he [Arius] says, not only does not precisely know the Father, for He is wanting in comprehension, but also the Son Himself does not know His own essence. And [Arius says] that the essences (*ousiai*) of the Father and of the Son and of the Holy Spirit are separate by nature (*physei*) and estranged and divided and alien and do not participate in each other; and so he asserts that they are unlike (*anomoioi*) altogether from each other by [their] essences and by glory into infinity. Thus as to likeness (*homoiotēta*) of glory and essence, he says that the Word is entirely foreign (*allotrion*) from both the Father and the Holy Spirit. For in such words has the impious one spoken; and he has said that the Son is distinct according to Himself and without participation according to anything of the Father. (I.6; Tetz (1998) 115, 1–19)

Athanasius asserts repeatedly that the interpretation of 'Arianism' that he presents here derives directly from 'the fables lying in the laughable writings of Arius' (I.6; Tetz (1998) 115, 19–20). This assertion has been the subject of considerable debate, to which I will return shortly, but what is beyond question is that these passages represent an explicit statement of Athanasius' own definition of 'Arian' theology. The fundamental elements of that definition precisely echo the description of 'Arianism' in the *Encyclical Letter* of Alexander quoted above, particularly the allegation that Arius separated the Son from the Father, denied that the Son was the true Word or Wisdom of God, and reduced Him instead to the level of a created and mutable being. Those same elements continue to occur consistently in Athanasius' later writings. The *Life of Antony* (69–70), the *De Decretis* (6), the *De Sententia Dionysii* (2), and most extensively the *Encyclical Letter* of 356 (12) all contain further Athanasian summaries of 'Arianism', each derived in turn from the *Orations against the Arians.* And just as Athanasius throughout his polemical works constructs his opponents as a single 'Arian party', so too his interpretation of their 'heresy' remains uniform and monolithic. In both the *De Decretis* and the *Encyclical Letter* of 356, and again in the *De Synodis* of 359, Athanasius continues to insist that the contemporaries whom he now condemns still hold the same theology that Arius is alleged to have taught in the beginning.

The Introduction to the *First Oration against the Arians* thus represents the blueprint for every Athanasian presentation of the doctrines that he condemns as 'Arian'. Near the end of that Introduction, Athanasius conveniently summarizes that definition:

What can they bring forward to us therefore from the infamous *Thalia*? ... That not always (*aei*) was God a father, but later He became so. Not always (*aei*) was the Son, for He was not until He was begotten (*ouk ēn prin gennēthē*). He is not from the Father, but He also came into existence out of nothing (*ex ouk ontōn*). He is not proper (*idios*) to the essence (*ousias*) of the

Father, for He is a creature (*ktisma*) and a thing made (*poiēma*). Christ is not true (*alēthinos*) God, but He also by participation (*metochē*) was made God. The Son does not know the Father exactly, nor may the Word see the Father perfectly, and the Word does not understand nor know the Father exactly. He is not the true (*alēthinos*) and only (*monos*) Word of the Father, but by name (*onomati*) only is called Word and Wisdom, and by grace (*chariti*) is called Son and Power. He is not unchangeable (*atreptos*), like the Father, but is changeable (*treptos*) by nature (*physei*), like the creatures (*ta ktismata*). (I.9; Tetz (1998) 118, 11–12; 14–22)

It is this construction of 'Athanasian Arianism' that in the analysis that follows I will compare to the known theological writings of Arius himself and of the 'Eusebians'.

'ARIANS' AND 'ARIANISM'? ARIUS, THE 'EUSEBIANS', AND THE 'DEDICATION' COUNCIL

In the *Search for the Christian Doctrine of God*, R. P. C. Hanson summarized what he believed to be 'the "Arian" school of thought'. His concise nine-point guide demonstrates succinctly the influence that the polemic of Athanasius has exerted upon modern conceptions of 'Arianism':

i) God was not always Father, He was once in a situation in which He was simply God and not Father;
ii) The Logos or Son is a creature. God made Him *ex ouk ontōn*;
iii) There are two *Logoi* and two Wisdoms (*Sophiae*), and several powers (*dunameis*) of God;
iv) The Son is variable by nature, but remains stable by the gift of God;
v) The Logos is alien from the divine Being and distinct; He is not true God because He has come into existence;
vi) The Son's knowledge of God is imperfect;
vii) The Son's knowledge of himself is limited;
viii) Anthropocentric Cosmology: the Son has been created for our sakes, as an instrument for creating us;
ix) A Trinity of different hypostases exists.[9]

[9] Hanson (1988*b*) 19–23, drawing upon the model of 'Arianism' constructed by Lorenz (1979) 37–49.

This nine-point guide, as Hanson himself acknowledges, is in fact a summary of Athanasius' monolithic construction of 'Arianism' as a theology held not only by Arius himself but by all those whom Athanasius defines as 'Arian'. Hanson is fully content to accept that construction. 'If we here reproduce what Athanasius alleges Arius to have taught, we must realize that it will also include much of what his early supporters taught rather than the exact teaching of Arius himself. For most of Athanasius' polemic the views of Arius and of his early supporters are identical. "Arius" is virtually interchangeable with "the Arians".'[10] 'But it is easy to see that the two cannot have been very different. What we have already seen of Arius' teaching compared with what Athanasius tells us is enough to establish that Arius' early disciples [among whom Hanson names Asterius and Eusebius of Nicomedia] enlarged and developed rather than altered his doctrine.'[11]

Hanson is far from being alone in his acceptance of Athanasius' construction of a distinct and clearly defined theological position that all those who are described as 'Arian' can be assumed to share. Despite the repeated cautions in recent scholarship concerning the uncertain reliability of our 'orthodox' sources, and Hanson's own emphasis that it is anachronistic to describe the fourth century in terms of established 'orthodoxy' and manifest 'heresy', the long-held conception of an 'Arian Controversy' has proved difficult to escape. Yet modern scholarly opinion has never reached a universally or even broadly agreed definition of the term 'Arian'. Taken at face value, such an appellation ought to indicate the teachings of Arius himself, but Maurice Wiles has demonstrated that Arius was never in reality a central figure in the controversies after Nicaea.[12] His name was not invoked as a founder or teacher,[13] except in the polemic of opponents

[10] Hanson (1988*b*) 19.

[11] Ibid. 19. See also Lorenz (1983), who, after repeating his earlier construction of 'Arianism' from the polemic of Athanasius and Alexander (11–19), emphatically concludes that all the doctrines that those men condemn 'auf Arius zurückgehen' and that therefore 'Der Arianismus ist keine Erfindung der orthodoxen Polemik' (35).

[12] Wiles (1996); see also Ayres (2004*b*): 'Arius' own theology is of little importance in understanding the major debates of the rest of the century' (56).

[13] The suggestion of Rowan Williams (1987) 82 that 'some anti-Nicenes may, in the early days, have been happy with the name of 'Arians', as a designation of their theological preference' must be rejected. Wiles (1993*b*) 42 is correct: 'titles deriving from the name of Arius were or would have been conscientiously disavowed by those on whom they were bestowed', as indeed occurred in 341.

like Athanasius.[14] Famously, the 'First Creed' of the eastern bishops who gathered at the 'Dedication' Council of Antioch in 341 explicitly declared that 'we have not been followers (*akolouthoi*) of Arius, for how could we, who are bishops, follow a presbyter?' (*De Synodis* 22; Opitz (1941) 248, 29–30). At the same time, it has been increasingly recognized that men previously described as 'Arian', in particular Asterius and Eusebius of Nicomedia, but also others including Eusebius of Caesarea, vary widely in their theology both from the teachings attributed to Arius and from each other. As Thomas Kopecek rather despairingly admitted, 'Arians did not always agree with one another about fundamental theological and christological propositions'.[15]

The immediate reaction of many scholars who have recognized these difficulties has been to create ever broader definitions of 'Arianism'. T. D. Barnes declares of Eusebius of Caesarea that 'even the most casual reader... cannot fail to see that it is an Arian orthodoxy which Eusebius represents as the accepted teaching of the Church'.[16] But the 'orthodoxy' that Barnes here describes as 'Arian' is little more than Eusebius' subordination of the Son to the Father, and as Hanson knew well, 'almost everybody in the East at that period would have agreed that there was a subordination of some sort within the Trinity'.[17] Rowan Williams, on the other hand, originally came to the conclusion that '"Arianism", throughout most of the fourth century, was in fact a loose and uneasy coalition of those hostile to Nicaea in general and the *homoousios* in particular'.[18] Similarly, Wiles argues that 'the Arian movement... is probably better understood as a loosely allied group of people with overlapping but by no means identical concerns, held together more by their opposition to certain Marcellan and Athanasian tendencies than by a single specific theological platform'.[19] These latter two perspectives do recognize the variety of doctrinal beliefs that can be traced within the ranks of those traditionally designated as 'Arian'. Yet they nevertheless remain

14 'The dead Arius was not even a whipping boy, but a whip' (Wiles (1993*b*) 43).
15 Kopecek (1981) 57.
16 Barnes (1981) 265.
17 Hanson (1988*b*) 287.
18 Williams (1987) 166.
19 Wiles (1989*b*) 159.

shackled by the assumption that a recognized 'Arian' position must in some sense exist. Williams and Wiles both attempt to define that position in negative terms, but in doing so they have still in effect adopted Athanasius' polemical polarization, defining as 'Arian' anyone who questioned the Nicene Creed or who opposed Athanasius himself.

All of these diverse modern interpretations of 'Arianism' thus accept, whether explicitly or implicitly, the construction of an 'Arian' party and an 'Arian' theology that underlies the polemic of Athanasius. But why do we employ terms like 'Arian' or 'Arianism' at all? Not only is the breadth of meanings attributed to these terms by different scholars confusing, but regardless of how they may be understood, such appellations must always be misleading. Taken at face value, they give to Arius a prominence that he simply did not possess in his own time, imposing his alleged theology upon other 'Arians' who held markedly different views. Yet, if 'Arianism' is to be redefined as a theological position broader than the teachings of Arius alone, then the very title merely increases the confusion and distortion.[20] Most importantly, to speak of an 'Arian Controversy' in any form is to impose upon the fourth century the polarized interpretation that is the product of our polemical sources, and above all of the writings of Athanasius. It is for this reason that Rowan Williams ultimately denied entirely the validity of 'Arian' terminology, for classifications such as 'Arian' tell us nothing and only 'make it harder to understand the period in its own terms'.[21]

It is against this background that my own analysis of Athanasius' construction of 'Arianism', and of the 'Eusebians' as 'Arian', must be set. In the previous pages I traced the definition of the theological position that Athanasius asserts that not only Arius himself but all those whom he names as 'Arian' held. Now it is necessary to assess the accuracy of that polemical assertion. As we shall see, there is certainly

20 Williams (1985) suggests that '"Arianism" as a system has less to do with the thought of the *Thalia* than with the sort of broadly-based position outlined in, say, Eusebius [of Nicomedia]'s *Letter to Paulinus*' (24). Vinzent (1993*a*) 32, on the other hand, asserts that 'Arianism' is better understood as the theology of Asterius 'the Sophist'. If such statements are true, however, one has to ask why such a 'system' should be called 'Arianism' at all.

21 Williams (1992) 104.

a degree of truth in Athanasius' presentation of the teachings of Arius. But there is also a strong element of distortion, and that element grows even stronger when we turn to the theology of the individuals whom Athanasius branded as an 'Arian party'. This distortion can only be demonstrated, however, by a careful comparison first between the Athanasian construction of the 'Arian heresy' and the extant writings of Arius, and then between both Arius' own theology and Athanasian Arianism and the still more fragmentary evidence for the teachings of the so-called 'Eusebians'. In this study I will draw when possible on the writings of all the known members of these 'Eusebians', but the vast bulk of our evidence derives from three men, the only men specifically named by Athanasius as 'heretics' in the *Orations against the Arians*. It is upon these individuals that my analysis must concentrate: Arius, Asterius 'the Sophist', and Eusebius of Nicomedia.

The Theology of Arius

The difficulties posed by the study of Arius' own theology are well known, and they do not need to be restated in detail here. Older attitudes that dismissed Arius as 'utterly illogical and unscriptural'[22] have now been almost universally rejected, but debate still rages over the content and origin of his doctrine and his place in the development of Christian thought. Arius has been described as both 'Antiochene'[23] and 'Alexandrian',[24] as an 'Aristotelian' and a 'Platonist',[25] as a unique and isolated thinker[26] and as 'a committed theological conservative'.[27] I will not attempt to do justice to all these modern

[22] Gwatkin (1882) 2. There is a summary of older scholarship on Arius in Lorenz (1979) 23–36.

[23] Pollard (1958).

[24] Wiles (1962), who wrote in part in response to Pollard. There are further discussions of the 'Alexandrian' background to Arius' thought in Barnard (1970) 296–310, Lorenz (1979) 67–122, and Kannengiesser (1986).

[25] On Arius' relationship to Platonism see especially Stead (1964), with brief summaries in Grillmeier (1975) 222–5 and Lorenz (1979) 62–5. On the more general question of Arius' philosophical antecedents, see Barnard (1970) 289–95 and Williams (1983).

[26] 'The lonely grandeur of the Alexandrian heresiarch' (Kannengiesser (1981) 24).

[27] Williams (1987) 175; see also Stead (1964) 30 and Young (1983) 64.

theories. Williams was almost certainly correct when he observed that 'it is perhaps a mistake to look for one self-contained and exclusive "theological school" to which to assign him',[28] and Hanson's conclusion that Arius was 'basically eclectic'[29] has a strong element of truth. Instead, I intend to contrast Arius' own words to the Athanasian construction of the 'Arian heresy', and so to identify both Arius' original teachings and the distortions inherent in Athanasius' presentation of the man whom he described as the greatest 'heresiarch' of all.

The surviving writings of Arius himself, however, are very limited indeed. Perhaps the least controversial texts, although still much debated, are three short works preserved by Athanasius and the ecclesiastical historians Theodoret and Socrates. These texts are the *Creed and Letter* that Arius sent to Alexander of Alexandria in 320/1 (*De Synodis* 16; Opitz, *Urkunde* VI); Arius' *Letter to Eusebius of Nicomedia* in *c.*321/2 (Theodoret I.5; Opitz, *Urkunde* I); and the *Creed* that Arius and Euzoius submitted to Constantine in an attempt to secure recognition of their 'orthodoxy', probably in 333 (Socrates, I.26; Opitz, *Urkunde* XXX).[30] Unfortunately, of these works, the *Letter to Eusebius* is brief, and concerned more with the rejection of Alexander's alleged beliefs than with stating Arius' own doctrines. The two *Creeds*, meanwhile, were both written in an attempt to secure reconciliation, and so could be accused of 'toning down' Arius' theological position.[31] Even collectively, these three texts cannot provide a full statement of the theology of Arius, and intensive scholarly attention has therefore been directed towards the most important, but also the most difficult, source for Arius' personal teachings, the fragments of his *Thalia* preserved in the works of Athanasius.

I have already reproduced earlier in this chapter the most extensive Athanasian 'quotation' that is said to come from Arius' *Thalia*, from

28 Williams (1987) 115.

29 Hanson (1988*b*) 88. See also Barnard (1970) 310–11.

30 For the chronology of the first two letters see Williams (1987) 56, and the discussion of the early 'Arian Controversy' in Ch. 3. On the last text see Stead (1994) 24, who like many scholars now rejects the date of 327 proposed for this creed by Opitz (1934).

31 The *Creed* submitted to Constantine in 333 has in particular been described by Williams (1987) 97 as 'almost entirely colourless'.

sections 5–6 of the *First Oration against the Arians* in *c.*339–46. But Athanasius also brings forward another collection of *Thalia* 'citations' in *De Synodis* 15, written some twenty years later in 359, and while this later collection shares a number of similarities with the material provided in the *First Oration*, there are also significant differences. In an important article first published in 1978, Christopher Stead rejected the traditional acceptance of these two Athanasian presentations of the *Thalia* as equally valid and mutually compatible.[32] He emphasized that a number of ideas attributed to Arius by Athanasius only appear in the alleged passages from the *Thalia* cited in the *First Oration*, which he identified as an Athanasian paraphrase rather than Arius' own words. The quotations given in *De Synodis* 15, on the other hand, would seem to correspond more readily to the other letters and creeds known to have been written by Arius.[33] However, in 1981 this analysis was challenged by Charles Kannengiesser.[34] Accepting and reinforcing the need to distinguish between the two Athanasian 'quotations', he argues that, although *Oration* I.5–6 'does not give us the *ipsissima verba* of Arius',[35] nevertheless these extracts remain our best indication of Arius' own doctrines. By contrast, Kannengiesser argues that *De Synodis* 15 represents a reworking of Arius' original ideas by a later 'Neo-Arian' editor,[36] and thus that this material sheds no direct light upon the thought of Arius himself.

[32] Stead (1978) 22–4. Stead particularly had in mind the collection of *Thalia* fragments in Bardy (1936) 246–74, in which equal weight is given to all Athanasius' 'quotations'.

[33] 'It is the more complex and less unorthodox presentation of Arius' teaching that is to be preferred; the simpler and more damning reports will be suspect' (Stead (1978) 24). Stead also argues in the same article that only the *De Synodis* extracts and the preface to the *Thalia* 'quotations' in *Oration* I.5 have a visible metre, as we would expect for genuine extracts from a work which Arius is believed to have written in verse. However, Stead later acknowledged ((1994) 27) that his own attempt to reconstruct that metre as anapaestic had failed, and upheld instead the argument of West (1982) that the metre is in fact 'Sotadean'. On this debate, see also Böhm (1992), esp. 334–7.

[34] Kannengiesser (1981), (1985*a*).

[35] Kannengiesser (1981) 14.

[36] In his initial argument (ibid.), Kannengiesser proposed Aetius as the 'Neo-Arian' 'editor'. In his later restatement of his hypothesis (1985*a*) 74, he favours instead the latter's pupil Eunomius.

No decisive verdict has yet settled this scholarly debate.[37] Rowan Williams[38] and Stuart Hall[39] have upheld the arguments of Stead, but Gregg and Groh[40] supported Kannengiesser, while R. P. C. Hanson ultimately declined to accept either position entirely.[41] My own conclusion, which the present study will seek to reinforce, is that *De Synodis* 15 does indeed provide the most reliable guide to the original words of Arius' *Thalia* and that Stead was correct to assert that in *Oration* I.5–6, Athanasius at several points 'has attributed to the Arians a view which is really his own inference'.[42] Given the prominent role that the presentation of the *Thalia* plays in Athanasius' construction of 'Arianism' in the Introduction to the *First Oration against the Arians*, it is surely significant that there are marked differences between that polemical construction of Arius' theology and the doctrines that can be substantiated from his other known letters and fragments. In order to assess the nature and extent of those differences, in the paragraphs that follow I have set the fundamental elements of Athanasian Arianism (as summarized in *Oration* I.9 quoted above) against the words of Arius himself, as they are recorded in his three extant letters and creeds and in the extracts from the *Thalia* quoted in *De Synodis* 15.[43]

Not always (*aei*) was God a father, but later He became so. Not always (*aei*) was the Son, for He was not until He was begotten (*ouk ēn prin gennēthē*).

No evidence supports Athanasius' allegation, also made by Alexander, that Arius taught that God was not always Father. It is possible that Arius believed either that God was always Father as He is the ultimate source of all, or that He was always Father *in potentia* even

37 To the two approaches to the *Thalia* discussed here, one might add the argument of Metzler (1991) that the original work was written at least in part as an acrostic. However, we simply do not possess sufficient evidence, either for Arius' words or for the possible content of that acrostic, for such an approach to resolve the argument between Stead and Kannengiesser, or to significantly assist a reconstruction of the genuine *Thalia*.

38 Williams (1985).

39 Hall (1985).

40 Gregg and Groh (1981) 83.n.19.

41 Hanson (1988*b*) 12.

42 Stead (1978) 32.

43 The same approach is adopted by Behr (2004) 143–6.

before the existence of the Son.[44] In any case, the accusation itself is nothing more than a hostile interpretation from the second statement attributed here to Arius, this time with complete justice. For Arius did deny explicitly that the Son could share the eternity of the Father. In his *Letter to Eusebius of Nicomedia*, he declares that 'He [the Son] was not, before He was begotten (*prin gennēthe*)' (Parmentier (1998) 27, 1–2), and in the *Letter to Alexander* he makes the same statement in greater detail. 'The Son, who is begotten apart from time (*achronōs*) by the Father, and who is created and established before the ages (*pro aiōniōn*), was not before He was begotten (*ouk ēn pro tou gennēthēnai*) . . . for He is not eternal (*aidios*) or co-eternal (*sunaidios*) or co-unbegotten (*sunagennētos*) with the Father' (Opitz (1941) 244, 9–11). Only the unbegotten (*agennētos*) Father is eternal, for all other beings must have a beginning of existence. In both his letters, Arius therefore repeatedly denies the teaching of Alexander that 'God always, the Son always', for this is to imply that there are two unbegotten beings. According to the *Thalia* fragments quoted in the *De Synodis*, 'we call Him unbegotten because of the one begotten in nature (*tēn physin*) . . . we adore Him as eternal because of the one born in time (*en chronois*)' (*De Synodis* 15; Opitz (1941) 242, 11–13).[45]

He is not from the Father, but He also came into existence out of nothing (*ex ouk ontōn*). He is not proper (*idios*) to the essence (*ousias*) of the Father, for He is a creature (*ktisma*) and a thing made (*poiēma*).

The belief that the Son was created 'out of nothing' (*ex ouk ontōn*) has always been held as a fundamental principle of 'Arianism', although Arius himself only uses this phrase once, at the end of his

[44] This latter doctrine was held by Asterius and also (according to Philostorgius, II.15) by Theognis of Nicaea, although Arius himself never makes such a statement in his extant words. According to the *Thalia* extracts in the *De Synodis*, Arius wrote that 'Understand then that the Unity was, but the Duality was not, before He existed. So it follows that even when there is no Son, the Father is God (*De Synodis* 15; Opitz (1941) 243, 1–2).

[45] It is difficult to reconcile Arius' statement in this final passage that the Son has a beginning '*en chronois*' with the emphasis in his *Letter to Alexander* above that the Son was begotten '*achronōs*', and thus the accuracy of the charge repeated by both Alexander and Athanasius that Arius taught that the Son was begotten temporally must remain uncertain.

Letter to Eusebius of Nicomedia.[46] Whatever the explanation for the omission of this idea from his other works,[47] in that letter Arius declares that 'He [the Son] is out of nothing (*ex ouk ontōn*) ... because He is neither part (*meros*) of God nor from any existing being' (Parmentier (1998) 27, 4–5). From this latter conclusion, Arius never deviates throughout his extant writings. In the *Thalia* extracts from the *De Synodis*, he insists that the Son 'has nothing proper (*idios*) to God according to personal subsistence (*idiotētos hypostasin*), for He is neither equal (*isos*) nor *homoousios* with Him.... The Father is alien (*xenos*) according to essence to the Son, because He exists without beginning' (*De Synodis* 15; Opitz (1941) 242, 16–17; 27).

Athanasius' statement that Arius denied that the Son was 'proper to the essence of the Father' is thus unquestionably correct. Just as Arius denied that the begotten Son could be co-eternal with the unbegotten Father, so too He cannot derive from the latter's *ousia*, as any such derivation must inevitably impose materialist or Sabellian ideas upon God.[48] Arius instead believed that the Son was created not from the *ousia* of the Father, but by His will alone.[49] However, while it is therefore also true that Arius did teach that the Son was in some sense a '*ktisma*', the assertion of both Alexander and Athanasius that Arius reduced the Son to the level of every other created being is again their own polemical interpretation. In his *Letter to Alexander*, Arius explicitly declares that the Son is the

46 The silence of Arius in the *Thalia* and the *Letter to Alexander* led Nautin (1949) to argue that the idea of creation '*ex ouk ontōn*' in the *Letter to Eusebius of Nicomedia* was a later polemical interpolation. However, this argument was strongly refuted by Simonetti (1965) 88–109, who emphasizes that all four extant manuscripts of Arius' *Letter*, two in Greek and two in Latin, all share the same original reading. For a useful summary of this debate, see Luibheid (1981) 22, who upholds the judgement of Simonetti.

47 It is often assumed, though without explicit evidence, that this omission represents a 'toning down' of Arius' beliefs under the influence of Eusebius of Nicomedia (e.g. Kannengiesser (1981) 10; Hanson (1985*a*) 79), who as we shall see did not endorse the idea that the Son was created 'out of nothing'.

48 The Son exists 'not as Valentinus pronounced that the offspring of the Father was an emanation; nor as Manichaeus taught that the offspring was a portion *homoousios* to the Father; or as Sabellius, dividing the Monad, speaks of a Son-Father' (Arius, *Letter to Alexander; Opitz (1941) 243, 35–244, 1).*

49 On the significance of the divine will to the theology of Arius, see Stead (1983) and Williams (1987) 98.

'perfect creature (*teleion ktisma*) of God, but not as one of the creatures' (Opitz (1941) 243, 33–4), and he did not describe the Son as a *poiēma*, a term that Arius is never known to have used.[50]

Christ is not true (*alēthinos*) God, but He also by participation (*metochē*) was made God.

In all his extant works, Arius does indeed deliberately avoid any reference to the Son as 'true (*alēthinos*) God'.[51] However, the allegation that Arius taught that therefore the Son was 'also made God by participation' cannot be substantiated. In the *De Synodis Thalia*, Arius declares that 'the Son who was not, but who existed at the paternal will, is only-begotten (*monogenēs*) God' (*De Synodis* 15; Opitz (1941) 243, 3–4). There is no reference to the Son becoming God by 'participation', and the emphasis that the Son is 'only-begotten' challenges Athanasius' assertion that Arius taught that the Son 'also' participates in the Divinity just as do others. Here once more we would seem to have the interpretation of Athanasius himself, derived from Arius' rejection of the term 'true God' and his doctrine that the Son was created by God's will.

The Son does not know the Father exactly, nor may the Word see the Father perfectly, and the Word does not understand nor know the Father exactly.

This synopsis of Arius' doctrine of the incomplete knowledge of the Son, although absent from his extant letters, would appear from the *Thalia* fragments in the *De Synodis* to be fundamentally correct. 'God is ineffable (*arrētos*) to the Son. ... For the Son Himself does not know His own essence; for, being Son, He truly came to be at His Father's will. What reason then permits the one who is from a Father to know by comprehension the one who begot Him? For it is clear that for one who has a beginning to encompass by thought or apprehension the one who is without beginning is impossible' (*De Synodis* 15; Opitz (1941) 243, 14; 18–23). That which is begotten cannot fully know the unbegotten, and the Son thus cannot perfectly know the Father,

[50] The only evidence that Arius ever did describe the Son as 'one of the creatures (*tōn ktismatōn*)' or as a 'thing made (*poiēma*)' derives from the polemic of Athanasius himself. I will return to this fundamental element of Athanasius' construction of 'Arianism' near the end of this chapter.

[51] In his *Letter to Alexander*, Arius describes the Father as 'one God ... alone true (*monon alēthinon*)' (Opitz (1941) 243, 28–9).

although Arius adds that the Son does know the Father 'in proper measure (*idiois metrois*)' to Himself (Opitz (1941) 242, 22)[52] and so presumably knows Him to a greater extent than any other being. Arius' doctrine of the Son's limited knowledge of His Father also contrasts sharply to the later arguments of Aetius and Eunomius that all beings could achieve knowledge of God. This again contradicts Kannengiesser's thesis that the *De Synodis Thalia* extracts derive from that 'Neo-Arian' circle, and reinforces instead the value of this source for Arius' own theology, which Athanasius here has accurately preserved.

He is not the true (*alēthinos*) and only (*monos*) Word of the Father, but by name (*onomati*) only is called Word and Wisdom, and by grace (*chariti*) is called Son and Power.

There is a degree of truth in Athanasius' claim that Arius denied that the Son was the only Word and Wisdom of the Father. As Stead observes, Arius taught a 'two-level theory' regarding the attributes of the Father and the Son.[53] All of the *epinoiai* ('aspects') by which the Son is known (such as Power, Wisdom, Truth, Image, Radiance, and Word) are in the theology of Arius qualities received by the Son from the Father, who possesses them inherently and eternally. Thus in the *De Synodis Thalia* Arius declares that 'God is wise, since He is Wisdom's teacher' and that 'Wisdom existed as Wisdom by the will of a wise God' (*De Synodis* 15; Opitz (1941) 242, 18; 243, 5).[54] In this sense, Arius did teach that the Son was not the only Wisdom, for there is also the distinct Wisdom inherent in the Father.[55] However, although Arius denies that the Son is proper to the essence of the Father, and therefore insists that the Son must possess His *epinoiai* through God's will and not by His own essential nature, at no point does he suggest that the Son is therefore only Word and Wisdom 'by name' or 'by grace'. This is Athanasius' own interpretation, that if the

[52] Arius possibly derived this conception of the Son's 'relative knowledge' from contemporary Neoplatonism (Williams (1987) 207–12; see also Kannengiesser (1981) 36–7). However, the hypothesis of any Neoplatonic influence upon Arius is rejected by Stead (1997), to whom Williams replies in (2001) 261–6.

[53] Stead (1964) 20.

[54] Vinzent (1993*a*) unconvincingly attributes this passage to Asterius (fragment 65).

[55] In his *Letter to Alexander*, Arius wrote explicitly that the Son received life and being and glory from the will of God, but that 'the Father did not, in giving to Him the inheritance of all things, deprive Himself of what He has ingenerately (*agennētōs*) in Himself' (Opitz (1941) 244, 6–7).

Son is not essentially God, then He cannot truly be called the Word, Wisdom or Power of God, and it is a conclusion that Arius himself would obviously have denied.

He is not unchangeable (*atreptos*), like the Father, but is changeable (*treptos*) by nature (*physei*), like the creatures (*ta ktismata*). This last and most controversial element of the construction of 'Arianism' that both Alexander and Athanasius attribute to Arius is at face value openly false. Not only does Arius emphasize the unique status of the created Son and distinguish Him from all other created beings, as we have already seen above, but in his letters Arius repeatedly and explicitly insists that the Son is 'unchangeable (*analloiōtos*)' (*Letter to Eusebius of Nicomedia*; Parmentier (1998) 27, 1) and 'immutable and unchangeable (*atrepton kai analloiōton*)' (*Letter to Alexander*; Opitz (1941) 243, 33). Only in the 'quotations' from the *Thalia* in *Oration* I.5–6 and in the *Encyclical Letter* of Alexander is Arius ever suggested to have taught that the Son could be mutable. Yet the assertion that Arius believed the Son to be changeable 'by nature' has largely been accepted by modern scholars, who often quote Wiles' description of the 'Arian Son' that 'while by nature He must be *treptos*, He can be and is in practice *atreptos*'.[56] It is not impossible that this view does in fact reflect the actual belief of Arius, for he never clarifies the source of the immutability that he attributes to the Son.[57] But by the same token, Arius never expresses this conclusion in his own words, and it is possible that here once more we see an interpretation that Athanasius (and Alexander) has drawn from Arius' original teachings, rather than the conclusion of Arius himself.[58]

[56] Wiles (1962) 345; Stead (1983) 246; Williams (1987) 114.

[57] The most common scholarly conclusion is that Arius' Son is mutable by nature, but immutable by His own will (e.g. Lorenz (1979) 200). This conclusion receives some support from the anathemas of the Council of Antioch in 325, on which see further below.

[58] Kopecek (1979) 124–5 observes that the 'Neo-Arian' Aetius apparently taught that the Son could be immutable by essence if so willed by God, a theory that he explains as Aetius' rejection of Arius' 'inconsistency'. Aetius chose 'to ignore Arius' frequent references to the Son's mutability in favour of two references to His immutability'. Of course, Arius' 'frequent references' to the mutability of the Son all occur in the polemic of Alexander and Athanasius, whereas the 'two references to His immutability' derive from Arius' own hand. But if Aetius did teach an essentially immutable yet created Son, then it is plausible (although it cannot be proven) that others, including Eusebius of Caesarea (see Lyman (1985) 264) and Arius himself, might have done likewise.

From this brief and somewhat schematic comparison between the polemic of Athanasius and the fragmentary evidence for Arius' own theology, it is evident that there are considerable elements of truth in Athanasius' construction of 'Arianism'. Arius did deny the eternity of the Son. He described the Son as a creature (*ktisma*), explicitly rejected that He could be proper to the *ousia* of the Father, and at least in one letter referred to the Son as created 'out of nothing'. Arius avoided the expression 'true God' in relation to the Son, denied in a sense that He was the only Wisdom of God, and taught that the Son could not fully know the Father. Nor were Athanasius and Alexander alone in denouncing several of these 'Arian' concepts. Both the Councils of Antioch and Nicaea in 325 anathematized the expressions 'there was when He was not' and that 'He came into existence out of nothing'.[59] In addition, Nicaea also anathematized any suggestion that the Son is 'subject to alteration or change', while the Council of Antioch insisted that the Son was immutable by nature and condemned those who teach that 'the Son is immutable by His own free will . . . and that He is not by nature immutable in the way the Father is' (Opitz (1934–5) 39, 19–40, 1).[60] The central clauses of the Nicene Creed are all intended to refute the conception of the Son attributed to Arius, and thus Nicaea proclaims that the Son is 'true God', and of course that He is '*homoousios*' with and 'from the *ousia*' of the Father.[61]

Yet alongside the genuine teachings of Arius that Athanasius condemns in his polemic stand an equally significant number of allegedly 'Arian' principles that in fact derive not from Arius' words but from the polemical interpretations of Athanasius and Alexander. The assertion that Arius taught that the Son was God only by participation and Word and Wisdom only by name and by grace,

[59] For the full texts of the anathemas of these two councils, see respectively Opitz (1934–5) 39, 16–40, 1 (Antioch, reproducing Schwartz's Greek retroversion from the Syriac original) and 52, 2–5 (Nicaea). On the respective interpretations of 'Arianism' at Antioch and Nicaea, see also Pollard (1960).

[60] This anathema supports the hypothesis that Arius attributed the immutability of the Son to His will and not His nature. However, it is difficult to ascertain if the Council of Antioch is actually drawing upon Arius' own writings here, or on the polemic of Alexander.

[61] According to Athanasius (*De Decretis* 20), Nicaea also anathematized the doctrine that the Son was 'created' (*ktiston*). However, there are good reasons for doubting the authenticity of this anathema (see below).

and most importantly the repeated charge that Arius rendered the Son mutable and reduced Him to the level of all other created beings, are all the product of such interpretation. In his construction of 'Arianism', Athanasius has thus combined Arius' own words and doctrines with implications and conclusions that Arius himself simply did not hold, a polemical approach that has proved all too influential on modern studies of 'Arian' theology.

In 1981, Robert Gregg and Dennis Groh published *Early Arianism—A View of Salvation.* They proposed that 'early Arianism is most intelligible when viewed as a scheme of salvation.... At the centre of the Arian soteriology was a redeemer, obedient to his Creator's will, whose life of virtue modelled perfect creaturehood and hence the path of salvation for all Christians'.[62] According to their thesis, Arius taught that 'the redeemer was not entirely unique. He was a representative creature',[63] who 'gains and holds his sonship in the same way as other creatures',[64] for whom he establishes a model for salvation. This argument has received support from a number of scholars,[65] and has done much to direct scholarly attention to the long ignored question of the role of soteriology in the fourth-century controversies. Yet the entire foundation of Gregg and Groh's work ultimately rests not on the actual words of Arius, but on the polemic of Athanasius that we have just examined.[66] Not only do Gregg and Groh assume the existence of a collective 'Arian movement, epitomized in its three central figures—Arius, Asterius the Sophist, Eusebius of Nicomedia',[67] but most importantly, their assertion that the 'Arian' Son was a representative and changeable creature depends solely upon Athanasius' interpretation of Arius' theology.

[62] Gregg and Groh (1981) x. A preliminary statement of this thesis had earlier been presented to the Patristics Conference of 1975 (though only pub. in 1984).

[63] Gregg and Groh (1981) 29–30.

[64] Ibid. 67.

[65] E.g. Kopecek (1979) 4 (responding to the earlier form of this thesis), and Frend (1984) 494. Lorenz, who had already argued independently that Arius' theology was in certain respects 'Adoptionist' ((1979) 122–7), also cites Gregg and Groh with approval when he repeats his argument in (1983) 48.

[66] This criticism of Gregg and Groh was made most explicitly by Kannengiesser (1981) 59–60, who observes that 'their presentation of Arius ... all rests exclusively on what Athanasius says in refuting the Arians in *C.Ar.*... [Athanasius] projects a doctrine of salvation that is unacceptable and calls it Arian'. See also Stead (1994) 36.

[67] Gregg and Groh (1981) 164.

Thus Gregg and Groh emphasize Athanasius' reduction of the 'Arian Son' to the level of the entire created order, and like Athanasius they ignore or dismiss Arius' own explicit description of the Son as a creature *not* as one of the creatures.[68] Only then can they proclaim that 'the burden of the evidence indicates that the assertion of the Son's fundamental identity with other creatures was from the beginning of the dispute axiomatic for Arian Christians',[69] and that Arius drew 'the closest possible links between Christ and fellow creatures'.[70] The 'burden of the evidence' in fact suggests nothing of the kind, for Arius' insistence that the Son was entirely unlike other creatures strikes at the heart of the Gregg and Groh thesis that the 'Arian Son' was a model for human salvation. This is equally true of the assertion that Arius taught that the Son was changeable and progressed in virtue. As has been amply demonstrated above, Arius in his extant works explicitly describes the Son as immutable, and the rather desperate attempt of Gregg and Groh to explain that 'in the one passage in which Arius terms Christ *atreptos* he means that unchangeability which comes to the perfected creature that holds unswervingly to the love of God'[71] has no support from the evidence at all. On the contrary, the 'Arian soteriology' that Gregg and Groh present is a direct product of Athanasius' construction of 'Arianism', and above all of his polarized interpretation of the 'Arian Controversy'. And so they can conclude that 'salvation, for orthodoxy, is effected by the Son's essential identity with the Father—that which links God and Christ to creation is the divine nature's assumption of flesh. Salvation for Arianism is effected by the Son's identity with the creatures—that which links Christ and creatures to God is conformity of will.'[72]

Can we really speak of such clearly defined and sharply contrasted 'orthodox' and 'Arian' conceptions of soteriology? Athanasius himself, in a much quoted passage, defines human salvation as 'deification'

[68] Gregg and Groh indeed argue that Arius only saw the Son as different from all creatures by degree rather than kind (ibid. 61), and they even complain that other scholars, particularly Stead, 'downplay Arius' own insistence that the Son was one of the creatures' (99.n.87). That insistence, of course, is not that of Arius, but of Athanasius.

[69] Ibid. 113. [70] Ibid. 13. [71] Ibid. 21.

[72] Ibid. 8. A similar but more nuanced soteriological polarization of the fourth-century controversies is presented by Lienhard (1999) 45.

(*theopoiēsis*) through Christ, for 'He became man, that we might become divine' (*De Incarnatione* 54; Thomson (1971) 268, 11–12).[73] For Athanasius, that deification is possible only through a Son who is true God by essence and nature, and the 'Arians' who deny those qualities to the Son thus deny in turn that the Son can deify man. It is this polemical conclusion that underlies the thesis of Gregg and Groh that Arius must therefore have held an entirely different model of salvation. That Athanasius and Arius differed significantly in their understanding of the Son and His divinity is not in question, but as Wiles in particular has emphasized, it is far from self-evident that Arius too could not nevertheless teach a soteriology of 'deification'.[74] The theological tradition that Christ became man so that we might become like Him reaches back at least as far as Irenaeus,[75] and the insistence of Athanasius that the Saviour must be God by essence and nature rests upon his own rigid ontological polarization between God and creation.[76] In his condemnation of the 'Arians', Athanasius has imposed upon his opponents this polarization, which they did not share. As I will argue elsewhere in this chapter, the very limited evidence that we have for the soteriology of the various men whom Athanasius condemns suggests that these men did in fact speak of salvation in terms of 'deification'. Their respective theological positions may still differ markedly from that of Athanasius, but the difference is not necessarily that which Athanasius (or Gregg and Groh) would construct.

The interpretation of 'Arianism' presented by R. P. C. Hanson raises similar difficulties, although in a rather different way. In a series of articles written in the mid-1980s,[77] culminating in the

[73] For two valuable recent studies of Athanasius' soleriology, see Widdicombe (1994) 223–49 and Anatolios (1998) 125–61.

[74] 'It does appear to me self-evident that only God can be the author of ultimate salvation ... similarly it appears self-evident that such salvation must reach down to where man is ... but this does not make it self-evident that the person of the agent of salvation must be either fully divine or fully human, let alone both' (Wiles (1966) 323; see also (1967) 96–7 and 107–8). For a partial reply to Wiles, see Anatolios (1998) 125–33.

[75] On this tradition, see Prestige (1956) 73–5, citing Irenaeus, *Adversus Haereses* III.19.1, and Nispel (1999) 291.

[76] I will return to this fundamental dimension of Athanasius' theology, and its significance for his construction of 'Arianism', below.

[77] See in particular Hanson (1985*b*) and, in a more abbreviated form, (1989) 145–6.

Search for the Christian Doctrine of God in 1988, Hanson argued that 'at the heart of the Arian Gospel was a God who suffered'.[78] The theology of Arius was an attempt to resolve the question of how Christ could be divine and yet also suffer for our sins when the Father Himself must be impassible, and thus 'Arianism in all its forms assumed that the Incarnation was a dispensation on the part of God which necessitated a reduction or a lowering of God so that it had to be undertaken by a being who, though divine, was less than fully divine'.[79] As this quotation demonstrates, Hanson like Gregg and Groh accepts the Athanasian construction of a single coherent 'Arian' theological position. And again like Gregg and Groh, Hanson's presentation of that position depends more upon the polemic of Athanasius than upon the words of Arius himself. This is true in particular of his repeated insistence that Arius' theology emphasized above all 'the weakness, ignorance and subjection to passion of the incarnate Logos, based on the universal Arian supposition that the Logos took the place of the *psyche* in Jesus Christ'.[80]

Did Arius truly apply the ignorance, hunger, and human weakness of the Incarnate Christ directly to the divine Logos? Certainly this is the position that Athanasius attributes to the 'Arians', alleging that they taught that the Son was as mutable and passible as every other creature. In his *Rule of Faith*, Eudoxius of Antioch and Constantinople declares that Christ 'became flesh, not man, for he did not take a human soul... [and] he was passible by the Incarnation'.[81] Eudoxius

[78] Hanson (1988*b*) 121.

[79] Hanson (1985*b*) 182; see also Grillmeier (1975) 247–8: 'the taking of the flesh is the ground [for the "Arians"] for assuming a change in the Logos. The consequent elaboration of this attitude then leads to the intolerable one-sidedness of the Arian heresy, which goes on to trace the weakness of the Logos throughout the Scriptures so as to be able to ascribe it to the Logos *qua* Logos'.

[80] Hanson (1988*b*) 604.

[81] Text in Hahn (1897) 261–2; translation from Hanson (1988*b*) 112. An alternative translation by Hall (1991) 154 interprets the final line as 'able to suffer by condescension (*di'oikonomian*)'. The only other 'Arian' text that Hanson brings forward in support of his model of 'Arianism' is the late and highly controversial Latin work known as the *Opus Imperfectum in Matthaeum* (Hanson (1985*b*) 202). Otherwise, Hanson's argument is derived entirely from polemical sources, including not only the works of Athanasius, but the *De Anima et Contra Arianos* of Eustathius of Antioch (a lost work from which six fragments are preserved in Theodoret's *Dialogues*), the *Contra Eunomium* of Gregory of Nyssa, and the 'orthodox' accounts of the alleged beliefs of the Western Latin 'Arians' in the late fourth and early fifth centuries.

was one of the men whom Athanasius asserts received the patronage of the 'Eusebians' in the *Encyclical Letter* of 356 (7) and *De Synodis* (12), and both Hanson[82] and before him Grillmeier[83] cite this passage as representative of 'Arianism'. Yet there is no evidence that Arius or any of the original so-called 'Eusebians' ever spoke explicitly of a suffering Son. The only statement of Arius that the Son 'took flesh and suffered (*pathonta*)' on our behalf occurs in the Creed that he and Euzoius presented to Constantine in 333 (Socrates, I.26; Hansen (1995) 74, 9). It is impossible to place any weight upon this reference, for a similar statement appears in almost every creed of this period (including Nicaea), without ever necessarily implying that this suffering was predicated of the Son's divinity. Moreover, although Hanson could declare that 'the doctrine that the incarnate Word assumed a *soma apsychon* is indeed one of the invariable characteristics of Arianism',[84] and so conclude that Arius had to attribute the Son's suffering to the Logos itself, there is no evidence in Arius' own writings that he held this position.[85] It is probable that Arius, like a number of his contemporaries, did in fact omit the human soul of Christ from his conception of the Incarnation,[86] but there is little sign that he (or Athanasius) considered this to be a question of any great

[82] 'Here we see into the heart of Arianism' (Hanson (1988*b*) 112).

[83] 'Eudoxius provides the clearest Arian formula of the incarnation' (Grillmeier (1975) 244).

[84] Hanson (1985*b*) 182. Elsewhere in the same article, Hanson opposes this argument to the thesis of Gregg and Groh, asserting that as the 'Arian Christ' lacked a human soul, He could not have been brought forward as a model for human salvation (204).

[85] The only contemporary to condemn Arius for denying the human soul of Christ is Eustathius of Antioch (Spanneut (1948) fragments 15, 17, 41). Eustathius' attribution of this doctrine to Arius was accepted by Grillmeier (1975) 239, Hanson (1988*b*) 111, and Lorenz (1979) 211–15, but it is striking that Eustathius' argument is not taken up by any other writer (including Athanasius) until much later in the fourth century. Epiphanius (*Ancoratus* 33.4) asserts that the so-called 'Lucianists' taught that the Son took a body without a soul (see below), and Theodoret (Epp. 104, 145, 151) likewise accuses Arius of such a teaching. The veracity of these later assertions is difficult to assess, however, for these authors were unquestionably influenced by the emergence of the theology of Apollinarius of Laodicea.

[86] Behr (2004) 146–7.

significance.[87] And while Arius certainly did subordinate the Son to the Father, and may have brought forward the suffering of the Incarnate Christ to demonstrate that by His association with human weakness the Son was different by nature from the Father,[88] this is not to say that Arius attributed that weakness directly to the divinity of the Son. Like the 'Arian soteriology' of Gregg and Groh, Hanson's conception of a 'suffering Arian god' would thus seem to be a product more of Athanasian Arianism than of the words of Arius himself.

It was never the primary intention of my argument to compose a new definitive presentation of the theology of Arius. The nature of our sources makes a full understanding of Arius' original arguments impossible, and 'we can never be sure that the theological priorities ascribed to Arius by his opponents were his own'.[89] From the extant fragments of Arius' writings, however, certain limited conclusions can be drawn. Arius places great emphasis on 'One God, alone unbegotten, alone eternal' (*Letter to Alexander*; *De Synodis* 16; Opitz (1941) 243, 28). The Son is God, but He is not eternal for He is begotten, and for the same reason He cannot share in the essence of the Father. The One God is transcendent and unknowable even by

[87] The degree to which the human soul of Christ was a subject of theological controversy before Apollinarius of Laodicea in the second half of the fourth century has been much debated, but despite the arguments of Hanson, it has increasingly been recognized that this question was simply not a central point at issue for either Arius or Athanasius (see Kannengiesser (1981) 31 and Stead (1994) 33). Indeed, Athanasius only appears to have begun to confront the significance of the human soul of Christ very late in his life, in *Tomus ad Antiochenos* 7 (on which text see Pettersen (1990) 193–8, although again I would question his belief that Christ's '*soma apsychon*' was an established 'Arian' doctrine, and Hall (1991) 152). The conclusion of a number of modern scholars is that Athanasius neither emphasizes nor denies Christ's soul (Louth (1985), Anatolios (1998) 77–8, and, from a slightly more positive perspective, Behr (2004) 215–16), and the same conclusion could probably be applied to Arius.

[88] It is a recurring assumption that if Arius or the 'Eusebians' did deny the human soul of Christ, which as we have seen is probable but unproven, then they must have attributed the sufferings of the Incarnation directly to the divine Logos. In addition to the argument of Hanson above, see Lorenz (1979) 211–15, and also Lienhard (1999) 150.n.53. Yet this assumption is not self-evident. Eusebius of Caesarea at least did deny the existence of a human soul in Christ, and yet nevertheless separated the Son's divinity from the suffering of the Incarnation (*De Ecclesiastica Theologia* I.20.41–3; *Demonstratio Evangelica* IV.13).

[89] Williams (1987) 95.

His Word; the Son is a creature, though not like any other. To quote the judgement of Christopher Stead, 'the traditional estimate of Arius is the right one. His main concern was to uphold the unique divinity of God the Father in the face of attempts to glorify the Logos, as he thought, unduly.'[90] The arguments of Gregg and Groh and Hanson, that Arius reduces the Son to a mutable and passible creature, derive from Athanasius, whose polemical interpretations of the words of Arius cannot be taken at face value. It is against this background that we must now assess the alleged 'Arian theology' of the men whom Athanasius brands as the 'Eusebians'.

The Theology of the 'Eusebians': The 'Lucianist School'

In order to evaluate Athanasius' construction of the 'Eusebians' as a collective 'Arian party', it is necessary to assess the theologies of the men whom Athanasius condemns as far as possible as individuals, particularly those men for whose writings the greatest evidence survives, namely Asterius 'the Sophist' and Eusebius of Nicomedia. But before such an analysis can begin, one highly significant legacy of the 'collective' interpretation of this 'party' must be acknowledged. Ever since the great work of Gustave Bardy, scholars have argued that the men named by Athanasius as 'Eusebians' represent a 'Lucianist school'.[91] According to Williams, 'the group described as *hoi peri Eusebion* is roughly the same as the group identified as pupils of Lucian of Antioch'.[92] Asterius and Eusebius of Nicomedia in particular are invariably named as members of this 'school', while in his letter to the latter, Arius famously referred to Eusebius as '*sulloukianista*' or 'fellow-Lucianist' (Parmentier (1998) 27, 7).[93] The theological

[90] Stead (1994) 36. As Stead had already observed in an earlier article ((1978) 38), 'Athanasius had the strongest possible motives for representing Arius' teaching in an unpopular guise . . . But Arius, once he had safeguarded the unique divinity of the Father, had no reason to go further and gratuitously humiliate the Son . . . Arius could not possibly have won the support of men like Eusebius of Caesarea if he had cast his teaching in the crude and offensive form which Athanasius presents to our view'.

[91] Bardy (1936), especially 185–210 on the 'Collucianist school'.

[92] Williams (1987) 63.

[93] For a recent discussion of this highly controversial phrase, see Brennecke (1993) 177, who emphasizes the unique isolation of this term and that we cannot know its context or precise implications.

position of Lucian and his 'pupils' has therefore been the subject of much scholarly debate in recent years.

Yet surprisingly little is actually known about Lucian of Antioch or his teachings.[94] Even his identity is a controversial subject,[95] and all our knowledge of his theology derives from later sources of highly doubtful value. The most frequently cited evidence, the statement of Sozomen (III.5) that the Second Creed of Antioch in 341 (to which I will return later in this chapter) was modelled on a creed composed by Lucian, is impossible to confirm, for Sozomen himself does not vouch for the veracity of the tradition that he reports.[96] Epiphanius (*Ancoratus* 33.4) in the late fourth century asserts that the 'school of Lucian' taught the doctrine that the Incarnate Christ did not possess a human soul. But despite the confidence of Hanson that 'this is one of the very few statements about Lucian of which we can be fairly sure',[97] the evidence that Lucian ever even referred to the soul of Christ is no more conclusive than for Arius above. Otherwise, our only evidence for Lucian's teachings derives (in a somewhat circular

[94] On the very sparse sources for the historical Lucian, see Bardy (1936) 3–32.

[95] In his *Letter to Alexander of Byzantium/Thessalonica*, Alexander of Alexandria refers to a Lucian who was the 'successor of Paul of Samosata'. Bardy, who initially identified this figure as Lucian of Antioch, eventually concluded that there were two different men of the same name. This conclusion has been supported by Barnes (1981) 194, Wallace-Hadrill (1982) 83, and Williams (1987) 162, but Hanson (1988*b*) 82 and Brennecke (1993) 178–9 are less convinced, while Stead (1994) 36.n.25 declares: 'I see no need to imagine two Lucians' (a view supported by Behr (2004) 49–51). Thus this debate remains unresolved, but given that the theology of Paul of Samosata is just as uncertain as that of Lucian, the assertion of Gregg and Groh (1981) 165 that Arius learnt a doctrine of Christ's ethical development from Paul through Lucian (an argument earlier put forward by Pollard (1958) 103–4 and Lorenz (1979) 128–35) must be rejected (Hanson (1988*b*) 71, Stead (1994) 26). Behr (2004) has now put forward instead the reverse argument, that Lucian was an opponent of Paul, and that the 'Lucianists' 'continued in the tradition that had begun to define itself in reaction to Paul of Samosata' (69).

[96] According to Sozomen, the bishops who gathered at Antioch in 341 'stated that they had found this formulary of faith, and that it was entirely written by Lucian... but whether they said this correctly or whether in order to exalt their own composition by the reputation of the martyr, I cannot say' (III.5.9; Hansen (2004) 346, 6–12). This claim was apparently unknown to Athanasius, and although accepted by Bardy (1936) 85–132 as genuine, more recent writers have tended to be more sceptical (Hanson (1988*b*) 289; Löhr (1993) 89–90; Brennecke (1993) 187–9).

[97] Hanson (1985*b*) 189; Behr (2004) 53. Both scholars wished to attribute to Lucian the same doctrine that Christ took a '*soma apsychon*' that they attributed to Arius and the 'Eusebians'.

argument) from the alleged theology of his 'disciples',[98] as they are recorded by the fifth-century 'Neo-Arian' ecclesiastical historian Philostorgius. In a fragment of this work preserved in the ninth-century summary of Photius, it is reported that

> Arius put forward that God is entirely unknown and incomprehensible . . . not only to men . . . but even to His own only-begotten Son of God. And he [Philostorgius] says that not only Arius but also many others were carried away into this absurdity at that time. For with the exception of Secundus and Theonas, and the disciples (*tōn mathētōn*) of the martyr Lucian, [namely] Leontius, Antony, [Maris of Chalcedon, Theognis of Nicaea, Menophantus of Ephesus, Asterius, Athanasius of Anazarbus][99] and Eusebius of Nicomedia, the rest of the impious band (*suntagma*) fell away into this opinion. (II.3; Bidez (1981) 14, 1–9)

Philostorgius' presentation of a distinct 'Lucianist party', from whom the 'Neo-Arians' would later arise, has received considerable acceptance from modern scholars.[100] Yet that presentation is ultimately no less distorted than Athanasius' construction of 'Arians' and 'Arianism'. As we shall see below, although it is probable that both Asterius and Eusebius of Nicomedia did reject Arius' belief that the Son could not perfectly know His own Father, there is no evidence that they shared the 'Neo-Arian' doctrines of Aetius and Eunomius, or that those doctrines originated from a 'Lucianist' theological position.[101] In the words of Wiles, 'Philostorgius may have created

[98] Much of the great study of Bardy (1936) follows precisely this circular approach, a methodology rightly criticized by Brennecke (1993) 173–4.

[99] The individuals added in square brackets, although not named in this passage, are included elsewhere among Philostorgius' 'Lucianists' (II.14, III.15). Several of Athanasius' 'Eusebians', it should be noted, are entirely missing (notably Narcissus, Theodore, Ursacius, and Valens), as too is Arius himself.

[100] 'There were real theological divergences between this group [the "Lucianists"] and Arius, and the later "Neo-Arians" of the mid-century traced their theological ancestry back to the Lucianists rather than Arius' (Williams (1987) 31; see also 63). In an earlier article, Williams (1985) 26 speaks explicitly of 'Arianism as it developed from Eusebius of Nicomedia to Eunomius', and both Kopecek (1979) 3 and Vaggione (1987*b*) xiii–xiv likewise speak of the 'Neo-Arians' as the 'descendants' of the 'Lucianists' and their leader Eusebius.

[101] It is particularly ironic that the very Second Creed of Antioch in 341 that may have come from Lucian, and whose connection to Eusebius of Nicomedia and Asterius cannot be questioned, not only bears simply no resemblance to 'Neo-Arian' teaching, but was itself to prove the favourite statement of the 'Homoiousian' foes of Aetius and Eunomius. The complaint of Philostorgius (II.15) that Asterius 'betrayed' his master Lucian by allegedly editing that formula testifies to the embarrassment of the 'Neo-Arian' historian, who had to explain the association with the Second Creed of men whom he wished to claim as the 'ancestors' of his own theological position.

an early Arianism in the image of his own later Neo-Arianism',[102] whose descent he traced back to Eusebius 'the great' of Nicomedia and his martyr-teacher Lucian. Most importantly, the only contemporary evidence for the collective identity of the 'disciples of Lucian' that Philostorgius constructs, and of whom Bardy could declare that they 'continued to make use of his [Lucian's] name and formed a homogeneous group, perfectly united',[103] rests solely upon Arius' ambiguous reference to Eusebius of Nicomedia as '*sulloukianista*'. Neither Eusebius nor Asterius, nor any other alleged 'Lucianist', is ever known to have used such a title, and indeed neither they nor Athanasius ever even mention Lucian's name.[104] The verdict of Williams, that 'Lucian himself remains largely an enigma, and it is difficult to avoid the conclusion that his individual significance in the background of the crisis in Alexandria has been very much exaggerated',[105] should also be extended to the 'Lucianist school'.

Asterius 'the Sophist' and Eusebius of Nicomedia

The individuals whom Athanasius names as 'Eusebians' include some men who probably were pupils of Lucian of Antioch, just as they include men who certainly did associate with Arius. But these men must be studied as individuals, not categorized as 'Lucianists' or dismissed as 'Arians'. Unfortunately, as we saw in Chapter 5, for the majority of these so-called 'Eusebians', our knowledge of their theology is extremely limited. Only for Asterius 'the Sophist' and Eusebius of Nicomedia himself does substantial (although still fragmentary) evidence survive. That there are similarities between their known writings and Arius' theology cannot be denied, yet there

102 Wiles (1985) 113 (see also Vaggione (2000) 44–7, although Vaggione essentially takes Philostorgius' account of the 'Lucianists' at face value).

103 Bardy (1936) 185. See also Wallace-Hadrill (1982): 'they called themselves Lucianists and their opponents called them Eusebians' (83), and Behr (2004): '"Lucianist" would in fact be an appropriate designation for those who rejected Nicaea and a description which they seem to have used for themselves' (49).

104 Brennecke (1993) 186 plausibly suggests that if there was a 'Lucianist' connection between some or all of the men usually known as 'Eusebians', that connection was created primarily through the cult of the martyr Lucian rather than through personal contact with the man or his theology.

105 Williams (1987) 167. Hanson (1988*b*) 83 put it rather more bluntly: 'too much fantasy has already been expended on Lucian of Antioch'.

are also significant differences. Only through the analysis of those writings can we assess Athanasius' polemical construction of these men, the true relationship of their own theology to the teachings of Arius, and their importance as individuals within the fourth-century controversies.

Asterius 'the Sophist' has often been described as the great theorist and theologian of the 'Eusebian party'.[106] Athanasius refers to him travelling the eastern Church with 'introductions' from the 'Eusebians' to teach from his *Syntagmation* (*De Synodis* 18), and in recent years Vinzent has rightly emphasized Asterius' importance within the fourth-century theological debates.[107] His attempt to define 'the theological system' of Asterius raises questions identical to those posed by the study of Arius.[108] As we saw in the brief discussion of Asterius' writings in Chapter 5, the bulk of the evidence for his theology (setting aside the disputed *Homilies on the Psalms*) lies in the fragments quoted by Athanasius (primarily in the *Orations against the Arians* and the *De Synodis*) and by Marcellus of Ancyra (preserved in turn in the *Contra Marcellum* of Eusebius of Caesarea).[109] The majority of these fragments seem to derive either from the *Syntagmation* or from the letter that Asterius wrote in defence of Eusebius of Nicomedia and Paulinus of Tyre, and as they are cited in isolation and only in hostile contexts they require very careful analysis. As Wiles observes, 'it is clear that Athanasius and Marcellus are

[106] Asterius 'ist der Systematiker, vielleicht *der* Systematiker, der Eusebianer und der Vordenker für Arius' (Vinzent (1993*a*) 22 (his italics); see also 24–5). Lienhard (1999) likewise describes Asterius as 'the ideologue of the Eusebian party' ((1987) 431).

[107] As Vinzent observes, Asterius was the primary target both of Marcellus in his *Contra Asterium* and of Athanasius in the *Third Oration against the Arians* ((1993*a*) 27–9; see also (1993*b*) 172–4 and (1994)).

[108] Vinzent (1993*a*) 38–58.

[109] In his original collection, Bardy (1936) identified 36 fragments from Asterius' writings, 16 in Athanasius and 20 from the works of Marcellus, which Vinzent (1993*a*) 82–141 expands to 77. However, both Bardy and especially Vinzent derive many of their Asterian 'quotations' from passages within Athanasius' polemic where the distinction between Asterius' own theology and Athanasius' polemical interpretations is not always as clear as their collections would suggest. It is for this reason that I am not entirely convinced by Vinzent's proposed 'systematic' model of Asterius' theology, for the reconstruction of such a 'system' from our fragmentary evidence must remain hypothetical. In the argument that follows, I have limited my own discussion to certain particularly well-attested fragments explicitly identified in our sources as quotations from Asterius.

commenting on the same writer and the same ideas. But what each objects to is an implication of Asterius' position that conflicts with a predominant concern of his own theological enterprise'.[110] Athanasius emphasizes the priority that Asterius attributed to the Father and His will, Marcellus the Asterian doctrine of three *hypostases* in the Trinity. In neither case can we assume that this emphasis was necessarily the central conception of Asterius himself.

Nevertheless, even a rapid survey of the theology of Asterius visible in these sources immediately reveals important similarities and differences between Asterius' own thought and both Athanasius' construction of 'Arianism' and the known teachings of Arius.[111] Thus, although there is no explicit evidence that Asterius ever used the phrase 'there was when He was not', he unquestionably shared Arius' belief that the Son is not eternal as is the Father, but is generated 'before the ages (*pro tōn aiōnōn*)' (Eusebius, *Contra Marcellum* I.4.28; fragment XXIII (Bardy), 17 (Vinzent)). Only the Father is unbegotten and without beginning, and Asterius rejects Athanasius' assertion that if the Son is not eternal then the Father was not always Father, arguing that He was Father *in potentia*, for 'before the generation of the Son, the Father had pre-existing knowledge how to generate' (*De Synodis* 19; fragment IV (Bardy), 14 (Vinzent)). Likewise, Asterius does not speak of Christ as 'true God', and he also shared with Arius the doctrine that the Son could not be materially generated from the Father's essence. Rather, 'being a thing made (*poiēma*), He has at His [the Father's] will come to be and been made' (*De Synodis* 19; fragment VI (Bardy), 16 (Vinzent)). Significantly, Asterius is willing to say explicitly that Christ was a *poiēma*, a term that as we saw Arius himself avoided. But despite Athanasius' interpretation that Asterius too therefore reduced the Son to the level of all created beings, the latter also specifically asserts the uniqueness of the Son, who is the only-begotten of the Father alone (*De Synodis* 18; fragment IIa (Bardy), 66 (Vinzent)). There is no evidence that

110 Wiles (1985) 120.

111 For an alternative comparison of the teachings of Asterius and Arius (not founded as is mine upon the contrast between Asterius' own theology and Athanasius' construction of 'Arianism'), see Vinzent (1993*a*) 63–71, who highlights in particular their different conceptions of the divine *monad* and the greater emphasis that Asterius placed on the proximity of the Father and the Son.

Asterius ever described the Son as mutable, or taught that He was created out of nothing, and according to Philostorgius (II.3, quoted above) he also rejected Arius' assertion in the *Thalia* that the Son did not perfectly know the Father.

The most notorious doctrine of Asterius, however, is that he taught that the Son was not the true Wisdom and Power of God.

The Blessed Paul did not say that he preached that Christ was His, that is, God's 'own Power' or 'own Wisdom', but without the article, 'God's Power and God's Wisdom' [1Corinthians 1:24], preaching that the proper (*idian*)[112] Power of God Himself was distinct (*allēn*), which was inherent (*emphuton*) and co-existent (*sunuparchousan*) with Him ingenerately (*agennētōs*).... He [Paul] tells us of another Power and Wisdom of God, namely, that which is manifested through Christ.... Many are those [powers] which are one by one created by Him, of which Christ is the first-born and only-begotten. (*De Synodis* 18 (see also *Oration against the Arians* II.37); fragment I, IIa (Bardy), 64, 66 (Vinzent)).

Even the locust and the caterpillar are named in the Scriptures as 'powers' of God. Asterius, like Arius, thus believed that the Son possessed Power and Wisdom not by His own nature or essence, but by derivation from the inherent properties of the Father.[113] In this sense Athanasius was correct that Asterius too denied that the Son was the only Power and Wisdom of God. Yet although Athanasius repeatedly cites this text as evidence that Asterius and the other 'Arians' therefore denied that the Son was Wisdom and Power except by name, and so reduced the Son to the level of the created order,[114] these conclusions again derive from Athanasius' own interpretation. The point of Asterius' argument (which we will also see expressed in a different form by Eusebius of Nicomedia in his *Letter to Paulinus of Tyre*) is not that the Son is like other creatures, but that even though He is the unique and only-begotten Power and Wisdom of God, He is

[112] '*Idian*' is the reading of Bardy (1936) 341. Vinzent (1993*a*) 124 reads '*idion*', and also notes the further possible reading of '*aidion*' (eternal).

[113] For a good brief discussion of this 'two level' theory of the Son as 'Power', see M. R. Barnes (1997) 211–12, and for a more detailed analysis of Asterius' view of 'Power' and 'Wisdom' as applied to the Father and the Son, see Kinzig (1991) 128–9 and Vinzent (1993*b*) 174–80.

[114] An interpretation of Asterius' theology accepted, as befitted their overall thesis of 'Arianism', by Gregg and Groh (1981) 112.

nevertheless Himself created[115] and possesses these attributes only by the Father's will. As the lowly locust and caterpillar can be termed 'powers', therefore the title 'Power' does not imply that the Son, though exalted above all creatures, must derive from the *ousia* of the unbegotten Father.

It is thus apparent that Asterius, in accordance both with the theology of Arius and with Athanasius' construction of 'Arianism', taught that the Son could not be eternal or derive from the *ousia* of the Father, for He was not unbegotten but created from the Father's will. Yet not only do the implications that Athanasius draws from these doctrines again distort the true content of Asterius' teachings, but there are also significant differences between the theological positions of Asterius and Arius. Asterius cannot be proven to have used the catchphrases 'there was when He was not' and 'He came to be out of nothing', or to have shared Arius' conception that the Son does not perfectly know His Father. Most importantly, however, in the fragments of Asterius' writings preserved in other sources we discover dimensions to his theology that Athanasius does not acknowledge at all. It is Marcellus of Ancyra, whose own controversial theology emphasized that the Godhead consisted of a single *hypostasis*, who in his polemic denounced Asterius because he taught emphatically that there were three *hypostases* in the Trinity. 'The Father is truly Father, and the Son truly Son, and the Holy Spirit likewise' (Eusebius of Caesarea, *Contra Marcellum* I.4.4; fragment XXc (Bardy), 60 (Vinzent)). And it is also Marcellus who records that Asterius described the Son as 'the exact image (*aparallakton eikona*) of His [the Father's] Essence and Will and Power and Glory' (Eusebius, *Contra Marcellum* I.4.33; fragment XXIa (Bardy), 10 (Vinzent)).[116] Both of these important Asterian expressions reappear in the Second Creed of the 'Dedication' Council of Antioch in 341, and the latter fragment in particular reveals an emphasis upon the uniqueness and divinity of the Son that conflicts directly with Athanasius' depiction of the 'Arians' throughout his polemic as *Christomachoi*.

115 'Asterius is only making the basic point of Christ's belonging to the created order' (Wiles (1985) 117).

116 It was for this doctrine that Philostorgius (II.15) condemned Asterius for his 'betrayal' of his 'master', Lucian of Antioch.

This contrast between the Athanasian construction of the 'Arianism' of Asterius and Asterius' own emphasis upon the divinity of the Son also raises a further question: how did Asterius conceive of the role of the Son as Saviour? None of the fragments considered above sheds any direct light upon Asterius' soteriology, and it was for this reason that Maurice Wiles entitled his study of the 'Asterian' *Homilies on the Psalms* 'A New Chapter in the History of Arianism?'. For those works seemed to offer precisely this insight, and indeed suggested that Asterius held a conception of salvation as 'deification' 'closer than has usually been recognized to that of Athanasius himself'.[117] This 'New Chapter', however, was emphatically closed by Kinzig when he denied the attribution of the *Homilies* to 'the Sophist',[118] and the most recent assessment of Asterian soteriology upholds that verdict. Vinzent argues that the true key to Asterius' conception of salvation is not 'deification' but the creaturehood of the Son.[119] For Asterius, Vinzent declares, only a Son who is a creature like ourselves and suffers Himself as a creature may be the instrument of our salvation.[120]

Yet Vinzent's conclusion ultimately derives once again not from Asterius' own writings but from the polemic of Athanasius, for it is Athanasius who represents the 'Arians' as reducing the Son to the level of the created order. Asterius, on the contrary, as we have just seen, places particular emphasis upon the divinity of the Son, whom he sets apart from all other creatures as the 'exact image' of the Father, and there is no evidence that he ever taught that the divine Son must Himself suffer. Although no interpretation of Asterius' soteriology can be conclusive in the light of the fragmentary evidence, I believe that it is just as plausible that Asterius did hold a conception of salvation through 'deification', and that Wiles was correct to suggest that the gulf between the soteriologies of

[117] Wiles (1985) 139. As Wiles observes, the theology of the *Homilies* is 'strongly Christocentric and soteriological' (126), and there is an explicit statement of 'deification' in *Homily* XXX.7: The Son 'took flesh and gave divinity (*sarka elabe kai theotēta edōken*)' (Richard (1956) 241, 21).

[118] Kinzig (1989) 15–16, (1990) 231–2. On the debate over the authorship of the *Homilies*, see the discussion of Asterius in Ch. 5.

[119] Vinzent (1993*a*) 52–6.

[120] 'Wie nur "der" Gott schaffen kann, so kann auch nur "der" Gott erlösen. Geschaffen aber hat Gott um der Geschöpfe willen durch ein Geschöpf, so erlöst er auch um der Geschöpfe willen durch ein Geschöpf' (ibid. 56).

Athanasius and Asterius may not be as great as is often assumed. Of course, this is not to question the manifest differences that did separate these two theologians in their respective interpretations of the eternity of the Son and His essential relationship to the Father. Nor would I defend 'the Sophist' as the author of the *Homilies* that Kinzig examines so thoroughly. But whereas Kinzig asserts that the theology of the *Homilies* is entirely incompatible with Asterius' known teachings, I would argue that such an evaluation, like the argument of Vinzent above or the assessments of Arius by Gregg and Groh and Hanson, reflects once more the influence of Athanasius' polemical interpretation of the theology of his opponents.[121] Not only does the imposition of Athanasius' construction of 'Arianism' upon Asterius distort the latter's true theological position, but this distortion in turn has partially concealed the true nature of the differences between these two men. As we shall now see, precisely the same distortions also occur in Athanasius' presentation of the theology of his greatest 'Eusebian' foe, Eusebius of Nicomedia himself.

'It is essential to recognize, as many apologists refuse to do, the difference between Eusebius' theological convictions on the one hand, and, on the other hand, the fact that he showed sympathy for Arius ... [and] had reservations about the *homoousion* formula.'[122] Yet to define the 'theological convictions' of Eusebius of Nicomedia raises difficulties still greater than for Arius and Asterius.[123] Aside from a few short fragments in the works of Athanasius (notably the

[121] There are indeed certain obvious differences between the theology of Asterius' known writings and the theology of the *Homilies*, most significantly of course the occurrence in the *Homilies* of the term *homoousios*. But Kinzig's conclusion that therefore the author of the *Homilies* 'is not an Arian, but an adherent of the Nicene Creed' ((1990) 227) adopts without question the polarized interpretation of the fourth-century controversies laid down by Athanasius. Such a conclusion misrepresents the theology of the *Homilies* themselves (for with the exception of the single word *homoousios* there is no explicit evidence that the author is by later definition 'Nicene'), and also raises serious doubts concerning Kinzig's assessment of the 'Sophist' as an 'Arian'. The assertion that Asterius primarily emphasized the difference between the Father and the Son (217–18) derives from Athanasius' polemic rather than Asterius' own writings, and so too does Kinzig's allegation that the prominence of the divinity of the Incarnate Christ in the *Homilies* further contrasts to the theology of the 'Sophist' who 'develops a Logos Christology interpreted in an Arian way' (136–7).

[122] Luibheid (1976) 5.

[123] For a brief discussion of the fragmentary surviving writings of Eusebius of Nicomedia, see Ch. 5.

three lines preserved from Eusebius' reply to the letter of Arius discussed earlier (*De Synodis* 17; Opitz, *Urkunde* II)) and elsewhere, the only extant statement from which such a definition can be derived is his *Letter to Paulinus of Tyre* in *c.*323 (Theodoret, I.6; Opitz, *Urkunde* VIII). This isolated text obviously cannot be assumed to represent the entirety of Eusebius' theological position. Nevertheless, a comparison between the known teachings of Eusebius and both the genuine doctrines of Arius and the Athanasian construction of 'Arianism' remains valuable, and yields nearly identical conclusions to the preceding analysis of Asterius' writings.

Eusebius of Nicomedia, in common with both Asterius and Arius, denied the eternity of the only-begotten Son. In the sole extant fragment from his response to the letter of Arius, in which Arius wrote that the Son was not eternal for He was not unbegotten, Eusebius approves of the latter's doctrine. 'Since your thoughts are good, pray that all may think thus; for it is plain to anyone, that what has been made was not before it was generated (*ouk ēn prin genesthai*), but that what was generated has a beginning of existence' (*De Synodis* 17; Opitz (1941) 244, 25–7). He does not himself use the expression 'there was when He was not', however, and nor does he ever describe the creation of the Son as 'out of nothing', and so in this regard he (like Asterius) does not entirely endorse the theology of Arius' original epistle.[124] But as the *Letter to Paulinus* makes explicit, Eusebius evidently did share in full the insistence of his two contemporaries that the Son was created, and therefore had a beginning and could not derive from the *ousia* of the eternal and unbegotten Father.

We have never heard that there are two unbegotten beings (*agennēta*), nor that one has been divided into two, nor have we learned or believed that it

[124] According to Eusebius, the manner of the Son's creation cannot be defined, for 'we believe that the mode of His beginning not only cannot be expressed by words but even in thought, and is incomprehensible (*akatalēpton*) not only to man, but also to all beings superior to man' (*Letter to Paulinus of Tyre*; Parmentier (1998) 28, 14–16). Eusebius in fact shares this emphasis on the ineffable generation of the Son with Alexander of Alexandria rather than with Arius (Luibheid (1976) 11–13), and although the only explicit evidence that Eusebius denied Arius' conception of the Son's limited knowledge of His Father is the dubious statement of Philostorgius (II.3) quoted earlier, it seems at least highly unlikely that Eusebius could have so emphasized the mystery of the Son's origin and then have taught the 'Neo-Arian' doctrine of the human knowledge of God (Stead (1973) 87, *contra* Kopecek (1979) 72).

has ever suffered anything material, but we affirm that the unbegotten is one, and one also that which exists in truth (*alethōs*) by Him, yet did not come to be from his essence (*ek tēs ousias*) and does not at all participate (*metechon*) in the nature (*physeōs*) of the unbegotten or exist from His essence (*ek tēs ousias*). (Parmentier (1998) 28, 7–12)

The Son is begotten, the Father is unbegotten. To teach that the Son is eternal and 'from the essence of the Father' is to imply the existence of two unbegotten beings and to impose material change and division upon the immaterial and indivisible God. Throughout the *Letter to Paulinus of Tyre*, any description of the Son as *ek tēs ousias tou Patros* is thus repeatedly condemned,[125] and the same motivation underlies Eusebius' hostility towards the term *homoousios* both before and after 325. Ambrose of Milan quotes from an otherwise unknown letter of Eusebius in which he declares that 'if we speak of a true (*verum*) and uncreated (*increatum*) Son of God, we begin to confess Him *homoousios* with the Father' (*De Fide* III.15; Opitz, *Urkunde* XXI). According to Ambrose at least, this letter was read out at Nicaea, and even helped to inspire the introduction of *homoousios* into the Nicene Creed.[126] Socrates likewise reports that at Nicaea itself Eusebius protested that 'that is *homoousios* which is from another either by division or derivation or emanation . . . the Son is from the Father in none of these ways' (I.8; Hansen (1995) 22, 32–23, 2), and a few years after 325 Sozomen describes another episode when Eusebius before Constantine again denied that the Son could be *homoousios* to the Father (II.21).[127] The truth or otherwise of these various fragments and anecdotes is difficult to ascertain, but although Eusebius did sign the Nicene Creed it seems

[125] See Stead (1977) 227–8.

[126] The precise source of Ambrose's quotation from Eusebius cannot be identified (it does not derive from the *Letter to Paulinus of Tyre*). Nor is it possible to assess with certainty the claim that this text was read at Nicaea, although it is quite likely that the known hostility of Eusebius (and of Arius) to such language did help inspire the much debated introduction of *homoousios* in 325 (Wiles (1965*a*) 454–5, Stead (1977) 226).

[127] Sozomen's anecdote is highly ambiguous, but would seem once again to suggest that Eusebius' rejection of *homoousios* was founded on his materialist interpretation of that term and its implications.

evident that he did so with considerable misgivings.[128] The recurring theme of all these passages is Eusebius' opposition to any language that he believed must compromise the immaterial nature of God, or render the Son a second eternal and unbegotten being.

In the theology of Eusebius, moreover, just as again for Arius and Asterius also, this denial that the Son can derive in any way from the *ousia* of the Father is inseparable from the affirmation of the Son as a 'created' being.

> If He [the Son] was of Him or from Him, as a part (*meros*) of Him or from an emanation of His essence (*ex aporroias tēs ousias*), it could not be said that He was created (*ktiston*) or established (*themeliōton*).... For that which exists from the unbegotten could not be said to have been created or established, either by Him or by another, since it exists unbegotten from the beginning. (*Letter to Paulinus*; Parmentier (1998) 28, 23–7)

But the Son is indeed created, and so cannot be eternal or share the *ousia* of the unbegotten Father. For 'the Lord Himself says, "God created (*ektise*) me in the beginning of His ways, and before the ages (*pro tou aiōnas*) he established (*ethemeliōse*) me" [Proverbs 8:22–3]' (*Letter to Paulinus*; Parmentier (1998) 28, 20–2). In Eusebius' interpretation of this much-debated passage, Proverbs 8:22 thus represents the fundamental proof-text that the Son is a creature (*ktisma*) and cannot be *ek tēs ousias tou Patros*. Therefore in turn, He must be created solely from the Father's will, for 'there is, indeed, nothing which is from His [the Father's] essence (*ek tēs ousias*), but all things have come to be by His will' (Parmentier (1998) 29, 10–11). And Eusebius specifically denies that the status of the Son as begotten requires an ontological union with the Father. 'If the fact that He is called begotten affords any ground for belief that he has come into being from the paternal essence (*ek tēs ousias tēs patrikēs*) and that he has from this identity of nature (*tautotēta tēs physeōs*), we perceive that it is not concerning Him alone that the Scriptures say "begotten", but that they also speak thus of those who are dissimilar (*tōn*

[128] The confused evidence regarding Eusebius' signature in 325 is summarized in Ch. 5. In his distrust of *homoousios* and *ek tēs ousias*, his attitude seems to have been very similar to that of his namesake of Caesarea, whose better documented interpretation of *homoousios* after Nicaea in his *Letter to his See* will be discussed below.

anomoiōn) to Him according to everything by nature' (Parmentier (1998) 28, 27–29, 5), including men (Isaiah 1:2, Deuteronomy 32:18) and even the drops of dew (Job 38:28).

At first sight, this argument that the Son is created by the Father's will and named begotten in the same manner as other creatures would appear to support the assertion of Athanasius that Eusebius entirely separated the Son from the divinity of the Father and reduced Him to the level of the whole created order.[129] The point of Eusebius' argument, however, is not to unite the only-begotten Son to all other created beings, but to emphasize that as He is a *ktisma* the Son too must be created from the Father's will and not from His *ousia*.[130] The fact that the Son is 'begotten' does not entail that He must exist *ek tēs ousias* of the Father, for even the drops of dew and other objects which are entirely unlike the Father by *physis* are described in the same terms.[131] But this is not to imply that the Son and the drops of dew are by nature alike. Although the Son is indeed a *ktisma*, He is also set apart from the rest of creation. Only the Son exists 'according to perfect likeness (*teleian homoiotēta*) of character and power to the Maker' (Parmentier (1998) 28, 13–14). And only the Son 'was created (*ktiston*), established (*themeliōton*), and begotten (*gennēton*) in the essence (*ousia*)[132] and the immutable and inexpressible nature (*analloiōtō kai arrētō phusei*) and in the likeness (*homoiotēti*) towards the Maker' (Parmentier (1998) 28, 18–20).

129 It was indeed for this reason that Gregg and Groh (1981) interpreted the *Letter to Paulinus* as evidence that Eusebius held their 'Arian soteriology' (100–1). However, this interpretation once again derives from Athanasius' polemic rather than Eusebius' own words, and although we have no direct evidence for the soteriology of the bishop of Nicomedia, it is not implausible that Eusebius in fact shared the same conception of salvation through 'deification' that I have tentatively attributed to Asterius above.

130 One of the few scholars to recognize this vital dimension of Eusebius' argument is Stead (1973) 87. Stead also rightly emphasizes that Eusebius thus 'stops well short of the later Anomoean position' ((1973) 87, *contra* Lienhard (1999) 83), for as we shall see, Eusebius then proceeds to emphasize the likeness of the Father and the Son.

131 As Lienhard (1999) 81–2 observes, Eusebius seems (at least on the evidence of this letter) to have had a particular concern for the precise use of language, especially the correct definition of terms like *gennētos*, *ousia*, and *physis* (the latter two, for Eusebius as for Athanasius, being fundamentally synonyms).

132 In this instance, *ousia* 'seems to have the sense of rank' or of 'metaphysical status' (Stead (1973) 87).

Eusebius in the *Letter to Paulinus* thus shares with Asterius an insistence upon the uniqueness and immutability of the divine Son.[133] This repeated emphasis on the Son as the 'likeness' (*homoiotēta*) of the Father is also taken up in another fragment attributed to Eusebius of Nicomedia, this time by Eusebius of Caesarea. According to the latter, Eusebius of Nicomedia described the Son as the Image (*eikōn*) of the Father, and held that 'the *eikōn* and that of which it is the *eikōn* are not of course conceived as one and the same; but there are two *ousiai* and two *pragmata* and two *dunameis*' (*Contra Marcellum* I.4.41; Klostermann (1972) 26, 18–20). As we have seen, Asterius too describes the Son as the '*aparallakton eikona*' of the Father, and Williams indeed concludes that this doctrine was the characteristic teaching of his 'Lucianist party', and that '"Lucianism"... is little more than a convenient label for a kind of pluralist *eikōn* theology'.[134] However, this '*eikōn* theology' was again not limited to alleged 'Lucianists', for Eusebius of Caesarea likewise placed great emphasis upon this term (*Demonstratio Evangelica* IV.2–3, V.1.19–21; *De Ecclesiastica Theologia* I.2, I.20), as did his successor Acacius.[135] Such language was in fact almost universal in

[133] Lienhard (1999) argues from the surviving fragments of Asterius' letter in defence of Eusebius that Asterius found the latter's *Letter to Paulinus* a 'theological embarrassment' (82). Certainly that letter evidently came under attack, notably from Marcellus of Ancyra, for Asterius felt the need to emphasize that Eusebius 'did not expound the dogma in the manner of a teacher when he composed the epistle, for the letter was not for the church or for the ignorant, but for the blessed Paulinus' (Eusebius of Caesarea, *Contra Marcellum* I.4.17; Asterius fragment XVII (Bardy), 7 (Vinzent)). But Lienhard underestimates the degree to which Asterius upholds and reinforces the theology of Eusebius' letter (which was indeed Asterius' stated aim, *Contra Marcellum* I.4.11, fragment XIX (Bardy), 6 (Vinzent)), and he exaggerates the theological differences between Asterius and Eusebius of Nicomedia (95–7).

[134] Williams (1987) 166. According to Vaggione (2000), the use of '*eikōn*' caused 'impassioned debate' (65) in 'Eusebian circles', and he asserts that 'almost all Eusebians... would have been very reluctant to say that he [the Son] was the image of the divine essence' (66), with the exception of 'one branch of the school' (66), that of Asterius. In fact, the only evidence that any so-called 'Eusebian' rejected this teaching derives from Philostorgius' construction of 'Neo-Arianism', which Vaggione has here followed. Almost every man named as a 'Eusebian' by Athanasius was present at the 'Dedication' Council of Antioch in 341, when as we shall see the doctrine that the Son was 'the *eikōn* of the essence of the Father' was explicitly proclaimed.

[135] On Acacius of Caesarea's now fragmentary *Contra Marcellum*, see Lienhard (1989).

the early fourth-century controversies,[136] and what is perhaps most striking is that all the men identified here differ markedly in their interpretation of *eikōn* from Athanasius, who insisted that an image did share the *ousia* of that from which the image was formed.[137] In any case, the emphasis of both Eusebius and Asterius on the 'likeness' of the Son to the Father directly contradicts Athanasius' construction of 'Arianism' and also differs at least in degree from the extant writings of Arius himself.

Yet the theology of Eusebius of Nicomedia, and in particular the *Letter to Paulinus of Tyre*, has almost invariably been characterized in modern scholarship as in some sense 'Arian'. Hanson concludes that the extant fragments of Eusebius' writings are 'enough to assure us that he was a strong supporter of Arius' theology'.[138] Kopecek declares that the *Letter to Paulinus* was 'a classic of early Arianism . . . a forceful statement of the early Arian position';[139] and Stead believes that in this letter 'Eusebius is clearly expressing a fairly radical form of Arian doctrine'.[140] All of these verdicts ultimately derive from Athanasius' polemical construction of a single 'Arian' theological position, and there is an extent to which the known writings of Eusebius, Asterius, and Arius do justify that presentation. Most significantly, as we have seen throughout the preceding pages, these three men uniformly and consistently subordinate the Son and deny that He is eternal or from the Father's *ousia*. As they each wrote in their letters and now fragmentary works, the Father alone is eternal and unbegotten, and to name the Son co-eternal or co-essential with His Father is to teach two unbegotten beings or to impose material division upon the immaterial and indivisible *ousia* of God. Eusebius' repeated rejection of any description of the Son as *ek tēs ousias tou*

136 Although '*eikōn* language' is absent from the Nicene Creed, the question of how the Son was the 'Image' of the Father was already a subject of debate before that council, in the *Encyclical Letter* of Alexander and in the Creed and anathemas of the Council of Antioch in 325.

137 There is a useful short discussion of the influence of Athanasius' definition of '*eikōn*' in the development of icon theology in Schönborn (1994) 8–13. But Schönborn does not do justice to the importance of the alternative '*eikōn* theology' of Athanasius' opponents.

138 Hanson (1988*b*) 31.

139 Kopecek (1979) 46.

140 Stead (1973) 87, (1977) 228; Lienhard (1999) 79.

Patros or *homoousios* with the Father is merely a particularly emphatic statement of a principle that he, Asterius, and Arius all shared, and thus they all concluded that the Son must be a *ktisma* and a product of the Father's will.

Neither the subordination of the Son to the Father nor distrust of the terminology of *ousia* and *homoousios*, however, were the sole preserve of an 'Arian' theology in the early fourth century. And most importantly, not only do Eusebius and Asterius never express in full the doctrines that Athanasius constructs as Athanasian Arianism, but there are also significant differences between their extant writings and the genuine teachings of Arius. Both Asterius and Eusebius avoided Arius' description of the Son as created out of nothing, just as they appear to have rejected his belief that the Son did not fully know the Father. They also place a far greater emphasis upon the unique divinity of the Son than Arius would seem to do, or than Athanasius acknowledges. In fact, to a remarkable extent the theological arguments of Asterius and Eusebius of Nicomedia parallel closely the better known doctrinal teachings of Eusebius of Caesarea.[141] The latter too denied that the Son could co-exist eternally with the Father, for 'how will the one be unbegotten (*agennētos*) and the other begotten (*gennētos*)?' (*Letter to Euphration of Balanae*; Opitz (1934–5) 4, 6). Elsewhere, he also described the Son as a perfect *ktisma* apart from all other *ktismata*, on the basis of Proverbs 8:22 (*Demonstratio Evangelica* IV.5.13, V.1.8–9), and as we have seen, he fully approved of his namesake's emphasis on the Son as the *eikōn* of the Father. At the same time, he rejected the creation of the Son out of nothing (*Letter to Alexander*; *Demonstratio Evangelica* V.1.25; *De Ecclesiastica Theologia* I.9–10, III.2.8) and emphasized that the Son's generation was ineffable to every created being (*Demonstratio Evangelica* V.1.8–9; *De Ecclesiastica Theologia* I.8, I.12). There are of course

[141] In his *Letter to Paulinus*, Eusebius of Nicomedia praises 'the zeal of my lord Eusebius [of Caesarea] ... in the cause of the truth' (Parmentier (1998) 27, 20–1), but the parallels between the theological writings of the two Eusebii have long been underestimated by scholars who have followed Athanasius' polarized polemic, and assumed a clear distinction must exist between the 'Arian' bishop of Nicomedia and his more 'conservative' namesake (e.g. Chadwick (1960) 173). However, Stead (1973) rightly rejects this traditional assumption that there was a 'noticeable difference of standpoint between the two Eusebii, and that Eusebius of Caesarea took the more moderate line' (92).

differences in emphasis, particularly that Eusebius of Caesarea is prepared, with careful qualification, to tolerate a description of the Son as *ek tēs ousias tou Patros* (*Demonstratio Evangelica* V.1.18). But the wider parallels between the two Eusebii and Asterius are too striking to be ignored. Yet Eusebius of Caesarea is now often regarded not as an 'Arian' but as broadly representative of a traditional Christian faith that could be accepted by the majority of the early fourth-century eastern Church.[142]

Whether the conclusions drawn here regarding the teachings of Asterius and Eusebius of Nicomedia can also be extended to the other men whom Athanasius identifies as 'Eusebians' is impossible to determine, for the evidence for their respective theologies is extremely limited (see Chapter 5). The isolated fragments of both Theognis of Nicaea, who denied that the Son is unbegotten,[143] and of Narcissus of Neronias, who taught that there are three *ousiai* in the Trinity (in Eusebius of Caesarea, *Contra Marcellum* I.4.39), suggest that these two men held similar positions to Eusebius of Nicomedia and Asterius on these points at least, but this is far too little to build a detailed comparison. A more complex problem is raised by the writings of George of Laodicea. As a presbyter before Nicaea, George wrote a letter in which he taught that the Son was created 'out of nothing' (*ex ouk ontōn*) and was 'a creature (*ktisma*) and one of the things made (*pepoiēmenōn*)', as He too is 'from God' (*De Synodis* 17; Opitz (1941) 245, 11). Some thirty years later, however, he also emphasized the 'likeness' of the Father and the Son in the 'Homoiousian' letter attributed to him by Epiphanius (*Panarion* 73).[144] And Athanasius of Anazarbus upheld the creation of the Son 'out of

[142] Thus Young (1983) introduces her study of Eusebius of Caesarea with the assertion that 'we can be pretty sure that he spoke for a solid mass of conservative churchmen' (1), and she acknowledges (in terms unfortunately influenced by the polarized polemic of Athanasius) that Eusebius' theology 'cannot be exactly identified with that of either side in the dispute' (17). Similar statements have also been made regarding other fourth-century bishops, including Cyril of Jerusalem (Young (1983) 124–33, Gregg (1985*a*)) and Eusebius of Emesa (Wiles (1989*a*)). Such 'difficult' individuals are in fact important precisely because they break down such polarized assumptions, a point well made by D. H. Williams (1996) 338–41 in his study of Germinius of Sirmium, the alleged ally of Ursacius and Valens.

[143] According to the Latin text edited by de Bruyne (1928) 110, Theognis taught that the Son is not '*ingenitus*' (*agennētos*).

[144] There is a useful discussion of the theology of this letter in Ayres (2004*b*) 158–60.

nothing', and declared in his *Letter to Alexander* that the Son was one of the 'things made' and one of the hundred sheep of Luke 15:3–7 (*De Synodis* 17). Hanson concludes from this that Athanasius of Anazarbus in particular was 'a consistent expounder of the theology of Arius',[145] but in reality we simply know too little of him or of any of these men to make such a decisive judgement. Any generalized conclusion once again risks imposing upon these individuals Athanasius' polemical construct of a collective 'Eusebian party'. But there is one important text that does represent a theological statement that all the diverse men whom Athanasius denounced as 'Arian' could apparently uphold: The Second Creed of the 'Dedication' Council of Antioch in 341.

The 'Dedication Creed' of Antioch

At some time within the period between January and September 341,[146] some 90 (*De Synodis* 25; Socrates, II.8) or 97 (Sozomen, III.5) eastern bishops gathered in Antioch with the eastern emperor Constantius to dedicate the 'Golden Church' of Constantine.[147] Four credal statements are traditionally associated with that council, preserved in the *De Synodis* of Athanasius. However, the four 'creeds' that Athanasius quotes are not of equal significance, nor in fact were they all composed by the same men. The 'First Creed' (Antioch I) is the letter of the council to Julius of Rome,[148] and contains little of theological substance. This creed is best known for the declaration of its authors, already quoted earlier in this chapter, that 'we have not been followers of Arius, for how could we, who are bishops, follow a presbyter?' (*De Synodis* 22; Opitz (1941) 248, 29–30). Antioch III was

[145] Hanson (1988*b*) 43.

[146] On the controversial chronology of the council, see Ch. 4.

[147] The primary sources for this council are Athanasius' *De Synodis*, and then the ecclesiastical historians Socrates (II.8, 10) and Sozomen (III.5), both of whom draw upon Athanasius' account but also possess independent material. Intriguingly, Theodoret (a bishop of the 'Antiochene school') omitted the council from his history entirely. For modern discussions of the 'Dedication' Council and its creeds, see Bardy (1936) 85–132, and particularly Schneemelcher (1977).

[148] Kelly (1960) 265; Schneemelcher (1977) 332. For the context of this letter, see Ch. 4.

the personal creed of Theophronius of Tyana, who presented this statement in his own defence against accusations of Sabellianism,[149] while Antioch IV was actually composed by a different Council of Antioch that met in the summer of 342.[150] Thus it is the Second Creed (*De Synodis* 23; Opitz (1941) 249, 11–250, 4), known in our sources as the 'Dedication Creed' or the 'Lucianic Creed', which represents the theology endorsed by this important gathering of the eastern Church. The parallels between this highly Scriptural creed and the writings of Asterius and Eusebius of Nicomedia are readily apparent.[151]

The 'Dedication Creed', after opening with the conventional assertion that the authors write 'in accordance with the evangelical and apostolic tradition' (Opitz (1941) 249, 11), explicitly rejects the more extreme elements that comprise Athanasius' construction of 'Arianism'. Yet the Creed does not teach either that the Son is co-eternal or co-essential with the Father. The Son is the 'only-begotten God... begotten before the ages (*pro tōn aiōniōn*) from the Father' (Opitz (1941) 249, 13–14). However, although any suggestion that 'time (*chronon*) or season (*kairon*) or age (*aiōna*) is or has been before the generation of the Son' (Opitz (1941) 249, 36–7) is anathematized, the Son is not explicitly described as eternal, but only as 'the firstborn of all creation, who was in the beginning with God' (Opitz (1941) 249, 18). A second anathema condemns the idea that the Son might be 'a creature (*ktisma*) as one of the creatures (*tōn ktismatōn*), an offspring (*gennēma*) as one of the offsprings (*tōn gennēmatōn*), or a thing made (*poiēma*) as one of the things made (*tōn poiēmatōn*)' (Opitz (1941) 249, 37–8). This doctrine excludes Athanasius' allegation that the 'Arians' reduced the Son to the level of all mutable creatures, but not

149 Athanasius alleges that all the bishops at Antioch 'subscribed (*hypegrapsan*)' to this statement (*De Synodis* 24; Opitz (1941) 250, 6), but as Barnes (1993) 58 observes, this claim is 'grossly tendentious: the rest of the bishops accepted Theophronius' creed as proof of his orthodoxy without in any sense adopting it as an authoritative statement of correct doctrine'. For a detailed discussion of this creed and its relation to the overall council, see Tetz (1989).

150 Barnes (1993) 230. This creed was to prove highly influential in the years that followed, and was repeated by Eastern Serdica, in the Macrostich Creed of 344, and at Sirmium in 351.

151 The parallels to Asterius were well demonstrated by Bardy (1936) 125–7 and Vinzent (1993*a*) 168–73.

the possibility that the Son is Himself a 'perfect creature', who is 'immutable and unchangeable (*atrepton te kai analloiōton*)' (Opitz (1941) 249, 17–18). The creed contains no explicit soteriological statement, but the declaration that '[we believe] in the Holy Spirit, who is given to those who have faith for comfort (*paraklesis*) and sanctification (*hagiasmos*) and perfection (*teleiōsis*)' (Opitz (1941) 249, 26–7) might suggest again a conception of salvation through 'deification'.

Most significantly, the divinity of the Son is here defined in terms that accord precisely with the known theologies of Asterius and Eusebius of Nicomedia, and which systematically omit all of the statements of the Nicene Creed that these two men were most reluctant to accept. The Son is 'God from God, whole from whole, sole from sole, perfect from perfect, King from King, Lord from Lord, living Word, living Wisdom, true Light, Way, Truth, Resurrection, Shepherd, Door' (Opitz (1941) 249, 14–16). But He does not hold these titles by His own essential nature.[152] Instead, as Asterius had already taught, He is the 'exact image (*aparallakton eikona*) of the Essence, Will, Power, and Glory of the Godhead of the Father' (Opitz (1941) 249, 17–18), who came down from heaven '"not to do my own will but the will of Him that sent me" [John 6:38]' (Opitz (1941) 249, 23–4). The Nicene expressions 'true God from true God', 'begotten not made', and above all '*homoousios*' and 'from the *ousia* of the Father' have been excluded. The creed concludes with a further statement that again echoes the extant fragments of Asterius, that there must be 'a Father who is truly Father, and a Son who is truly Son, and the Holy Spirit who is truly Holy Spirit... so that they are three in subsistence (*hypostasei*) and one in agreement (*symphōnia*)' (Opitz (1941) 249, 30–1; 33).

By the standards of later 'orthodoxy', there are still evident flaws in the theology expressed in this 'Dedication Creed'. *Homoousios* is omitted; the eternity of the Son is left unspoken; and the doctrine of the Trinity is openly subordinationist, for the identities of the Father, Son, and Holy Spirit 'denote accurately the peculiar subsistence,

[152] In this creed, as in the writings of Asterius, it seems that these clauses teach instead a 'two-level' theory of the titles of the Son, and that the Son derives titles from the eternal properties inherent in the Father (M. R. Barnes (1997) 215).

rank, and glory (*hypostasin te kai taxin kai doxan*) of each that is named' (Opitz (1941) 249, 31–2). But the Second Creed of Antioch cannot be described as 'Arian'. Hilary of Poitiers famously described the Council of 341 as a '*sanctorum synodus*' (Hilary, *De Synodis* 32), and Sozomen observed that the Second Creed in particular 'very nearly resembled that of the council of Nicaea' (III.5.8; Hansen (2004) 344, 26–346, 1). In the words of Hanson, 'true-blue Arians would have found it impossible to accept the statement that the Son is the "exact image of the substance...of the Godhead of the Father"'.[153] Therefore he declares that the 'Dedication Creed' 'deliberately excludes the kind of Arianism professed by Arius and among his followers by Eusebius of Nicomedia'.[154]

Yet not only are there a number of obvious parallels between the creed itself and the theological writings of both Eusebius and Asterius, but certainly Eusebius and probably Asterius as well were in fact prominent members of the very synod that composed this creed.[155] Indeed, the register of the leading bishops of the 'Dedication' Council provided by Sozomen (III.5.10) represents a veritable roll-call of the men whom Athanasius condemned as 'Eusebians' and 'Arians'. In addition to Eusebius himself (now bishop of Constantinople) and Flacillus of Antioch, these names include Acacius of Caesarea, Patrophilus of Scythopolis, Theodore of Heraclea, Eudoxius of Germanicia, Gregory of Alexandria, Dianius of Cappadocian Caesarea, and George of Laodicea.[156] The 'Dedication Creed' must therefore be

[153] Hanson (1988*b*) 287.

[154] Ibid. 290.

[155] The presence of Eusebius is attested by Socrates (II.8) and Sozomen (III.5), and as the bishop of Constantinople he was presumably a highly influential figure in 341. The evidence for Asterius' attendance is less conclusive (he is not named by the ecclesiastical historians, but according to the often unreliable *Libellus Synodicus* he accompanied Dianius of Cappadocian Caesarea to the council). As Hanson (1988*b*) observes, however, the theological parallels between Antioch II and Asterius' known writings (whether or not they derive from a common 'Lucianic' source) make it 'impossible to avoid the conclusion that Asterius had some influence on the composition of the Second (Dedication) Creed' (289).

[156] One of the few scholars to give proper weight to this register of names is Schneemelcher (1977): 'Die Zahl der Teilnehmer zeigt doch, daß es sich nicht um eine kleine Provinzialsynode gehandelt haben kann. Die bei Sozomenus gennanten Namen lassen erkennen, daß die führenden Bischöfe des Ostens anwesend waren' (339).

recognized as an important guide to the theology both of Eusebius himself[157] and of all these individual 'Eusebians' (many of whom, as Sozomen observes, were leading metropolitans and so to some extent representatives of their regions). This carries important implications for the significance of that creed, a creed that appears to represent a widespread theology within early fourth-century eastern Christianity.

To quote once more from Hanson, the 'Dedication Creed' 'represents the nearest approach we can make to discovering the views of the ordinary educated Eastern bishop who was no admirer of the extreme views of Arius but who had been shocked and disturbed by the apparent Sabellianism of N[icaea].'[158] 'The Second Creed shows us [the views of] the hitherto silent majority... they constituted a widespread point of view, but we can hardly call them a party'.[159] Such a statement cannot be confirmed, for the 'silent majority' are by definition unknown and often nameless. But I believe that Hanson is correct that the Second Creed of Antioch does represent a theology that a considerable proportion of the eastern Church in 341 could endorse. To appreciate the full significance of this fact, however, we must break free from the recurring assumption of earlier scholars, restated explicitly by Hanson, that it is possible to divide that eastern Church between the 'ordinary bishops' represented by the

[157] Hanson (1988*b*) 290, following the hypothesis of Simonetti (1975) 153–5, argues that the 'Dedication Creed' reveals the degree to which Eusebius had developed his theological position since the beginning of the controversy and his *Letter to Paulinus of Tyre*. Doubtless Eusebius' theology and his expression of that theology did develop throughout the years that followed the Council of Nicaea, but I believe that the Simonetti–Hanson thesis underestimates the continuity between the Second Creed of Antioch and the earlier writings of both Eusebius and Asterius.

[158] Hanson (1988*b*) 290.

[159] Ibid. 291; see also Kelly (1960), who describes the 'Dedication Creed' as 'frankly pre-Nicene in its tone' (271), and as 'a faithful replica of the average theology of the Eastern Church, the theology of which Eusebius of Caesarea was a spokesman' (274). Hanson's interpretation of the creed has recently been challenged by Parvis (2003), who emphasizes that even 97 bishops was certainly not a majority of the eastern Church, and by Ayres (2004*b*), who limits 'eastern' to 'Asia Minor, Syria, and Palestine' (120). But even so, the statement of such a bloc (which included a number of leading metropolitans) must represent at the least a widespread and significant theological viewpoint within eastern Christianity.

'Dedication Creed' and the 'Arian party' of the 'Eusebians'.[160] This division is yet again a product above all of Athanasius' polemic and his polarized construction of the 'Arian Controversy', in which every bishop must choose between the alleged poles of 'Arianism' and 'orthodoxy'. In Chapter 3, we saw how Athanasius and his supporters sought to impose that polarization upon the eastern bishops at the Council of Tyre, urging them to accept the existence of the 'Eusebian party' that he had constructed and in turn to defend his innocence against an 'Arian conspiracy'. In his doctrinal works, Athanasius imposes that same polarization upon the wider theological controversies of his time, and so again appeals to the eastern 'majority' to separate themselves from the 'Eusebians' and to unite with himself and the 'orthodox' against the 'Arian heresy'.

Once the polarized divisions of that polemical construction have been removed, it is possible to define the 'Dedication Creed' not through comparison to 'Arianism' or 'Nicene orthodoxy', but as a broadly representative statement of a theology that prevailed in much of the eastern Church in the first half of the fourth century, and indeed beyond.[161] At the Council of Seleucia in 359, it was this creed and not Nicaea that those eastern bishops now usually known as the 'Homoiousians' invoked as the traditional faith of the Church.[162] These 'Homoiousians' were themselves accepted by Athanasius as 'orthodox' in his *De Synodis*, despite their distrust of the term *homoousios*, but he never acknowledged their dependence upon a creed that he wished to condemn as 'Arian'. Various eastern bishops continued to appeal to the Second Creed of Antioch in the 360s and even as late as 381.[163] These appeals suggest once more that the 'Dedication Creed' was held as representative by a considerable portion of the eastern Church, and reflects the influence that the legacy of Eusebius of

160 This distinction between 'conservative' and 'Arian/Eusebian' received its clearest exposition in Gwatkin (1882), esp. 53 and 61, and remains visible in Hanson and (albeit with a broader definition of 'Eusebian') in Lienhard (1999) who describes the 'Dedication Creed' as 'a classic statement of Eusebian theology' (169; see also Ayres (2004*b*) 120).

161 For a survey of the subsequent history of the 'Dedication Creed' in the fourth-century controversies, see Bardy (1936) 96–119.

162 Socrates, II.39–40; Sozomen, IV.22.

163 Socrates, IV.4, V.8; Sozomen, IV.7, IV.12, VII.7.

Nicomedia and other so-called 'Eusebians' exerted upon the continuing fourth-century controversies.[164]

It is against this wider eastern theological background that the teachings of Asterius and Eusebius of Nicomedia must also be understood. The exact extent to which these men can themselves be viewed as representative is difficult to determine, for each of the individual bishops at Antioch in 341 must have possessed their own particular theological emphases. But within the writings of Asterius and Eusebius certain principles can be identified that all of the ninety or more bishops who attended the council would seem to have shared. All were reluctant to describe the Son as eternal, or to speak of Him as *homoousios* to the Father, or as having derived from His *ousia*. The Son is God, and the Word, Wisdom and Power of God, but He possesses His divinity through the will of the Father, of whom He is the *Eikōn*. Thus the union of the Father and the Son is not ontological, and great emphasis is placed on the distinct identities of the individual *hypostases* of the Trinity, an emphasis that was apparently aroused by fears of the Sabellian implications of *homoousios*, especially as revealed in the theology of Marcellus of Ancyra.[165]

[164] The various blocs that emerged within the eastern Church in the middle of the fourth century all claimed to be the heirs of traditions represented by the men whom Athanasius condemned as 'Eusebians'. In addition to the 'Homoiousian' emphasis upon the 'Dedication Creed', on which see Löhr (1993) 88, one should also note again Philostorgius' construction of a 'Neo-Arian' 'succession' from Eusebius and Lucian, and the conflict over the legacy of Lucian of Antioch himself (see Brennecke (1993) 186–7, 191). All of these later theological positions could claim with some justification to trace their doctrines back to the writings of individual 'Eusebians'. There is thus perhaps some truth in the hypothesis that Eusebius of Nicomedia held together a tradition that included a variety of diverse positions, and that this tradition increasingly divided following his death shortly after the 'Dedication' Council.

[165] On the influence of Marcellus upon the 'Dedication' Council, see Hanson (1988*b*) 285–92, Tetz (1989), and Lienhard (1999) 167–71. The Second Creed is actually the only Antiochene creed that does not contain the expression 'His kingdom shall have no end', which was intended to refute Marcellus (although whether Marcellus truly taught the contrary is open to much doubt) and which appears in the other three creeds of 341–2. The emphasis upon the three distinct *hypostases* of the Trinity in the 'Dedication Creed', however, is at least in part intended to be a refutation of Marcellus' doctrine of one *hypostasis* in the Godhead, and the Sabellianism that his teaching was alleged to imply.

This broad theological position, within which considerable individual divergences could and did exist, is not 'Arian'. As we have seen, such a label exaggerates both Arius' importance within the ongoing doctrinal debates of the 330s and 340s and the degree to which his teachings were ever representative of the wider Church. At the same time, this theology is not the 'Nicene orthodoxy' of the later writings of Athanasius, and to refer to a 'non-Nicene' or 'anti-Nicene' position equally exaggerates the contemporary significance of Nicaea. All these titles ultimately derive from the polemical polarization of our sources.[166] The same difficulty is also inherent in the alternative model proposed by Joseph Lienhard, who avoids these older labels, but imposes his own polarized and artificial categories upon the fourth-century controversies.[167] Yet some terminology must be employed to describe this theology. As Rowan Williams has observed, 'the problem for students of this period is, in part, the lack of a convenient theological designation for a theology which takes for granted some sort of hierarchical pluralism in its talk of God'.[168] 'Eusebian' itself is too loaded and polemical a term,[169] as this entire

[166] 'The standard classifications of 'Arian' and 'Nicene' are not only inaccurate as a means of determining the doctrinal allegiances of those groups to which they usually refer, but the terms also tend to cloud, rather than illuminate, our ability in distinguishing the nuances of their beliefs. Either classification runs the risk of creating a typology which assumes a degree of theological homogeneity or uniformity that did not exist' (D. H. Williams (1996) 335).

[167] Lienhard ((1987), repeated (1999) 28–46) argues that 'the conflict in the fourth century was one between two theological traditions' (420), which he identifies as 'miahypostatic and duohypostatic theology, the theology of one *hypostasis* and two *hypostaseis* respectively' (422). Lienhard's model raises a number of important questions, but his categories simply do not hold, for the two 'traditions' that he defines are each compounded from various writers (as he himself acknowledges) and represent positions that no individual in the fourth century would recognize (not least because, despite his later claim that the word *hypostasis* was 'the one linguistic symbol that became the rallying-point of the two opposing groups' ((1993) x), many of the participants in the controversies never even used this term). Above all, Lienhard's model rests on just as polarized a foundation as the polemical construct of Athanasius himself, and assumes the same distorted interpretation of a single rigidly divided 'Arian Controversy'.

[168] Williams (1987) 167; see also Wiles (1989*a*) 267–8.

[169] Lienhard (1987) declares that 'as a historical phenomenon, it would be most accurate to call the "Arian" theology "Eusebian" understood as a way of thought shared and fostered by Eusebius of Caesarea and Eusebius of Nicomedia among others' (419). In his *Contra Marcellum* (1999), he employs that title throughout to designate Marcellus' opponents, whose theology he defines as representative of his

monograph demonstrates. Other terms proposed in recent scholarship, like 'Origenist'[170] and 'Lucianist',[171] are also inadequate, as indeed is 'conservative', which frequently implies little more than the subordination of the Son and a fear of Sabellianism. I cannot propose a solution here to the problem that Williams has outlined. But I would emphasize that, whatever terminology we may use to describe these controversies, it is essential that we avoid the polarization that Athanasius above all has constructed and which has so effectively concealed the wide theological spectrum that existed within the fourth-century Church.

proposed 'duohypostatic' tradition (101–3). Although his definition of 'Eusebian' is not precisely that of Athanasius, Lienhard's arguments amply demonstrate the polemical nature of such a title, which again rests on his polarized interpretation of the fourth-century controversies. A slightly more nuanced version of Lienhard's use of 'Eusebian' occurs in Ayres (2004*b*) 52, who emphasizes the range of views within what he describes as a 'broad Eusebian trajectory' (60). But here again Ayres' acceptance of the construction of the 'Eusebians' as in some sense a uniform theological tradition renders him unable to do full justice to the diversity of theological positions held by the men on whom this polemical title has been imposed, a limitation particularly visible in his description of the 'Eusebians' as 'Theologians of the "One Unbegotten"' (52).

170 Both Young (1983) 1 and Kannengiesser (1983*b*) 466 refer respectively to 'popular Origenism, the faith of the ordinary educated Christian' and 'the Oriental moderate forms of Origenism in the east of the fourth-century empire'. Frend (1984) 524 declares explicitly that the 'Eusebians', who he elsewhere describes as 'Arian', 'represented what had become the traditional Origenism of the majority of the Eastern bishops' (see also Wallace-Hadrill (1982), who simply describes the 'Eusebians' as 'the Origenists' (77)). However, although the teachings of Origen (*c.*185–254) unquestionably exerted great influence on fourth-century Christian theology (see esp. Hanson (1987)), this influence affected all those involved in the controversies, while at the same time 'no "Origenist" theologian took over and unreservedly argued for Origen's system in its entirety' (Williams (1987) 149; see also Hanson (1987) 413–14). Unless we reduce the title 'Origenist' to mean little more than 'subordinationist', a reduction that does justice neither to Origen's own teachings nor to the diversity of fourth-century theology, such a title can only be misleading.

171 This term was employed by Williams (1987) 166: 'if any comprehensive name could be given to at least the leaders of resistance to Nicaea, and perhaps also to the vague consensus on which they relied, "Lucianist" and "Lucianism" are not bad designations'. However, quite aside from the problems we have already traced in defining the theological position of Lucian of Antioch or the existence of a 'Lucianist school', such terminology once again creates an artificial division between the alleged 'Lucianists' and the other eastern bishops with whom they clearly shared much common ground, as the 'Dedication' Council of 341 reveals.

The men whom Athanasius condemns as 'Eusebians', particularly Asterius and Eusebius of Nicomedia, but also the entire body of bishops who attended the 'Dedication' Council in 341, cannot be described as 'Arian'. On the contrary, the teachings of these men (and indeed the doctrines of Arius himself) must be understood within the broad theological framework, widespread across the eastern Church, which the writings of Asterius and Eusebius and the Second Creed of Antioch all to a significant extent represent. Yet because of the polemic of Athanasius, the parallels between those writings and the wider eastern theology visible in the 'Dedication Creed' have for too long been ignored. Not only does Athanasius construct an entirely artificial polarization between the alleged 'Arianism' of his opponents and the 'orthodoxy' that he presents as the traditional faith of the Church, but through that polarization Athanasius in effect denies the very existence of the theological position proclaimed in 341. Within Athanasius' construction of the 'Arian Controversy', no alternatives can exist between his two 'poles' of 'Arianism' and 'orthodoxy'. Thus in the *Orations against the Arians*, and in all his theological polemical works, he separates the 'Eusebians' from the main body of the eastern Church and appeals to that 'majority' to denounce the 'heresy' of those he condemns and embrace his own 'orthodox faith'. In the final pages of this chapter, I wish to look more closely at the precise methodology through which Athanasius has achieved this construction and its full implications.

THE THEOLOGICAL POLEMIC OF ATHANASIUS: POLARIZATION, DEFINITION, AND IMPOSITION

The theology of Athanasius has received much attention from scholars past and present,[172] and a detailed discussion of the complexity of his thought is not my intention here. However, as we have seen, Athanasius' construction of the 'Arianism' of his opponents is formulated against the background of the polarized vision of the

[172] For good recent discussions of the theology of Athanasius, see Widdicombe (1994) 145–249, Pettersen (1995), Anatolios (1998), and Behr (2004) 168–259.

'Arian Controversy' that underlies his polemic. His own definition of 'orthodoxy' is presented, particularly in the *Orations against the Arians*, in opposition to the 'heresy' that he attributes to his foes. To understand his construction of 'Arianism', and the methodology by which it is composed, it is therefore necessary to survey briefly the fundamental principles of the theology that Athanasius presents as the traditional faith of the Church.

For behold, we speak openly from the divine Scriptures concerning the pious faith, and we hold [it] as a lamp on a lampstand, saying that He is true (*alēthinos*) by nature (*physei*) and legitimate (*gnēsios*) Son of the Father, that He is proper (*idios*) to His essence, only-begotten Wisdom, and true (*alēthinos*) and only Word of the Father. He is not a creature (*ktisma*), nor a thing made (*poiēma*), but proper offspring (*idion gennēma*) of the essence (*ousias*) of the Father. Therefore He is true (*alēthinos*) God, existing *homoousios* with the true Father.... For this again the Lord said, 'he who has seen Me, has seen the Father'. Always (*aei*) He was and is, and never He was not. For since the Father is eternal, eternal (*aidios*) also must be His Word and Wisdom. (*Oration* I.9; Tetz (1998) 117, 1–6; 118, 9–11)

Throughout his many writings, Athanasius never significantly deviates from this conception of Christian 'orthodoxy', although the terminology that he employs does develop over time. Already in his earliest treatise, the *Contra Gentes-De Incarnatione*,[173] the central doctrine of the theology of Athanasius is the full divinity of the Son and His ontological unity with the Father. Only if the Son is truly God, eternally and essentially the Son of the Father, can He promise the revelation of God and the salvation of man that lay at the heart of Athanasius' understanding of the Christian message. In the later *De Decretis* and *De Synodis*, Athanasius expresses this ontological unity through the Nicene term *homoousios*, a term which he almost entirely avoids in his earlier writings. Yet this shift in language

[173] The exact date of composition of this dual treatise, which I omitted from my catalogue of Athanasian works in Ch. 1, has been much debated (see Leemans (2000) 132–5). However, whether we place this text in *c.*318 (the traditional date) or in the early–mid-330s (as modern scholars have increasingly argued), Athanasius clearly wrote the *Contra Gentes–De Incarnatione* before the *Orations against the Arians*, and so had already formulated his ontological doctrine of the Son before he began to write directly against the 'Arian heresy'.

is not the product of any notable shift in Athanasius' thought. The word *homoousios* appears only once in the three authentic *Orations against the Arians*, in the passage quoted above. But throughout those *Orations* as throughout his later works Athanasius consistently proclaims that it is because the Son is the proper offspring of the *ousia* of the Father that He is able to reveal the Father through the Incarnation and make possible the 'deification' (*theopoiēsis*) of mankind.

Just as the polemic of Athanasius constructs a polarization between 'Arianism' and 'orthodoxy', so Athanasius' own theology, and above all his conception of the divinity of the Son, is itself founded upon a polarized ontological division between God and the world created from nothing. The Godhead, eternal and immutable by *ousia* and by *physis*,[174] is separated by a vast gulf from the created order, brought into existence in time and mutable by nature. This separation lies at the heart of Athanasius' doctrinal position, and in turn of his construction of the 'Arian heresy'. Either the Son is eternal and immutable God, or He is a creature like any other. Either He is the true and essential offspring of the Father, or He is entirely unlike God by essence, created from nothing and mutable by nature. Either 'the Saviour is neither God nor Word nor Son' or 'He is the Word of the Father, and true Son, and He is God from God' (*Oration* I.10; Tetz (1998) 119, 3–6). And if only a Son who is ontologically God can be the source of revelation and deification for man, then a Son who is a creature, however unique in comparison to other creatures, cannot be our Saviour, for He cannot bridge the gulf that separates God from the created order to which He too belongs. For Athanasius, the 'created Son' of Arius thus compromised his entire understanding of salvation, and represented a 'heresy' that had to be opposed. Yet the construction of Athanasian Arianism that we have traced throughout this chapter in fact derives from the imposition of

[174] For Athanasius' use of the terms *ousia*, *physis*, and also *hypostasis*, see Torrance (1995) 206–12. In Athanasius' writings all three terms are virtually synonyms, but there are nuances between them, and by the time of the *Tomus ad Antiochenos* (362) Athanasius is increasingly aware of the development within eastern theology of a distinction between *ousia* and *hypostasis*.

Athanasius' own polarized theological principles upon the men whom he condemns.[175]

In the penultimate paragraph of the introduction to the *First Oration against the Arians*, in a passage that follows directly from the statement of his own 'orthodoxy' quoted earlier, Athanasius lays down the polarized consequences of his polemic in the most explicit form.

> If someone then, after inquiring into the doctrines of both (*ta para amphoterōn*), might be asked the faith of which of the two he would choose, or the words of which he would say to be befitting of God . . . that He was, or that He was not; that He was always (*aei*), or before His generation (*prin genesthai*); eternal (*aidion*), or since this and from then; true (*alēthinon*), or by adoption (*thesei*) and by participation (*metochē*) and according to thought (*kat' epinoian*); to call Him one of the generated beings, or to join Him to the Father; [to call] Him unlike (*anomoion*) according to the essence (*ousian*) of the Father, or like (*homoion*) and proper (*idion*) of the Father; a creature (*ktisma*), or Him through whom the creatures (*ta ktismata*) came to be; that He is the Word of the Father, or that there is another besides him and through that one this one came to be and through another Wisdom, and that this one is called Wisdom and Word only by name (*onomati*) and is a partaker (*metochon*) of that Wisdom and second to it? (I.9; Tetz (1998) 118, 25–7; 29–36)

All of the individual elements within this summary of Athanasian Arianism, and the theological principles that Athanasius presents as 'orthodox' in contrast to this 'heresy', originate from Athanasius' ontological polarization of God and the created order. And as we have already seen, although certain of the beliefs condemned here were taught by Arius, Asterius, and Eusebius of Nicomedia, the vast majority of these 'Arian' doctrines ultimately derive from Athanasius' own polemical interpretations. Thus in the final two clauses of this passage, Athanasius repeats his recurring assertion that the 'Arians' taught that the Son is not the true Word and Wisdom of the Father. This is to a certain extent correct, but the conclusion that Athanasius then draws, that the 'Arians' assert that the Father was once without His Word and Wisdom entirely (*Oration* I.17, I.19), derives from the

[175] 'Athanasius means us to interpret Arius from the point of view of his own theology. For Athanasius, Father, Son and Spirit are a coequal Trinity separated by an unbridgeable gulf from all originate beings; and in this connection, and for controversial purposes, he can speak as if all originate beings were on a level; and he represents Arius as placing the heavenly Son within this homogeneous mass' (Stead (1978) 31).

imposition upon his opponents' theology of Athanasius' own assumption that the Son is the only Word of the Father.[176] The men whom he condemns simply did not hold the position that Athanasius attributes to them, but through their condemnation, Athanasius implies that only his interpretation of the Son can be valid and 'orthodox'. This is the methodology that recurs throughout Athanasius' theological polemic, and above all in his constant assertion that the 'Arians' reduce the Son to the level of all creatures.

For Athanasius, and so in turn for later generations, the reduction of the Son to a *ktisma* would become the essential characteristic of the 'Arian heresy'.[177] However, although it is true that Arius and indeed almost all the so-called 'Eusebians' did describe the Son by that term, the implications of this position that Athanasius develops at great length in his polemic again derive almost exclusively from the imposition of his own theological principles. According to Athanasius, if the Son is not co-eternal and co-essential with the Father then He is no different from all other mutable creatures, whose attributes he shares. Thus Athanasius insists that every 'Arian' must believe that the Son, like any other creature, was created 'from nothing', a doctrine that Arius himself did express once, but which is not found in the writings of Asterius or Eusebius of Nicomedia. Athanasius' repeated emphasis that the 'Arians' render the Son mutable also rests upon this same polemical foundation,[178] while from the 'Arian'

176 This Athanasian construction represents what was described by Stead as a 'Mosaic Argument'. The alleged 'Arian' conception of an 'unwise God' 'is reached by combining the Arian denial of eternal generation with the Athanasian principle that God's Word and Wisdom are wholly identified with His Son. This argument... becomes wholly specious when directed against the Arian position, which (for what it is worth) is that God eternally possesses reason and wisdom as impersonal attributes' (Stead (1976) 136, see also (1978) 39). The final sneer against the 'worth' of the 'Arian position' reflects Stead's discomfort at his own criticism of Athanasius (whom he goes on to defend against charges of 'bad faith' (1976) 136), but his conclusion is indisputable.

177 'Athanasius called "Arian" anyone who could be understood to mean that the Son is a creature' (Anatolios (1998) 96). For the continuity of this attitude in later centuries, see Slusser (1993) and Wiles (1996).

178 See especially *Oration against the Arians* I.35–52, in which Athanasius develops in full his argument that the 'Arians' attribute changeability, ethical advancement and suffering to the divine Son. It is these passages above all that underlie the reconstructions of 'Arianism' proposed by Gregg and Groh and Hanson. A new translation of the text in question has now been produced by Anatolios (2004) 91–110, although the accompanying commentary is somewhat uncritical, primarily because Anatolios accepts at face value Athanasius' polemical assertion that Arius made the Son mutable (89–91).

denial of the eternity of the Son, Athanasius concludes that his opponents taught that the Son was created in time (*Oration* I.11)[179] and was not the creative Word of the Father (*Oration* II.21).[180] None of these alleged doctrines were ever taught by any of the men whom Athanasius condemns. Consequently, the 'Arian heresy' that he refutes at such length in the *Orations against the Arians* is largely a product not of the words of Arius or of the 'Eusebians', but of Athanasius' own polemical construction.

Athanasius knew well that neither Arius nor any of the men he described as 'Arian' actually taught that the Son, although a *ktisma*, was no different from every other created being. In *De Synodis* 16, he quotes Arius' explicit insistence in his *Letter to Alexander* that the Son is a '*ktisma*' but not as one of '*tōn ktismatōn*'. But Athanasius' own polarized ontology will not permit such a distinction to be made. His denunciation of this 'Arian' argument in the *Second Oration against the Arians*, set near the beginning of his exegesis of the crucial text of Proverbs 8:22, provides a particularly vivid demonstration of the methodology of his polemic and its inherent distortions:

Let us behold what it was that they replied to the blessed Alexander in the beginning, when their heresy was formed. They wrote then saying that, 'He is a creature (*ktisma*), but not as one of the creatures (*tōn ktismatōn*); He is a thing made (*poiēma*), but not as one of the things made (*tōn poiēmatōn*); He is an offspring (*gennēma*), but not as one of the offsprings (*tōn gennēmatōn*)'. Therefore let everyone behold the treachery and deceit of this heresy. For, knowing the bitterness of its own folly, it tries to embellish itself with persuasive words, and it says what indeed it thinks, that He is a '*ktisma*', but it believes that it is able to conceal itself by saying 'but not as one of *tōn*

[179] As we have already seen, not only is 'there was when He was not' a statement that Eusebius and Asterius at least avoided, but more importantly no 'Eusebian' theologian ever taught that the Son was generated temporally, a doctrine explicitly anathematized by the bishops in Antioch in 341.

[180] This is the example of Athanasian *reductio ad absurdum* that Stead (1976) 135–6 selects to demonstrate his 'Mosaic Argument'. 'If we combine the (Athanasian) proposition that the Son does everything that the Father does with the (Arian, or supposedly Arian) proposition that the Son is created by the Father, we are in a dilemma; either we get the absurd result—for which, of course, the Arian proposition is held responsible—that the Son is his own maker and creator; or else the Arian proposition has to be given up. But presumably the Arians would not, and need not, accept the Athanasian part of this artificial combination.'

> *ktismatōn*'... [Yet] this so great sophism of yours is shown to be foolish. For once again you still say that He is one of the creatures, and the things that someone might say about the other creatures, you also attribute to the Son, being truly foolish and blind. For indeed, in what manner is any one of the creatures such as another, so that this [i.e. to be unlike other creatures] you can speak of concerning the Son as a distinctive feature (*exaireton*)? (II.19; Tetz (1998) 195, 1–196, 8; 196, 16–20)

All creatures may differ from each other in kind (*genos*), but nevertheless all are creatures by nature. Therefore

> either let the Word be distinguished from the things made (*tōn poiēmatōn*), and as Creator be restored to the Father, and let Him be confessed to be Son by nature (*physei*). Or, if He is simply a creature (*ktisma*), [then] let Him be confessed to have the same rank (*taxin*) as the other [creatures] have in relation to one another... for even if the Son may transcend the others by comparison (*sugkrisei*), nevertheless He is a creature, just as they are. (II.20; Tetz (1998) 196, 1–3; 197, 6–7)

Either the Son is a *ktisma* like any other or He is proper offspring (*idion gennēma*) of the essence of the Father, for although all the *ktismata* may be distinct from each other in 'kind' or 'quality', nevertheless they are alike by 'nature'. The distinction of Arius, that the Son is a creature but not as one of the creatures, is nothing more than a rhetorical 'sophism'. Such a conclusion is the inevitable and logical consequence of Athanasius' own ontology, but it is also a manifest distortion of the actual theology of the men whom Athanasius wishes to condemn. Indeed, the very 'quotation' that he here attributes to the 'Arians' is a product of his own polemic and not of the writings of his foes. What Arius actually wrote in his *Letter to Alexander* (quoted by Athanasius himself in *De Synodis* 16) is that the Son is 'the perfect creature (*teleion ktisma*) of God, but not as one of the creatures, offspring (*gennēma*), but not as one of the offsprings'. In the version of this text presented in the *Second Oration against the Arians*, however, while Athanasius cites the final clause correctly, he inserts the line 'a thing made (*poiēma*), but not as one of the things made', and he omits the term *teleion*, with which Arius qualified his description of the Son as a *ktisma*. In effect, Athanasius has rewritten the words of Arius according to his own polarized theological principles. He imposes upon Arius his own definition of *ktisma* and *poiēma* as synonyms,[181] a definition which there is no evidence that Arius shared, for he does not name the Son a *poiēma* anywhere in his extant writings.[182] And Athanasius ignores the concept of a 'perfect' creature, an irrelevant distinction if all created beings, including the 'Arian Son', are alike by *physis* in contrast to the divine essence and nature of the Father.

Yet the doctrine that the Son was 'a perfect creature, not like other creatures' was not empty rhetoric. It was an essential component of a widespread eastern theology that understood the Son as a unique and divine *ktisma*, a theology that Arius, Asterius, the two Eusebii, and many of the bishops who attended the 'Dedication' Council of 341 would appear to have shared.[183] All of the men whom Athanasius condemns did indeed deny that the Son was eternal or from the *ousia* of the Father, but there is no evidence that any of these so-called 'Arians' ever taught that the Son, although a creature, possessed the same attributes, essence, and nature as those beings who were created by the Father through His Word.[184] Instead, I would contend that all

[181] 'Once it has been shown that the Word is not a *poiēma*, it is also shown that He is not a *ktisma*. For it is the same to speak of a *poiēma* and a *ktisma*, so that indeed the proof that He is not a *poiēma* is proof also that He is not a *ktisma*' (*Oration* II.18; Tetz (1998) 195, 15–18). Athanasius goes to great lengths in the *Orations against the Arians* to insist that these two terms must be understood as synonyms, but Arius' avoidance of the term *poiēma* suggests that he at least did not share that assumption.

[182] The formula that Athanasius denounces here is in fact closer to the teaching of Eunomius (*Liber Apologeticus* 28) than to that of Arius. There is a discussion of this Eunomian teaching in Vaggione (1987*a*), although Vaggione seems unaware that Arius himself does not use the term *poiēma*.

[183] Earlier in this chapter we saw that both Arius and Asterius explicitly refer to the Son as a unique creature, while this doctrine can also be inferred from Eusebius of Nicomedia's *Letter to Paulinus*, and from the anathema of the Second Creed of 341 against those who teach that 'the Son is a creature as one of the creatures' (which at least implies the possibility of a creature *not* like other creatures). The clearest statement of this position, however, is in the writings of Eusebius of Caesarea, who insists upon the importance of Arius' distinction between the Son as a 'perfect creature' and the rest of the created order in his *Letter to Alexander* (quoted in the *Acta* of the Second Council of Nicaea in 787; Opitz, *Urkunde* VII). Here he complains that Alexander has falsely alleged that the 'Arians' taught 'that the Son came to be like one of the creatures (*tōn ktismatōn*), when they did not say this but, making a clear distinction, they proclaim that He was not like one of the creatures' (Opitz (1934–5) 14, 14–15, 1).

[184] Athanasius 'incessantly confronts the Arians with the crude alternative, either a Son fully equal to the Father, or a creature just like any other creature; he dismisses any suggestion that the Son enjoys some sort of intermediate status . . . is it really certain that God's originative power is restricted to one of two alternative processes, either generating a being fully equal to himself, or creating beings radically inferior?' (Stead (1976) 129–30).

the individuals whose theological positions I have examined in this chapter, and particularly Asterius and Eusebius of Nicomedia, defined the Son as a 'perfect *ktisma*', an immutable mediator separate by *ousia* and *physis* both from the unbegotten Father and from the created order. Thus they bridged the gulf that separates God and creation not through the Incarnation of an ontologically divine Son, but through a mediator who was both a *ktisma* and God.[185] Athanasius' theology was to prove the more enduring, and the logic of his position is perhaps the more compelling. But contrary to his polemic, the men whom he condemned did nevertheless uphold the existence of a divine Son, who they believed was the source of the creation[186] and salvation[187] of man.

That this conclusion is impossible to prove, and indeed flies in the face of the traditional interpretation of the theology of the men named by Athanasius as the 'Eusebians', I would attribute both to

[185] It is a recurring theme of modern scholarship that the 'Arian Controversy' can be understood in terms of two contrasting models of the relationship between God and the world, and that Athanasius placed the 'demarcation line' between God and creation, whereas the 'Arians' placed that line between the Father and the Son (see Florovsky (1962) 47; Grillmeier (1975) 228–9; Widdicombe (1994) 154; Torrance (1995) 188; and Vaggione (2000) 123–4). Yet for those theologians who defined the Son as a 'perfect *ktisma*', there was not in fact one 'demarcation line' at all, for the Son was distinct both from the Father and from all other creatures. The rigid polarization of 'God' and 'creation' by *ousia* and *physis* derives from the theology of Athanasius, and does not do justice to the doctrines of those he condemned or to the complexity of the wider fourth-century debates (a point well made by Ayres (2004*b*) 4).

[186] In the *Second Oration against the Arians*, almost immediately following the passage that I quoted earlier, Athanasius declares that Eusebius, Arius, and Asterius all taught that the Father created the Son as a mediator because creation itself could not endure His untempered hand (*Oration* II.24; Asterius, fragment VIII (Bardy), 26 (Vinzent)). Athanasius condemns this doctrine as 'raving impiety', for if creation could not endure the Father's hand, nor could the created Son (*Oration* II.26). Yet if the statement that he attributes to his foes is genuine, then his own evidence would rather suggest once more that the men he condemns interpreted the Son as a unique *ktisma*, distinct both from the Father and the world which is created by the Father through the Son.

[187] As we have already seen, Athanasius repeatedly insists that only a Son who is co-essential and co-eternal with the Father can promise 'deification' to man, for a created Son must hold His divinity only by grace and adoption like other creatures, and cannot therefore deify others. Here again, however, it is far from self-evident that Athanasius' conclusion must necessarily be true, nor that a created but unique Son cannot Himself unite man to God.

the enduring influence of Athanasius' polemic and to the degree to which that polemic has distorted our knowledge of the fourth-century controversies. Athanasius reduces the 'Arian Controversy' to a polarized conflict divided between two clearly defined theologies, for either the Son is God by *ousia* and *physis*, or He is a mutable *ktisma* and part of the created order. If the latter position is manifest 'heresy', then the former doctrine must be the 'orthodox truth'. As we have seen throughout this chapter, however, the men whom Athanasius condemns did not hold the theology that he defined as 'Arianism', and nor was his own understanding of the Christian faith necessarily 'orthodox' at the time in which he wrote.

The real doctrinal issues that separated Athanasius from those whom he names as 'Arian' did not in fact concern the actual divinity of the Son, which every individual involved in the controversy upheld. The primary question at stake was rather how that divinity could be expressed without compromising either the status of the Son Himself or the indivisible and immaterial Godhead. To resolve so complex a question involved the need to define or redefine a number of crucial terms, including *ousia*, *physis*, *hypostasis*, *ktisma*, and *agennētos*, and it is important to remember that none of these terms possessed in the early fourth century the fixed definitions that Athanasius in particular would gradually attach to them. Indeed, the distorted presentation of 'Arian' theology in Athanasius' polemic derives to a considerable extent from his imposition of his newly emerging definitions upon the arguments of his foes. This has already become apparent in the preceding pages in Athanasius' condemnation of the 'Arian' created Son, and is equally true of his repeated attempts to refute the emphasis that Arius, Asterius, and Eusebius of Nicomedia all placed upon the term 'unbegotten' (*agennētos*).[188] Athanasius sought to deny the underlying assumption of his opponents that the begotten Son could not be co-eternal or co-essential with the unbegotten Father. In doing so, he moved towards the later distinction between *agennētos* (without a father) and *agenētos* (eternal), a definition that he in turn then sought to justify by imposing the consequences of his

[188] *Oration against the Arians* I.30–4, *De Decretis* 28–32, and *De Synodis* 46–7.

new distinction between 'unbegotten' and 'eternal' upon those he condemned.[189]

There *were* of course fundamental differences between the theological positions of Athanasius and of the diverse individuals whom he collectively brands as 'Eusebian'. Arius, Asterius, and Eusebius of Nicomedia all maintained the distinction between the Father and the Son to a degree that for Athanasius compromised the essential Christian doctrines of revelation and salvation. But both these genuine differences and the respective theologies of the men in question have been drastically distorted by his polemic. Athanasius not only condemns the 'Arians' as 'heretics' whom every Christian must condemn, but through the imposition of his own definitions and ontological principles upon his foes, he denies the very possibility of the broad theological position that these individuals shared. Instead, he constructs his own definition of 'Arianism' which he then attributes to Arius and to the 'Eusebians', and through contrast to that 'heresy' he presents his own in many ways novel and controversial faith as the only 'orthodox truth'.

I will conclude this chapter with a brief look at one final element of Athanasius' construction of the 'Eusebians' and of the 'Arian Controversy' which requires consideration both for its own intrinsic significance and as a further demonstration of the methodology of his polemic: Athanasius' presentation of the Council of Nicaea and of the Nicene Creed. As I have already observed, Athanasius scarcely refers to Nicaea or to *homoousios* in his early works, particularly the *Orations against the Arians*. Yet from the *De Decretis* (*c.*350–5) onwards, the Nicene Creed becomes in his writings the only 'orthodox' safeguard against the 'Arian heresy'. Whatever the motives for this

189 Athanasius himself does not appear to have employed this precise textual distinction between these two terms (see Prestige (1923) and (1933)), but his argument already reflects the conceptual definition on which that distinction rests. One should add that some justification for this Athanasian definition was certainly necessary at the time in which he wrote, for modern analyses of the history of the term *agennētos* in Christian writings (Prestige (1956) 38–52, Kopecek (1979) 244–65, Patterson (1982) 920–1) suggest that contrary to Athanasius' claims it was his position and not that of his opponents which was untraditional.

development,[190] its most striking consequence for the study of Athanasius' polemic is that neither his own theology nor his construction of 'Arianism' undergoes any significant change. *Homoousios* rather than 'proper offspring of the *ousia* of the Father' becomes Athanasius' preferred expression for the ontological unity of the Father and the Son, and within his polarized 'Arian Controversy', Nicaea now represents the 'orthodox truth'. But in his later works, Athanasius does not reinterpret his own position in the light of the Nicene Creed. On the contrary, he redefines Nicaea according to his own theological and polemical principles. In opposition to 'Athanasian Arianism', Athanasius constructs an 'Athanasian Nicaea'.[191]

In the *De Decretis*, Athanasius describes how at Nicaea 'the Eusebians were examined at great length' (18; Opitz (1935) 15, 9) by the assembled bishops.

The Council wished to banish the impious statements of the Arians and to write the confessed language of the Scriptures, that the Son is not out of nothing (*ek ouk ontōn*) but 'from God', and is 'Word' and 'Wisdom' and neither a creature (*ktisma*) nor a thing made (*poiēma*), but proper offspring (*idion gennēma*) from the Father. But the Eusebians, compelled by their inveterate heterodoxy, understood His being 'from God' to be in common (*koinon*) with us. (19; Opitz (1935) 15, 36–16, 2)

The fathers, perceiving their treachery and the cunning of their impiety, were then forced to express more clearly the sense of the words 'from God', and to write 'the Son is from the essence (*ek tēs ousias*) of God', in order that 'from God' might not be thought to apply in common (*koinon*) and equally (*ison*) to the Son and to generated beings, but that it may be confessed that everything else is a creature (*ktisma*) and the Word alone is from the Father... [and] that it may be confessed that the Word is other than the nature (*physin*) of the generated beings and alone is truly from God. (19; Opitz (1935) 16, 4–8; 23–4)

They immediately added, 'But those who say that the Son of God is out of nothing (*ek ouk ontōn*), or created (*ktiston*), or alterable (*trepton*), or a thing

[190] Hanson (1988*b*), who likens Athanasius' initial silence regarding *homoousios* to 'the words of Sherlock Holmes about the dog not barking' (436), places the *De Decretis* in 356/7, and links the shift in Athanasius' language to the policies of Constantius 350–5 (438). Kopecek (1979) 116–17, who dates this work to *c.*350, believes that Athanasius came to uphold the Nicene Creed gradually in the years that followed the Council of Serdica in 343, and particularly after the Macrostich Creed of 344.

[191] For a very similar argument, although with less polemical emphasis, see Ayres (2004*a*).

made (*poiēma*), or from another essence, these the holy and catholic Church anathematizes'. By saying this, they showed clearly that *ek tēs ousias* and *homoousion* are destructive of the catchwords (*logariōn*) of the impiety, that He is a creature (*ktisma*) and a thing made (*poiēma*) and a generated being (*genēton*) and changeable (*trepton*) and that He was not before He was begotten (*ouk ēn prin gennēthē*). (20; Opitz (1935) 17, 21–5)

Athanasius' account is a crucial source for our knowledge of the Council of Nicaea and its proceedings, yet his highly influential presentation of the Nicene debates once again derives from the imposition of his own theological and polemical principles, this time upon the bishops assembled in 325. The distinction that Athanasius draws here between the 'Nicene fathers' and the 'Eusebians' is yet another retrojection of his polemical model of an 'Arian party'. No such clear distinction existed at Nicaea itself, where the 'Eusebians' of course were themselves among those 'fathers'.[192] And while the 'Eusebians', as throughout Athanasius' polemic, are represented as spokesmen for a 'heresy' that none of these individuals actually held, the Nicene Creed is now interpreted according to Athanasius' theological definitions. If the Son is *homoousios* to the Father, then He is the 'proper offspring' (*idion gennēma*) of the Father's *ousia* and 'neither a *ktisma* nor a *poiēma*', but separate by *physis* from all created beings. This is the language of Athanasius, and not of Nicaea. The terms '*gennēma*' and '*physis*' do not even appear in the Nicene Creed, and nor indeed does the word *ktisma*. Although the Nicene anathemas appear to condemn the teaching that the Son was created (*ktiston*), this is in fact only true of those versions of the Nicene Creed 'quoted' by Athanasius himself. In every other version of the text, and particularly those that derive directly from Eusebius of Caesarea,

[192] The account of Nicaea by Eustathius of Antioch (quoted in Theodoret, I.8) represents a similar polemical division of the bishops at the council into distinct factions, although Eustathius speaks of three 'factions' rather than two (the 'Ariomaniacs', the 'peace party', and 'those who spoke best' (Parmentier (1998) 34, 9–11)). The fifth-century historians (see Lim (1995) 182–216) all depict Nicaea in similarly polarized terms (Socrates, I.8; Sozomen, I.17; Theodoret, I.7), and until recently modern reconstructions of the council still tended to assume the existence of a distinct bloc at Nicaea led by Eusebius of Nicomedia and in some sense 'Arian' (e.g. Stead (1973) 94–100, Grant (1975) 6–8). However, such assumptions derive directly from our polemical sources, and the imposition of this polarization creates too rigid divisions, concealing the diverse spectrum of positions that actually existed in 325.

this anathema is absent.[193] It would seem that even the Nicene anathemas were not immune to Athanasian interpolation, and the imposition of his condemnation of the 'Arian created Son'.

Athanasius would become the champion of Nicaea for later Christian generations. But neither in 325, nor at the time when he wrote the *De Decretis*, was his definition of 'Nicene orthodoxy' by any stretch of the imagination the only possible or accepted interpretation of that Creed. The *Letter to His See* that Eusebius of Caesarea wrote immediately following the Council, which Athanasius quotes in the *De Decretis*, is explicit testimony that at least one bishop among the 'fathers' of 325 did not define the Creed or *homoousios* on Athanasius' terms. Despite Athanasius' attempt to claim that Eusebius' *Letter* confirms his own interpretation of the Nicene Creed,[194] the bishop of Caesarea in fact understood *homoousios* and *ek tēs ousias* very differently. Eusebius accepted these terms only in the broadest possible sense, as a safeguard for the unity of the Father and the Son.[195] He has often been accused of 'misrepresenting' the Nicene Creed,[196] and it is certainly true that Eusebius was uncomfortable with the decisions of the Council. But to accuse him of misrepresentation assumes the existence of a 'correct' definition of Nicaea against which Eusebius' letter may be compared, namely that of Athanasius.[197] While Athanasius' interpretation of Nicaea would

[193] Wiles (1993*a*).

[194] 'Although he was ashamed at that time to write these phrases, and excused himself to his Church in his own way (*ōs ēthelēsen*), yet because he does not deny the '*homoousios*' and '*ek tēs ousias*', he clearly wishes to signify this in his Epistle' (*De Decretis* 3; Opitz (1935) 3, 15–18). For the parallels between the arguments of Eusebius and Athanasius over the definition of Nicaea, see Ayres (2004*a*) 350–3.

[195] Eusebius justified his argument by citing the authority of the Emperor Constantine, a justification that is no less tendentious than the arguments of Athanasius.

[196] A claim made particularly vigorously by Higgins (1966), and also by Barnes (1981), who declares that the bishop of Caesarea explained the Nicene Creed 'in a fundamentally Arian sense ... [and] accepted the word *homoousios* by disregarding its implications' (226).

[197] This assumption that it is possible to speak of a single 'true' definition of Nicaea valid throughout the fourth-century controversies is visible for example in Grillmeier (1975) 266–73, or in the uncritical image of Athanasius as the 'Nicene champion' in Pettersen (1995) 146–62. The same assumption of a single Nicene definition is inherent in John Behr's recent books, *The Way to Nicaea* (2001) and *The Nicene Faith* (2004), for Behr's primary focus is very much 'the Nicene faith, as articulated by its main protagonists, Athanasius, Basil, Gregory of Nazianzus, and Gregory of Nyssa' ((2004) 475). However, Behr is fully aware of the difficulties that such terminology can pose.

eventually become recognized as 'orthodox', however, this recognition only developed gradually and cannot be imposed upon the decades immediately following the Council. Eusebius' interpretation of Nicaea in fact has equal or greater authority than that of his younger contemporary, given that he was actually a bishop in 325.[198] And it is not inconceivable that Eusebius of Nicomedia and other so-called 'Eusebians' understood the Nicene Creed in very similar terms.[199]

Different bishops could understand the Nicene Symbol in very different ways, and neither Athanasius nor Eusebius of Caesarea can be assumed to be representative of the wide array of interpretations of Nicaea that must have existed in the eastern Church throughout the fourth century.[200] It was against this background of diverse attitudes towards the Nicene Creed and its terminology that Athanasius first began to invoke Nicaea as confirmation of his own 'orthodox' position. Thus he felt obliged to compose a work like the *De Decretis Nicaenae Synodi*, simultaneously upholding and defining the Nicene Creed,[201] for that Creed could not be brought forward into a debate within which it had hitherto played little part without a careful definition of the theology that it was now claimed to represent. In the *De Decretis*, the only interpretation of Nicaea that Athanasius will acknowledge is his own, and it is essential that we do not allow the eventual triumph of that Athanasian interpretation to conceal the distortions inherent within his presentation of the

[198] A point well made by Stead (1977) 241.

[199] In the '*Letter of Recantation*' of Eusebius of Nicomedia and Theognis of Nicaea in late 327 (Socrates, I.14.2–6; Opitz, *Urkunde* XXXI), the two bishops declare that 'after having closely considered the import of the term *homoousios*... [and] after suggesting whatever entered our thought for the security of the churches, and fully assuring (*plērophorēsantes*) those under our influence, we subscribed (*hypesēmēnametha*) to the declaration of faith' (Hansen (1995) 52, 15–19). Those lost 'reassurances' may not have differed markedly from that of Eusebius of Caesarea, for certainly all these men shared the same distrust of '*homoousios*' and '*ek tēs ousias*'.

[200] This diversity is well demonstrated by Ayres (2004*b*) 85–92, who also rightly emphasizes that a single accepted definition of the Nicene Creed, which he describes as 'pro-Nicene' theology, only emerged very gradually across the fourth century, and was by no means a simple continuation of an existing 'Nicene faith' (236–40). 'Athanasius' theology in the 340s and 350s is not *the* "original" Nicene theology, but a development from *one of* the original theologies that shaped Nicaea' (239; his italics).

[201] See Ayres (2004*a*) 338–40.

Council. His definition of Athanasian Nicaea is in fact no less tendentious than the Athanasian Arianism whose distortions we have traced throughout this chapter. The Council of Nicaea has become a further vehicle for the polarized polemic of Athanasius, for only then can he conclude that 'he who does not hold the doctrines of Arius necessarily holds and intends the doctrines of the [Nicene] Council' (*De Decretis* 20; Opitz (1935) 17, 26–7).[202]

[202] In the *De Synodis* Athanasius for the first time significantly qualifies this rigid polarization, when he acknowledges that the 'Homoiousians' of Basil of Ancyra (*De Synodis* 41) are not 'Arians', and yet do not accept the Son as *homoousios* to the Father. This acknowledgement contradicts Athanasius' own rhetoric earlier in the same work, when he asked 'who are they whom you allege are scandalised and troubled at these [terms, i.e. '*homoousios*' and '*ek tēs ousias*']? Of those who are pious towards Christ, not one' (*De Synodis* 34; Opitz (1941) 261, 19–21). And Athanasius never admits in the *De Synodis* that in the *Encyclical Letter* he wrote just three years earlier he had named Basil among the 'Arian' 'heirs' of the 'Eusebians', nor that at the Council of Seleucia in 359 the creed invoked by the 'Homoiousians' as the symbol of the traditional 'orthodoxy' of the Church was not Nicaea, but the 'Dedication Creed' of 341.

Conclusion

It has never been my intention, either in the preceding chapter or in this monograph as a whole, to question that Athanasius was sincere in his denunciation of men whom he believed held a theology that struck at the very heart of the Christian faith. The 'Arianism' that he condemned blasphemed God and denied the salvation of man, reducing the Son to the level of all created beings. Against such a 'heresy', every Christian had to rally to defend the 'orthodox' doctrine of the Son and Saviour, who is the true Word and Wisdom, co-eternal and co-essential with the Father. Yet Athanasius' polarized presentation of this 'Arian Controversy' is a rhetorical device with a long history in Christian heresiological tradition, and the polarization that he constructs cannot be assumed to represent the actual teachings of the men upon whom it is imposed. The 'Arian party' of the 'Eusebians' never existed as a distinct ecclesiastical or theological entity, and the 'Arianism' that Athanasius attributes to those men does not reflect either the doctrines of Arius himself or the known writings of any of the individual 'Eusebians'. The Athanasian definition of 'orthodoxy', on the other hand, was far from being the traditional faith of the eastern Church that he would like to claim. Athanasius' theology and in particular his interpretation of the Nicene Creed would become almost unanimously accepted by later Christian generations, but this remarkable achievement must not be retrojected back upon the period in which he himself wrote.

There were, of course, fundamental differences that did separate the theological positions of Athanasius and Arius, and the extant writings of Eusebius of Nicomedia and the other 'Eusebians' confirm that their doctrines stood significantly closer to those of Arius than to those of the bishop of Alexandria. Arius, Eusebius, and Asterius 'the Sophist' shared the conviction that the begotten and created Son could neither be eternal nor derive from the unbegotten *ousia* of the Father, and they distrusted the language of the Nicene Council and above all the term *homoousios*, which they believed implied a materialist and modalist conception of God. But the individuals whom Athanasius brands as the 'Eusebians' also differed from each other and from Arius in the expression and interpretation of their beliefs. The 'Arianism' that Athanasius attributes to these men bears no resemblance to their diverse teachings, but is a product of the imposition upon them of Athanasius' own theological definitions. The ontological polarization of God and creation through which Athanasius interprets the arguments of his foes reduces the 'Arian Son' to the level of all other mutable and created beings, against which 'heresy' he presents his own doctrine of the co-essential Word as the only 'orthodox truth'. But these two alternatives were not the only theological positions that existed within fourth-century Christianity. The men whom Athanasius condemns did not degrade the Son, but taught that He was a 'perfect creature' and mediator between God and the world, a position that the 'Dedication Creed' of Antioch attests was accepted in some form by a considerable proportion of the eastern Church in 341. The doctrinal debates of the fourth century were far more complex than Athanasius is prepared to admit, and only when we have broken free from his polarized polemic and his construction of 'Arianism' can we begin to understand fully these controversies and their participants.

I have placed particular emphasis upon the theological dimension of Athanasius' polemic against the 'Eusebians', both because this dimension was the most important element of that polemic, and because it is here that we have sufficient external evidence, however limited, for a meaningful comparison between Athanasius' construction of his opponents and their own writings. In this one instance where such a comparison is possible, the scale and implications of the distortions that Athanasius' polemic has created are striking. Those distortions must at the least raise very serious doubts before we can accept at face value the image of the 'Eusebians' that Athanasius constructs elsewhere, when such alternative evidence is lacking. Equally importantly, the distortions in question are by no means limited to the presentation of the men whom Athanasius condemns. As we have seen, Athanasius' construction of the 'Arians' and 'Arianism' is inseparable from his construction of himself and of his contemporary environment, and this is true not only of his theological polemic but also of his interpretation of his ecclesiastical career.

Athanasius' presentation of the conspiracies of the 'Eusebians' is no less tendentious than his presentation of the 'Arianism' that he alleges motivated their actions. Every element within this Athanasian condemnation of his opponents is a rhetorical *topos*, from letter-writing to patronage, imperial favour to violent persecution. A *topos* is not necessarily false, but such accounts of 'Arian' actions must be handled with great care. It is possible to trace within Athanasius' own writings a number of inconsistencies and developments that suggest that his polemic evolved according to the context that each given work was intended to meet. This is most obviously true of the first appearance of the 'Eusebians' within his polemic, at the Council of Tyre in 335 when Athanasius was himself condemned. That initial appearance then led to the role of the 'Eusebians' being retrojected back on to the events preceding the council, in order to construct Athanasius' defence of his own innocence in the *Apologia Contra Arianos* narrative as the victim of an ongoing 'heretical conspiracy'. Likewise, his representation of an 'Arian purge' against the 'orthodox' in the decades after Nicaea steadily increases in scale in the works of his third exile (356–62), while across the same period his attitude to imperial involvement in the Church also undergoes a remarkable shift in accordance with his own changing situation. Such developments over time are by no means surprising, but they do render Athanasius' presentation of these alleged actions of his opponents subjective and tendentious. That presentation is founded upon the greatest of all Athanasius' polemical distortions, his construction of his opponents as a collective 'heretical party': '*hoi peri Eusebion*'.

The fundamental purpose of Athanasius' construction of the 'Eusebians' remains consistent throughout his polemic from its initial inception at the Council of Tyre. Athanasius sought to impose upon the fourth-century Church his own polarized division between himself, as the innocent representative of 'orthodoxy', and the 'Eusebians' whose conspiracies against him were motivated solely by their desire to spread their 'heresy'. Through this presentation of himself as the victim of an 'Arian party', Athanasius appealed to all Christians not only to uphold his innocence but to endorse his polemic, separating themselves from the 'heretics' and thus turning his rhetoric of polarization into reality. Although that appeal failed to avert his condemnation at Tyre, Athanasius' interpretation of his career and of the 'conspiracy' of his 'Arian' foes would eventually come to exert great influence, first upon the western bishops and then gradually upon the eastern Church and upon subsequent generations.

Yet it is this Athanasian interpretation of the fourth-century controversies, and above all Athanasius' polarized distinction between the 'Eusebians' and the eastern Church, that I have argued throughout this monograph must be rejected. Despite the eventual triumph of Athanasius' polemic within Christian tradition, the existence of the 'Eusebians' as a separate party is a polemical construct, not a reflection of reality. This is not to deny the near certain probability that the individuals whom Athanasius describes as 'Eusebian' did know each other, write to each other, and shared similar ecclesiastical and theological concerns. Nor is it in doubt that in all the evidence that we possess, Eusebius of Nicomedia-Constantinople is a prominent and influential figure, whose role in the controversies of his lifetime and whose relationship first with Constantine and then with Constantius merit further study. But the idea that 'church politics after Nicaea are party politics' must be treated with caution. It is the polemic of Athanasius that has created the construct of the 'Eusebians' that dominates our sources, and that construct serves a definite purpose within his writings in his presentation both of his opponents and of his own career and theology.

The polemical writings of Athanasius will always be of fundamental importance for our knowledge of the fourth-century controversies and their participants. It is therefore essential that we better understand the principles that underlie that polemic and the factors that determine how Athanasius presents events and individuals. This monograph is intended to be a step towards that better understanding. Through this study of Athanasius' construction of the 'Eusebians', the polemical distortions that have long been suspected in Athanasius' writings have been confirmed, and can be demonstrated in almost every instance in which we have external evidence (particularly theological) against which Athanasius' presentation can be compared. Of course, such external evidence may itself be equally distorted, and once again I would emphasize that to question the interpretation of a given episode by Athanasius is not to assume that another account is necessarily true. But when that alternative evidence does not exist, then Athanasius' unsupported narrative cannot be accepted at face value, and this is no less true of Athanasius' presentation of himself than of his construction of the 'Eusebians'.

The purpose of this monograph has been essentially a negative one, a deconstruction of the polemical writings of Athanasius to emphasize the distortions that his polemic creates. I have not attempted to do justice to the wider importance of Athanasius' own career and theology within Christian tradition, and I have made only a very limited attempt to begin the reconstruction of the events and participants of the fourth-century controversies towards which I believe my conclusions here must lead. The recognition of the polemical nature of party constructs like the 'Eusebians' raises important questions concerning the networks of friendship and patronage that certainly existed within the Church in this period, just as the interaction of Church and State and particularly the much-debated concept of a 'court bishop' in the crucial years following the conversion of Constantine still require further examination. The removal of polemical labels like 'Arian' or 'Nicene', and the abandonment of the polarization inherent in such language, is already opening great new opportunities for the reinterpretation of the doctrinal controversies of these years in modern scholarship. The broad eastern theological position represented by a number of the 'Eusebians', and in particular by the 'Dedication Creed' of 341, was to develop in many different directions in the decades that followed that council, and played a role in the gradual formation of 'orthodoxy' that is still not properly understood. No less importantly, if perhaps ironically, it is only through a more complex and balanced interpretation of the debates that have for so long been misnamed the 'Arian Controversy' that we can fully recognize the achievement of Athanasius himself in the definition of the 'Nicene faith' of which he was to become the champion.

Bibliography

1. Editions, Textual *Critica*, and Translations

i) The Writings of Athanasius

Bartelink, G. M. J. (1994). *Athanase d'Alexandrie: Vie d'Antoine, Sources Chrétiennes* **400**, Paris.

Burgess, H. (1854). *The Festal Letters of Saint Athanasius*, Oxford.

Bright, W. (1881). *The Historical Writings of Athanasius*, Oxford.

Camplani, A. (1989). *Le Lettere Festali di Atanasio di Alexandria*, Rome.

—— (2003). *Atanasio di Alessandria. Lettere festali. Anonimo. Indice delle Lettere festali*, Milan.

Cureton, W. (1848). *The Festal Letters of Athanasius*, London.

Heil, U. (1999). *Athanasius von Alexandrien: De Sententia Dionysii. Einleitung, Übersetzung und Kommentar*, Berlin and New York.

Lefort, L. T. (1955). *Saint Athanase: Lettres festales et pastorales en Copte, Scriptores Coptici* **19**, 1–72; **20**, 1–55.

Lorenz, R. (1986). *Der zehnte Osterfestbrief des Athanasius von Alexandrien*, Berlin and New York.

Martin, A. (ed.) (1985). *Histoire 'Acéphale' et Index Syriaque des Lettres festales d'Athanase d'Alexandrie, Sources Chrétiennes* **317**, Paris.

Meijering, E. P. (1996–8). *Athanasius, die dritte Rede gegen die Arianer: Einleitung, Übersetzung, Kommentar*, 3 Vols, Amsterdam.

Müller, G. (1952). *Lexicon Athanasianum*, Berlin.

Opitz, H.-G. (1935). *Athanasius Werke II.1.* Vol. 3. *Die Apologien: 1. De Decretis Nicaenae Synodi*, Berlin and Leipzig.

—— (1936). *Athanasius Werke II.1.* Vol. 4. *Die Apologien: 2. De Sententia Dionysii, 3. Apologia De Fuga Sua (1–18)*, Berlin and Leipzig.

—— (1938*a*). *Athanasius Werke II.1.* Vol. 5. *Die Apologien: 3. Apologia De Fuga Sua (19–27), 4. Apologia Secunda (1–43)*, Berlin.

—— (1938*b*). *Athanasius Werke II.1.* Vol. 6. *Die Apologien: 4. Apologia Secunda (43–80)*, Berlin.

—— (1940*a*). *Athanasius Werke II.1.* Vol. 7. *Die Apologien: 4. Apologia Secunda (80–Schluß), 5. Epistula Encyclica, 6. De Morte Arii, 7. Ep. Ad Monachos, 8. Historia Arianorum (1–32)*, Berlin.

—— (1940*b*). *Athanasius Werke II.1.* Vol. 8. *Die Apologien: 8. Historia Arianorum (32–Schluß), 9. De Synodis (1–13)*, Berlin.

Opitz, H.-G. (1941). *Athanasius Werke II.1.* Vol. 9. *Die Apologien: 9. De Synodis (13–55), 10. Apologia ad Constantium (1–3)*, Berlin.

Robertson, A. (1892). *Select Writings and Letters of Athanasius, Bishop of Alexandria. Nicene and Post-Nicene Fathers*, Second Series 4, London.

Seiler, R. (1932). *Athanasius, Apologia Contra Arianos (Ihre Entstehung und Datierung)* (Diss. Tübingen).

Stockhausen, A. von (2002). *Athanasius von Alexandrien, Epistula Ad Afros: Einleitung, Kommentar und Übersetzung*, Berlin and New York.

Szymusiak, J. M. (1987). *Athanase d'Alexandrie. Deux Apologies: A L'Empereur Constance, Pour sa Fuite, Sources Chrétiennes* **56**, rev. edn., Paris.

Tetz, M. (1988). 'Ein enzyklishes Schreiben der Synode von Alexandrien (362)', *ZNW* **79**, 262–81; repr. in id. (1995) 207–25.

—— (1996). *Athanasius Werke 1.1. Die Dogmatischen Schriften.* Vol. 1. *Epistula ad Episcopos Aegypti et Libyae*, Berlin and New York.

—— (1998). *Athanasius Werke 1.1. Die Dogmatischen Schriften.* Vol. 2. *Orationes I et II Contra Arianos*, Berlin and New York.

—— and Wyrwa, D. (2000). *Athanasius Werke 1.1. Die Dogmatischen Schriften.* Vol. 3. *Oratio III Contra Arianos*, Berlin and New York.

Thomson, R. W. (1971). *Athanasius, Contra Gentes and De Incarnatione*, Oxford.

ii) Other Primary Sources

Bidez, J. (3rd edn. by F. Winkelmann) (1981). *Philostorgius Kirchengeschichte mit dem Leben des Lucian von Antiochien und den Fragmenten eines arianischen Historiographen*, Berlin.

Cameron, Averil and Hall, S. G. (1999). *Eusebius: Life of Constantine. Introduction, Translation and Commentary*, Oxford.

Casey, R. P. (1935). 'An Early Homily on the Devil ascribed to Athanasius of Alexandria', *JThS*, OS, **36**, 1–10.

De Bruyne, D. (1928). 'Deux Lettres inconnues de Theognius l'évêque arien de Nicée', *ZNW* **27**, 106–10.

Hahn, A. (1897). *Bibliothek der Symbole und Glaubensregeln der alten Kirche*, Breslau.

Hansen, G. C. (1995). *Sokrates Kirchengeschichte*, Berlin.

—— (2004). *Sozomenos Historia Ecclesiastica Kirchengeschichte: Übersetzt und Eingeleitet*, Turnhout.

Klostermann, E. (2nd edn. by G. C. Hansen) (1972). *Eusebius Werke, Volume 4. Gegen Marcell, Über Die Kirchliche Theologie, Die Fragmente Marcells*, Berlin.

Metzler, K. (1991). 'Ein Beitrag zur Rekonstruktion der "Thalia" des Arius', in K. Metzler and F. Simon (eds), *Ariana et Athanasiana: Studien zur*

Überlieferung und zu philogischen Problemen der Werke des Athanasius von Alexandrien, Opladen, 13–45.
Nautin, P. (1949). 'Deux interpolations orthodoxes dans une lettre d'Arius', *Analecta Bollandiana* **67**, 137–41.
—— (1963). 'Note critique sur la lettre d'Eusèbe de Nicomédie à Paulin de Tyr', *VC* **17**, 24–7.
Opitz, H.-G. (1934–5). *Athanasius Werke II.1.* Vols 1–2. *Urkunden zur Geschichte des arianischen Streites 318–328*, Berlin and Leipzig.
Parmentier, L. (3rd edn. by G. C. Hansen) (1998). *Theodoret Kirchengeschichte*, Berlin.
Richard, M. (ed.), (1956). *Asterii Sophistae Commentoriorum in Psalmos*, Oslo.
Spanneut, M. (1948). *Recherches sur les Ecrits d'Eustache d'Antioche*, Lille.
Tetz, M. (1952–3). 'Eine Arianische Homilie unter dem Namen des Athanasius von Alexandrien', *ZKG* **64**, 299–307.
Turner, N. (1963). *A Grammar of New Testament Greek* 3, Edinburgh.
Vinzent, M. (1993*a*). *Asterius von Kappadokien: Die Theologischen Fragmente. Einleitung, Kritischer Text, Übersetzung und Kommentar*, Leiden, New York and Köln.
—— (1996). *Pseudo-Athanasius* Contra Arianos IV: *Eine Schrift gegen Asterius von Kappadokien, Eusebius von Cäsarea, Markell von Ankyra und Photin von Sirmium*, Leiden, New York, and Köln.

2. Modern Authors

Abramowski, L. (1975). 'The Synod of Antioch 324/25 and its Creed' (German original, *ZKG* **86**, 356–66), trans. in id. (1992) III, 1–12.
—— (1982). 'Dionysius of Rome (d.268) and Dionysius of Alexandria (d.264/5) in the Arian Controversies of the Fourth Century' (German original, *ZKG* **93**, 240–72), trans. in id. (1992), XI, 1–35.
—— (1991). 'Die dritte Arianerrede des Athanasius: Eusebianer und Arianer und das westliche Serdicense', *ZKG* **102**, 389–413.
—— (1992). *Formula and Context: Studies in Early Christian Thought*, London.
Allen, P. (1990). 'The Use of Heretics and Heresies in the Greek Church Historians: Studies in Socrates and Theodoret', in G. Clarke (ed.), *Reading the Past in Late Antiquity*, Rushcutters Bay, 265–89.
Amidon, P. R. (2002). 'Paulinus' Subscription to the *Tomus ad Antiochenos*', *JThS*, NS, 53, 53–74.
Anatolios, K. (1998). *Athanasius: The Coherence of His Thought*, London and New York.

Anatolios, K. (2001). 'The Influence of Irenaeus on Athanasius', *StP* **36**, 463–76.
—— (2004). *Athanasius*, London and New York.
Arnold, D. W-H. (1989). 'Sir Harold Idris Bell and Athanasius: A Reconsideration of *London Papyrus* 1914', *StP* 21, 377–83.
—— (1991). *The Early Episcopal Career of Athanasius of Alexandria*, Notre Dame, Indiana.
Ayres, L. (2004*a*). 'Athanasius' Initial Defence of the Term *'Omooúsios*: Rereading the *De Decretis*', *JECS* **12.3**, 337–59.
—— (2004*b*). *Nicaea and its Legacy: An Approach to Fourth-Century Trinitarian Theology*, Oxford.
Bagnall, R. S. (1993). *Egypt in Late Antiquity*, Princeton.
Bardy, G. (1936). *Recherches sur Lucien d'Antioche et son École*, Paris.
Barnard, L. W. (1970). 'The Antecedents of Arius', *VC* **24** (1970) 172–88; repr. in id. (1978) 289–311.
—— (1971). 'Pope Julius, Marcellus of Ancyra, and the Council of Sardica—A Reconsideration', *Recherches de Theologie ancienne et medievale* **38**, 69–79; repr. in id. (1978) 341–53.
—— (1973). 'Athanasius and the Meletian Schism in Egypt', *JEA* **59**, 181–9.
—— (1974*a*). 'Athanase et les empereurs Constantin et Constance', in Kannengiesser (ed.) (1974), 127–43; repr. in revised English translation in Barnard (1978) 312–28.
—— (1974*b*). 'The Date of S. Athanasius' *Vita Antonii*', *VC* **28**, 169–75.
—— (1975*a*). 'Some Notes on the Melitian Schism in Egypt', *StP* **12**, 399–405.
—— (1975*b*). 'Two Notes on Athanasius', *Orientalia Christiana Periodica* **41**.ii, 344–56; repr. in id. (1978) 329–40.
—— (1978). *Studies in Church History and Patristics*, Thessaloniki.
—— (1983). *The Council of Serdica 343* AD.
—— (1989). 'Athanasius and the Emperor Jovian', *StP* **21**, 384–9.
—— (1993). 'Did Athanasius know Antony?', *Ancient Society*, 139–49.
Barnes, M. R. (1997). 'One Nature, One Power: Consensus Doctrine in Pro-Nicene Polemic', *StP* **29**, 205–23.
—— (1998). 'The Fourth Century as Trinitarian Canon', in L. Ayres and G. Jones (eds), *Christian Origins: Theology, Rhetoric and Community*, London and New York, 47–67.
—— and Williams, D. H. (eds) (1993). *Arianism after Arius: Essays in the Development of the Fourth Century Trinitarian Conflicts*, Edinburgh.
Barnes, T. D. (1978). 'Emperors and Bishops, AD 324–344: Some Problems', *AJAH* **3**, 53–75; repr. in id. (1984) XVIII.
—— (1981). *Constantine and Eusebius*, Massachusetts and London.
—— (1984). *Early Christianity and the Roman Empire*, London.

—— (1989). 'The Career of Athanasius', *StP* **21**, 390–401.

—— (1990). 'The Consecration of Ulfila', *JThS*, NS, **41**, 541–5; repr. in id. (1994) X.

—— (1993). *Athanasius and Constantius: Theology and Politics in the Constantinian Empire*, Massachusetts and London.

—— (1994). *From Eusebius to Augustine*, London.

—— (1998). 'Constantine, Athanasius and the Christian Church', in S. Lieu and D. Montserrat (eds) (1998), 7–20.

Bauer, W. (1971). *Orthodoxy and Heresy in Earliest Christianity* (German original 1934, English translation from the 2nd German edn. (ed. G. Strecker, 1963) eds R. A. Kraft and G. Krodel), Philadelphia.

Baynes, N. H. (1925). 'Athanasiana', *JEA* **11**, 58–69; partially repr. in id. (1960).

—— (1926). 'Alexandria and Constantinople: A Study in Ecclesiastical Diplomacy', *JEA* **12**, 145–56; repr. in id. (1960) 97–115.

—— (1948). 'Sozomen, *Ecclesiastica Historia* I.15', *JThS*, OS, **49**, 165–8.

—— (1960). *Byzantine Studies and Other Essays*, London.

Behr, J. (2001). *The Way to Nicaea*, The Formation of Christian Theology, Vol. 1, New York.

—— (2004). *The Nicene Faith*, The Formation of Christian Theology, Vol. 2, New York.

Bell, H. I. (1924). *Jews and Christians in Egypt*, London.

Böhm, T. (1991). *Die Christologie des Arius. Dogmengeschichtliche Überlegungen unter besonderer Berücksichtigung der Hellenisierungsfrage*, Ottilien.

—— (1992). 'Die *Thalia* des Arius: Ein Beitrag zur frühchristlichen Hymnologie', *VC* **46**, 334–55.

Brakke, D. (1994). 'The Authenticity of the Ascetic Athanasiana', *Orientalia*, NS, **63**, 17–56.

—— (1995). *Athanasius and the Politics of Asceticism*, Oxford.

—— (1998). ' "Outside the Places, Within the Truth": Athanasius of Alexandria and the Localization of the Holy', in D. Frankfurther (ed.), *Pilgrimage and Holy Space in Late Antique Egypt*, Leiden, Boston, and Köln, 445–81.

—— (2001). 'Jewish Flesh and Christian Spirit in Athanasius of Alexandria', *JECS* **9**, 453–81.

Brennan, B. R. (1976). 'Dating Athanasius' *Vita Antonii*', *VC* **30**, 52–4.

—— (1985). 'Athanasius' *Vita Antonii*: A Sociological Interpretation', *VC* **39**, 209–27.

Brennecke, H. C. (1984). *Hilarius von Poitiers und die Bischofsopposition gegen Konstantius II: Untersuchungen zur dritten Phase des arianischen Streites* (337–361), Berlin and New York.

Brennecke, H. C. (1988). *Studien zur Geschichte der Homöer: der Osten bis zum Ende der homöischen Reichskirche*, Tübingen.

—— (1993). 'Lukian von Antiochien in der Geschichte des Arianischen Streites', in Brennecke, Grasmück, and Markschies (eds) (1993), 170–92.

—— Grasmück, E. L., and Markschies, C. (eds) (1993). *Logos: Festschrift für Luise Abramowski zum 8. Juli 1993*, Berlin and New York.

Brent, A. (1993). 'Diogenes Laertius and the Apostolic Succession', *JEH* **44**, 367–89.

Bright, W. (1877). 'Athanasius', in W. Smith and H. Wace (eds), *A Dictionary of Christian Biography*, Vol. I, London, 178–203.

Brown, P. (1971). *The World of Late Antiquity*, London.

—— (1992). *Power and Persuasion in Late Antiquity: Towards a Christian Empire*, Madison, Wisconsin.

Buell, D. K. (1999). *Making Christians: Clement of Alexandria and the Rhetoric of Legitimacy*, Princeton.

Burgess, R. W. (1999). *Studies in Eusebian and Post-Eusebian Chronography*, Stuttgart.

—— (2000). 'The Date of the Deposition of Eustathius of Antioch', *JThS*, NS, **51**, 150–60.

Burrus, V. (1991). 'The Heretical Woman as Symbol in Alexander, Athanasius, Epiphanius and Jerome', *HThR* **84**, 229–48.

Cameron, Averil (1991). *Christianity and the Rhetoric of Empire: The Development of Christian Discourse*. Sather Classical Lectures 55, Berkeley and Los Angeles.

—— (1993). *The Later Roman Empire*, London.

Chadwick, H. (1948). 'The Fall of Eustathius of Antioch', *JThS*, OS **49**, 27–35; repr. in id. (1982) XIII.

—— (1958). 'Ossius of Cordova and the Presidency of the Council of Antioch, 325', *JThS*, NS, **9**, 292–304; repr. in id. (1982) X.

—— (1960). 'Faith and Order at the Council of Nicaea: A Note on the Background of the Sixth Canon', *HThR* **53**, 171–95; repr. in id. (1982) XII.

—— (1967). *The Early Church*, London.

—— (1972). 'The Origin of the Title "Ecumenical Council" ', *JThS* NS, **23**, 132–5; repr. in id. (1982) XI.

—— (1982). *History and Thought of the Early Church*, London.

—— (2003). *East and West: The Making of a Rift in the Church*, Oxford.

Clark, E. A. (1993). *The Origenist Controversy: The Cultural Construction of an Early Christian Debate*, Princeton.

Cross, F. L. (1945). *The Study of Saint Athanasius*, Oxford.

Davis, S. J. (2004). *The Early Coptic Papacy: The Egyptian Church and its Leadership in Late Antiquity*, Cairo and New York.

De Clercq, V. C. (1954). *Ossius of Cordova: A Contribution to the History of the Constantinian Period*, Washington.

Di Maio, M. (1996). '*Imago veritatis aut verba in speculo*: Athanasius, the Meletian Schism, and Linguistic Frontiers in Fourth-Century Egypt' in R. W. Mathisen and H. S. Sivan (eds), *Shifting Frontiers in Late Antiquity*, Aldershot, 277–84.

—— and Arnold, D. W-H. (1992). '*Per Vim, Per Caedem, Per Bellum*: A Study of Murder and Ecclesiastical Politics in the Year 337 AD', *Byz* **62**, 158–211.

Drake, H. A. (1986). 'Athanasius' First Exile', *GRBS* **27**, 193–204.

—— (2000). *Constantine and the Bishops: The Politics of Intolerance*, Baltimore and London.

Drijvers, J. W. (1992). *Helena Augusta: The Mother of Constantine the Great and the Legend of Her Finding of the True Cross*, Leiden.

Edwards, M. J. (1995). 'The Arian Heresy and the Oration to the Saints', *VC* **49**, 379–87.

—— (1997). 'Simon Magus, the Bad Samaritan', in M. J. Edwards and S. Swain (eds), *Portraits: Biographical Representation in the Greek and Latin Literature of the Roman Empire*, Oxford, 69–91.

—— Goodman, M., and Price, S. (eds) (1999). *Apologetics in the Roman Empire: Pagans, Jews, and Christians*, Oxford.

Ehrhardt, C. T. H. R. (1980). 'Constantinian Documents in Gelasius of Cyzicus, *Ecclesiastical History*', *JAC* **23**, 48–57.

Elliott, T. G. (1988). 'The Date of the Council of Serdica', *Ancient History Bulletin* **2**, 65–72.

—— (1992). 'Constantine and "The Arian Reaction after Nicaea" ', *JEH* **43**, 169–94.

—— (1996). *The Christianity of Constantine the Great*, Scranton.

Elm, S. (1997). 'The Polemical use of Genealogies: Jerome's Classification of Pelagius and Evagrius Ponticus', *StP* 33, 311–18.

Eltester, W. (1937). 'Die Kirchen Antiochias im IV. Jahrhundert', *ZNW* **36**, 251–86.

Florovsky, G. (1962). 'The Concept of Creation in Saint Athanasius', *StP* **6**, 36–57.

Fowden, G. (1994). 'The Last Days of Constantine: Oppositional Views and their Influence', *JRS* **84**, 146–70.

Frend, W. H. C. (1974). 'Athanasius as an Egyptian Christian Leader in the Fourth Century', *New College Bulletin* **8**, 20–37; repr. in id. (1976),

Religion Popular and Unpopular in the Early Christian Centuries, London, XVI.

Frend, W. H. C. (1984). *The Rise of Christianity*, London.

—— (1991). *The Early Church*, 3rd edn., London.

Gero, S. (1981). 'The True Image of Christ: Eusebius' Letter to Constantia Reconsidered', *JThS*, NS, **32**, 460–70.

Grant, R. M. (1975). 'Religion and Politics at the Council of Nicaea', *Journal of Religion* **55**, 1–12; repr. in id. (1983), *Christian Beginnings: Apocalypse to History*, London, XI.

—— (1997). *Irenaeus of Lyons*, London.

Gregg, R. C. (ed.) (1985). *Arianism: Historical and Theological Reassessments*, Philadelphia.

—— (1985*a*). 'Cyril of Jerusalem', in id. (1985), 85–105.

—— and Groh, D. E. (1981). *Early Arianism—A View of Salvation*, Philadelphia.

—— —— (1984). 'The Centrality of Soteriology in Early Arianism', *StP* **15**, 305–16.

Griggs, C. W. (1990). *Early Egyptian Christianity: From its Origins to 451 CE*, Leiden.

Grillmeier, A. (1975). *Christ in Christian Tradition, Volume One: From the Apostolic Age to Chalcedon (451)*, 2nd rev. edn. (trans. J. Bowden), Oxford.

Gwatkin, H. M. (1882). *Studies of Arianism*, Cambridge.

Gwynn, D. M. (1999). 'Constantine and the other Eusebius', *Prudentia* **21.2**, 94–124.

—— (2003). 'The Construction of a "Heretical Party" in the *Apologia Contra Arianos* of Athanasius of Alexandria', *Prudentia* **35.2**, 161–87.

Haas, C. (1991). 'The Alexandrian Riots of 356 and George of Cappadocia', *GRBS* **32**, 281–301.

—— (1993). 'The Arians of Alexandria', *VC* **47**, 234–45.

—— (1997). *Alexandria in Late Antiquity: Topography and Conflict*, Baltimore and London.

Hall, S. G. (1985). 'The *Thalia* of Arius in Athanasius' Accounts', in Gregg (ed.) (1985), 37–58.

—— (1991). *Doctrine and Practice in the Early Church*, London.

—— (1998). 'Some Constantinian Documents in the *Vita Constantini*', in Lieu and Montserrat (1998), 86–103.

Hanson, R. P. C. (1962). *Tradition in the Early Church*, London.

—— (1982). 'The Transformation of Images in the Trinitarian Theology of the Fourth Century', *StP* **17**; repr. in id. (1985*c*), 253–78.

—— (1984). 'The Fate of Eustathius of Antioch', *ZKG* **95**, 171–9.

—— (1985*a*). 'Who taught *ΕΞ ΟΥΚ ΟΝΤΩΝ?*', in Gregg (ed.) (1985), 79–83.
—— (1985*b*). 'The Arian Doctrine of the Incarnation', in Gregg (ed.) (1985), 181–212.
—— (1985*c*). *Studies in Christian Antiquity*, Edinburgh.
—— (1987). 'The Influence of Origen on the Arian Controversy', in L. Lies (ed.), *Origeniana Quarta* (1987), Innsbruck, 410–23.
—— (1988*a*). 'The Source and Significance of the Fourth *Oratio Contra Arianos* attributed to Athanasius', *VC* **42**, 257–66.
—— (1988*b*). *The Search for the Christian Doctrine of God: The Arian Controversy 318–381*, Edinburgh.
—— (1989). 'The Achievement of Orthodoxy in the Fourth Century AD', in Williams (ed.) (1989), 142–56.
Harnack, A. von (1898). *History of Dogma*, Vol. 4 (trans. N. Buchanan from 3rd German edn.), London and Edinburgh.
Hauben, H. (1998). 'The Melitian "Church of the Martyrs": Christian Dissenters in Ancient Egypt', in T. W. Hillard, R. A. Kearsley, C. E. V. Nixon, and A. M. Nobbs (eds), *Ancient History in a Modern University, Volume 2: Early Christianity, Late Antiquity and Beyond*, Macquarie, 329–49.
—— (2001). 'Le Papyrus London VI (P. Jews) 1914 dans son contexte historique (mai 335)', *Proceedings of the Twenty-Second International Congress of Papyrology*, Florence, 605–18.
Haugaard, W. P. (1960). 'Arius: Twice a heretic? Arius and the Human Soul of Jesus Christ', *CH* **29**, 251–63.
Hess, H. (2002). *The Early Development of Canon Law and the Council of Serdica*, Oxford.
Higgins, M. J. (1966). 'Two Notes', in P. Wirth (ed.), *Polychronion: Festschrift Franz Dölger zum 75 Geburtstag*, Heidelberg, 238–43.
Holland, D. L. (1970). 'Die Synode von Antiochien (324/25) und ihre Bedeutung für Eusebius von Caesarea und das Konzil von Nizäa', *ZKG* **81**, 163–81.
Honigmann, E. (1939). 'La Liste Originale des Pères de Nicée', *Byz* **14**, 17–76.
Hunt, E. D. (1982). *Holy Land Pilgrimage in the Late Roman Empire AD 312–460*, Oxford.
—— (1989). 'Did Constantius II have "Court Bishops"?', *StP* **19**, 86–90.
Jalland, T. G. (1944). *The Church and the Papacy: A Historical Study*, London.
Jones, A. H. M. (1954). 'The Date of the *Apologia Contra Arianos* of Athanasius', *JThS*, NS, **5**, 224–7.
—— (1964). *The Later Roman Empire 284–602*, Oxford.

Kannengiesser, C. (1964). 'Le temoignage des Lettres Festales de saint Athanase sur la date de l'Apologie *Contre les Paiens, Sur l'Incarnation du Verbe*', *RSR* **52**, 91–100; repr. in id. (1991) V.

—— (1970). 'La date de l'Apologie d'Athanase *Contre les Paiens* et *Sur l'incarnation du Verbe*', *RSR* **58**, 383–428; repr. in id. (1991), VI.

—— (ed.) (1974). *Politique et Théologie chez Athanase d'Alexandrie*, Paris.

—— (1981). 'Holy Scripture and Hellenistic Hermeneutics in Alexandrian Christology: The Arian Crisis', *Colloquy* **41** of the Centre for Hermeneutical Studies, Berkeley (pp. 1–40 repr. in id. (1991) I).

—— (1982). 'Athanasius of Alexandria: *Three Orations against the Arians*: A Reappraisal', *StP* **17.3**, 981–95; repr. in id. (1991) IX.

—— (1983*a*). *Athanase d'Alexandrie eveque et ecrivain*, Paris.

—— (1983*b*). 'Arius and the Arians', *ThS* **44**, 456–75; repr. in id. (1991) II.

—— (1985*a*). 'The Blasphemies of Arius: Athanasius of Alexandria *De Synodis* 15', in Gregg (ed.) (1985), 59–78; repr. in id. (1991) III.

—— (1985*b*). 'The Athanasian Decade 1974–1984: A Bibliographical Report', *ThS* **46**, 524–41; repr. in id. (1991) XI.

—— (1986). 'Athanasius of Alexandria vs. Arius: the Alexandrian Crisis', in B. A. Pearson and J. E. Goehring (eds), *The Roots of Egyptian Christianity*, Philadelphia, 204–15; repr. in Kannengiesser (1991) XII.

—— (1989). 'The Homiletic Festal Letters of Athanasius', in D. G. Hunter (ed.), *Preaching in the Patristic Age*, New York, 73–100; repr. in Kannengiesser (1991) XV.

—— (1991). *Arius and Athanasius: Two Alexandrian Theologians*, London.

—— (1993*a*). 'Athanasius' so-called *Third Oration against the Arians*', *StP* **26**, 375–88.

—— (1993*b*). '(Ps.-) Athanasius, *Ad Afros* Examined', in Brennecke, Grasmück, and Markschies (eds) (1993), 264–80.

—— (1995). 'Die Sonderstellung der dritten Arianerrede des Athanasius', *ZKG* **106**, 18–55.

—— (2002). *Prolegomena to the Biography of Athanasius*, Victoria.

—— (2003). 'The Dating of the Double Apology and of *Contra Arianos* I–III' (Paper presented to the Fourteenth International Patristics Conference, Oxford).

Kelly, J. N. D. (1960). *Early Christian Creeds*, 2nd edn., London.

—— (1977). *Early Christian Doctrines*, 5th edn., London.

Kennedy, G. A. (1983). *Greek Rhetoric under Christian Emperors*, Princeton, New Jersey.

Kinzig, W. (1989). 'Asterius Amasenus, Asterius Sophista or Asterius Ignotus? Reflections on the Authorship of the *Homilies on the Psalms* (ed. Marcel Richard)', *StP* **20**, 15–23.

—— (1990). *In Search of Asterius. Studies on the Authorship of the Homilies on the Psalms*, Göttingen.

—— (1991). 'Asterius Sophista oder Asterius Ignotus? Eine Antwort', *VC* **45**, 388–98.

—— and Vinzent, M. (1999). 'Recent Research on the Origin of the Creed', *JThS*, NS, 535–59.

Klein, R. (1977). *Constantius II und die christliche Kirche*. Darmstadt.

—— (1982). 'Zur Glaubwürdigkeit historischer Aussagen des Bischofs Athanasius von Alexandria über die Religionspolitik des Kaisers Constantius II', *StP* **17.3**, 996–1017.

Kopecek, T. A. (1979). *A History of Neo-Arianism*, Vols I–II, Massachusetts.

—— (1981). 'Response' in Kannengiesser (1981) 51–68.

Le Boulluec, A. (1985). *La Notion d'heresie dans la literature greque II–III siècles*, Paris.

Leemans, J. (2000). 'Thirteen Years of Athanasius Research (1985–1998): A Survey and Bibliography', *Sacris Erudiri* **39**, 105–217.

Lienhard, J. T. (1982). 'Recent Studies in Arianism', *Religious Studies Review* **8**, 331–7.

—— (1985). 'The Epistle of the Synod of Ancyra, 358: A Reconsideration', in Gregg (ed.) (1985), 313–19.

—— (1987). 'The "Arian" Controversy: Some Categories Reconsidered', *ThS* **48**, 415–37.

—— (1989). 'Acacius of Caesarea's *Contra Marcellum*: Its Place in Theology and Controversy', *StP* **19**, 185–8.

—— (1993). 'Did Athanasius reject Marcellus?', in Barnes and Williams (eds) (1993), 65–80.

—— (1999). Contra Marcellum: *Marcellus of Ancyra and Fourth-Century Theology*, Washington.

Lieu, S. N. C. (1998). 'From History to Legend and Legend to History: The Medieval and Byzantine Transformation of Constantine's *Vita*', in Lieu and Montserrat (eds) (1998), 136–76.

—— and Montserrat, D. (eds) (1998). *Constantine: History, Historiography and Legend*, London.

Lim, R. (1995). *Public Disputation, Power, and Social Order in Late Antiquity*, Berkeley, Los Angeles, and London.

Logan, A. H. B. (1992). 'Marcellus of Ancyra and the Councils of AD 325: Antioch, Ancyra and Nicaea', *JThS*, NS, **43**, 428–46.

Löhr, W. (1986). *Die Entstehung der homöischen und homöusianischen Kirchenparteien—Studien zur Synodalgeschichte des 4. Jahrhunderts*, Bonn.

—— (1993). 'A Sense of Tradition: The *Homoiousian* Church Party', in Barnes and Williams (eds) (1993), 81–100.

Löhr, W. (2003). 'Arius Revisited' (paper presented to the Fourteenth International Patristics Conference, Oxford).

Loose, U. (1990). 'Zur Chronologie des arianischen Streites', *ZKG* **101**, 88–92.

Lorenz, R. (1979). *Arius Judaizans? Untersuchungen zur dogmengeschichtlichen Einordnung des Arius*, Göttingen.

—— (1983). 'Die Christusseele im Arianischen Streit. Nebst einigen Bemerkungen zur Quellenkritik des Arius und zur Glaubwürdigkeit des Athanasius', *ZKG* **94**, 1–51.

Louth, A. (1985). 'Athanasius' Understanding of the Humanity of Christ', *StP* **16**, 309–18.

—— (1989). 'The use of the term ιδιος in Alexandrian theology from Alexander to Cyril', *StP* **19**, 198–202.

Luibheid, C. (1976). 'The Arianism of Eusebius of Nicomedia', *IThQ* **43**, 3–23.

—— (1978). 'Finding Arius', *IThQ* 45, 81–100.

—— (1981). *Eusebius of Caesarea and the Arian Crisis*, Dublin.

—— (1982). *The Council of Nicaea*, Galway.

—— (1983). 'The Alleged Second Session of the Council of Nicaea', *JEH* **34**, 165–74.

Lyman, J. R. (1985). 'Substance Language in Origen and Eusebius', in Gregg (ed.) (1985), 257–66.

—— (1989). 'Arians and Manichees on Christ', *JThS*, NS, **40**, 493–503.

—— (1993*a*). *Christology and Cosmology: Models of Divine Activity in Origen, Eusebius and Athanasius*, Oxford.

—— (1993*b*). 'A Topography of Heresy: Mapping the Rhetorical Creation of Arianism', in Barnes and Williams (eds) (1993), 45–62.

MacMullen, R. (1970). *Constantine*, London.

Martin, A. (1974). 'Athanase et les Mélitiens (325–335)', in Kannengiesser (ed.) (1974), 31–61.

—— (1989). 'Le fil d'Arius 325–335', *Revue d'histoire ecclésiastique* LXXXIV, 297–333.

—— (1996). *Athanase d'Alexandrie et L'Église d'Égypte au IVe siècle (328–373)*, Rome.

May, G. (1994). Creatio ex Nihilo: *The Doctrine of Creation out of Nothing in Early Christian Thought* (German original 1978, trans. A. S. Worrall), Edinburgh.

Meijering, E. P. (1968). *Orthodoxy and Platonism in Athanasius: Synthesis or Antithesis?*, Leiden.

Millar, F. (1992). *The Emperor in the Roman World (31BC–AD337)*, 2nd edn., London.

Minns, D. (1994). *Irenaeus*, London.

Murray, C. (1977). 'Art and the Early Church', *JThS*, NS, **28**, 303–45.

Newman, J. H. (1833). *The Arians of the Fourth Century* (1968 edn., Westminster).

Ng, N. K.-K. (2001). *The Spirituality of Athanasius: A Key for Proper Understanding of This Important Church Father*, Bern.

Nichols, A. (1992). *Rome and the Eastern Churches: A Study in Schism*, Edinburgh.

Nispel, M. D. (1999). 'Christian Deification and the Early *Testimonia*', *VC* **53**, 289–304.

Nordberg, H. (1964). *Athanasius and the Emperor*, Helsinki.

Nyman, J. R. (1961). 'The Synod of Antioch (324–325) and the Council of Nicaea', *StP* **4**, 483–9.

Odahl, C. M. (2004). *Constantine and the Christian Empire*, London and New York.

Opitz, H.-G. (1934). 'Die Zeitfolge des arianischen Streites von den Anfangen bis zum Jahr 328', *ZNW* **33** (1934), 131–59.

Orlandi, T. (1975). 'Sull'*Apologia Secunda* (*Contra Arianos*) di Atanasio di Alessandria', *Augustinianum* **15**, 49–79.

Parvis, S. (2003). 'The Strange Disappearance of the Moderate Origenists: the Arian Controversy, 326–341' (paper presented to the Fourteenth International Patristics Conference, Oxford).

—— (2004). 'A Rainy Day in Rome 340: How Athanasius and Marcellus Invented Arianism' (unpublished).

—— (2006). *Marcellus of Ancyra and the Lost Years of the Arian Controversy*, Oxford.

Patterson, L. G. (1982). 'Methodius, Origen, and the Arian Dispute', *StP* **17.2**, 912–23.

Peeters, P. (1945). 'L'épilogue du Synode de Tyr en 335', *Analecta Bollandiana* **63**, 131–44.

Pettersen, A. (1982). 'A Reconsideration of the Date of the *Contra Gentes–De Incarnatione* of Athanasius of Alexandria', *StP* **17.3**, 1030–40.

—— (1984). ' "To Flee or Not to Flee": An Assessment of Athanasius' *De Fuga Sua*', in W. J. Shiels (ed.), *Persecution and Toleration*, Oxford, 29–42.

—— (1990). 'The Arian Context of Athanasius of Alexandria's *Tomus ad Antiochenos* VII', *JEH* **41**, 183–98.

—— (1995). *Athanasius*, London.

Pohlsander, H. A. (1993). 'Constantia', *Ancient Society* **24**, 151–67.

Pollard, T. (1958). 'The Origins of Arianism', *JThS*, NS, **9**, 103–11.

—— (1959). 'The Exegesis of Scripture and the Arian Controversy', *Bulletin of the John Rylands Library* **41**, 414–29.

Pollard, T. (1960). 'The Creeds of AD 325: Antioch, Caesarea, Nicaea', *SJTh* **13**, 278–300.

Prestige, G. L. (1923). '*Αγεν(ν)ητος* and *γεν(ν)ητος*, and kindred words, in Eusebius and the early Arians', *JThS*, OS, **24**, 486–96.

—— (1933). '*ΑΓΕΝ(Ν)ΗΤΟΣ* and Cognate Words in Athanasius', *JThS*, OS, **34**, 258–65.

—— (1956). *God in Patristic Thought*, 2nd edn., London.

Radt, S. (1980). 'Noch einmal Aischylos, Niobe Fr. 162 N, 2nd edn. (278 M)', *ZPE* **38**, 47–58.

—— (1988). 'Hoi (ai, etc) peri + acc. nominis proprii bei Strabo', *ZPE* **71**, 35–40 and 'Addendum', *ZPE* **74**, 108.

Rapp, C. (2005). *Holy Bishops in Late Antiquity: The Nature of Christian Leadership in an Age of Transition*, Berkeley, Los Angeles, and London.

Reynold, H. R. (1880). 'Eusebius of Nicomedia', in W. Smith and H. Wace (eds), *A Dictionary of Christian Biography*, Vol. II, London, 360–7.

Ritter, A. M. (1978). 'Arianismus', *Theologische Realenzykolpädie*, Berlin and New York, 692–719.

Rusch, W. R. (1974). 'A la recherche de l'Athanase historique', in Kannengiesser (ed.) (1974), 161–77.

—— (1985). 'Some Comments on Athanasius' *Contra Arianos*, Book I, 3', in Gregg (ed.) (1985), 223–32.

Schäferdiek, K. (1980). 'Zu Verfasserschaft und Situation der Epistula ad Constantinam de imagine Christi', *ZKG* **91**, 177–86.

Schneemelcher, W. (1950). 'Athanasius von Alexandrien als Theologe und als Kirchenpolitiker', *ZNW* **43**, 242–55; repr. in id. (1974*b*), 274–89.

—— (1954). 'Zur Chronologie des arianischen Streites', *Theologische Literaturzeitung* 79, 393–400.

—— (1974*a*) 'Die Epistula Encyclica des Athanasius' in id. (1974*b*), 290–337.

—— (1974*b*) *Gessammelte Aufsätze zum Neuen Testament und zur Patristik*, Thessaloniki.

—— (1977). 'Die Kirchweihsynode von Antiochen 341', *Bonner Festgabe Johannes Straub zum 65. Geburtstag am 18.October 1977*, Bonn, 319–46.

Schönborn, C. (1994). *God's Human Face: The Christ-Icon* (French original 1976, trans. L. Krauft), San Francisco.

Schwartz, E. (1935). 'Zur Kirchengeschichte des vierten Jahrhunderts', *ZNW* **34**, 129–213.

—— (1959). *Gesammelte Schriften* 3. *Zur Geschichte des Athanasius* (first pub. in *Nachrichten der königlichen Gesellschaft der Wissenschaften zu Göttingen*, 1904–11), Berlin.

Seeck, O. (1911). *Geschichte des Untergangs der antiken Welt* 4, Berlin.

Seibt, K. (1994). *Die Theologie des Markell von Ankyra*, Berlin and New York.
—— (2000). 'Markell von Ankyra (*ca.* 280–374 n.Chr.) und Asterius Sophista (*ca.* 270–*ca.* 350 n.Chr.): Ammerkungen zu einer neuen Edition der Markell-Fragmente und der Epistula ad Iulium', *ZKG* **111**, 356–77.
Sellers, R. V. (1928). *Eustathius of Antioch: And His Place in the Early History of Christian Doctrine*, Cambridge.
Setton, K. M. (1941). *Christian Attitudes towards the Emperor in the Fourth Century: especially as shown in addresses to the Emperor*, New York.
Simonetti, M. (1965). *Studi sull'Arianesimo*, Rome.
—— (1975). *La Crisi Ariana nel Quarto Secolo*, Rome.
Sivan, H. (1996). 'Ulfila's Own Conversion', *HThR* **89**, 373–86
Skarsaune, O. (1987). 'A Neglected Detail in the Creed of Nicaea (325)', *VC* **41**, 34–54.
Slusser, M. (1986). 'Athanasius' *Contra Gentes* and *De Incarnatione*: Place and Date of Composition', *JThS*, NS, **37**, 114–17.
—— (1988). 'The Exegetical Roots of Trinitarian Theology', *ThS* **49**, 461–76.
—— (1993). 'Traditional Views of Late Arianism', in Barnes and Williams (eds) (1993), 3–30.
Spoerl, K. M. (1993*a*). 'Apollinarius and the Response to Early Arian Christology', *StP* **26**, 421–7.
—— (1993*b*). 'The Schism at Antioch since Cavallera', in Barnes and Williams (eds) (1993), 101–26
—— (1997). 'Anti-Arian Polemic in Eusebius of Caesarea's *Ecclesiastical Theology*', *StP* **32**, 33–8.
Stead, G. C. (1961). 'The Significance of the *Homoousios*', *StP* **3**, 397–412; repr. in id. (1985*a*), I.
—— (1964). 'The Platonism of Arius', *JThS*, NS, **15**, 16–31; repr. in id. (1985*a*), III.
—— (1973). ' "Eusebius" and the Council of Nicaea', *JThS*, NS, **24**, 85–100; repr. in id. (1985*a*), V.
—— (1975). 'The Concept of Divine Substance', *VC* **29**, 1–14; repr. in id. (1985*a*), VII.
—— (1976). 'Rhetorical Method in Athanasius', *VC* **30**, 121–37; repr. in id. (1985*a*), VIII.
—— (1977). *Divine Substance*, Oxford.
—— (1978). 'The *Thalia* of Arius and the Testimony of Athanasius', *JThS*, NS, **29**, 20–52; repr. in id. (1985*a*), X.
—— (1981). 'Response' in Kannengiesser (1981) 73–6.
—— (1983). 'The Freedom of the Will and the Arian Controversy', *JAC.E.* 10, 245–57; repr. in id. (1985*a*), XVI.
—— (1985*a*). *Substance and Illusion in the Christian Fathers*, London.

Stead, G. C. (1985*b*). Review of Kannengiesser (1983*a*), *JThS*, NS, **36**, 220–9.
—— (1988). 'Athanasius' earliest written work', *JThS*, NS, **39**, 76–91; repr. in id. (2000), X.
—— (1994). 'Arius in Modern Research', *JThS*, NS, **45**, 24–36; repr. in id. (2000), IV.
—— (1997). 'Was Arius a Neoplatonist?', *StP* **32**, 39–52; repr. in id. (2000), V.
—— (1998). 'The Word "From Nothing" ', *JThS*, NS, **49**, 671–84; repr. in id. (2000), VII.
—— (2000). *Doctrine and Philosophy in Early Christianity*, Aldershot.
Steenson, J. N. (1985). 'Basil of Ancyra on the Meaning of *Homoousios*', in Gregg (ed.) (1985), 267–79.
Telfer, W. (1936). 'Arius takes refuge at Nicomedia', *JThS*, OS, **37**, 60–3.
—— (1946). 'When did the Arian Controversy begin?', *JThS*, OS, **47**, 129–42.
—— (1949). 'Sozomen I.15, A Reply', *JThS*, OS, **50**, 187–91.
—— (1950). 'Paul of Constantinople', *HThR* **43**, 31–92.
Tetz, M. (1975). 'Über nikäische Orthodoxie. Der sog. *Tomus ad Antiochenos* des Athanasios von Alexandrien', *ZNW* **66**, 194–222; repr. in id. (1995), 107–34.
—— (1979*a*). 'Athanasius von Alexandrien', *Theologische Realenzyklopädie*, Vol. 4, 333–49; repr. in id. (1995), 1–22.
—— (1979*b*). 'Zur Biographie des Athanasius von Alexandrien', *ZKG* **90**, 304–38; repr. in id. (1995), 23–60.
—— (1989). 'Die Kirchweihsynode von Antiochien (341) und Marcellus von Ancyra', in D. Papandreou, W. A. Bienert, and K. Schäferdiek (eds), *Oecumenica et Patristica. Festschrift für Wilhelm Schneemelcher zum 75. Geburtstag*, Stuttgart, Berlin, and Köln, 199–217; repr. in Tetz (1995), 227–48.
—— (1993). 'Zur strittigen Frage arianischer Glaubenserklärung auf dem Konzil von Nicaea (325)', in Brennecke, Grasmück, and Markschies (eds) (1993), 220–38.
—— (1995). *Athanasiana: Zu Leben und Lehre des Athanasius*, Berlin and New York.
Torrance, T. F. (1995). *Divine Meaning: Studies in Patristic Hermeneutics*, Edinburgh.
Twomey, V. (1982). Apostolikos Thronos: *The Primacy of Rome as reflected in the Church History of Eusebius and the Historico-apologetical Writings of Saint Athanasius the Great*, Münster.
Ulrich, J. (1994). 'Einige Bemerkungen zum angeblichen Exil des Ossius', *ZKG* **105**, 143–55.
—— (1997). 'Nicaea and the West', *VC* **51**, 10–24.
Uthemann, K.-H. (1991). Review of Kinzig (1990), *VC* **45**, 194–203.

Vaggione, R. (1987*a*). '*Οὐχ ὡς ἐν των γεννημάτων*: Some Aspects of Dogmatic Formulae in the Arian Controversy', *Studia Patristica* **17.1**, 181–7.

—— (1987*b*). *Eunomius: The Extant Works*, Oxford.

—— (2000). *Eunomius of Cyzicus and the Nicene Revolution*, Oxford.

Vanderspoel, J. (1999). 'Correspondence and Correspondents of Julius Julianus', *Byz* **69**, 396–478.

Vinzent, M. (1993*b*). 'Gottes Wesen, Logos, Weisheit und Kraft bei Asterius von Kappadokien und Markell von Ancyra', *VC* **47**, 170–91.

—— (1994). 'Die Gegner im Schreiben Markells von Ankyra an Julius von Rom', *ZKG* **105**, 285–328.

Vogt, H.-J. (1973). 'Parties in the History of the Church: Athanasius and his Contemporaries' (trans. F. McDonagh), *Concilium* **8.9**, 37–49.

Walker, P. W. L. (1990). *Holy City, Holy Places? Christian Attitudes to Jerusalem and the Holy Land in the Fourth Century*, Oxford.

Wallace-Hadrill, D. S. (1982). *Christian Antioch: A Study of Early Christian Thought in the East*, Cambridge.

Warmington, B. H. (1985). 'The Sources of Some Constantinian Documents in Eusebius' *Ecclesiastical History* and *Life of Constantine*', *StP* **18.1**, 93–8.

—— (1986). 'Did Athanasius Write History?', in C. Holdsworth and T. P. Wiseman (eds), *The Inheritance of Historiography 350–900*, Exeter, 7–16.

—— (1989). 'Did Constantine have "Religious Advisers"?', *StP* **19**, 117–29.

—— (1997). 'Eusebius of Caesarea and Some Early Opponents of Athanasius', *StP* **32**, 59–64.

West, M. L. (1982). 'The Metre of Arius' *Thalia*', *JThS*, NS, **33**, 98–105.

Widdicombe, P. (1994). *The Fatherhood of God from Origen to Athanasius*, Oxford.

Wiles, M. (1961). 'Eternal Generation', *JThS*, NS, **12**, 284–91.

—— (1962). 'In Defence of Arius', *JThS*, NS, **13**, 339–47.

—— (1965*a*). '*ΟΜΟΟΥΣΙΟΣ ΗΜΙΝ*', *JThS*, NS, **16**, 454–61.

—— (1965*b*). 'The Nature of the Early Debate about Christ's Human Soul', *JEH* **16**, 139–51.

—— (1966). 'Soteriological Arguments in the Fathers', *StP* **9.3**, 321–5.

—— (1967). *The Making of Christian Doctrine: A Study in the Principles of Early Doctrinal Development*, Cambridge.

—— (1977). *The Christian Fathers*, 2nd edn., London.

—— (1985) (with Gregg). 'Asterius: A New Chapter in the History of Arianism?', in Gregg (ed.) (1985), 111–51.

Wiles, M. (1989*a*). 'The Theology of Eusebius of Emesa', *StP* **19**, 267–80.

—— (1989*b*). 'Eunomius: Hair-Splitting Dialectician or Defender of the Accessibility of Salvation?', in Williams (ed.) (1989), 157–72.

Wiles, M. (1993*a*). 'A Textual Variant in the Creed of the Council of Nicaea', *StP* **26**, 428–33.

—— (1993*b*). 'Attitudes to Arius in the Arian Controversy', in Barnes and Williams (eds) (1993), 31–43.

—— (1996). *Archetypal Heresy: Arianism through the Centuries*, Oxford.

Williams, D. H. (1992). 'The Anti-Arian Campaigns of Hilary of Poitiers and the "*Liber Contra Auxentium*" ', *CH* **61**, 7–22.

—— (1995*a*). 'Polemics and Politics in Ambrose of Milan's *De Fide*', *JThS*, NS, **46**, 519–31.

—— (1995*b*). *Ambrose of Milan and the End of the Nicene-Arian Conflicts*, Oxford.

—— (1996). 'Another Exception to Later Fourth-Century "Arian" Typologies: The Case of Germinius of Sirmium', *JECS* **4**, 335–57.

—— (1997). 'Necessary Alliance or Polemical Portrayal? Tracing the Historical Alignment of Arians and Pagans in the Later Fourth Century', *StP* **29**, 178–94.

Williams, G. H. (1951). 'Christology and Church–State Relations in the Fourth Century', *CH* **20.3**, 3–33 and **20.4**, 3–26.

Williams, R. D. (1983). 'The Logic of Arianism', *JThS*, NS, **34**, 56–81.

—— (1985). 'The Quest for the Historical *Thalia*', in Gregg (ed.) (1985), 1–35.

—— (1986). 'Arius and the Melitian Schism', *JThS*, NS, **37**, 35–52.

—— (1987). *Arius: Heresy and Tradition*, London; (2001*a*). 2nd Impression, London.

—— (ed.) (1989). *The Making of Orthodoxy: Essays in Honour of Henry Chadwick*, Cambridge.

—— (1992). 'Article Review: R. P. C. Hanson's *Search for the Christian Doctrine of God*', *SJTh* **45**, 101–11.

—— (1993). 'Baptism and the Arian Controversy', in Barnes and Williams (eds) (1993), 149–80.

—— (2001*b*). 'Defining Heresy', in A. Kreider (ed.), *The Origins of Christendom in the West*, Edinburgh and New York, 313–35.

Woods, D. (2001). Review of Burgess (1999*b*), *JThS*, NS, **52**, 900–3.

—— (2002). 'Eusebius on Some Constantinian Officials', *IThQ* **67**, 195–223.

Young, F. (1971). 'A Reconsideration of Alexandrian Christology', *JEH* 22, 103–14.

—— (1982). 'Did Epiphanius Know what He Meant by Heresy?', *StP* **17.1**, 199–205.

—— (1983). *From Nicaea to Chalcedon: A Guide to the Literature and its Background*, Philadelphia.

—— (1991). *The Making of the Creeds*, London and Philadelphia.

Index of Athanasian Texts

General Index